Fanny Brice

Herbert G. Goldman

Fanny Brice

 The Original Funny Girl

New York   Oxford

OXFORD UNIVERSITY PRESS

1992

Oxford University Press

Oxford   New York   Toronto
Delhi   Bombay   Calcutta   Madras   Karachi
Petaling Jaya   Singapore   Hong Kong   Tokyo
Nairobi   Dar es Salaam   Cape Town
Melbourne   Auckland

and associated companies in
Berlin   Ibadan

Published by Oxford University Press, Inc.
200 Madison Avenue, New York, New York 10016

Oxford is a registered trademark of Oxford University Press

Library of Congress Cataloging-in-Publication Data
Goldman, Herbert G.
Fanny Brice : the original funny girl / Herbert G. Goldman.
p. cm.   Includes bibliographical references.
Discography: p.   List of stage productions: p.
Includes index.   ISBN 0-19-505725-2
1. Brice, Fanny.   2. Comedians—United States—Biography.
3. Singers—United States—Biography.
4. Actors—United States—Biography.   I. Title.
PN2287.B69G65   1992
792.7'028'092—dc20
[B]   91-17373

9 8 7 6 5 4 3 2 1

Printed in the United States of America
on acid-free paper

To
META SUSAN SCHECHTER GOLDMAN
my sister-in-law
a real mensch

Preface

This is the first attempt at anything approaching a definitive biography of Fanny Brice. *The Fabulous Fanny,* Norman Katkov's 1952 book based on Fanny's otherwise unpublished memoirs, did not attempt to cover Brice's show-business career, and bore the marks of censorship by her family. That family is headed by Ray Stark, the phenomenally successful producer and former Hollywood agent, married to Fan's daughter, Frances.

Anyone attempting a biography of Brice is beset by problems. Fanny died at fifty-nine after having been in virtual retirement for fourteen years. This declaration may sound strange to those who recall her as "Baby Snooks," the *enfante terrible* of radio's Golden Age. However, *Baby Snooks,* which went through several incarnations from 1937 to 1951, took her but three days a week to rehearse and then perform. This was in marked contrast to her stage career (1906–1937), which saw her travel and do eight shows weekly. Brice's life in those days was a matter of public record, especially when her second husband, Nick Arnstein, was a fugitive from the law in 1920. Brice's private life was seldom news once the professional Fanny "disappeared" into her mischievous baby. Her social life was likewise centered around family and friends, whose homes she decorated with a taste and feeling for decor unrivaled by the greatest of professionals.

Then there is the surprising nature of Fan's stage career itself. She was a Yiddish dialect comedienne for whom vehicles were hard to find. Fanny Brice, despite her popularity and talent, was never a full-fledged Broadway star who had her name above the title. (Ironically, her first film, *My Man,* gave her that star vehicle and billing. Movies never were Miss Brice's medium.) Interviews, articles, and news items exist, but not in the great numbers they do for Al Jolson, Ed Wynn, Eddie Cantor, or other male contemporaries.

The number of old-timers along Broadway who remember the "good old days" before World War II (and, specifically, before the Depression), has dwindled to a handful in the past ten years. My great thanks, then, to Mae Clarke, Jerry Hausner, the late Tish Lee, Judy Altman, Gary Stevens, Barbara Barondess, and Vyola Vonn.

Thanks must also go to Miles M. Kreuger, president of the Institute of the American Musical; Jim Curtis; Richard Halpern; Audrey Kupferburg; Lillian (Libby) Tudiver; and, of course, Sheldon Meyer, senior vice-president of Oxford University Press; Gail Cooper, my line editor; and Karen Wolny, my photo editor.

Special thanks go to Larry F. Kiner and Peter Tatchell, who provided valuable audio and research assistance for the "Baby Snooks" years of Miss Brice's life. A very special thanks is due to Bonnie Corso, whose encouragement and feeling for the subject were important in the final months of writing.

And my great thanks to George Russell of *Variety* for allowing me to use quotes from the "old show business Bible."

My greatest debt, however, is to Sime Silverman, Joshua Lowe, Hobe Morrison, and numerous, sometimes unnamed correspondents on *Variety*, the *New York Clipper*, *Dramatic Mirror*, *Billboard*, and other show-business trade periodicals who covered Fanny's stage career—and, sometimes, her private life—for more than forty years.

The spelling of Miss Brice's first name has vexed theatrical historians for decades. Early programs spell it "Fannie," but Brice herself, as years rolled on, gave it as "Fanny." The truth is that name derivatives like "Jimmy" were usually spelled "Jimmie" before 1930. This biography uses the more modern "Fanny" spelling throughout. ("Fanny" is simply a diminutive of "Fania," a common Jewish female name.)

Believing that the writing of a book should express the spirit of its subject, I have modified the racy, rather colloquial style I employed in *Jolson*, my last book. Fanny Brice was nonetheless a "show biz gal." I have written accordingly. If this book invokes the spirit of her theatrical era at the same time it delineates the character, career, and art of Fanny, it will have served the wishes of its author.

New York   Herbert G. Goldman
May 26, 1991

Contents

Fanny Brice

Listen, kid! I've done everything in the theatre except marry a property man. I've been a soubrette in burlesque and I've accompanied stereopticon slides. I've acted for Belasco and I've laid 'em out in the rows at the Palace. I've doubled as an alligator; I've worked for the Shuberts; and I've been joined to Billy Rose in the holy bonds. I've painted the house boards and I've sold tickets and I've been fired by George M. Cohan. I've played in London before the king and in Oil City before miners with lanterns in their caps.   FANNY BRICE

Introduction

T housands of stagestruck girls know Fanny Brice as the subject of *Funny Girl,* the 1960s show and film that gave the world the hit song "People" and made a superstar of Barbra Streisand. Their aging parents and grandparents remember Fanny as "Baby Snooks," the incorrigible tot of network radio from 1936 to 1951. A handful of old-timers and show biz aficionados know her as a great comedienne and Yiddish dialectician, laughing hit of the *Ziegfeld Follies* and other Broadway shows from 1910 to 1936. Fanny's daughter, Frances Stark, remembers her mother as a polished lady with the manner of Queen Mary.

She was, indeed, a lady, one who dressed in perfect taste, knew antiques and fabrics, entertained with lavish dinner parties, and lived like a nineteenth-century duchess. But to describe her only as a lady is like describing Boss Tweed as a statesman. She also cussed like a sailor, called everybody "kid," and was honest to the point of sheer brutality. She fell asleep—and snored—at Broadway shows that held no interest for her and once, at a Hollywood premiere, delivered a series of loud, critical remarks that drove her artist son out of the theatre. Fanny didn't care where the "hell" the leading lady was sitting—which happened to be right in front of them. Yet withal, she never seemed offensive—perhaps the true mark of a lady.

Talking to Fanny was an experience. She walked around the room quite quickly as she spoke, and her comments—about people, rarely things and almost never abstractions—were amazingly accurate and devastatingly perceptive. As one of Broadway's great performers, Fanny was an intelligent observer of the show world and a great judge of special material. Sylvia Fine, for one, would never give a song to husband Danny Kaye unless it first passed the Brice muster.

Fanny was a woman of amazing honesty—especially in show business, a field seldom known for its veracity and evenhanded dealings. She brought people up or down to her own social level, terming George Gershwin "a silk herring" when he started having ego problems and calling Ernest Hemingway a "schmendrick" when that great author was being lionized by the world. But if she liked you, doors would open. People of all backgrounds trusted Fanny's judgment.

Like many show biz people from before the first World War, she hated "phonies." A Broadway producer once insisted he would give her "my right arm."

"Listen, kid," Fan told him. "I happen to know you got a whole drawer full of right arms."

The onstage Fanny Brice was a comedienne, a satirist, a woman who used her great powers of observation to detect the weaknesses and falsities of life and people to create both the most riotously ridiculous characterizations in Broadway history and the most pointedly barbed thrusts at Jewish pretension launched before the advent of Philip Roth. At the start of her career, she portrayed young, awkward Jewesses beset by problems ranging from catty friends, to worthless beaux, to people who objected to her improbable occupations as Salome dancer or nude model in Washington Square. Later, she included blasts at nouveau riche artistic affectations and pseudo-intellectual dissimulation. All were brought down to earth and reduced to absurdity.

Nor did she spare herself in that regard. Fanny belonged to that wave of immigrant and first-generation Americans who sought the "finer" things in life possessed by older, more established classes and tried to emulate them in every possible way. She was always flawlessly groomed, from her perfectly manicured fingernails to her slender figure, from her coiffed hair to her ankles. Fanny's sense of comedy allowed her to direct a servant in the arrangement of the silverware for a big dinner, then turn to an intrigued house guest and belch. Self-satirization was a Bricean trademark, her method of acknowledging the roots of her success. She wanted—and obtained—all of the fine things, never forgot her origins, and saw the humor in the contrast between the two.

An amazingly strong person, Fanny had a sense of integrity that left her both unspoiled by her friendships with the cream of society and unsullied by her contacts with eccentric criminals like "Large Face the Safecracker." Despite a lack of interest in political affairs—Fanny believed in people but not politics—she was a Renaissance woman who made efforts in a fairly wide variety of fields. Always an instinctive artist (she had virtually no formal education) Fanny flew by the seat of her pants when push came to the inevitable shove. That "seat" was invariably right.

She was about five-foot-seven in an era in which most women were under five-four, was surprisingly slender, and had a face that never seemed to look the same from one photograph to another. A pleasant-looking girl while in her twenties, Fanny let herself go "character" as soon as she reached forty. Yet she remained sexual and vibrant, a woman loved by some, admired by many, and respected by all.

Fanny belonged to that breed of "do as I say, not as I do" women who, while independent herself, thought most women's recipe for happiness lay in being good wives and helpmates. "Because if a woman has a career, she misses an awful lot," she said. "If you have a career, then the career is your life." This attitude, which sounds at odds with current women's rhetoric, is nonetheless in keeping with the Fanny who would shut her eyes on stage and sing "My Man." Fanny Brice was the greatest comedienne America has ever known, as well as its first truly great "torch singer." Her versatility was the marvel of Broadway fifteen years before the birth of "Baby Snooks."

Fanny's early years were spent in what was probably the most interesting epoch in the history of American entertainment. Fanny was aware of that, and intensely proud of the traditions that had spawned her.

"The performer is different today," she said in 1946. "Years ago we had a school. The school was vaudeville and burlesque. You knocked around. So it seasoned you. Made a mensch of you. So it gave you an interesting background before you clicked. Today, they go into pictures from nowheres. Somebody sees a girl flipping hamburgers in a drive-in joint, so right away she gets a screen test and she photographs good so they develop her and give her a face and clothes. But they can't give you a real personality or give you a natural technique of acting to hold an audience or your own school. If they had put me in front of a camera thirty-five years ago when I was starting out, I had such a kisser the camera would have stood up and walked away in disgust."

She began her stage career as a stagestruck and ambitious girl who buttonholed producers and ran errands for a burlesque queen in 1908. By 1920, she was tough enough to stand up to police and prosecutors when "her man," Nick Arnstein, was one of the most wanted fugitives in the United States. By the age of forty-seven, she was independent enough to give her third husband a divorce, announce her intention never to marry again, and spend the rest of her years as a five-thousand-dollar-a-week radio star, interior decorator, and grandmother—supremely independent in both mind and pocketbook.

Fanny was a strange mixture of elegance and earthiness—a woman women admired who could hold her own with any man. She laughed loudly, and was one of the few comedy performers who would rather hear others tell a good funny story than tell one herself. She told some tales of dubious veracity, but never said anything she did not believe *represented* the truth. Extroverted on the surface, she was private with regard to her own feelings—which were deeply hurt by the men in her life. There were certain subjects, like her sex life, that she simply would not talk about.

She almost never spoke about her father.

Self-aware and self-perceptive, Fanny once said she had always been aware of "two people within me. Almost like a mother and child. I have felt like I was my own mother, and when I would think about Fanny, I would always think about myself as a child."

Fanny's great-niece, Judy Altman, said she was a typical Hungarian Jewess—interested in the occult, very wise, and able to detach from herself. Fanny had a fascination with kineticism, hypnotism, and the spirit world that might have been unhealthy in a women less earthy and sensible. She may have been among the most sensible women who ever lived—except where it concerned her life with men. Fanny always went for what she called "the bastards," and her ultimately unhappy experiences paved the way for the maturity, and loneliness, that graced her later years.

Fanny's story is to some extent that of a loss of innocence. There is some sadness in the stagestruck girl's loss of awe and wonder, and the disillusionment of the woman in love. If Fanny really was two people—Fanny the child and Fanny the mother—it seems quite clear the "mother" really won.

Fanny's mother was named Rose; coincidentally, since the girl in many of her songs, "Rose of Washington Square," Rosie Rosenstein in "I'm an Indian," "Second Hand Rose," and others, had the same name. Rose Borach was Hungarian, the watchful, practical, hard, and cynical matriarch whom her daughter partially identified with but never truly admired. Her father was Charles Borach—"French Charlie," the elegant, mustachioed romantic who would rather play pinochle and listen to his daughter sing than work and pay the bills. The "child" Fanny loved French Charlie and the romance he embodied.

This is the story of those two Fannys—the wise mother and the romantic child—along with the stage world and times in which "both" women lived.

CHAPTER *I*

A Borach

The Jewish family has been called a patriarchy in theory and a matriarchy in practice. Fanny Brice's family was matriarchal in the extreme, and Fanny, independent woman though she was, somehow never really liked it.

Fanny's mother, Rose, was born in Hungary on June 14, 1867, the daughter of Philip Stern, a poor Jewish villager who died when she was still a little girl. Philip's destitute widow sent their ten-year-old daughter to America with an aunt in 1877. The aunt was the mother's own sister, to whom she gave three feather beds as payment.

Rosie's mother wanted her to have more than a hut with a leaky roof, dirt floors, and a cow in the kitchen. That had been her home in Hungary. What Rosie found in America, however, was not wealth, but work: constant, low-paying labor as a nurse for the two-year-old child of an Irish family on New York's East Side, and, later, as a needle worker in a fur factory—the sort of sweatshop Fanny would sing of in "The Song of the Sewing Machine."

Rosie's best friend there was Bertha, a girl of her own age who married an Irishman named John Brice. Rose boarded with the Brices until she caught John in a restaurant with a young woman. She hastened to tell Bertha, and John, who knew that a best defense was a good offense, turned on his accuser. Either Rosie went, John told his wife, or he did. Rosie had to move.

Rose now met a tailor by the name of Seymour Cohen, a short, thin, ungainly youth who still lived with his mother. Rose and Seymour went for walks through the East Side and talked of marriage. Their major obstacle was money. Seymour only made two dollars weekly, and even in the 1880s that was not enough to marry and have kids.

While waiting for her boyfriend to advance himself, Rose continued working in the fur factory and took a room in the apartment dwelling of Frank Grant and his wife, Selma Borach, an Alsatian immigrant with a brother known as "Pinochle" Charlie.

Charles Borach had been in the French Army until a letter from his sister offered him the promise of an easier life in New York City. Whether he was discharged or (as Fanny once maintained) deserted, matters little. By 1885, however, he was living with his sister on New York's Lower East Side.

Rose was no romantic. She came from a poor background, worked a hard job, and had few illusions about happy endings. When a year had passed, and Cohen's fortunes had not prospered, the eighteen-year-old Rose told Seymour she was sorry and left him in the middle of a walk on New York's Houston Street.

Charlie Borach, in the meantime, had become her other suitor. He was now a bartender making eighty dollars a week in the largest saloon on the Bowery. When Charlie wasn't working, he was playing pinochle or sitting in the kitchen of the Grants' apartment drinking beer with Frank and Selma. He was a good-natured, rather dreamy sort of sot—completely unlike Rose, the girl he wished to marry.

There was no real courtship, and no love on Rosie's part. Charlie proposed through his sister, Selma, and Rose, who took a week to think it over, finally accepted. She had broken up with Seymour and, at nineteen, had no time to lose. Eighty dollars a week was nothing to sneeze at in 1886.

Romantic love had lost by seventy-eight dollars. Fanny's mother was a very practical woman.

The Borachs set up housekeeping at 179 Second Avenue, a respectable address in a not-too-run-down section of the Lower East Side that would become a hub of Jewish culture in the early 1900s. Four children followed in the next six years: Philip (named for Rose's father, 1887); Carolyn, or "Carrie" (1889); Fania (1891); and Louis, or "Lew" (1893). They were living at 102 Forsyth Street at the time of Fanny's birth on October 29, 1891, a far-from-Orthodox Jewish family in what was then an Irish neighborhood.

Fanny's first vivid memories were not of the East Side, but of Europe. In the summer of 1896, when she was four and a half, the family went to visit her paternal grandfather in Alsace, a French province ceded to Germany by the Treaty of Frankfurt in 1871.

Charles Borach's father was then a white-haired gentleman easily un-nerved by his grandchildren's runny noses. Fanny recalled that he spoke no English, but had done well enough in the wine business to give the family a substantial gift of money before the end of their visit. The elder Borach gave the cash to Rosie, who seemed much more responsible than Charlie, his own son.

The Borachs did not travel first-class, and Fanny remembered a stair-case that went up to a different level of their ocean liner. She saw a lady sitting in a deck chair there, and found that looking sad could make the woman give her a piece of orange. She started going up there every day, getting oranges from the woman, watching other people, and wearing the same sad expression. One first-class passenger gave her something like an ice cream soda.

That was how Fanny discovered performing—the key to a kinder and better life than the one she knew at home with a loveless marriage be-tween a cold mother and an increasingly ineffectual father.

Back from Europe, the Borachs moved across the Hudson River to New-ark, where Rosie opened a cigar, candy, and stationery store with the money received from her French father-in-law. The family lived upstairs from the store, and Fanny remembered a huge glass sliding showcase containing chewing gum. One night, she crept down, stole several pack-ages of gum, and proceeded to chew it in bed. When the sweetness passed from one small packet, she would open up another and stuff that into her mouth as well. In the morning, Rose discovered her with gum stuck in her hair.

The store drove Pinochle Charlie into a short-lived early retirement—playing cards in the back room while his wife took care of business in the front. This arrangement endured for two years, until Rose took her hard-won profits and purchased a bar at 26 Lafayette Street—partly for the increased income a saloon offered and partly to entice her husband back to work.

She was, however, badly disillusioned. Charlie just refused to work, leaving it to Rose to tap the kegs, make the "free lunches" that accom-panied the nickel beers, and keep tabs on expenses. "Mom was very good in business," Carrie recalled. "Once we had seven saloons in Newark. Mom would go from one to the other."

That statement gives the wrong impression; the Borachs only paid rent for the one saloon on Lafayette Street. "In those days," Fanny said, "a saloon keeper bought his beer and other liquors from one company, and the brewers paid the rent." Rose Borach simply hired enough bartenders and bouncers to run each place. Then she dropped in to each bar to count the till.

And while Rose counted, Charlie played pinochle and drank. They rarely slept together anymore, as Charley, an asthmatic, often choked if he laid down in bed. Fanny remembered him putting a pillow on the table and sleeping on his arm. Charlie claimed that whisky "let him breathe," and let his drinking and card playing make up for his absent sex life. Rose, increasingly resentful, had only her work.

The summer of 1900 saw Charles and Rose Borach go to Europe with Lew, the youngest child, leaving Fanny and her two other siblings with the Klein family on Jones Street. What impressed, and infuriated, Fanny most about them was the way Mrs. Klein doted on her husband—waiting on him hand and foot when he got home from work. If the family had hamburger for dinner, Mr. Klein got steak. He was the master of the house, and Mrs. Klein saw to it that the children spoke in whispers while he ate, or read, or napped before their bedtime. The patriarchy angered and bewildered the young Fanny, whose own home, of course, was nothing like the Kleins'.

Fanny's early feeling for women's rights was only one vivid memory of Jones Street. Her penchant for going through garbage cans for things that she could fashion into toys and other items led the kids in that neighborhood to call her "The Hogan's Alley Rag Picker." Her other nickname there was "Shit Behind the Coal Box." The coal box in question was in front of Stafford's Grocery. It was simply a matter of expediency; Fanny had to go but was "too lazy" to return to the Klein home.

The Borach family moved uptown to Camden Street when Charlie, Rose, and Lew returned from Europe. It was in this new neighborhood that Fan met Hattie Levy, her "first chum."

Hattie had what Fanny remembered as "seven or eight brothers and sisters. She was born the same year, the same day, and almost the same hour that I was. We felt like twins. She didn't like school any more than I did. We played hooky from the first year on."

One of their big hooky occupations was Blaney's Theatre, Newark's home of "ten-twent'-thirty" melodrama. In a world without radio, television, or even movies, the stage was more a center for mass entertainment than a citadel of art. Theaters devoted to plays, musicals, melodramas, vaudeville, burlesque, and other live forms of popular amusement were a part of daily life in every city, and the top stars spent more time on tour than on Broadway. Fanny first became aware of Blaney's when her parents, who allowed bill posters for it to be hung in their saloons, began to get two tickets for each play. She wanted to go, too, along with Lew and Hattie, but Rose Borach was not overly indulgent. Fanny and Hattie finally contrived to sneak in at nine o'clock in the morning while the theatre was being aired, and stay hidden in the balcony until the afternoon performance. By themselves or with young Lew, the girls saw all the old-time thrillers every week for months until they were discovered. Neither child pulled the stunt again.

Fanny was not sheltered. In her childhood, her best friends were from poorer families, and Fanny never hesitated to raise their standard of living with items from the Borach family kitchen.

"I hate to think what a pest I was to my mother," Fanny said in later years. "Cans of coffee, loaves of bread, dozens of eggs, even bottles of beer used to disappear from our kitchen. I took them over to Hattie's. I took the bottles of beer because I had heard someone say that beer was good for nursing mothers and Hattie's mother always had a new baby." The loaves of bread were usually days old and stale. Fanny would tell Hattie that her mother had bought too much "by mistake."

Fan and Hattie shared much more than simply the same birthdate. Both girls' fathers were French Jews who liked to drink and gamble. The difference was in the mothers. Where Rose Borach was strong—they called her "Tiger" in the neighborhood—Hattie's mother was weak, and there finally came a time when Fanny noticed Mrs. Levy putting clothes out on the line to dry, taking them off, and putting them out again.

Mrs. Levy's relatives had her put in "Ward Eight" of a local hospital, where Fanny often visited with Hattie. Mrs. Levy never remembered Fanny, but seemed to recall the name "Rose Borach."

"Yes," she'd say. "She sent me stale bread."

The Borach home was certainly never high on the social ladder, although Rose liked to dress well and enjoyed entertaining. Fine food was especially important, and her recipe for Hungarian goulash was a family treasure.

Despite the press yarns spun by Broadway PR people, Fanny Brice did not have a poor childhood. Her family was actually middle-class, and the Borachs' two annual trips to Coney Island were made, not by streetcar, but by horse-drawn cab. Fanny always felt sorry for the poor horse, which struggled pulling seven people.

The Borach household usually had servants, immigrants Rosie would hire fresh from Ellis Island. For eight dollars monthly and room and board, they worked all day and well into the night, got no day off, and were content with an occasional new dress or suit of clothes. Their rooms were on the top floor, and Fanny, ever curious about all sorts of people, got them to tell her, in very broken English, of their life in the "old country," often Poland.

The Polish words she learned from the servants complemented the German and Hungarian she picked up in the neighborhoods. Irish had predominated on the Lower East Side, but the most common dialect on Rankin Street in Newark was one from western Germany called *bleu-Deutsch*.

The Borachs lived among few Jews, and Fanny never knew more than a hundred words of Yiddish.

Fanny had little in common with Phil and Carrie, her two elder siblings. She remembered Phil as a terrible tease. She once threw a pair of scissors at him, and they stuck into his neck as he went running through the house.

Carrie was "Miss Prim," the well-behaved "class" of the family whom Rosie took along on vacations. She never dared take Fanny, who had graduated from swiping groceries for poor friends to stealing change from Rosie's pocketbook. Like Baby Snooks, the character she would immortalize in hundreds of radio broadcasts, Fanny the child was good-hearted but mischievous—a school truant and, it must be noted, an incorrigible thief.

And just as Snooks would make her baby brother, Robspierre, the victim of her mischief, Fanny commandeered her brother Lew for her pilfery—and trouble. If Rose took them to somebody's house at night, they sneaked into the kitchen and raided the sugar bowl, a frequent depository for household money. The punishment for any such offense was swift and sure: Rosie beat the living daylights out of them.

Fanny always remembered her mother throwing Lew up so he crashed against the ceiling. They rarely were repeat offenders after being caught. But there always was new mischief to get into. One scheme involved selling the same stolen music box to different people in the neighborhood, stealing it back, and selling it again.

The only thing Lew had in common with Phil and Carrie was the asthma they inherited from Charlie. Fanny, of all the siblings, did not suffer from it.

Fan was always, as she later put it, "scheming"—opening a sewing school for her girlfriends or, with Lew, selling lemonade on the sidewalk at a penny a glass. Rosie never figured out where all the sugar went, and a nail driven through a stick was an effective way of spearing lemons off a local fruitstand.

Fanny's frequent truancy resulted in low grades—twos and threes, the lowest marks possible—in everything but drawing. Paint sets, crayons, pencils, pads, and other art supplies were readily available in Newark's leading department store. Shoplifting hence became the new phase of Fan's childhood thievery.

Fan dressed Lew in one of Carrie's outfits, thinking that the department stores would not suspect two girls. When they were caught, the guilty and scared Lew blamed Fanny for "making me do it." Fanny then proceeded to blame Lew.

They were finally released, but told to stay out of the store. It was the closest Fanny ever came to actual arrest, and wrote *finis* to her career of theft.

Childhood thievery, while certainly illegal and regularly punished, was nonetheless quite commonplace in cities of the era. Its roots are quite discernible in Fanny's case, however—a mother too preoccupied with business and two older children (Phil, the oldest and a boy, was Rose's pride, joy, and hope for the future) to give her attention, and a father who loved her, but was weak—a fool for alcohol, endless pinochle games, and Fanny's own theatrics.

Fanny was a "ham" (so called after the non-kosher meat that actors used to remove greasepaint), meaning, not necessarily a lack of talent, but a built-in need to get up and perform. But if the instinct, first discovered on that voyage back from France and further sparked by plays she saw at Blaney's, was there to begin with, Fanny's father nourished it, and, quite unknowingly, set his daughter's life on a firm course.

On Sundays, when all the bars were closed, the Borach family would gather in their Lafayette Street saloon after breakfast. Fanny could not resist getting up on the bar and performing, the mirror in back adding to the "show" atmosphere. She sang, she "danced," and she acted little playlets based on fairy tales or melodramas she had seen at Blaney's.

Rosie was usually annoyed by Fanny's efforts, but French Charlie encouraged his daughter to perform. At the close of Fanny's song or playlet, he would applaud and toss her a dime or nickel. Rosie, who earned every penny, seethed.

A much more cynical Fanny, hurt by men and speaking from a vantage point of fifty years, might take her mother's side. But Fanny at the age of nine saw "Daddy" as a handsome, gallant knight in shining armor who loved life and little princesses and theatre.

Fanny's mother found French Charlie less of a white knight each day.

Their marriage fell further apart with every newly acquired saloon and every pinochle game, and if Charlie's drinking irritated Rosie, it was her husband's growing refusal to do any work that finally wrecked their marriage. Rose had married Charlie chiefly for his income. Now it was her own work that brought in the money, and her lack of feeling for him was replaced by sheer contempt.

As her mother turned from Charlie, Fanny's own love for him deepened. In a way, she worshipped the French immigrant who coupled the ambitions of a barroom loafer-dreamer with the soul of a Lord Byron.

Fanny got a job as a wrapper in Newark's leading department store during the Christmas season in 1901. It seemed a good way to get money for theatre tickets, but the boredom of wrapping scores of packages drove the ten-year-old Fanny into her now-common flights of fantasy. Before two days had passed, she told her fellow workers a fantastic yarn in which her mother was dead, her father was blind and needed false teeth, her older brother Phil needed a brace for his crippled leg, Carrie was epileptic, and she was their sole support.

The next day, when Fanny came to work and opened her assigned locker, she found old clothes, stale rolls, and other items her co-workers had brought for her to take back home to her poor blind father, crippled brother, and epileptic sister.

Fanny now felt guilty for probably the first time in her life. The following day, she showed up in her best clothes and two sets of little diamond earrings. Fanny told her gaping fellow workers she had just been "saying" that her family was poor. In fact, she almost bragged, they were quite well-to-do—as they could surely see.

One of the astonished, rather angry wrappers went to the floor manager, who reported the incident to the main office, which knew Rose Borach as one of the store's best customers. A phone call to the bar on Lafayette Street brought Rose running to the store.

Fanny's outraged mother almost slapped her silly. It was the end of Fanny's job in the department store, and Rose even refused to give her the $2.50 that the store sent for the time she worked.

Rosie simply never understood.

Rosie took her children to see her family in Hungary the following summer, leaving Charlie to run things in Newark. Fanny found Budapest interesting, but was saddened when Rose took her brood to her native Migletz, a village with straw roofs and naked gypsy children. Fanny's most memorable experience was helping her mother's 102-year-old blind aunt to the outhouse.

That vacation, that return to her old roots, spurred Fanny's mother to take action. Shortly after their return to Newark, Rosie sold the bar without her husband's knowledge, bought a house on St. Mark's Avenue in Brooklyn, and moved there with the children. Later, she obtained a separation. The Borachs never were divorced; Rosie had simply decided to end sixteen years of unhappy marriage and become the "head of household" in name as well as fact.

Charles Borach followed his family to Brooklyn, taking a room in the Graveside section, next to the famed racetrack where the Brooklyn Handicap was run, and becoming a bookmaker, a perfectly legal occupation in New York State until a new anti-gambling law was passed in 1908. Rosie went into the real estate business, leaving her children in the nominal care of a housekeeper during the day.

Pinochle Charlie visited his children often—always in the daytime, when his wife was not near their house on St. Mark's Avenue, and always with presents. Carrie remembered him as tall, gallant, and handsome. She and her two brothers always asked him not to leave, but Fanny would invariably vanish with her present. Seeing him for only a few minutes was too painful.

The removal of her father, Fanny's one-man audience, might have turned a less adventurous girl into a very frustrated actress. Fanny solved her problem by putting on plays for her friends in the cellar of the Borach home. A penny or an orange or some other piece of fruit was the admission price kids paid to see Fan re-create the melodramas she had seen at Blaney's. She would always be the heroine, usually on a bridge with a shawl over her shoulders, pretending she had a child and nothing to eat. Fanny found that she could actually weep, not just look sad, and she liked crying even better than making the ten or twenty cents her performances netted. Fanny was astounded to find that she could weep easily while acting, and the spellbound reactions of her young audience soon became her triumph and delight. If the performances allowed her to shed tears over the loss of her father, tears she could not bear to shed before Rose or French Charlie, Fanny never knew it.

Fanny also found a way to make the trips to Coney Island without either of her parents. Filling a handkerchief with rocks, she would get on the Vanderbilt Avenue trolley with Lew—her invariable accomplice—and "accidentally" drop the hankie out the window. The handkerchief supposedly contained their fare, and Fanny would cry real tears until a fellow passenger offered to give them the necessary money.

From then on, Fanny would get cash enough for cotton candy, ice cream, hot dogs, rides, and every other thing available at Coney Island by walking up to selected fat men, asking for directions, and then breaking into tears. For some reason, she found, fat men stuffing their faces with hot dogs seemed to be the most sympathetic.

Fanny and Lew made that trip to Coney many times during the summer of 1903—until they met a fat man who was also a detective. That ended their excursions.

Fanny's success with Coney Island fat men had convinced her she was as good an actress as most of the professionals she saw on Brooklyn stages. Her visits to the theatre were continual, and she saw some of the greatest actors and performers of the day at theaters like the Montauk, the Amphion, and the Gayety—E. H. Sothern and Julia Marlowe in Shakespearean repertory; Frank Daniels, Eddie Foy, and Anna Held in popular musical comedies. Her truancy was continual as well. At one point, she answered an advertisement calling for an errand girl in a dressmaking shop. She got the job and made six dollars a week until her mother found out and made her return to school.

Such vigilance on Rosie's part, however, was occasional at best. Like most people of her age and background, she saw education as important for boys but a mere nicety for girls. Fanny very may well have agreed. She hated school, and would invariably show up with her nose painted red and, never one to pass a dare, draw pictures of the teacher on the blackboard. At thirteen, Fanny was in Grade 4B, along with kids of nine. And the older she got, the more she played hooky, earning money for her own use with a run of short-lived jobs.

She worked as a receptionist in a chiropodist's office, but quit after one day because she could not stand having to remove a fat woman's stockings. (Fanny took a pair of manicuring scissors as her "payment" for the day.) Then she got a job in a candy store, ostensibly so she could "eat candy all day." The store had a supply of penny sticks of peppermint that had gone unsold for months because the kids did not think they were worth the money. Fanny cut each stick in sixteen pieces, wrapped each piece in tissue paper, and put them in the window with a sign, "Sixteen Pieces For One Cent." All were sold within a day.

Fanny lost that job when she told the proprietor his wife was "sweet on the corner policeman." As in Newark, she was always telling stories, making up little dramas that invariably boomeranged.

Fanny's closest friend in Brooklyn was an Irish girl named Hannah Ryan. Together with Lew, they spent their summer evenings in impromptu entertainments on the front stoops of neighborhood homes. Hannah did an Irish jig, Lew danced (he had natural talent) and Fanny sang the verses of popular songs. The other kids would join her in the choruses, but Fanny's strong and plaintive voice rang out above the others on last lines.

Fanny had once thought of being a designer, but her need to perform grew as she reached puberty—and, not incidentally, lost her father. She could sing, her friends admitted, but she was a ham. Both points were quite true.

Fanny Borach—her friends called her "Borax," "Twenty Mule Team Borax," and, in "tribute" to her stage ambitions, "Bore Act"—was still fourteen years old in the summer of 1906. She stood five feet six inches tall, almost her adult height, and weighed about one hundred pounds. Her light brown, naturally curly hair came down to her waist, though Fanny tied it at her neck with an enormous ribbon. Her green eyes were easily her most attractive feature.

She was not terribly unlike the ungainly girl in Noël Coward's "Don't Put Your Daughter on the Stage, Mrs. Worthington." In Fanny's case, however, it was she and not her mother who had stage ambitions. Rosie was not against her younger daughter's going on the stage—acting was not quite the totally unfeasible profession it would later be—nor was she in favor of it. Fanny was fourteen, still too young to get married, and Rose was too busy selling real estate and setting Phil up in the dairy business to bother much with her one way or another. (Phil, Rose had determined, would be quite the opposite of Charlie. Named for her own father, he was looked upon by her as the "important one.")

Nor was physical beauty a prerequisite for a career in theater. With the exception of several male matinee idols and some leading actresses, stage people of the early 1900s were not particularly gorgeous. Talent, dedication, and native intelligence were the essentials then demanded in the theater. Fanny Borach had all three.

Fanny's career started when Jo Hennessey, one of her neighborhood friends, mentioned something about amateur night at Keeney's Theatre. "Amateur Night"—which, ironically, paid money to the winners—was a good way to break into show business in 1906, and Thursday was amateur night at Keeney's Theatre on Fulton Street in Brooklyn. Fanny became curious about these shows, and decided to see one with Hannah Ryan.

Keeney's Theatre, owned and managed by Frank Keeney, was Brooklyn's leading vaudeville theatre in the early 1900s. The inimitable Al Jolson, certainly the leading male musical variety performer of the 1910s and '20s, had made his first blackface appearance there in late 1904. Now, about a year and a half later, it would be the site of the debut of Fanny Brice, the leading female musical variety performer of the first quarter of the twentieth century. Neither appearance was considered historically noteworthy at the time. Fanny's debut, in fact, was completely unexpected—by the audience, by Keeney, and by Fanny.

Economic necessity provided the scenario. Fanny and Hannah had a quarter each when they arrived at Keeney's, but found the only tickets left were fifty cents apiece. Fanny, though, was nothing if not streetsmart. Sizing up the situation, she said that her friend and she were putting on an act in that night's show. The girls were then directed to the stage door, where they got in free.

Fanny planned to see the show and leave before their turn came. But Frank Keeney never followed an order of entrance on amateur nights, and Fanny never knew when she and Hannah would be thrust onstage. She kept on asking when their turn would come, but got no satisfactory reply.

Finally, without much warning, the stage manager pushed Fanny out onstage. The laughing Hannah did not follow.

Fanny was terrified, and almost started weeping when someone in the gallery yelled, "Come on, Fanny." It was someone from around St. Mark's Place.

What saved Fanny—and began, not incidentally, her career—were the orchestrations then available from publishers at ten cents a song. It was not uncommon for performers at amateur nights, or patrons at restaurants, to go up to an orchestra conductor and request a certain well-known number. Out would come the simple orchestration, and the request would be granted.

Fanny asked the orchestra at Keeney's to play "When You Know You're Not Forgotten by the Girl You Can't Forget," a popular ballad by Fred Helf and Ed Gardenier. Fanny swayed throughout the introduction until one of the kids in the balcony hollered, "If you're going to jump, jump." Fanny laughed and sang, her voice filling the theatre. She had one of those clear, vibrant voices that the early 1900s cherished. Fanny made a few of the exaggerated gestures that had sometimes brought laughter from the front stoop loungers. At Keeney's, though, they brought approval, and several well-to-do patrons in the front rows threw coins up on the stage. She sang the ballad very sadly, stooping down to pick up the money and say "Thank you" without missing a beat. This half intentionally funny gesture got big laughs, and Fan, who got a huge ovation when her song was over, picked up a total of four dollars in change by the time she left the stage. She also won first prize—ten dollars—at the end of the evening.

"It took me three-quarters of an hour to get to the theater," she told Charles Darnton of the *New York Herald Tribune* some years later. "But going back I made it in ten minutes—zip!" Fanny bought a pair of white canvas shoes and a willow plume the next day.

Frank Keeney now told Fanny about other amateur contests, some at theaters in which he had a part interest. He also told her not to pick her money up until she finished singing.

Fanny's life as a performer had begun, although French Charlie had not seen the launching. The *bon vivant* French Jew who nurtured Fanny's stage ambitions would live several more years. His effect on Fanny, however, would last decades, shaping both her stage work and her preference in men. Fanny, thanks to Charlie, was an artist. Unlike him, however, she was practical and strong. The talent would enable her to triumph on the stage. The strength, though, would allow her to survive.

CHAPTER *2*

Enter Miss Brice

F rank Keeney had interests in two other Brooklyn theaters besides the one he owned on Fulton Street, and Fanny's next amateur night appearance was at one on Flatbush Avenue. This time, she did not pick her money up until she finished singing. The result was that she missed the laughs she had gotten at Keeney's. Fanny soon went back to picking up the money.

The next six months saw Fanny enter one Brooklyn amateur night after another, usually, though certainly not always, walking home with the first prize. "I started getting smug about it, and I finally let it carry over on the stage. You could cut the audience resentment with a knife. I never let myself get smug again."

Fanny's songs included "Cheer Up, Mary," "Once in a While," and three or four other equally forgotten numbers. As her confidence grew, she expanded her act and did an imitation of Joe Welch, the Yiddish-dialect comedian, when she sensed the mood was right.

Fanny's bent for comedy was nurtured, not by just the Jewish need for humor, but the very nature of popular theatre. That nature was, of course, pure entertainment, with comedy its backbone. In vaudeville, a medium built around individual performers, anything was "okay if it made them laugh"—providing one did not offend. Sex and religion were officially taboo, but ethnic and racial humor was accepted. So was born the blackface, the green-bearded Irish comic, and the dialectician. Fanny, with her multi-ethnic background, ready ear, and natural curiosity about all sorts of people, was naturally inclined toward dialects—not only Yiddish, but the hybrid Irish-German dialect heard so often in the greater New York area in the early 1900s. In 1906, however, she was principally a singer, singing mostly ballads, with brief forays into novelties and comedy songs like "In My Merry Oldsmobile," "Will You Love Me in December As You Do in May?" and "If The Man in the Moon Was a Coon."

"The amateur night audience is primitive," Fanny said years later. "It is a thing of large proportions. It is either terribly cruel or vastly appreciative, leaping like a wild animal on the weak, praising to the skies those who please it, and always admiring a fighter. I learned to watch its every move and to beat it to that move. When it wanted sentiment, I gave it tears by the bucketful. When it wanted funny stuff, I clowned to the best of my ability."

In contrast to the world of New York theater in the late twentieth century, in which skilled, professional union actors work for nothing in "showcase" productions that lead nowhere, some "amateurs" of Fanny Brice's girlhood managed to make comfortable livings off cash prizes and the coins thrown by appreciative patrons. Fanny sometimes netted more than thirty dollars weekly, a respectable wage for a white-collar worker and a fortune for a girl of fourteen and a half in 1906—even if she gave most of her earnings to her mother.

When the master of ceremonies at one amateur show introduced her as "the Brooklyn favorite, Miss Fanny Borach," Fanny thought she'd gone as far as possible in Brooklyn. Rose was no stage mother, but she thought a singer who could make thirty dollars a week in Brooklyn would probably make fifty in New York. "My mother couldn't read or write," remembered Fanny, "but she could count like a bugger."

Phil, now nineteen and the owner of a fledgling dairy business, stayed in the house on St. Mark's Avenue in Brooklyn. Rose and the rest of her children moved to an apartment at 147 East Eighty-second Street in the Yorkville section of Manhattan.

Charlie, who still visited his children, moved to New York, too. Unsuccessful as a bookie, he had gone into the real estate business and moved to 300 West 130th Street in the city's newest "boom" neighborhood, Harlem. (The boom eventually went bust, and Harlem apartments were increasingly offered to poor black families fleeing the revived Ku Klux Klan in the South.)

Rose would sometimes visit Charlie there along with Carrie, Fanny, and Lew. One time, late at night, Fan overheard her parents discuss sex, a subject she had learned about from girlfriends, but had not discussed at home.

The more that Fanny heard that night, the more she knew that sex—not just French Charlie's laziness—had wrecked her parents' marriage.

Fanny loved French Charlie but did not respect him. She conversely respected but did not like Rosie. This curious dual ambivalence toward both her parents was an important part of Fanny's inner makeup. The necessity of seeing herself as her own role model built her confidence and forced her to make her life with outside friends.

Fanny, now completely self-reliant, pursued show business with a vengeance once the Borachs moved into Manhattan. All her love, ambition, energy, and hopes, previously scattered among charities and money-making schemes, now were channelled into learning songs and making contacts. Fanny's gung-ho attitude about her new career seemed down-right funny to many, and her single-minded purpose behind making social contacts might have seemed quite boorish had it not been tempered by a genuine interest in people.

Fanny did not *like* people as much as she was fascinated by them. What made them act and think in different ways, their diverse personal dislikes and different skills, intrigued her by the hour. Show biz people, with their egos, intense jealousies, and childlike insecurities, seemed to be most interesting of all.

One of Fanny's friends among the "amateurs" was a pretty Irish girl named Kitty Flynn. Fan and Kitty started buying the theatrical trade papers—*Dramatic Mirror, Clipper,* and a new one called *Variety*—and haunting the offices of Tin Pan Alley music publishers on Twenty-eighth Street. Becoming friendly with professional performers, they heard about *A Millionaire's Revenge,* a new melodrama being produced by the Mittenthal Brothers Amusement Company. Fan and Kit went to their office and were hired.

Their parts, of course, were merely "bits." The idea of two untrained teen-aged girls with no agents or professional experience landing acting jobs within a few short weeks may seem remarkable today. One must bear in mind, however, that the theatre of the early 1900s was a thriving business. In a world without television, and where the motion picture had not yet begun to toddle, the stage had the task of supplying entertainment for the masses. The 1906–07 season would prove to be the most active in the history of the American theatre, with hundreds of professional touring shows, more than a thousand active vaudeville theatres, minstrelsty, burlesque, stock companies, and a dozen circuses. More than thirty thousand people made their livings as performers.

A Millionaire's Revenge was a four-act melodrama by Hal Reid, a successful and prolific hack whose other plays had launched Gladys Smith (later known as Mary Pickford) as a child actress. Clumsily exploiting the then-recent shooting murder of famed architect Stanford White by Harry K. Thaw, jealous husband of Evelyn Nesbit, *A Millionaire's Revenge* featured characters named "Harold Daw," "Stanford Black," and "Emeline Hudspeth Daw," and sought to make a hero of the deranged Thaw by depicting White as an obnoxious debauchee who takes part in blatant orgies and brags of his previous intimacy with Nesbit.

Fanny, Kitty, and two other girls (Grace Smith and Maysie Harrison) played "artist's models" who fearfully enter the "Black" studio and do a little singing and dancing turn. One of the play's highlights was a model popping out of a pie, and Fanny agreed to be the model—costumed in the barest of chiffon.

A Millionaire's Revenge opened at the Lyceum Theatre in Elizabeth, New Jersey, on Monday evening, September 10, 1906. Fanny, under the stage name "Jenny Waters," proved to be the sole diversion in what everyone considered Hal Reid's worst play. Not yet fifteen, skinny and underdeveloped, Fanny had to wear "symmetricals" beneath her tights in the girls' singing and dancing turn—"falsies" for the legs and breasts that had a way of falling from position. Even Fanny's singing voice was hampered by a cold. As luck would have it, Kitty Flynn had the same cold, so only two girls out of four did any singing. The "four models" were as comically inept as the entire play.

The climax to the disaster came in Pittsburgh, the Thaw family's hometown, when one of the actors bumped into Fanny's pie and overturned it on the stage, its built-in light bulbs cutting Fanny. Forced to withdraw from the cast, she headed home to Harlem, recovery, and more amateur contests.

Rosie, who had gone into the insurance business on Eighty-second Street, now went back into real estate and moved the family to 26 Beekman Place on the ritzy East Side of Manhattan. The new location, though, was not lucky for Fanny. Amateur nights did not seem as popular—or numerous—in New York as in Brooklyn, nor was Fanny Borach as triumphant. Feeling she needed more experience, and ever on the lookout for more money, Fanny scanned the newspapers for advertisements about amateur shows in New York, Brooklyn, and Newark. One of her successes in Manhattan was at Hurtig & Seamon's Music Hall at 125th Street and Seventh Avenue, where her younger brother Lew had already won third place under the name "Willie Green." Lew had been taking dancing lessons from a soft-shoe pro named Bower, and could do eight variations on one step.

Amateur contests, some of which were looked upon as "rackets" by disgruntled losers, were always held at night, so Fanny, as practical as Rosie, took her friend Harry Green's offer of a day job at a movie house on East Eighty-third Street. "In those days," she recalled, "they were featuring illustrated songs. A stereopticon view of two lovers, the title of the song over their heads in big letters, would be thrown on the screen.

Someone had to sing the song as long as the picture stayed before the crowd. That was my job. Afterwards, the chorus of the song was thrown on the screen and everybody joined in the singing and had a good time.

"I sang. I sold tickets. I painted signs. I played the piano. The audiences in those days liked to be annoyed. I didn't know how to play. They didn't care."

Fanny became friendly with the theater's cashier, a young woman ten years older than she. That summer, one year after Fanny's stage debut at Keeney's, the cashier heard that George M. Cohan and Sam H. Harris needed chorus girls for their new show, *The Talk of New York*. She relayed the news to Fanny, and suggested they apply.

Cohan, the cocky, brilliantly versatile Irish-American who had rocketed to wealth and fame in *Little Johnny Jones* in 1904, and Harris, the affable manager of former world featherweight boxing champion Terry McGovern, had formed Cohan & Harris Productions one year earlier to produce *Popularity,* Cohan's first play without music and first flop. *Forty-Five Minutes from Broadway,* the only previous Cohan show not to have George M. in its cast, had elevated Victor Moore to stardom as racetrack character Kid Burns, the role he was reprising in *The Talk of New York*.

The salary for chorus girls in *The Talk of New York* was eighteen dollars a week—below what Fanny had been earning as an "amateur," but quite good for an untrained chorine in her first production. Unwilling to jeopardize her job at the movie theatre, Fan had her mother phone and tell the manager she had a fever—while she herself went downtown to Cohan & Harris.

There was no audition. The twenty-five-year-old cashier was dismissed as too old, but Fanny was told to leave her name and address with a production assistant. Two weeks later, she received a postcard telling her to report for rehearsals on the roof of the New Amsterdam Theatre on Forty-second Street. Only then did Fanny quit her movie theatre job.

Victor Moore was the star of *The Talk of New York,* but the chief figure at rehearsals was the twenty-nine-year-old Cohan—co-producer, librettist, lyricist, composer, and director of the show.

"Rehearsals were called," Fanny remembered. "George M. Cohan and Sam Harris sat down in the orchestra in the front row. Somebody handed out songs and we were ordered to get around the piano." The song young Fanny and her sister chorines had to learn that day was "Won't You Put a Little Bet Down for Me?" a modest ensemble number that worked well within the context of the show.

Fanny, ever the ham, was chagrined because Cohan and Harris were neither able, nor particularly interested, to hear her sing. Determined to be noticed, Fanny held the last notes of each closing line with all her might.

She was noticed all too quickly. Cohan jumped out of his seat, pointed a sharp finger at her, and barked out "No solos! Don't you hold those notes."

Young Fanny took this rebuke with mixed feelings. She had been chastised, but noticed, and was ham enough to feel proud at having sung a "solo" in a Broadway rehearsal.

Things went smoothly from that point until the beginning of the second week, when the girls (chorines tended to be in their teens) were shown the dance steps. Few chorus girls of that day were trained dancers, but Fanny was so gawky and awkward that her efforts to pick up the steps were actually comic. "I didn't know my left foot from my right," she later said. "Everytime someone said 'Right,' I had to stop to think which hand I wrote with and then carry the idea down to my toes." Fanny's rather fanciful account just underscores the pitiful reality: a disoriented, floundering teen-ager trying pitifully to keep up with the action and sometimes lapsing into comedy in an attempt to deal with an awful situation.

Cohan, every bit as witty and fiery as James Cagney played him in *Yankee Doodle Dandy,* thought the fifteen-year-old girl was either cutting up or totally lacking in coordination. "All right, that's it," he finally shouted. "I can't stand it," he said to Sam Harris; "she's holding up the whole works. You—with the St. Vitus Dance," he said, pointing to Fanny. "Back to the kitchen!"

Fanny, thunderstruck at Cohan's action, went backstage, sat down, and wept. She cried for fully half an hour, stopped, and sat for a few minutes, wondering what her next move would be. Then the rehearsal ended and she heard George M. approach.

Fanny quickly spat on her hands, rubbed her eyes, and started to weep all over again. Cohan was sympathetic, but he told the girl she simply could not dance. "I know," said Fanny, putting down her handkerchief. "But I can sing."

Cohan stressed his need for dancers, but gave Fanny the address of a man casting a show who needed singers. Fanny went to the address and found a third-rate company in a broken-down rehearsal hall. "I decided," Fanny later said, "that it was not for me."

Returning home, she told her mother that Cohan had decided she was "too skinny" after seeing her in tights. Rosie believed her, and the episode was closed. But Fanny, ever practical and willing to work hard, thought the time had come to learn to dance.

An advertisement in a trade paper said that Rachel Lewis trained people for the stage and gave them "practical experience." Fanny saw it as a wise investment, and went down to Rachel's office at Sixth Avenue and Thirty-fourth Street. Rosie, who controlled the purse strings, went down with her.

Rachel Lewis, a woman in her thirties, was willing to train Fanny for the theatre for the modest sum of two hundred and fifty dollars in 1907 money. Rosie argued the price down to thirty-five, and Fanny was told to report the next day.

Fanny did, expecting to get training and meet other young performers. But the only person there was Rachel Lewis. "She just talked," remembered Fanny. "Then, the next day, she measured me for a costume."

Rachel Lewis was something more—or less—than an acting teacher. She put shows together for the road, making money from her share of the receipts (the "student actors" were paid nothing) as well as from tuition. After a few days, other "students" showed up, and rehearsals for *The Ballad Girl,* a rags-to-riches play about a little chorus girl who takes the place of an obnoxious leading woman, were begun.

The leading man was Charles O'Neill, not a student actor, but a drunk and Rachel's lover. Rachel gave Fanny a tiny part and a yellow cheesecloth dress she remembered as "ten inches above my knees." Fanny had already reached her adult height of five-seven and weighed less than one hundred pounds. "Imagine," she said later, "how I looked."

Rachel, Gene, Fanny, and the other "student actors" went out on the road with *Ballad Girl,* playing one-night stands in Pennsylvania. The ever-eager Fanny was exploited as a workhorse, cleaning out whatever dirty, run-down theatres Rachel booked and taking care of Sunday, the leading lady's dog in *Ballad Girl.* Rachel paid her rent and gave her twenty-five cents a day for meals. "The dog cost me ten cents a day," remembered Fanny. "I never got any salary."

But she did get laughs. Fanny's first appearance saw her tugging at her dress in an effort to cover her fifteen-year-old legs. She did not know the cause of all the titters until later.

The Ballad Girl failed to do business, and Rachel, deciding heavy melodrama would be much more commercial, sent the scenery and costumes back and got *A Royal Slave* by Clarence Bennett. Fanny now became a seamstress in addition to her other duties. "Rachel had me up until three or four o'clock every morning sewing tassels on corduroy pants," she recalled. To partially reward her for her efforts, Rachel gave Fanny the lead in *Royal Slave.*

Fanny played a girl forced into marriage by her stepmother, her costume the same yellow cheesecloth dress with a sash tied around the middle. A wedding dress, needed for the final scene, consisted of a slightly altered window curtain.

"We opened," recalled Fanny. One night, the manager of the hotel came to the theatre with a policeman and pointed out the curtain. Rachel settled the account by paying the hotel manager three dollars.

A Royal Slave did better business than *The Ballad Girl,* but not enough to suit Rachel or keep Charley O'Neill in liquor. Several weeks after the play opened, Fan was sitting writing letters at a long table in the lobby of the Hotel Randall in Hazleton, Pennsylvania. A woman and her daughter, also in the show, were seated close by.

At one point, Fanny looked into a mirror and saw Rachel and Charley making for the front door, carrying valises. They were obviously trying to desert the company, which meant their "student actors" would be stranded.

Fan, the mother, and her daughter followed Lewis and O'Neill to the train station and into the same car. When the conductor came for their fares, they said the "lady up front" had them.

"Rachel was sure surprised when she turned around and saw us," recalled Fanny. "She paid our fares."

Fanny felt sorry for the woman and her daughter, who were without money or a place to live. She suggested that they come and stay at her house.

"They did," remembered Fanny. "They seemed to be ready to stay there for the rest of their lives. We had to get a policeman to throw them out.

"For a long time after that, whenever I went away, Mama'd say, 'Don't bring home any more actresses, Fanny.'"

Rachel Lewis had taught her almost nothing but a cheap imitation of a Spanish dance, but Fanny had decided not to pursue further instruction. Three months' training was more than most stage aspirants received in 1907, and the determined teen-ager had already decided her next course of action. Broadway shows, she reasoned, were beyond her at the moment, but burlesque, then called the "break-in ground" of show business, was not. Fanny went to see Joe Hurtig at Hurtig & Seamon's Music Hall the day after she returned from Hazleton.

Burlesque from the 1890s to the onset of the Great Depression in the early 'thirties was controlled by a handful of individuals who owned more than twenty shows between them, the shows rotating between thirty cities on a self-contained circuit known as the Columbia Wheel. The all-important owners were Ed Rush, L. Lawrence Weber, Sam Scribner, and the six Hurtig brothers—Ben, Joe, Lou, Jules, Israel, and Harry.

The enthusiastic teenager reminded Joe Hurtig of the amateur contest she had won at Hurtig & Seamon's Music Hall the previous season, and of how her strong, clear voice had won his praise. Now, Fanny assured him, she had obtained "experience" as well. Proceeding to make *The Ballad Girl* and *A Royal Slave* sound like triumphs touring the capitals of Europe, she asked him for a place in one of the four Hurtig shows.

Fanny Borach was no beauty, and would have had far more difficulty breaking into show business in a later era. But producers were accessible to aspiring performers in the early 1900s, and Hurtig took a liking to this gregarious young Jewess with the strong, clear singing voice. He finally said he would find room for Fanny in the *Trans-Atlantic Burlesquers,* a Hurtig show then playing the Olympic Theatre in Brooklyn.

Fanny still knew nothing about dancing, but Joe Hurtig told the company manager to work her into the chorus, and Fanny was put into the back row. She did her best to ape the steps of other dancers, and if the results were dismal, the presence of fifteen other chorines covered all her flaws. No one ever saw the feet of the tall girl in the back row.

The salary was fifteen dollars a week, less than half of what Fanny had been clearing from her amateur night triumphs a year earlier. But she had broken into "real show business"—which was all that mattered to the stagestruck girl.

Much has been written of the many great performers who came out of vaudeville into Broadway, radio, and movies. But the notion of vaudeville as a training ground might have seemed downright insulting to variety performers and managers of the early 1900s. Vaudeville headliners earned salaries ranging from $150 (in the "small-time") to $3,000 a week, and stars of the legitimate theater, from Ethel Barrymore to Mrs. Patrick Campbell, often toured vaudeville in one-act "tabloid" versions of their stage successes, earning more than they could make on Broadway.

The training ground, if any, was burlesque. This was not the burlesque of the 'thirties, when the strip tease was promoted to attract business at the height of the Depression. This was burlesque in its literal sense, a theatrical art form that poked fun—in opening and closing "travesties" sandwiched around a series of variety acts called an "olio"—at plays and topics of the day.

Like most stagestruck people, Fanny worshipped talented performers.

The leading "soubrette" of the *Trans-Atlantic Burlesquers* was Lizzie Freligh, a veteran of five years in burlesque who had once played boys' parts for Weber and Fields.

Lizzie had reportedly been raised in convents in Georgetown, D.C., and upper New York State. Originally intending to make singing her career, she had damaged her voice by performing in the open air as vocal soloist with one of the big turn-of-the-century marching bands. While with Weber and Fields, Lizzie substituted for Frankie Bailey, known for her attractive legs.

Lizzie told a writer for the Pittsburgh Post that she "just happened to get into burlesque . . . made somewhat of a success and . . . found no reason to change. The salary, and that is what we are after when all is said and done, is large and treatment couldn't be better." Nor was Lizzie's attitude unique. Performers of the early 1900s viewed the stage in much the same way that law enforcement officials viewed the police force. The theatre was a way of life, but also a trade or profession in which one expected to earn a living. A real "trouper" loved the stage in much the same way as the dedicated "copper" (there were many) loved the police force. Lizzie was with the *Bowery Burlesquers,* another Hurtig show, before joining the *Trans-Atlantic Burlesquers* for the 1907–08 season.

Sophie Tucker, roughly five years Fanny's senior, remembered Fanny's taking her to a hotel on Twelfth Street in New York to meet Lizzie, "a tiny, dainty creature, adored by the galleries for her roguish smile and her gift for being naughty in a nice way. Fanny thought the world of her and ran her errands with the devotion of a schoolgirl for an older girl crush."

"The Flubb-Dubb Conspiracy" was the first part of the *Trans-Atlantic* show. This "burletta" had been in use for a few seasons, but the *New York Clipper* said it had been "embellished with some pretty new numbers" upon reviewing the show at the Murray Hill Theatre in New York. The show's olio included the Sisters De Graff, who sang "up-to-date songs in the latest style," Eddie Fitzgerald and John Quinn in a comedy sketch, the Kalinowski Brothers (European acrobats), Normal Bell in "operatic selections, assisted by her musical ponies," Clay Smith and Eddie Convey in a "talking and singing act," and a trio composed of Val Rayner, James Whitely, and Eddie Nugent singing various songs in "excellent harmony." "The Gay Modiste" was the closing burlesque, with Lizzie as Jean De Resky.

In the chorus, Fanny faked along as best she could and gave support to Lizzie in two numbers, "My Irish Rosie" and "I'm Happy When the

Band Plays Dixie," the finale of "The Flubb-Dubb Conspiracy," in which Miss Freligh delighted her male admirers by appearing in tights.

Fanny learned a lot about stage basics in the six months she spent in the chorus of the *Trans-Atlantic Burlesquers.* She learned about such things as backstage discipline, how scenes are played, and how an entire show is run and performed before an audience. Moreover, she made friends with Lizzie Freligh. Burlesque stars were known as "bitches" to the chorus girls, but Lizzie was reputedly as charming off the stage as on, and was as fond of Fanny as the young and gawky Jewess was of her.

Fanny learned a lot; but she did not learn how to dance.

The *Trans-Atlantic Burlesquers* closed its season at the Gayety Theatre in Milwaukee on May 16, 1908. Rosie, still dealing in real estate, had bought a house at 154 West 128th Street, and Fanny spent the next two months basking in the glory of her girlfriends' admiration. She was in "show business"—a virtual celebrity to "non-professionals" like John and Bertha Brice, who lived near the new Borach house and had rekindled their old friendship with Fan's mother.

Fanny continued to buy the trade papers and make the rounds of agents and producers. But she knew she was not good enough to dance in Broadway chorus lines, and vaudeville booking agents had no use for skinny teenagers without saleable acts. Fanny, then, was only too glad when Joe Hurtig agreed to put her in the chorus of *The Girls from Happyland,* another of the Hurtig brothers' shows. The stars were Billy W. Watson, who had come to prominence as principal comedian of *Me, Him, and I,* and, to Fanny's delight, Lizzie Freligh.

A black man—Fanny could never remember his name—staged *The Girls from Happyland.* He wanted a good chorus, and was driven to distraction by Fanny's gawky fumbling of basic instructions and her ignorance of fundamental dance steps. He frankly told Joe Hurtig that the girl was hopeless, but Fanny pleaded and her job was saved.

Fanny was taken out of the chorus and used strictly as a singer. Joe Hurtig was no fool. Playing Fanny strictly to type as a persistent ham anxious to break into show business, he had her sing unexpected second choruses from the boxes, aisles, and seats in different parts of the theatre. It was a rather unique role, but Fanny was more insulted than honored. Singing from the house was something done by "stooges," amateur "plants" installed to help an act or show. And a stooge was not considered a professional performer. Odd as it may seem, young Fanny was determined to get back into the chorus.

To sooth her battered ego and discourage further references to her as

"Fanny 'Bore-Act,'" Fanny changed her name. She had already told John Brice she would adopt his surname for the stage. Now she thought the time had come, and theatrical trade rosters listed "Fanny Brice" in *The Girls from Happyland* company for the 1908–09 season. The name had character, was easy to remember and pronounce. It was euphonious, and not overtly ethnic in its day. There was, what's more, a well-known actress known as Fanny Rice.

The Girls from Happyland was scheduled to open the new season in Birmingham, Alabama, on August 30, 1908. Fanny told her mother she would need extra underwear, and proceeded to grab every brassiere, pair of panties, and petticoat in the Borach household. She had a plan.

"My mother had made me some chemises, the kind with ribbons running through them, and a lot of shirtwaists. Choosing the best dancer in the chorus, I offered her a chemise in payment for a lesson in dance steps."

That was not all. "I bought a pair of wooden shoes and went about learning how to dance by bribing the stage hands and the other girls. Most stage hands know a few dancing steps, and whenever I saw one practicing his favorite, I would give him a quarter to teach it to me. I bribed the girls with shirtwaists and other wearing apparel. So finally there came a day when I could dance well enough to work in the chorus, and when that day came I demanded loudly that I be admitted."

That was in St. Louis, only four weeks after the start of the season. Two weeks after that, Fanny was promoted from the back row to the second.

Lizzie Freligh left the show in late November, and the resulting shakedown in the company lifted Fanny to the front row of the chorus and a rather brief part as a maid. Fan, however, was not altogether happy. She had become close to Lizzie and missed her friendship deeply. Fanny was relieved and joyful when Lizzie rejoined the show two months later.

Some accounts of Fanny's life say that she became Lizzie's understudy at this point. But Mabel Leslie had taken Lizzie's place during her absence and continued as her standby for the balance of the tour. Fanny, though, was given a small part to understudy, a job that grew important when Lizzie took another, final leave of absence in the spring.

The woman Fanny understudied was the wife of the stage manager, a huge woman who seemed as healthy as the horses that still pulled the bulk of the nation's traffic. In Chicago, Fanny noticed that the woman had an abscess on the back of her right ear. It grew all week, and burst before *The Girls from Happyland* opened a one-week engagement at Cincinnati's Standard Theatre on Sunday, May 3, 1909.

The woman was carried back to her room at the Sinton Hotel, and Fanny went on as a principal for the first time.

Fanny played her small part well. She had a gift for fun, and the stage intelligence to sense the inherent humor of a line, a scene, or a moment on the stage. Frank Livingston, the company manager, was particularly impressed with her comedic talents, ideally suited as they were to farce and burlesque theatre. The audience seemed to catch her pleasure at being onstage, and to trust her judgement if she thought something was funny.

Fanny sent a wire to her brother, Lew, in Cleveland, proudly boasting of her Cincinnati "triumph." Lew and the other two members of his "Newsboys Trio" were working in the olio of *The Trocaderos,* a show whose tour had been extended to the end of May.

The sending of that telegram proved fortunate for Fanny. One of *The Trocaderos'* female leads was leaving the show, and Lew recommended Fanny to replace her. With *The Girls from Happyland* slated to close in Cincinnati, Fanny wired her acceptance, and a copy of the script was hurriedly delivered. Fanny learned the part in two days and played it— to the management's relief—in Buffalo, Toronto, and Boston.

It had been a season of great progress for young Fanny. From being thrown out of the chorus in rehearsals, she had worked her way from stooge to back-row chorus girl, to front-row chorus girl, to understudy, to principal. She had made valuable friendships, and impressed many with her hard work, willingness to learn, and success under pressure. In a theatre that rewarded guts and talent, teen-aged Fanny Brice had won acceptance. She had shown, in the then-current parlance, she "belonged."

CHAPTER 3

College Girl

T he show business of the early 1900s was both larger and more closely knit than it would be three quarters of a century later. The average actor, whether vaudeville, burlesque, or "legit," knew literally hundreds—maybe thousands—of people in his chosen field, ranging from other actors to theatre managers, stagehands to advance agents, prop men to dressers. Cohan, as producer, director, author, and performer, knew so many people in show business that he started calling everybody "kid." Fanny, as her show biz circles widened, soon got into the same habit.

Fanny kept up with the latest show biz gossip, continued reading the trade papers, and made the rounds of song publishers like Leo Feist on Thirty-seventh Street and the new Ted Snyder Company on Thirty-eighth, where she became friendly with Snyder and his staff lyricist, twenty-one-year-old Irving Berlin. She was becoming known in certain show business circles, not so much for her work as for her enthusiasm. Few in New York, at this point, had seen Fanny Brice perform. Everyone, however, seemed to know the gawky but ambitious young singing comedienne with the mobile face, slim figure, and burning ambition.

Fanny had been back in New York just three weeks before she heard Frank Livingston had been made manager of *The College Girls,* a new burlesque show on the Columbia Eastern Wheel. Determined to land a principal role in the new company, she had Frank recommend her to Max Spiegel, one of the co-owners.

There was no audition; Spiegel simply asked Fanny if she had a "specialty," a song or dance or routine she could do in the olio. Fanny, although not a seasoned pro, had learned one of the first rules of show business: if someone asks if you can do something—say yes! She knew she had given the right answer when Spiegel engaged her at a salary of twenty-five dollars a week, but was mortified when, one week into re-hearsals, he instructed her to report to the Arverne (Long Island) Thea-tre on Thursday night and do her nonexistent specialty at the Friars' special benefit show.

Doing what she could to hide her panic, Fanny left Spiegel's office and ran down to the Ted Snyder Music Publishing Company at 112 West Thirty-eighth Street. Irving Berlin was there when she rushed in.

Fanny said she needed a specialty, and Berlin, still making only twenty-five dollars a week against royalties, taught her his two latest composi-tions—"Sadie Salome, Go Home" and "Wild Cherries." He sang "Sadie Salome" with a Yiddish accent that had "all the intonation of Hester Street." The song concerned a Jewish girl who does the daring Salome "Dance of the Seven Veils," then the rage of vaudeville due largely to Eva Tanguay's notorious interpretation.

Fanny had done imitations of Yiddish comedian Joe Welch on ama-teur shows and, later, chorus girl nights while with Hurtig & Seamon. (Welch, one of the best of the "Jew" comics, played a godforsaken type who suffered one misfortune on top of another.) But "Sadie Salome" sparked something in Fanny. Her sense of fun, of the risqué, was made for Berlin's song, as was her proclivity for eye-rolling comment on out-rageous situations. Sophie Tucker later claimed that Fanny learned her Yiddish dialect from Harry Delf, "a grand Jewish comedian who used to play the joints in Brooklyn and Coney Island." Fanny was familiar with Delf's work, as well as that of Ben Welch, Barney Bernard, Alexander Carr, and many other Yiddish dialect comedians. But "Sadie" marked her start as a comedienne, and Berlin, himself only a youth on the threshold of greatness, was Fanny's show-business godfather.

The program at the Arverne had her sandwiched in between Lew Fields (of Weber and Fields fame) and Raymond Hitchcock, one of the biggest musical comedy stars of the period. "In those days," recalled Fanny, "if the audience was surprised at anything I did, they weren't any more so than I was, as I never had a routine or knew what I was going to do until I hit the stage. I had only instinct to go by." Fanny rolled her big green eyes and used her hands in oblique, grotesque gestures as she sang.

> Don't do that dance, I tell you, Sadie.
> Dat's not a business for a lady.
> Most ev'rybody knows that I'm your loving Mose.
> Oy, oy, oy, oy, where is your clothes?
> Sadie Salome, go home.

"Before I reached the second verse, it happened," Fan remembered. "The thing that begins to change your life—the clangor, the first thunder on the mountaintop!"

What really happened was more startling than thunder; Fanny's starched white sailor suit had gathered in a most strategic place. Fanny squirmed as the suit goosed her, and the more she squirmed, the more the audience laughed. Fanny finished "Sadie Salome," sang "Wild Cherries" (a good ragtime song with music by Ted Snyder) and was forced to give an encore.

"Perhaps," she later said, "this was one of the few occasions in his life that an audience made Raymond Hitchcock wait."

Fanny had now found her niche. Her progress from here on would be extremely rapid in a day in which careers were based on years of trouping, all the more incredible because she did not stem from a theatrical background. Fanny, due to talent, drive, good fortune, and the niche Berlin had given her, would rise to the top of show business like a cork.

Max Spiegel wanted to sign Fanny to a three-year contract after seeing her perform in Arverne. Since she was still seventeen, and therefore underage, he said to take the contract home and have her mother sign it.

Fanny told Spiegel her mother could not write and signed the contract herself. Rose could sign her name, but Fanny, still ambitious, did not want to mortgage her future for three years. Fanny's ego at this time and sense of her own worth would pave the way for her debut on Broadway.

Fanny Brice was now a signed professional, a teen-aged woman of the theatre. Far from a raving beauty, she felt vindicated by her success, and was proud to be young and an actress. The face that her success was in burlesque, the despised "bottom rung" of the theatrical profession, did not bother Fanny, who saw Broadway as the next step on her own professional ladder.

Fanny may have been the most ambitious teen-ager in America.

Although what was then known as an "antic" comedienne, relying on her face and body to get laughs, Fanny played what was called a "comedy-soubrette" part in *The College Girls*. "On and Off," the title of the show's feature-length musical playlet, was a travesty on *The College Widow*, a well-known play of the day that later served as inspiration for *Horse Feathers*, the 1932 Marx Brothers film vehicle. Act One concerned two college boys in love with each other's sisters. Their fathers, very German Heine Schmitz and very Irish Dennis McFadden, will not let them marry, so the boys get Lillian Lloyd, the college widow, to ensnare them. The second act, set in the "Gambling Rooms at the Chalet Noir in Paris," sees the arrival of the widow's French husband—played by R. G. Knowles, who had been "Professor Bunyon" in the first act.

The show's musical numbers were all catchy and well rendered: "Love

Thy Neighbor," sung by Joe Fields and George Scanlon as the fathers; "College Boy," sung by Willie Weston; and "O.I.C.," sung by the four sweethearts, Weston, Ed Harris, Fanny, and Grace Childres.

The College Girls opened the season at the Gayety Theatre in Brooklyn on Monday, August 21, 1909. Fanny's part was large, but nowhere near as crucial as that played by Weston, a curious victim of stage fright who was often funnier offstage than on. Weston was also in the olio, introducing several bright songs and winning fine applause with his impersonations of Cliff Gordon, the well-known "Dutch" or German comic; and Bert Williams, the great black comedian who worked behind a layer of burnt cork.

As time went by, however, Weston received competition. Fanny's rendition of "Sadie Salome" had, if anything, improved, her green eyes bugging out in comic shock as she intoned the lines reproaching Sadie's dance. "Wild Cherries" provided her the perfect upbeat encore.

There was a great turnover in burlesque, the owners shifting actors from one show to another with almost feudal expediency. Klara Hendrix replaced Grace Childres in mid-season, necessitating changes in the show that gave Fanny a new song, "Music Man," in which she led the chorus "with various lively moves and bright grimaces." Fanny was already doing a song called "The Girl with the Diamond Dress," in addition to "Sadie Salome" and "Wild Cherries" in the show's olio.

By February 1910, Fanny Brice was the most well-received and valued member of the company—not excepting Willie Weston. She roamed with Klara Hendrix, and the two soubrettes were soon inseparable friends, sharing everything from stage makeup to secrets.

Actors of those days had little formal education. Chorus girls, while not nearly as promiscuous as stage-door Johnnies liked to imagine, were mostly teen-aged girls with no formal training and little ambition past marriage. Principals like Fanny were cut from different cloth, but few of them envisioned themselves "single women."

Fanny was eighteen when *The College Girls* opened a three-night engagement at the Empire Theatre in Albany, New York, on Thursday, February 3, a girl who lived for the stage only and whose social life was bounded by letters from her family on one side and platonic friendships on the other. She later claimed men "never made passes" at her. In fact, men did make passes; Fanny did not catch them.

In light musical entertainment, a field in which gorgeous women are more the rule than the exception, Fanny was not beautiful and knew it. And like many women who feel unattractive, she refused to accept compliments with grace. Her response was to say something totally absurd and make a comic gesture. This would defuse the compliment and disconcert the courter.

She felt patronized by men, possibly exploited as an easy, quick convenience, or maybe even laughed at on the sly. She thus felt anger at unwanted suitors, feeling they had unmitigated gall in trying for her favors. Faced with Fanny's attitude, prospective lovers generally vanished.

Except one named Frank White, a barber Fanny met through Klara. "My God, he smelled nice," Fanny told Hettie Jithian Cattell in 1928. "I guess he used everything he had in the shop on himself." White, in fact, owned three barbershops, including one in Albany's Kenmore Hotel, and seemed sophisticated to the two teenaged performers.

What made Frank White successful was his sheer persistence. He followed Fanny and *The College Girls* from Albany to Boston, taking Fanny out to restaurants and almost smothering her with attention. Fanny thought a man who went to all that trouble simply had to really like her. In truth, White had a passion for young actresses, and Fanny was a talented young soubrette with considerable charm, if not beauty. After they had dinner for the fourth or fifth time—young Fanny never passed up a free meal—Frank proposed that they be married.

Fanny, street-smart but a virgin and naïve about men, gave him no reply, and Klara, who liked Frank, thought that she was crazy. Marriage was the norm, she argued; Frank was a nice guy, and why not take what one was offered? Fanny, to whom friends were all-important, had to listen.

The show moved on to Springfield, Massachusetts, and White, who also owned a barbershop in that town, moved right with it. On Sunday, February 13, he corralled Fanny and talked her into getting married. Full of doubts about men, not loving Frank, but needing love herself, she finally said yes.

Fanny was confused, but more afraid for her career than anything else, and added a condition to the nuptial agreement: Frank was not to consummate the marriage until June, when the season was over. Fanny had heard that girls who lost their virginity could not walk for several days, and did not want to risk losing her job in *The College Girls*.

White obtained a marriage license the next day, rented an open barouche, and went to pick up a reluctant Fanny. She feigned illness in a bid to postpone matters, but White had ordered a big wedding dinner for the company, and Fanny, not wishing to be ostracized by her fellow performers, resigned herself to the inevitable and got into the barouche.

The wedding service was performed, the company had dinner, White went back to Albany, and Fanny went to Holyoke and New York with *The College Girls*. Klara, who accepted Fanny's invitation to stay in the house on 128th Street, told Rose that Fanny had married a barber.

The family was flabbergasted, not just by the wedding, but by its suddenness and White's persistent, odd courting behavior. Carrie was now married, and Michael Radice, Fanny's new Italian brother-in-law, opined that Frank had married Fanny for her stage income. He even doubted White owned any barbershops.

The family sent White a wire demanding that he come down to New York. He obeyed, and, failing to impress his new in-laws, was assigned to a small room on the top floor. Rosie, still the "tiger," said she would have the marriage annulled.

"You had nothing to do with him," she told her younger daughter. Fanny was, if anything, relieved. She did not care about Frank White or any other man at this point—only about songs and other parts of the show business she had worked so hard to enter.

The College Girls played a week at the Gayety Theatre in Philadelphia following its engagement in New York. One night, as Fanny came out the stage door, Frank White grabbed her by the wrist and said he would call the police if she did not come with him. Young, poorly educated, unsure of the law, and anxious to avoid humilitation, Fanny went.

White made Fanny move her things to his hotel room. Trying to stall, Fan had Frank buy her a pineapple at a fruit stand on the way. In the room, Fan got into the long-sleeved cotton nightgown Rose had bought her at Siegel & Cooper, and, anxious to forestall the inevitable, slowly ate the pineapple as Frank watchfully cut pieces with his long, sharp penknife.

As soon as the last piece had been consumed, Frank got into bed with Fanny and consummated the marriage with considerable passion but little love. He grunted and groaned happily, but Fanny felt like she was having a tooth pulled. At the finish, her nightgown was stained with blood, and the satisfied White said he would take it home and show it to his "folks."

Frank and Fanny lived together for two days before *The College Girls* moved on to Newark. Three nights of sex with unresponsive Fanny was enough for White, who went back to his other barbershop in Schenectady, New York.

Fanny never saw Frank White again. Rose still tried to get the marriage annulled, but the now-deflowered Fanny had been three months past her eighteenth birthday when she married Frank—which meant they had to settle for divorce.

They got it more than two years later. Fanny, in the meantime, lived for her career and her friends.

In March, when *The College Girls* played Hurtig & Seamon's Music Hall on 125th Street, Fanny went back to the Ted Snyder Music Publishing

Company in search of new material. Berlin was not there this time, but Fanny met a young woman eight years her senior who would prove to be a valued lifelong friend.

Polly Moran, the raucous comedienne who later formed a rather short-lived but heralded screen comedy team with Marie Dressler, had seen Fanny when *The College Girls* played the Buckingham Theatre in Louisville. Polly was herself performing "Sadie Salome" in vaudeville—wiggling her finger in the air, but failing to capture the strong parody of Jewish discomfiture that underscored the Brice rendition. Following a critical suggestion, Polly watched Fanny perform in *The College Girls*.

Polly was impressed, and asked Ted Snyder to introduce her to Fanny when she saw her in his office. She always recalled Fanny in her sailor suit with its blue coat, white collar, and long skirt. Polly asked Fanny to Schrafft's at Thirty-seventh Street and Broadway for an ice cream soda. The two girls talked of songs and shows, laying the beginning of a lasting friendship.

Fanny once said that she "duplicated" friendships, and that Polly Moran was an adult, show-business version of Hannah Ryan, her Irish chum in Brooklyn. Fanny would have other duplicate relationships in the ensuing years.

Fanny now knew every publisher in Tin Pan Alley—F. B. Haviland at 125 West Thirty-seventh Street, F. A. Mills at 122 West Thirty-sixth, Leo Feist at 134 West Thirty-seventh, Jerome H. Remick & Company at 131 West Forty-first, and more than half a dozen others. The same week she met Polly Moran, Fanny got a note from Helen Ziegfeld, secretary for Joseph W. Stern & Company, asking her to come and hear some songs the firm was "plugging." Fanny showed the note to Klara and some other members of the company.

"Look," she told them, covering the "Helen," "Ziegfeld wants me." The trouble was that Fanny's colleagues knew she was half serious. Fan's ambitions were still soaring, and the *Ziegfeld Follies* seemed, to her, a realistic goal.

Three weeks later, *The College Girls* was back in New York, playing the brand-new Columbia Theatre.

The opening of the Columbia Theatre in January 1910 had been seen as the ultimate triumph of "reformed" burlesque by Weber, Scribner, and the other major cogwheels of the Columbia Amusement Company. Managers and actors from the legitimate theater and vaudeville attended, and even political and social names lent their presence to give sanction to what the late nineteenth century had seen as "lewd" and "vulgar."

Fanny's progress in the last year had been nothing short of remarkable, and the *New York Clipper*, long established as the leading journal of the entertainment business, touted her as a "major find and talent," saying that some smart manager was bound to "sign her up before too long." It came to pass quite soon—and on a higher plane than the *Clipper* had imagined.

The name of Ziegfeld has stood as the symbol of grand opulence, taste, and quality in theatre for more than three quarters of a century. The son of "Dr." Florenz Ziegfeld, head of the Academy of Music in Chicago, Florenz Ziegfeld, Jr., entered theatrical production when his father sent him to Europe to engage talent for the school's exhibition at the Chicago World's Fair of 1893. While in New York, young Ziegfeld signed up Sandow, Europe's greatest strongman, whom he managed for three years. Another trip to Europe brought Ziegfeld into contact with Anna Held, a young French music-hall performer he promoted to American stardom with the aid of outrageous publicity stunts—notably her celebrated "milk baths."

By 1907, when the forty-year-old Ziegfeld produced his first *Follies*, he was one of the best-known producers in the country, spending money on himself, his surroundings, and his productions with a lavishness not seen outside Versailles. "No one," Eddie Cantor said, "had less regard for money than Flo Ziegfeld." The theatrical world was thus enriched; as was, temporarily, Flo Ziegfeld. He finally died broke, a victim of the changing times and his own disregard for money.

Like those kings credited with poetry and music written by their courtesans and troubadors, a host of works his underlings accomplished have been credited to him. Joseph Urban, not Ziegfeld, created the lavish, tasteful sets and backgrounds that became the hallmark of the *Ziegfeld Follies* in 1915, and Gene Buck not only wrote much of the annual revue's material, but discovered much of the talent it was famous for and laid it before Ziegfeld.

Ziegfeld's only contact with burlesque was through a man named Jerry Siegel, an expert in the field who saw every show that played New York. Aware of Fanny through his reading of the *Clipper*, Siegel found her gift for mimicry, her wide, crooked smile, and the way she would make comment on a given situation with the raising of an eyebrow, not just funny, but "class" enough for Ziegfeld and a natural contrast for the far-famed *Follies* beauties.

Siegel saw the show on Monday evening, April 11, and spoke to Bert Cooper the following afternoon. Cooper, one of Fanny's many friends and a successful agent, told him all about her contract with Max Spiegel—signed when she was three months shy of eighteen and, as such, not binding.

Siegel, thus informed, called Ziegfeld. The *Follies* had never had a real comedienne (Bayes, Tanguay, and Tucker were more on the order of musical entertainers), and Ziegfeld felt that he was ready to discover new talent after relying on established names to carry the first three editions. Trusting Siegel's judgment, Ziegfeld sent a telegram to Fanny at the Columbia Theatre: WILL YOU COME TO SEE ME AT YOUR EARLIEST CONVENIENCE STOP FLORENZ ZIEGFELD.

Fanny was certain that a member of the cast had sent the telegram; the timing seemed too good after her joke about Helen Ziegfeld. But she called the Ziegfeld office just in case.

Assured the telegram had come indeed from Florenz Ziegfeld, Fanny flew down to the office, effervescently telling all she met along the way of her good fortune. When at last she stood before Flo Ziegfeld, she felt proud but anxious, dressed in the white outfit she wore in order not to look "burlesquey."

Ziegfeld was then a forty-three-year-old Midwestern gentleman who wore an ascot and spoke in what Fanny later described as a "twangy, whiny voice—even I have never been able to imitate it." (Surviving sound films make the Great Glorifier look and sound more like the head of a Chicago labor union than the Great White Way's revered producer of good taste and glamor.) "He spoke for a few minutes, telling me he thought there would be a place for me in the *Follies*."

Ziegfeld then produced two copies of a two-year contract calling for Fanny to receive seventy-five dollars a week for the first year and one hundred dollars a week for the second. Fanny signed, received her copy, and then left the office slowly, as she thought befit a lady. She thanked Ziegfeld's secretary, thanked the doorman, ran to Forty-seventh Street and Broadway—near the site on which the Palace would be opened three years later—and spent the next two hours showing passersby the contract. In those days, actors, agents, managers, and others in the theatre could be found on Broadway any minute of the day, and Fanny signalled everyone she knew was in show business. "Hey, Ziegfeld signed me," she would call, "a hundred a week"—quoting the second season's salary.

Fanny never went back to *The College Girls*. For the next few days, she stood on that street corner, the hub of the theatrical universe, showing the precious contract to everyone she thought had some connection with the theatre. Within a week, the stiff and shiny paper was in pieces, and Fanny had to ask Ziegfeld for another copy. She needed still another by the time the *Follies* went into rehearsal.

Fanny Brice was not the only major talent in the *Ziegfeld Follies* of 1910. Bert Williams, the deft and marvelous black comedian who had already enjoyed a great career while partnered with George Walker, was making his own *Follies* debut, and a sketch on the upcoming Johnson–Jeffries fight was written in which Bert would play Jack Johnson.

Williams was then thirty-five, a tall, broad-shouldered, and soft-spoken individual with the manners of the South Seas gentleman he, in fact, partly was. Seventeen years Fanny's senior, he invariably greeted her by asking, "How is Miss Fanny today?" A Mason, well-read, and respected throughout the theatrical profession, he was nonetheless subject to the same humiliations as less-celebrated black men. Fanny recalled that he insisted on using the back elevator if he stayed in first-rate "white" hotels when the *Follies* went on tour. That was to spare himself the indignity of being told he *had* to use it. "It wouldn't be so bad," he once confided, "if I didn't still hear the applause ringing in my ears."

The appearance of Williams as the first black performer ever featured in a major "white" Broadway musical led Ziegfeld to engage the talented black song-writing team of Will Marion Cook and Joe Jordan to write numbers for the show. (Williams provided his own numbers, and Gus Edwards, famed for his "kid" acts in vaudeville, was hired to write additional songs.) Fanny was cast in two scenes but had not been provided with "specialty" material by the time rehearsals started. When she questioned Ziegfeld about songs, he pointed out Cook and Jordan, who were surrounded by performers wanting more songs and additional lyrics for · encore choruses.

The tunesmiths told her they had nothing new as yet except the chorus of "Lovey Joe," a song named after Jordan, its composer. Fanny was impressed by what she heard. By the next morning, a complete song had been written that foreshadowed black blues numbers of a later decade. Fanny's introduction of it was a high point of rehearsals, and Ziegfeld gave her a good spot to sing it in the *Follies*.

The rest of the rehearsals were marked by squabbling for individual material, petty quarrels, and a major fight that centered around Bert Williams. Some of the principals objected to the black man's presence in the show, and Ziegfeld had to threaten to dismiss several people before the trouble stopped. A further problem occurred when Ziegfeld demanded that director Julian Mitchell add certain electrical effects to the show and then failed to give him the necessary money. Ziegfeld, ever cool, averted that one with a compromise. But more headaches would follow.

Fan herself caused trouble of a minor sort by making herself scarce during rehearsals. Whenever she was called, it seemed, she was out having a soda. And Ziegfeld's backer, A. L. Erlanger, bullyboy of the powerful Theatrical Syndicate, seemed to constantly upbraid her for her background in burlesque—which, though not then considered smutty, was still looked upon as "low class" theatre.

The *Ziegfeld Follies* of 1910, like its last two predecessors, tried out at Nixon's Apollo Theatre in Atlantic City prior to its opening on Broadway. Erlanger decided to take charge in Atlantic City, and Sunday, June 12, was set aside for dress rehearsal. The company was called for 10:00 A.M., and everyone was on time except Fanny.

When she finally arrived at 10:15, Abe Erlanger was furious. A squat, bald man of fifty, not known for his kindly disposition, he had threatened and browbeaten scores of producers into entering the fold of the Syndicate, a combine that included (Marc) Klaw and Erlanger, producer Charles Frohman, western theatre magnate Al Hayman, and theater owners Samuel F. Nixon and J. Frederick Zimmerman. By the turn of the century, Klaw & Erlanger had made it impossible to book a show or play without going through the Theatrical Syndicate, which extorted money from local theatre managers to guarantee first-class attractions and (off the record) from theatrical producers to ensure good routes. Abraham Lincoln Erlanger was not a man to cross.

"Look here, young woman," he told Fanny, "you're late. Don't you know you should have been here at ten o'clock?"

Fanny said "I know it," coolly, and Erlanger was enraged. "Then why weren't you here on time?" he demanded. Fanny, though, said nothing.

"Why don't you answer?" he continued. "Don't you know who I am?"

"Yes, I know who you are," Fanny replied. "But I don't care. I am not used to being talked to in any such manner, and until you change your tone I won't reply. We are treated like ladies in burlesque."

Erlanger almost exploded and told Fanny she was in imminent danger of losing her engagement. "I don't care if I am," said Fanny. "I am not going to be treated in this manner for any engagement. Burlesque is waiting for me any time I want to go back, and I will go back before I'll stand for any of this sort of thing."

The company was shocked, but Fanny stood her ground, and A. L. let the matter drop. Theatrical employment was far more plentiful in 1910 than it would be eighty years later, and neither Fanny's ego nor her shrewd cynicism were tempered by her thrill at being in the *Follies*. Her gall was also traceable, in part, to youth and quick success.

Abe Erlanger had a long memory. When Fanny's specialty was called at dress rehearsal, she sang the first verse and followed with the chorus:

> Lovie Joe, that ever lovin' man
> From 'way home in Birmingham

He can do some lovin' an' some lovin' sho',
An' when he starts to love me I jes' hollers "Mo"!

As soon as Fanny sang that line, Erlanger jumped up and yelled out "Stop! . . . Just a minute. Will you please sing that chorus over and pronounce those words 'sure' and 'more'?"

"But this is a coon song," Fanny said.

"I know it's a coon song, but where do you think you are, in a burlesque show? The people who come to my theatre pay two-fifty a seat, and they want to know what you're singing about."

Fanny went down to the footlights where she could see the famous "Honest Abe." "I live on 128th Street," she told him. "It's on the edge of Harlem. They all talk that way. No Negro would pronounce those words the way you did. I can't sing them any other way."

Erlanger exploded. "Put something else in place of that specialty! You're out! No one says 'No' to me on my stage when I say 'Yes'!"

Fanny had integrity—especially as it applied to art. As a middle-aged woman playing Baby Snooks on radio, she would at times refuse to say a line because "Snooks wouldn't say that." She showed that same integrity when she stood up to Erlanger in 1910.

Fanny went to the back of the theatre, sat down, and spent the rest of the rehearsal weeping bitter tears at life's unfairness. Hours later, back in her hotel room, a messenger told Fanny to report to Mr. Ziegfeld.

Ziegfeld, Fanny learned, had convinced Erlanger that her specialty was needed in order to make the scene, set in the "Office of a Music Publisher," run long enough for the preparation of the show's next segment. Fanny would sing "Lovey Joe" until a suitable replacement could be found—but only at the first performance in Atlantic City; she would probably not sing the song on Broadway.

The first performance of the *Ziegfeld Follies* of 1910 was given at Nixon's Apollo Theatre in Atlantic City on Monday night, June 13, 1910. Fanny came out to sing "Lovey Joe" at 9:30, what was later described as the "crux of the evening, when the audience was swimming in boredom because of the (untried) show's lack of rhythm and gait."

Fanny, dressed in a fashionable white satin gown, sang "Lovie Joe" her way—not Erlanger's—and stopped the *Follies* as cold as Ethel Merman stopped *Girl Crazy* with "I Got Rhythm" twenty years later. Theatrical convention then allowed for encores, and Fanny, by report, gave half a dozen. Abe Erlanger was standing in the wings as she came off, and held out his straw hat. "You owe me ten dollars," he laughed. "I broke this applauding you."

"You owe me an apology," said Fanny.

Many chroniclers have said that Fanny was the unqualified hit of the 1910 *Follies,* walking off with the reviews and audience acclaim when the show opened in New York. That is a slight exaggeration, though "Lovey Joe" went over big and Fanny was again forced to give encores. Adolph Klauber of the New York *Times* said that Fanny, "not especially prepossessing elsewhere, scored a hit with 'Lovey Joe,' for which her eccentric facial expression and queer vocal interpolations were largely responsible." Sime Silverman, founder of *Variety,* was more prophetic:

> Toward the ending of the performance, Julian Mitchell and Luise Alexander gave a "Vampire Dance," quite fierce in conception and execution. Also around eleven o'clock, Fanny Brice, who had previously made a big hit with her own style of singing a "coon" song, tempted the fates again with a "Yiddish" number that couldn't get over. Miss Brice entered the Follies from burlesque. She left a good impression, and will safely be continued a member of the organization if merit counts.

In truth, no one performer dominated that year's *Follies.* Bert Williams was "warmly welcomed," but found himself handicapped by poor material. The most commended member of the cast was probably young Lillian Lorraine, the showgirl who sang Victor Hollaender and Ballard MacDonald's "Swing Me High, Swing Me Low" while being swung out over the orchestra. (Miss Lorraine, already having problems with the bottle, scored an even bigger hit the night she forgot to wear drawers while performing this number.)

The general consensus was that the 1910 *Follies* was a long show with good and bad material that took a nosedive after Miss Lorraine's swing song in the second scene of Act II. Many of the actors and chorines made their entrances by way of the auditorium, reached through special staircases and trap doors. The novelty failed to impress, but the new *Follies* was successful—chiefly due to the indulgent attitude reviewers took toward musicals, the annual revue's growing reputation, its undeniable good parts, and the fact that the 1910 *Follies,* at the "Jardin de Paris" (a roof garden atop the New York Theatre at West Forty-fourth Street) was an overall improvement on the 1909 edition, providing good escapist entertainment from the searing summer heat.

Fanny Brice had not become a star, but had shown that she belonged among the very best performers. In those days of continuity on Broadway, it meant the teen-aged Fanny was established.

CHAPTER 4

Shubert Sonata

T he *Ziegfeld Follies* was and remains the ultimate in theatrical glamor. It was Broadway at its finest—the most gorgeous sets and costumes, the most beautiful women, the greatest use of lights and color, and the greatest comedians in theatre history. Being in the *Follies* was a source of pride and great success to all the performers— especially to the teen-aged girls.

But though remembered chiefly for "Glorifying the American Girl," the *Follies* were largely satirical revues that threw their gentle barbs at leading celebrities of the day—society leaders, businessmen, and politicians who, thanks to Broadway's status as the nation's showplace, were often in the audience laughing at themselves. Performers in the *Follies,* most of them from poor or lower-middle-class backgrounds, would find themselves adopted, after a fashion, by the rich and famous.

Fanny was thus ushered into a new world, one she had barely touched while on tour in *The College Girls*. It was a curious world, without what we would now call social conscience, yet with codes of loyalty, honor, and personal generosity that have baffled later generations. Many top stars of this era lost their fortunes when the show world they knew died at the same time the stock market crashed in 1929. Almost as important in their falls, however, were the "free and easy" ways with money that social pressure then demanded in the theatre. One was expected to "spread it around."

No one spread it quite like Diamond Jim Brady, a former hotel bellhop who had made his fortune selling railway equipment in the early 1880s. He was fifty-four in 1910, but Fanny thought he "had a natural childish quality. . . . If you hadn't known how generous he could be to down-and-outers, how no one ever left him empty-handed, you would have found him ridiculous."

Brady threw a party for the cast of the *Follies* after the show opened in Atlantic City. Brady's love of diamonds had earned him his nickname, and Fanny was astounded when he showed her the ten-carat diamonds he used for buttons on his underwear, and the hundred-dollar bills he put under the plates of every guest "for no reason at all except that you were on the stage"—and in the *Follies*.

The *Follies* world, like the show world of most eras, was an amalgam of naïveté and sophistication. Where the chorines Fanny knew in burlesque had been virgins, the *Follies* girls, most of them in their late teens, were sexually experienced, with rich boyfriends who kept them well supplied with money, furs, and jewels.

Jewelry was a prestige symbol to performers of the early 1900s. Men in show business were identified by the rings and diamond stickpins that went in and out of hock as fortunes changed, and no actress with pretensions to success was without a jewel box and sets of necklaces and bracelets. Fanny soon began her own jewelry collection, buying most of it herself. She was neither jealous nor contemptuous of the showgirls kept by boyfriends. "They may have said poor Fanny," she recalled years later. "But I knew what I was doing, and I knew I'd wind up better off than they were."

Fanny's new-found friends included Lillian Lorraine, Ziegfeld's own paramour and probably the best-known of his showgirls before World War I. Born in San Francisco of French-Irish parents in 1892, she had made her stage debut at four and had lost her virginity at thirteen. Willful, childishly selfish and coquettish, Lillian also had a voracious sexual appetite that seldom focused on one man for long. "She never wore any make-up," Fanny recalled. "Everything about her was glowing and fresh, a sort of blooming newness like you see in a very young girl. Her hair rolled off her forehead in simple lines and swung into lovely folds. I have never seen a woman in the theatre with so little artificiality." She was, at the same time, a silly and self-centered girl whose fickle ways and drinking soon destroyed her. In short, she was the opposite of Fanny, a fact that made them close friends for a year.

Fanny received considerable publicity during the show's run on Broadway, much of it either laughably inaccurate (such as the press stories about her selling newspapers beneath a tower of the Brooklyn Bridge to help her "poor" family) or outrageously stereotyped (such as those that featured two fictitious brothers, "Pincus Brice" and "E. Rosenbaum Brice," the latter named after the *Follies'* real-life company manager, Ed Rosenbaum). Rosie now felt Fan deserved more money, and interfered with her daughter's professional life for what would prove the only time. Going down to the producer's office with a somewhat embarrassed Fanny in tow, she persuaded an indulgent Ziegfeld to give her a new contract calling for one hundred dollars a week for the balance of the first year and $150 for the second.

Fanny and her mother shed their middle-class ways a short time later, taking space in the posh Albany Apartments at Broadway and Fifty-second. The rooms were large (30′ × 30′) and consisted of two bedrooms, a living room, a maid's room, and a kitchen. Rosie and Fanny lived alone, Fan's social life being confined to girlfriends and an occasional drink with a stage-door Johnny who found tall, Jewish comediennes more attractive than the most Glorified Girls in the World.

The *Follies* ran in New York through the summer before opening a national tour at Chicago's Colonial Theatre in September. Fanny roomed with Lillian on this tour at the request of Ziegfeld, who thought her a good influence on his promiscuous girlfriend. Fanny liked neither the job nor her implied position as her friend's "plain Jane" attendant. Nor was it an easy job.

Ziegfeld took Lillian and Fanny out to dinner in Chicago, an evening Fanny looked at as the high point of her social life so far. New clothes for it were a must.

Clothes were all-important to the women in show business. Audiences wanted to see gorgeous costumes, but where Sophie Tucker and others knew the value of a great stage wardrobe, Fanny thought of clothing as an emblem of success.

She was new to the twin worlds of fashion and the *Follies,* and her inclinations were toward clothes that loudly proclaimed her new status in the Broadway theatre—dresses and fur coats from Simon's, a second-hand shop that sold five-hundred-dollar dresses for sixteen and seventeen bucks. For her evening with Lillian and Ziegfeld, Fanny bought an ostentatious sapphire-blue satin dress, an orange coat, and a big blue hat with a vegetable garden and an ostrich plume. The ensemble did little more than make Ziegfeld lose his appetite. He finally asked Lillian to show Fanny how to dress, giving her two hundred and fifty dollars for the purpose.

Fanny's first lesson in clothing bore almost immediate results. Before the *Follies* finished its run in Chicago, Fanny had her first affair, her first sexual experience since the three days she had lived with Frank White.

The man in question was Fred Gresheimer, tall, handsome, muscular, and possessed of a charmingly rich vocabulary that disguised a baser nature. Fanny met him when the heir to the Schlitz brewery fortune brought her to the Hotel Sherman's College Inn, then one of Chicago's well-known night spots. Fred was at a nearby table with a friend of his, making pointed cracks about the *Follies* that had Fanny laughing. Young Schlitz, who had met Gresheimer and his friend some hours earlier, naïvely brought them over to meet Fanny. Within an hour, they had left the College Inn, rid themselves of "sucker" Schlitz, and taken Fanny on a round of cabarets and other hot spots that included the Eberle Club, a notorious Chicago brothel.

The top whorehouses of the major cities in the early 1900s were a far cry from the dingy places later generations would associate with theatres of prostitution. They were usually well furnished and well lit, with a piano player on twenty-four-hour duty. The pianist was usually a black man, although a black woman served the same function at the Eberle. "In those days," recalled Eubie Blake, "the only places where a black piano player could find work were churches and brothels." Fanny was soon singing up the proverbial storm for the Eberle's employees.

Fanny never considered herself married to Frank White, never used the name "Mrs. White," and, while certainly not what the times labeled a "loose" woman, acted very much the single girl in show biz, circa 1910. Gresheimer appealed to her ever-present need for the exotic, the suave, and the sophisticated—tastes that had been whetted by her success in the *Follies*.

Gresheimer, the wastrel son of a rich family and a "man of the world," to Fanny's way of thinking, wrote her entertaining letters when the *Follies* left Chicago—letters Fanny read to Lillian. Miss Lorraine was interested, especially after Fanny showed her a photograph of Freddy in a swimsuit, and asked for more readings whenever she saw Gresheimer's handwriting on an envelope.

The 1910 *Ziegfeld Follies* played the major theaters in the country—the Euclid Avenue Opera House in Cleveland, the Nixon in Pittsburgh, and the Chestnut Street Opera House in Philadelphia, along with more than twenty others. The company, which numbered well over a hundred, travelled in a special ten-car train, stayed in the best hotels, and inhabited a world of glamor known to only the top television and film stars of today. Most of the big musical attractions went no farther west than Chicago or St. Louis, but the *Follies* of 1910 played Davenport, Des Moines, and Kansas City before heading out to California. Comedian and singer Bobby North was a local favorite in San Francisco, and Lillian Lorraine was the subject of a feature story in the *Chronicle* when the show opened a two-week engagement at the Columbia Theatre.

Ralph E. Renaud thought the 1910 *Follies* was

stronger individually in its men than its women, but it would be a poor appreciation indeed that would pass Fanny Brice. This strange and fantastic young woman of the willowy form and the elastic face doesn't sing her songs at all—she just sort of kind of remembers them. Her gestures and facial play mark the climax insanity, but she is bubbling with natural fun and life.

Most of the important song numbers were handed to Miss Lillian Lorraine, a pretty young woman with a graceful presence, but not much voice, though what there was of it was pleasing enough.

The show played Oakland, Fresno, and Los Angeles before swinging back east by way of Salt Lake City. Fanny, Lillian, and several other principals gave their parts to understudies after the first performance in Omaha on June 1 and returned to New York, where the *Ziegfeld Follies* of 1911 had already gone into rehearsals.

Ziegfeld, who came to the train station, was aghast to see Lillian's maid wearing the same awful hat Fanny had bought in Chicago. The sociable and enterprising Fanny had sold it to her in St. Louis.

Ziegfeld gave the startled maid twenty-five dollars to get rid of the offending hat once and for all.

Fred Gresheimer arrived in New York while the new *Follies* was still in rehearsals. A total playboy, he was soon ensnared by the coquettish Lillian. While the show was still in tryouts in Atlantic City, they sneaked back to New York and married.

Fanny, although charmed and fascinated, had not been in love with Freddy, and was nowhere near as distraught as Ziegfeld, whom she frequently met for a late breakfast in the days that followed. She remembered him "standing before a large photograph of Lillian on the mantelpiece. . . . He could not bear to be alone."

It would be years before she understood his grief.

Critics, while respectfully reporting the weak parts of each year's *Follies,* had been practically unanimous in saying that each one of the first four editions of the annual revue was better than its predecessor. Such was not the case, however, with the *Ziegfeld Follies* of 1911. While it was a good show, professionally done, with songs by Irving Berlin and a cast including Fanny, Bert Williams, Bessie McCoy, the Dolly Sisters, and rubber-legged Leon Errol in his *Follies* debut, it nonetheless failed to excite like the 1910 edition. Bert Williams walked away with the individual notices, singing Berlin's "Woodman, Spare That Tree" and showing his usual comic artistry in a sketch set in New York's Grand Central Station (then under construction) with Errol.

Fanny appeared to best advantage as "Rachel Rosenstein, alias Little

Buttercup" in "H.M.S. Vaudeveel," a take-off on *H.M.S. Pinafore,* which opened the second act. She also had two songs, "Doggone That Chilly Man" in Act I, which Sime Silverman said "had little to recommend it," and Berlin's "Ephraham Played Upon the Piano" in "New Year's Eve on the Barbary Coast," an eighteen-minute "cabaret" that closed the show.

Fanny hated "Ephraham," and blamed it for her failure to repeat her former triumph. "(Ziegfeld) couldn't pick songs for me," she later declared. She recalled the song as being just a chorus with no verses, but the fact is that the verse was overlong, with a short chorus that recalled popular songs of the nineteenth century.

> Ephraham played upon the piano.
> Ephraham, he had a great left hand.
> Ephraham in his fancy manner,
> Made an upright sound like a "Baby Grand."

Berlin, the man who gave her "Sadie Salome" and made her a Yiddish dialect comedienne, was unable to give her another hit in the 1911 Follies. Fanny, it was now apparent, needed certain types of songs, as well as specialists to write them. It would take three years to find one.

Nor was the run of the 1911 edition nearly as exciting to young Fanny as her first *Follies* had been. Lillian, who had enjoyed a less-than-scintillating wedding night with Gresheimer and was starting to drink heavily, accused Fanny of still seeing Freddy. It was a bad situation that erupted during a performance.

Fanny and blond showgirl Vera Maxwell shared lines in a patter song in the Barbary Coast cabaret scene. On the night in question, Fanny's large hoopskirt caught in a chair and dragged it along just as Lillian made her entrance. Lillian, who did not see the chair, tripped over it, and the audience, thinking it was part of the show, just howled. Hearing laughter, Fan than made a show of trailing the chair. It ruined Lillian's scene, and she confronted Fanny in the wings with her eyes blazing.

"Why didn't you pick up the chair?"

"Why should I have? It was getting a laugh."

Lillian pulled Fanny's hair, and the two young women were wrestling on the floor by the time Lillian's cue came to re-enter. The performers onstage froze for a few moments until Fanny appeared, dragging Lillian behind her by the hair.

Abe Erlanger fired Lillian from the cast a short time later when she missed an entrance during a rehearsal called to add new songs. She was back, at Ziegfeld's insistence, the following year.

Fanny at this time had neither lovers nor, it seemed, much interest in men. She had unwittingly become one of those women who, not thinking themselves beautiful, become the "best friend" of a truly gorgeous woman. After Lillian and she stopped speaking, Fanny found a new best friend in Vera Maxwell, then a teen-aged showgirl, who would be called "the most beautiful young woman in the world" by French artist Paul Huillon in 1914. Known as the "Blonde Venus," she was actually more beautiful than Lillian, and far more congenial. The daughter of a lawyer who had lost and partially regained a family fortune, Vera was as practical as Fanny. The two girls took a vow of mutual assistance in case either became poor. Neither ever did.

The *Follies* of 1911 closed its Broadway run on September 2 and, like the 1910 edition, opened its tour in Chicago the following Monday. Fanny's mother, Rosie, travelled with the show for a few weeks as Fanny's guest. At other times, Fan roomed with Vera Maxwell and the Dolly Sisters (Yansci and Roszika), the four taking a big "travelling salesman's room" with two double beds wherever possible. A man in Indianapolis invited all four young women to a party in the country where the dress was blue jeans and straw hats. Vera and the Dollys found the party dull, but Fanny loved it and stayed long after her roommates wished to leave. Vera, Yansci, and Roszika, who had no transportation without Fanny, finally decided to walk back to town.

Fanny found her trunk out in the hall when she returned to the hotel in the middle of the night. Her three roommates, furthermore, refused to let her in until she banged on the door for half an hour. Even then, an argument ensued that lasted until breakfast.

Fanny was then twenty—and the eldest of the four. Few of Ziegfeld's girls were any older, which should explain a lot of their behavior.

The show went to St. Louis and then swung back east, playing Philadelphia at New Year's and then heading for New England. Just before the tour ended, in Binghamton, New York, on March 30, 1912, Ed Rosenbaum, the company manager, came into the hotel restaurant where Fanny as breakfasting with Vera. "When you get into town," he said to Vera, "Mr. Ziegfeld wants to see you." Then he looked at Fanny. "He doesn't want to see you!!"

Fanny made no show of the tremendous hurt she felt, but the chance that Ziegfeld would not offer to re-sign her had long been apparent. She blamed the song "Ephraham," the absence of other good songs, and the show itself—cloaking herself in the ego that is every actor's courage. Making matters far worse was the news that her father had died. French Charlie had succumbed to the effects of asthma and a lifetime of drinking. He was barely fifty, but had lived to see his daughter reach the *Follies*.

Fanny felt defeated and alone. Talking to her mother was impossible; Rosie had hated Charlie, and loved theater only as a source of money.

Strength, not talent, sustained Fanny now. She had seen the bottle destroy young showgirls, and the oft-heard stories about down-and-out actors only made her vow to come back fighting. It was 1912; she had Broadway credits, and could take comfort in the knowledge that show business offered an abundance of work for qualified performers. The one important thing was not to weaken.

She certainly had money saved, enough to live in style with her mother for at least a year. Going to the theatre in the meantime was essential, and the following Monday night found Fanny watching the acts from a box at Hammerstein's Victoria, the leading vaudeville theatre in New York. Seated next to her was Morris Gest, an eccentric Broadway figure who had made his mark in association with David Belasco and was also involved with the Shuberts—brothers from Syracuse who were challenging the Theatrical Syndicate for control of the American theatre.

Gest lost little time in asking Fanny what she had planned for next season. Lee Shubert, he explained, was interested in signing her. Gest soon offered to take Fanny to Lee's office, advising her to ask for five hundred dollars a week.

Fanny hedged her bets, asked for four hundred and fifty, and realized she had made a mistake when Lee quickly agreed. Lee's late-working secretary typed up the contract. Fanny signed, and was told to be ready the third week in August.

"Much as I loved money," Fanny said, "it meant more to me to have that sum in black and white on a contract so I could show Ziegfeld what other managers thought of me." She walked into Flo's office the next day and put the contract on his desk.

Ziegfeld shook his head and said, "That's gratitude!" Fanny, who was not much of a weeper, burst right into tears and told him what Rosenbaum had said. When Ziegfeld expressed innocence, she asked him to call Vera Maxwell to confirm it. Ziegfeld did, and said he felt "just awful. . . . I thought sure you'd come in and see me."

Fanny, with considerable hindsight, said she thought there was "something" to Rosenbaum's statement. Her relationship with the company manager was a good one (Rosenbaum later served the Shuberts and eventually became a top Broadway press agent, claiming to have been Fanny's mentor in her early years), and Fanny did not think he made the statement without reason. Ziegfeld, she was sure, must have said "something."

Her tenure with the Shuberts would not start until late August. Fanny, in the meantime, needed work, so Max Hart, a major agent until he lost a five-million-dollar lawsuit against the all-powerful United Booking Office, got her into big-time vaudeville. Fanny opened at Hammerstein's Victoria on Monday afternoon, April 22, 1912. Hammerstein's, on Forty-second Street and Seventh Avenue, had supplanted Keith's Union Square Theatre as New York's premier variety theatre shortly after the turn of the century, and would continue as the "Mecca of Vaudeville" until Martin Beck opened the Palace in 1913.

Fanny's vaudeville debut was a qualified success. Joshua (Jolo) Lowe said she was "unquestionably 'the goods' for vaudeville," but added that her act was "badly put together. . . . She starts slowly with two songs, out of which she gets comparatively little, then puts over a 'wallop' with a 'Yiddish' ditty that makes most of the present day soubrettes who essay that kind of material look foolish, and finally spoils it all by changing to a silly costume consisting of white satin trousers of eccentric design with an equally inconsistent red coat. . . . Miss Brice is chock full of unction and has a keen sense of travesty. But the last two numbers are inane, and the first two not worthy of her talents as a comedienne."

Fanny continued playing vaudeville for almost three months. Prior to beginning her work for the Shuberts, she took time out to divorce Frank White.

Fan had gotten all the evidence she needed from two anonymous male homosexuals who identified themselves as the night clerk and bellhop at the Mohawk Theatre Hotel in Poughkeepsie, New York. Neither wanted money, although both seemed out for some kind of revenge.

Fan took them to see her lawyer. White did not contest the case, which came before the Honorable Mitchell Erlanger (brother of A. L.) in August. The bellhop's testimony, in which he told of serving White in bed with an actress named May Dale, was enough for "Mitch" (as Fanny called him) to cut in and say divorce was granted. Judge Bischoff gave the final decree exactly twelve months later, and Frank White spent the remainder of his life as an obscure businessman and hotel manager. Until his death in Florida in February 1940, White never ceased to boast of his marriage to Fanny, and even listed her as his beneficiary in a major building project in the 1930s—a rather strange gesture for a man who ran out after just three days of marriage.

Fanny Brice reported for rehearsals of the Shuberts' *Whirl of Society* on Monday, August 19, 1912. The show, with Al Jolson and Stella Mayhew, had enjoyed a healthy run at the New York Winter Garden that spring,

and with Jolson still in tow, the Shuberts now looked forward to a lucrative road tour.

With Fanny as "Marcelle, a maid," a Yiddish dialect role written in
especially for her, *The Whirl of Society* opened its tour at the Lyric Theatre
in Chicago on Sunday night, September 1, 1912. "Miss Brice," wrote Jack
Lait in the *Chicago Evening American,* "as a Yiddish servant maid, works
hard and earnestly. She need not labor so arduously, for I assure her she
is funny and pleasant without such honest exertion. Once she went so
far for a laugh that she transcended politeness in a song ("Fol de Rol
Dol Doi," by Jean Schwartz and Edward Madden) chorus, and this is
deplorable, for neither she nor the show needs to become over frank to
please." Jolson walked away with the good notices, but still complained,
by telegram to New York of a "coon song" done by Brice. Fanny, forced
to cut the number, disliked Jolson from then on.

She more than got along with others in the cast, particularly Willie
Weston of *The College Girls,* who played the part of "Baron von Shine"
in his inimitable German dialect. Willie and his wife, Mae, were Fanny's
closest friends throughout the tour; the two young women spending
their days cooking, shopping, or talking over coffee in hotel rooms.

Fanny became ill in mid-September, and Gussie White ("a little Jewish girl," in the words of company manager Stanley Sharpe) took her
place at that time in Chicago. Gussie made twenty dollars a week as
Fanny's understudy, with an extra five bucks added when she actually
performed.

Fanny was learning. While the Shuberts might pay higher salaries
than Ziegfeld, they were chiselers who made money in underhanded ways.
J. J. (Lee's younger brother and the man in charge of Winter Garden
shows) had been rankled by *The Whirl of Society*'s "not doing business,"
despite the fine reviews garnered by Jolson, and Fanny was told the company would be put on half salary during Christmas week. "Brice claims
no clause in contract about half salary," Sharpe wired J. J. in New York.
"Absolutely refuses to accept salary, said if you break contract with her
she will do same by leaving this Saturday night. Advise you wiring her
to accept half salary and you will adjust her claims in office. Impossible
to do so now on account of it being Winter Garden Co. and it will get
over." A follow-up wire from Sharpe said he had "had long talk with
Brice before receiving your wire, and got her to sign for half salary. Told
her to take it up with you in New York."

Few performers cherished money as Fanny Brice did. But dealing
with the Shuberts, Fanny now felt, was not worth what it cost.

One way Fanny differed from most other women in show business was
the pride she took in cooking. Especially adept at Rosie's native Hun-

garian cuisine, she could also prepare a remarkably wide variety of dishes. Fan did all of her own cooking on the road with what were then twenty-five-cent alcohol stoves. Her greatest triumph came when she prepared a six-pound duck on one and served nine people (including Al Jolson, Oscar Schwartz, Willie Weston, and their wives) while on tour with *The Whirl of Society*. Jolson, who loved duck, said it was the best he'd ever tasted.

The Whirl of Society underwent a transformation on Sunday, November 17. Gaby Deslys, the legendary French musical star noted for her "Ooh, naughty boy!" phrase, blonde beauty, and celebrated (fictitious) romance with Manuel II of Portugal, had opened a disastrous tour in *Vera Violetta* in Trenton, New Jersey, the previous Monday. J. J. Shubert closed the show after one performance and sent Gaby to join the cast of *The Whirl of Society* in Baltimore, dropping the then-less-expensive Jolson down to secondary billing. Fanny liked Gaby, who she felt had a "certain soundness of character about her despite her flamboyant reputation." Gaby also brought along her American dancing partner, Harry Pilcer, who had been with Fanny in the *Ziegfeld Follies* of 1910. Pilcer, the short, dark, handsome son of an Austro-Hungarian Jewish tailor, would enjoy a sexually mysterious relationship with Gaby, whom he practically worshipped, until her death in 1920.

It was now, in Baltimore, that Fanny met "a man who stood then and forever after for everything that had been left out of my life—manners, good breeding, education, and an extraordinary gift for dreaming."

It was racing season in Baltimore, and the "wise guys" were in town. Among them were Frank McGee and one Nick Arnold, a strikingly tall (6′ 6″), thin man with a moustache who might have been described years later as a Jewish William Powell.

McGee, who knew Fanny's roommate, chorine Rosie Seballis, asked both girls to dine with them in their suite in the Hotel Canon. Fanny found Nick Arnold "good looking" and "smart . . . but I was never susceptible like many other girls. He was merely a handsome fellow. I learned he was a promoter of inventions. I liked his manner and his sense of humor."

Matters got more interesting the following week, when *The Whirl of Society* opened a five-week engagement at the Lyric Theatre in Philadelphia and Fanny and her roommate had an after-the-show supper with McGee and Arnold in their suite in the Bellevue Hotel.

They had a fine meal, far different from the club sandwiches and chicken à la king the girls were used to. Fanny was terrifically impressed with the "Gold Suite." "Everything in that room—piano, furniture, taffeta draperies—was golden." It seemed to sum up the man's fire and his zest for life—a zest that Fanny, fatherless and working for the Shuberts, found particularly attractive.

Fan was really floored when she went to the bathroom. The gentleman was fond of deluxe toiletries in leather cases. His dull silk pajamas bore his monogram, J.W.A., in tastefully small letters. Everything in Fanny's sight bespoke a man of breeding and true "class."

Fanny was "born again" in that bathroom. Charged, animated, and wanting to know more about the handsome man with the fine taste, she joked, and mugged, and laughed for the remainder of the evening. They stayed up almost until dawn—the handsome, tall man with the mustache almost doubled over in hysterics at Fan's stories and expressions.

The full name of the man of breeding, manners, and leather toiletries was Jules Wilford Arnstein. "Arnold" was one of several aliases he employed from time to time. His friends, however, called him "Nick."

CHAPTER 5

Nick Arnstein

He was born Julius Wilford Arndstein in Norway on July 1, 1879, the son of a German Jew named Moses Arndstein and his Dutch wife, Thekla Van Shaw. Brought to the United States in babyhood, he received a good education and worked as a contractor for a time. But Nick was like French Charlie; he quickly became bored.

Only certain women called him "Jules," an Anglicization that he much preferred to "Julius." To friends, acquaintances, and "business" partners, he was Nick, a diminutive of "Nickelplate," the nickname he had gotten in his teens because the wheels of his bicycle had nickel-plated spokes.

Bicycle racing was a major sport in the 1890s, its "professionalism" stemming, for the most part, from the gambling that then ran every sport from boxing to horse racing. The atmosphere was exciting to Nick, who regarded throwing races as romantic, and doubtless saw himself as a young Count of Monte Cristo. Throwing those bike races drew Nick into permanent alliance with professional gamblers, confidence men, and various interconnecting parts of the sports underworld. He felt at home in their world, and they quickly saw how this well-educated, polished young man could be valuable in many operations.

Between 1909 and 1912, Nick was arrested in London, Paris, and Monte Carlo on swindling charges. In London, he was accused of swindling a man out of fifteen thousand dollars in connection with a ring of confidence men that reached as far as Hong Kong. Extradited to the States, he managed to stay out of prison.

Nick told Fanny that he was a "businessman," but never spelled out the true nature of his business beyond saying he was a "promoter of inventions." He told her about his arrest record shortly after they became intimate in Philadelphia, but did not yet mention Carrie Greenthal, the

Jersey City woman he had married on May 5, 1906, and left three years later. The arrest record did not bother Fanny. She was still a romantic, and Nick was charming; he spoke French, and knew fine food, good clothes, and furnishings. She soon found out that he had seven brothers, Jewish-Norwegian-American businessmen who looked on "Julius" as the "black sheep" of the family.

Nick was a dreamer—not the ineffectual type who seeks to escape his ever humdrum, failure-ridden life with fantasies of fame and fortune, but a man who seemed already to inhabit an exciting world of luxurious surroundings and titled aristocrats. It was never easy to separate reality from fiction in the story of Nick Arnstein, since his conversation mixed both facts and falsehoods in an ever-brewing cauldron that left real truth impossible to find. He was the quintessential romantic con man, and, according to Eddie Cantor, "the best actor Fanny ever saw. The performance never faltered and the curtain never fell."

Nick and Fanny went to New York after *The Whirl of Society* closed its run in Philadelphia on Saturday night, December 28, 1912. Nick said he had business in the city, and Fanny did not want to be apart from her new lover for a day if she could help it. The only thing that marred a perfect weekend came when Fanny missed her train to Montreal, where *The Whirl of Society* was scheduled to open a six-day engagement at the Princess Theatre on Monday night. Gussie White played "Sadie" at the first performance, and Fanny was docked by the Shuberts, losing twelve percent of that week's paycheck.

When the company returned to New York in January 1913, Fanny rejoined Rosie at the Albany Apartments.

Nick soon moved in with them.

Rosie "hated Nick from the beginning," according to Fan's sister, Carrie. Fanny's mother saw right through the polished charm, the manners, and the studied pose of wealth and good connections. To Rosie, Nick Arnstein was a bum who had no money and had never done a day's work in his life.

But Fanny had fallen for him like the young and still impressionable stage-door Johnnies fell for Mr. Ziegfeld's showgirls. Rosie's damning accusations fell on ears that did not want to hear.

That Rosie would not like Nick is not surprising; he was too much like French Charlie. That very similarity was doubtless a large element in Fanny's love for Arnstein. Nick, who wore a mustache like French Charlie, was a charming, wistful dreamer like French Charlie, and who, like Charlie, tried to dodge whatever real work he could, doubtless touched the part of Fanny that felt deprived of her father. Fanny, although blessed with an ability for "feeling" an audience and possessed of great instinctive taste, was at the same time a practical and sensible person. It was only with one man—Nick Arnstein—that she was hopelessly romantic, giving without reason, and almost incredibly naïve. Nick, in short, touched—and ultimately became—her Achilles heel.

"I was in heaven, that's all," was Fanny's own description of her early days with Nick. Unwilling to do anything that might disturb what seemed a dream, she never directly questioned Nick about his background. She did, however, hire some detectives to investigate his past. Before a week had passed, they told her that Arnstein was married.

Fanny kept the information to herself and tried, as best she could, to totally ignore it. She could not give up Nick, not even after Rosie, who learned about his marriage through some sources of her own, reproached her for living with "a married man."

Nick put his knowledge of good furnishing to use as soon as he moved in with Fanny. Declaring the apartment tasteless, vulgar, and depressing, he went to Gimbel's department store, ordered ten thousand dollars' worth of furnishings, and asked that everything be sent C.O.D. He then told Fanny to say she wanted to pay in monthly installments when the furniture arrived. That way, Nick explained, she'd save the cost for credit Gimbel's would have charged.

Rose fumed. Fanny paid. And Nick remained composed, the classic gentleman.

In December, while *The Whirl of Society* was still in Philadelphia, Fanny and other key members of the cast received scripts for a new Shubert production called *The Honeymoon Express*. Fanny again played a maid, "Marcelle," who figured little in the plot but sang three songs: "Syncopatia Land," "My Coca-Cola Belle," and "My Raggyadore."

The show needed more rehearsals when it opened at the New York Winter Garden on February 6, 1913, and Sime Silverman said that nervousness "unsettled the entire company. . . . It was almost pitiful to see the state of Fanny Brice. She did not recover herself until the second act, when Miss Brice led 'My Raggyadore' (the 'Toreador' song from Carmen, 'ragged') with a good swing to her swaggering walk as the bull fighter." Ada Lewis, formerly of Harrigan and Hart shows, played the part of Gaby's aunt and walked away with most of the laughs scored by the show's women. Acton Davies, writing in the *New York Evening Sun*, said Yansci Dolly, the soubrette, had "a delicacy about her work which

Miss Fanny Brice, for instance, might do well to follow. Miss Brice, for reasons for which she had only herself to blame, did not hit it off any too well with her audience last night."

The run of *Honeymoon Express* was notable, to Fanny, for the good times that she shared with Nick and for a brief incident involving her mother. One night, three strange men knocked on the door of the apartment and asked her where "the girls" were. The average citizen in his or her apartment in the New York of that era did not live in fear, nor think in terms of violence. Rosie simply told the men, "Mine Fanny is at the Winter Garden und mine Carrie is married." It was only when they started searching the apartment that she realized the men were drunk, and thought that her apartment was a whorehouse. She ran down to the manager's office, and the three men were ejected.

The Winter Garden was only a block away, and Rosie ran there to tell Fanny what had happened. The next day, Fanny spoke to the landlord, who reduced the rent from $130 to one hundred dollars a month in order to keep the incident out of the newspapers.

It marked the first time Rosie—"The Tiger"—had seemed even partly terrified or helpless. From this point on, she gradually relinquished family leadership to Fanny and retreated to a life of card games, cooking, and benign domesticity. Few who met Rose Borach in her later years could believe the "Tiger" she had been before the age of fifty.

Fanny, as the years went on, assumed her mother's toughness.

If Fanny's opening-night failure in *The Honeymoon Express* increased her dislike of working for the Shuberts, she nonetheless was shocked to learn they would not pick up her weekly option after April 26. "Lee 'n' Jake" were making a clean sweep at this point, replacing Gaby Deslys with the cheaper Grace LaRue, and Gaby's partner, Harry Pilcer, with Charles King.

Talented, versatile, and dainty Ina Claire would replace Fanny. Miss Claire had scored a triumph in the title role of *The Quaker Girl*, and was then a bigger name than Fanny. The role of Marcelle was actually expanded for young Ina, who was given some of Gaby's numbers and a few new ones as well.

Fanny, now hardened to setbacks, went back into vaudeville. Her act included the song "You Made Me Love You," in which she sang the second chorus in Yiddish dialect, and a parody of "Be My Little Baby Bumble Bee," which closed her turn.

Part of Fanny's success was due to the delight she put into her work. Her Yiddish character was a woman sharing her fun with the audience, arching her eyebrows with a mischievous glint as she described her latest beau or interest in the arts. It was this quality that made Fan's parody of "Bumble Bee" so funny. She was only twenty-one, and had not yet peaked as a *farceuse*. But great comedy performance stems from comment—the very subtle "Look, I'm dancing" commentary Fanny put into her work.

Two weeks after she broke in at Shea's in Buffalo, Fanny played the Fifth Avenue Theatre in New York. "Fanny Brice is always growing better," wrote Sime Silverman. "Some day if Fanny will take care of herself she is going to be a great comedienne, for Fanny has a naturally humorous streak in her composition. . . . Let it here be recorded that in a fast playing bill and following 'singles' and 'doubles,' Fanny Brice was the hit of the bill. She made them like it." One seldom got a better review from the honest Sime, but Fanny was more worried about Nick than about her career in vaudeville. Arnstein dealt with Rosie's ever-increasing hostility with a mixture of charm and bored indifference. More and more, however, he seemed tired and distracted. He professed a longing for "the shores of England" and, for the first time, told Fanny of his marriage.

Nick said that Carrie, who had a daughter by a previous marriage, would not give him a divorce, that she had detectives watching him, and that they knew he was living with Fanny Brice at the Albany Apartments. More important to Fanny, Nick told her that he did not love his wife.

Fan already knew about the marriage. Now that he had brought it into the open, she resolved to wait—and fight, if need be—until Nick obtained that divorce and they could be married.

Despite her toughness and her career, Fan valued a home life and family. She was determined Nick would be the father of her children. No one, not her mother and not Carrie Greenthal Arnstein, would change that.

Nick made plans to sail in July. He never specified what deals were awaiting him in England, but Fanny bought him a matched set of luggage, helped him pack, and explained she would not see him off because of professional commitments. Fanny now looked forward to two months, or more, without Nick Arnstein. The prospect seemed more unbearable as sailing day approached. Once, when Nick was out of town on "business," Fanny slept with Rose and dreamed she was with Nick. Still asleep, she grabbed and kissed her mother, until Rosie woke her up by saying, "This ain't Nick."

She finally decided to sail along with him. Now bereft of money, thanks to Nick's taste for the finer things and Rosie's insistence on banking every other available penny, Fanny pawned her jewels, told her mother she was going to spend the remainder of the summer at a friend's mountain retreat, and joined a surprised Nick on the *Homeric*.

Fanny remembered the voyage as "wonderful and heavenly and enchanting . . . I was never happier in my life." Nick took a flat for them on Jeremyn Street when they reached London. Fanny knew few people in the city, but Nick had a friend in Clifford C. Fischer, who needed a replacement for Anna Held in *Come Over Here*, a revue at the London Opera House. It was a rather small revue—really nothing more than a good vaudeville show that included baritone solos by Wilfred Douthitt, soprano solos by Julia Caroli, dances by Oscar Schwartz (who had worked with Fanny in *The Whirl of Society*), and several other acts.

Fanny, billed as the "refinement of ragtime," had no "name" in England, and, in order not to accept a small "show" price, she arranged to appear without salary for the first three nights of her engagement. A price would then be put on her services.

She opened at the London Opera House on Monday, August 4, 1913. The audience response was overwhelming, and Fanny was described as "a sure favorite" in a special cable to *Variety*. Fischer agreed to pay her what was then $650 a week in American money, but *Come Over Here* closed less than three weeks later.

Fanny, however, now had her own contacts. Gaby Deslys and Harry Pilcer, in London waiting to go into *À la Carte*, a music hall "revue" quite similar in form and content to *Come Over Here*, introduced her to producer Alfred Butt, who engaged Fanny at a salary equivalent to $800 a week. Fanny joined a cast that included Joe Jackson, the well-known American "tramp comedian" and bicyclist.

Fanny ran into a problem when *À la Carte* opened at the Victoria Palace on October 27. On August 4, the same night she had opened in *Come Over Here*, Grace LaRue had scored a big hit with "You Made Me Love You" at that theater. When Fanny sang the same song at the Palace, the audience thought she was stealing from Miss LaRue.

The English particularly resented performers who lifted material, but Fanny was not sure of what the problem was when she heard buzzing amongst members of the audience. She overcame all difficulties, though, when she began to kid the number in the second chorus. Fanny had been doing it that way in the States for months; but she pulled out all the stops at the Victoria Palace. She winked; she ad-libbed, inviting men in the audience to meet her after the show; she even grabbed the curtains and swung on them as she sang. By the time she hit the final line, the audience was hers.

In command, she then proceeded with her act. She was, if anything, a bigger hit than she had been in August.

Nick celebrated Fanny's stage success in London by moving them to larger quarters at No. 1, Marble Arch. Fanny was all set to do the cooking, but Nick said that was not the way decent people lived in England. He installed a butler and a cook, asking Fan for money until his own "plans" were realized. Throughout their stay in England, Fanny paid the bills, the rent, and the cost of two racehorses Nick persuaded her would earn huge sums of money.

À la Carte closed on November 8. One week later, Fanny went into rehearsals for *Hullo, Ragtime!,* a new edition of a revue that had been enormously successful at the London Hippodrome. The new version, produced by Harry Day and Edward Lauri, opened at the London Palladium on Monday, December 1, 1913, and was reviewed by *The Era*.

> Several of the entertaining incidents originally presented at the Hippodrome are, of course, retained in this new, up-to-date version; and it is only therefore necessary to record that a large share of the success of the revue last night was due to Miss Fanny Brice and Mr. Sam Sidman. The major portion of the work falls upon these two accomplished artistes—who from the outset won the favour of the audiences at both the first and second houses.

Hullo, Ragtime! played one week at the Palladium and went on tour; Fanny's last performance was at the Empire Theatre in Bristol on January 17, 1914. She and Nick (whose "business deals" had proved nonexistent) sailed back to New York on the *Mauretania* two weeks later and, at Nick's insistence, moved out of the Albany Apartments to a more prestigious address: West Fifty-eighth Street between Fifth and Sixth avenues, next door to the Vanderbilts and directly opposite the Plaza, one of the world's truly swank hotels.

The move was a benign but calculated way of distancing themselves from Rosie, who remained at the Albany as Fanny's lifetime pensioner. Legally or not, Fan was now Nick's wife for all intents and purposes. Girlhood was long over.

She now began to entertain, earning a reputation for good food and witty conversation at the parties she threw for both show people and the social set that now surrounded her and Nick on every side of Fifty-eighth Street. The Charles B. Alexanders, cream of society's "old guard," lived two doors away, and gracious Mrs. Alexander soon became a friend—of sorts—to Fanny.

People of the theatre—let alone Yiddish dialect vaudeville comediennes—were not then accepted in top social circles. Fanny said New York society people liked her because she was "natural"—unimpressed by their importance and unawed by their great wealth. Fanny treated everyone the same, be they king or vagabond, grand dame or prostitute.

Department store heir John Wanamaker, Jr., was Fanny's favorite person "in society." She first met him in 1910, when Johnny began paying attention to a friend of Fanny's in the *Ziegfeld Follies* chorus. Fanny's mother took part in a floating poker game on Thursdays. One night, when it was at Fanny's place on Fifty-eighth Street, she introduced Johnny to Rosie and her friends. Wanamaker sat down to play their penny-ante game and wound up losing about three and a half dollars. Fanny assured Rosie that he would survive the loss.

Fanny's parties soon became the "in" thing with the social set. Averell Harriman, the distinguished financier and later U.S. Ambassador to Britain, Secretary of Commerce, and Governor of New York, became a friend of Fanny's, as did Mrs. Borden Harriman, future American ambassador to Denmark.

Arnstein did not like the parties, thinking it was Fanny, and not him, that people came to see. He probably was right, but Fanny always claimed Nick "would be surrounded by people ten minutes after he entered a room." Arnstein was a fine speaker, with a charm and a line of talk that fascinated men as well as women. Few realized that half of what he said was barefaced lies.

Nick had been living largely off of Fanny for more than a year. Carrie still refused to give him a divorce, and Nick remained vague about the various "business deals" he had brewing. Fanny still refused to press him about anything, afraid that his displeasure would destroy the happiness she could not live without. In the meantime, Fanny paid the bills. To do so, she kept working.

Fanny opened what would prove to be a fifteen-month vaudeville tour with a week's engagement at New York's Palace Theatre on Monday afternoon, February 23, 1914. It was her first appearance at the fabled Palace, which was driving Hammerstein's Victoria out of business and would soon become known as the "Mecca of Vaudeville." "May I never play the Palace" was a saying among vaudevillians of the 1920s, and perhaps a bit too much has been made of the theatre's status as the greatest variety house in the world. Some historians have pointed with amazement at the names who never played there—George M. Cohan, Al Jolson, and Harry Lauder. But Cohan and Jolson left vaudeville years before the Palace opened its doors in 1913, and Harry Lauder's tours from that date on were independent "concerts" booked by his trusted American manager, William Morris. The Palace, in short, was nothing more—or less—than the midtown New York theatre of the United Booking Office vaudeville combine. Every established big-time act of the 1913-to-1928 period played it if the act in question managed to avoid the U.B.O.'s feared blacklist.

Fanny made her Palace debut billed as "direct from her eight months' run at the Palace Music Hall, London," following Eddie Foy and the Seven Little Foys on the second half of the bill. "Her 'Fol De Rol' and 'Yiddish' kidding still remain the most effective portion of her turn," Joshua (Jolo) Lowe wrote in *Variety*, "and she was a bigger hit than ever. Miss Brice opened with a song in which she displayed a perceptible English accent, but soon dropped it."

Fanny had sung "Fol de Rol Dol Doi," by Jean Schwartz and Edward Madden, in *The Whirl of Society*. Partially inspired by the "Krazy Kat" cartoon strip, and partially by the same writers' "Rum Tum Tiddle," "Fol de Rol" presented Fanny as a lovesick Jewess driven "skid-diddish" by her boyfriend Ignatz's singing of the song. Comically flapping her arms as she implores her "Yiddisher turtle dove" to flap his wings and "crow mit love," Fanny's depiction of a young girl on the verge of sexual ecstasy proved to be her biggest song success since "Lovey Joe" more than two years earlier.

Fanny Brice's act and art were based on a strong bond between the audience and herself. Once it was established, by a look or a smile, she created characters—the Jewess doing the Salome dance, an improbable vamp, or a woman jilted by "that fellow, Nathan." The next phase was the comment; Fanny's exclamation point or "Look at me, I'm byootiful" accent on the subject's self-image and blissful unselfconsciousness.

At times, there was the shattering of all illusion by the abrupt jump to another plane, as when, playing "The Vamp," Fanny recited the first four lines of a Kipling poem and then said, "I can't get over it" in Jewish New Yorkese. Or, to cite a good example from a future year, "Mrs. Cohen" listing the sandwiches she'd brought to the beach for her children: "salami, bologna, liverwurst, and . . . (joyously but slyly) we got ham!"

Fanny's work was mostly farce, with an occasional element of satire, as when she punctured the bourgeois pretensions of women whose ethnicity betrayed them. (Fanny's character, however, seemed delightfully aware of her Jewishness.) Gilbert Seldes noted how "her spirits mount and intensify with every moment on the stage. She creates rapidly and her characterizations have an exceptional roundness and fulness; when the daemon attends she is superb."

Fanny continued in vaudeville for five months, ending with a week at Hammerstein's Roof Garden (atop the Victoria) in July. She was scheduled to open at Morrison's Theatre in Rockaway the following week, but Fanny abruptly cancelled her remaining bookings and made plans to sail on the *Aquitania* on July 21.

Her agent, Max Hart, may have been puzzled, but the reason for

Fan's action was comparatively simple: Nick was then in London and had cabled her to join him.

Fanny, on arrival, found that Nick's friend, Clifford Fischer, was about to produce a new music-hall revue. Nick, in truth, had cabled her to join him partly as a source of revenue; he needed money badly. All plans were scrapped, however, within days of Fan's arrival. The European war had broken out.

Fanny and Nick sailed back home less than three weeks later, and Brice went right back into vaudeville, opening at the Orpheum in Brooklyn on August 31. Max Hart was still her agent, but Nick said she needed publicity, and Fanny decided to give C. F. Zittell, vaudeville critic of the *New York Journal,* one thousand dollars to serve as her press agent.

Zittell, or "Zit," as he was known in show business circles, promptly got his client into what was arguably the most embarrassing situation of her career. Writing in his column, he announced she would appear at the Palace the entire week of September 28, 1914—including Yom Kippur, holiest day of the Jewish year.

Leaders of several Jewish societies wrote to the *Journal,* protesting the wording of the advertisement, which they considered a direct slap in the face at their faith. They also wrote the Palace, and the United Booking Office considered taking Fanny's name off their sheets for giving the vaudeville establishment bad public relations.

Zittell quickly jumped into the breach, saying that the printer had misread his copy and made "including" out of "excluding" in the Yom Kippur line. Zittell got away with this excuse—which reconciled Fanny with the U.B.O. and the Jewish community leaders.

That same year—1914—Fanny got a maid.

Having a maid was more than just a luxury and comfort; it was a symbol of stardom. Adele Moon came to Fanny when her previous employer, Yansci Dolly, went to Europe for the summer. She remained for twenty-three years.

Adele was very much a product of her era: a young black woman who preferred the company of whites, particularly those whites in the theatre. She idolized "Miss Fanny," a worship that grew with the passing years.

Adele, or "Dell," as Fanny called her, had a passion for good clothes, and spent much of her money buying things she never wore. Later, when the clothes went out of style, she would spend more money having them remodelled—and still never wear them.

Fanny thought that Dell found her own people "dull." In fact, it was show business—and successful people, white or black—she found attractive. Dell worked in Fanny's dressing room as well as in her home, and she knew all the backstage gossip. Fanny found her wonderful, and loyal beyond telling.

There was an air of mystery about Nick Arnstein, and his penchant for sudden disappearances—and equally sudden reappearances—made that mystique all the stronger. He would often show up, without warning, in whatever city Fanny happened to be playing, and then take her out to dinner with all the amenities—flowers, wine, and fascinating light conversation.

Arnstein's so-called business in New York involved a former boxer known as Sam "Cheats" Ginsburg. Nick, dressed to the nines, would meet girls in Pabst's Columbus Circle Café and lure their boyfriends into crooked games of dice and cards with Ginsburg. No one ever failed to pay up.

In addition to this and other clandestine activities Fanny never cared to know about, Nick was involved in several mundane business ventures—all financed by Fanny. First he had a "shirt hospital" on Broadway. Then he sold renovated cars and promoted a fire detector. All these enterprises failed because Nick lacked the tenacity to see them through. He would work ten hours a day at the beginning of each new project, and then taper off to eight . . . and six. As weeks went by, he simply took to stopping in now and again to see how things were being run and sit in his big office.

When the business ended and the furnishings were sold, he'd disappear again. Fanny remonstrated against Nick's business habits, but, at this point, never nagged him. Nor did she object to his long absences on unnamed "business deals." Nick was like a daddy who came home from some mysterious "job" at sudden intervals, and Fanny, usually so streetwise, acted like his little girl.

It was somewhat like a dream—a magic time in which Nick would call her from New York, listen to her talk about the audience that night, and discuss when he "might" meet her for an after-theatre supper.

And then it was all over. Nick and two other members of the "Gondorf Ring" were indicted on a wiretapping charge.

CHAPTER 6

Into Her Own

T he Gondorf Ring was a cartel of swindlers and con men built up and headed by the Gondorf brothers of Atlantic City. Charley Gondorf was a legend, and "Henry Gondorff" was the name used for Paul Newman's character in the 1972 motion picture *The Sting*.

Fanny had already signed to play a featured role in Lew Fields' *Hands Up*, a "musico-comico" melodrama about the theft of a necklace that opened at the Shubert Theatre in New Haven, Connecticut, on June 7, 1915. The *New York Dramatic Mirror* said Fanny was "the hit of the show," but the production failed to come up to expectations, and was closed in Albany a week and a half later. (Fields sold it outright to the Shuberts, who opened a revised version on Broadway with a different cast.) Fanny returned to New York as Nick's case came up for trial. She was nervous and afraid, as if to counterpoint Nick's outward coolness.

The case against him was airtight, and neither machinations by the Gondorf mob nor the best lawyers Fanny hired could sway the jurors' minds. On June 28, 1915, Jules W. Arnstein was sentenced to from two years and ten months to three years in Sing Sing prison.

Fanny pawned her jewels again and put herself in debt to raise Nick's $25,000 bail. Nine months of appeals on his case would follow. Fanny, pressed for funds, returned to vaudeville on July 19, playing dates in and near New York in order to be close to Nick.

Fanny now had a new act, consisting of four parts—a ragtime song, delivered in a white dress trimmed with fur, two character songs, and a "stop buck" dancing routine for which she wore a man's full-dress evening suit.

The character numbers were "If We Could Only Take Their Word" and "Becky Is Back in the Ballet." Both songs were the work of Blanche

Merrill, a twenty-year-old special material writer who had started writing songs for Eva Tanguay while in high school.

Merrill thought in terms of themes, not words or music, and published versions of her songs do not do justice to her sense of travesty and the special way she tailored songs to individual performers. "Becky Is Back in the Ballet" featured Fanny in a tutu, acting out the efforts of a child at ballet school and her bragging mother.

"Push up the foot, sweetheart. And don't break the toes. Look how she goes around. She goes around and around and she never gets dizzy. Do for Mama the dying duck like Pavlova. She's what you call a Russian ballet. What ballet. What balance. I can't get over it. Her father should have such a ballet. Honeysuckle, don't forget the twist. For that I pay two dollars a lesson. Look out, darling. Look out you don't break your technique."

"If We Could Only Take Their Word" contained a monologue in which Fanny impersonated first a millinery salesgirl and then a gay designer. ("If you don't buy this hat, dear, you are *sick!*") Of greater interest is the next verse, in which she did (1) a Jewish woman boasting of her child and then (2) the child singing. It was the first time Fanny played a child.

The idea had been born four months earlier, at a party thrown during Fanny's engagement at the Temple Theatre in Detroit. Fanny never liked performing at parties, feeling that material designed for use onstage was not as effective when done in a living room. Pressed to do something at this time, she sang a current song called "Poor Pauline" (inspired by the film serial *The Perils of Pauline*, starring Pearl White and written by Charles McCarron and Raymond Walker) in the manner of a child. Her fellow guests thought it was frankly hilarious, and Fanny mentioned it to Blanche on their first meeting. The result, as heard on a Columbia recording of "If We Could Only Take Their Word," captures perfectly the joyless, inwardly projected, half rebellious spirit of a child forced into performing.

Years would pass before Fanny's next attempt at child impersonation. Years would pass again before the start of Baby Snooks.

Fanny played her third engagement at the Palace in September and spent the following week uptown at the Colonial. *Hands Up*, in the meantime, had wound up a six-week run at the Forty-fourth Street Theatre with a cast headed by Irene Franklin. It started touring on September 6, but suffered from a feud between Franklin and dancer Florence Walton. On Monday night, October 11, Franklin "fainted" onstage at the Lyric Theatre in Philadelphia; Fanny was brought in to fill her role.

Fanny played "Violet Lavender" (with an incongruous Yiddish accent) for the remainder of the show's two weeks in Philadelphia, after which the Shuberts simply closed *Hands Up.* The show, however, gave Fanny a small, brief toehold in musical comedy. Producer F. Ray Comstock offered her the role of "Miss Tony Miller, the Winter Garden star" in *Nobody Home,* the Jerome Kern–Guy Bolton musical that had opened in New York the previous season and was now on tour.

The engagement, Fanny thought, might pave the way for a career as a comedienne-soubrette in book musicals. *Nobody Home* was the first in a charmingly intimate series of Princess Theatre musicals that would eventually include *Very Good Eddie* and *Oh, Boy!* The plot revolved around the efforts of a "society dancer" to secure the blessings of his girlfriend's domineering aunt for their impending marriage—a situation made more difficult because he has been seen in Tony's company. Fanny joined a cast headed by Lawrence Grossmith ("one of England's foremost comedians"), Maude Odell, and Charles Judels.

This was Fanny's first "straight" (non-dialect) role since *The College Girls,* and she differed from her predecessor, Adele Rowland, mainly in her pace. Stated simply, Brice would not work slow, and Grossmith, in the role of Freddy Popple, went through torture keeping up with his new "Tony."

The anonymous critic for the *Baltimore Sun* said Fanny was "in a class wholly by herself" as Tony, "and quite able to keep any audience sitting up and taking notice whenever her magnetic smile beams upon the stage. Her songs, 'The Magic Melody' and 'Any Old Night,' were tremendous successes, and when Mr. Lawrence Grossmith added to the evening's repertoire his heartfelt and moving lyric eulogy to his 'Bed, Wonderful Bed,' the success of the evening was assured."

The production followed its six-day booking at Baltimore's Academy of Music with similar engagements in Pittsburgh and Cleveland before opening a six-week run at the Princess Theatre in Chicago on Sunday night, November 28.

Tuesday, December 21 proved the most memorable night of the entire run. Near the end of the first act, Fanny had a scene with veteran Thomas Graves, who played the part of "Maurice," assistant manager of the "Hotel Blitz" in New York City. On this night, Graves looked at her strangely in the middle of the scene and backed off toward the wings. Fanny saw him fall into somebody's arms offstage.

Reacting quickly, Fanny turned the rest of the scene's lines into a monologue, shouting at "Maurice" offstage. Upon exiting, she was told Graves had taken sick, but would recover.

Graves' dressing room was next to Fanny's, and during intermission,

Dell peeped into it through a hole in the old wall. A doctor had the old actor stretched out over his trunk.

Graves had died of a heart attack, but . . . the show had to go on. Stage manager Frank Ross informed the company of Graves' death after the performance.

Fanny had secured whatever professional advancement she could ever have expected from a tour in *Nobody Home*. She gave her two weeks' notice after Christmas, and was replaced by Mildred Elaine, another refugee from J. J. Shuberts' Winter Garden shows, at the end of the Chicago run.

Fanny returned to New York, where Nick was awaiting word on his final appeal. In between her times with Nick, she had her first recording session for the Columbia Graphophone Company, cutting "I Don't Know Whether to Do It or Not," "If We Could Only Take Their Word" (in two parts), and "Becky Is Back in the Ballet," which Columbia did not elect to issue.

"I Don't Know Whether to Do It or Not," which Fanny performed in a wedding gown, was one of her most popular specialities in the years before America's entry into World War I. The song was never published, but Fanny's recording has survived. Instead of Yiddish dialect, she sings it in the hybrid Irish-German accent then common among first-generation Americans growing up in polyglot New York. The lyrics, by Blanche Merrill, are the words of a young woman full of serious doubts on the day of her wedding:

> I don't know whether to do it or not
> I'm thinking it out with all the brains I got
> Should I be a wife or lead the single life
> One's a coise, the other's woise
> How can a woman make a choice?
> I promised him I'd marry him today
> But why? Why should I throw myself away?
> I'll be sorry if I do it, but what'll I do?
> If I don't do it, then I'll be sorry, too.
> Should I go, go. Yes, no, I don't know.
> Don't know whether to do it or not.

Blanche Merrill's arrival as Fanny's special-material writer marked a new development in Fanny as an artist. Whereas before she had confined herself to farce and ragtime, a new element of satire came into her work; often, as in "Becky," aimed at Jewish mothers. Fanny never said whether her own mother, Rosie, was the target of these thrusts.

She would continually broaden her material in the years to come, embracing, not just comedy, but torch songs and "The Song of the Sewing Machine," a serious ballad about the wretches who worked in the sweatshops.

Fanny left New York immediately following her session for Columbia, opening her first tour of the Orpheum vaudeville circuit in Omaha on February 20. The Orpheum Circuit consisted of the finest vaudeville theatres in the West and, with harps in every orchestra, was looked on as the "class" chain of the nation. The original Orpheum Theatre was in San Francisco, and Fanny was accorded a fine reception when she opened there in April, to judge from Walter Anthony's review in the *Chronicle*.

> The audience last night gave it to Fannie Brice, who earned the distinction by the amiability of her manner, her fantastic sense of humor and her caricatures and characterizations. Fannie doesn't care what she does, nor how she looks, nor what she says. She is the irresponsible queen of high burlesque and an artist into the bargain. She is a female Eddie Foy, but with an authentic comedy genius. There is brain back of her nonsense.

In March, while Fanny was in Calgary, Nick's last appeal was exhausted. He arrived in Sing Sing on the eighteen of the month, where Professor George W. Kirchway was serving as warden pending the outcome of charges against former warden Thomas Mott Osborne.

Nick soon had the best of everything in Sing Sing. He became a trusty in the warden's residence, where he had more leeway, better food, and far more desirable living conditions than an ordinary convict. Fanny and his friends had pulled whatever strings they could.

In April, while playing the Orpheum in San Francisco, Fanny got a wire from Ziegfeld offering her a scant two hundred dollars a week to appear in the *Follies*. Ziggy received the following telegram in reply:

FANNIE BRICE FOUND DEAD IN HER ROOM IN THE HOTEL STOP THE ONLY CLUE IS A TELEGRAM SIGNED BY F. ZIEGFELD JR. WHICH WAS CLUTCHED IN HER HAND

The prestige of being in the *Follies* was worth a drop from the thousand dollars a week Fanny could command in vaudeville, but two hundred dollars a week was plainly ridiculous. They settled for about five hundred and fifty before Fanny returned east to start rehearsals for the *Follies*.

The 1915 *Follies* had seen Ziegfeld glorify the American girl as never before. Previous editions of the *Follies* had been well-produced topical and satirical revues with great comedians, good musical performers, and beautiful young women. Beginning with the 1915 show, however, Ziegfeld created a new world of exquisite taste, illusion, and unparalleled glamor. The difference was Joseph Urban, a forty-three-year-old Viennese scenic designer who had come to America as stage director for the Boston Opera in 1912. Urban's sets, exuding oriental majesty and an exotic, sensual splendor, coupled with Ziegfeld's own fine color sense and subtle use of lighting, made the *Follies* the great repository of visual magnificence Ziegfeld always dreamed it would be. Show biz had, at long last, become art.

The 1916 edition was, if anything, a comedown. The major weakness, said contemporary critics, was George Hobart's book. But if the show lacked literary brilliance or cohesiveness, the individual talents of the comedians more than carried the day. Ina Claire offered impersonations of Jane Cowl, Geraldine Farrar, and Billie Burke in the course of a scene at "Puck's Pictorial Palace," W. C. Fields presented a croquet game "On the Lawn at Lallypoosa," Ann Pennington impersonated Mary Pickford, and Bert Williams appeared in a travesty of Othello. Fanny did a take-off on Theda Bara, famous "vampire" siren of the screen.

"Alas for Theda Bara when Miss Brice has done," wrote John DeKoven, reviewing the show in New York for the *Cleveland Leader*.

> Theda is thrown, eyes and all, to the lions to make a Ziegfeld holiday. It is a symphony of so many snakey maneuvers, so staggering an assortment of amorous wiggles, so lucious a collection of lip twisting and eye rolling—in fine, so gorgeous and grim a grotesquery that it is almost libel, and the original Theda might be ill over it.
>
> Miss Brice appears in a few yards of black something—something that clings to her like a wet bathing suit. It starts with all propriety well at the bottom, but starts very early on the upward climb. Thus emphasized, she proclaims herself a six-cylinder 1916 model of Sappho, ready to meet all flappers, any weight or complexion, in a flapping contest to be held then and there. Or words to that effect. Then she forthwith vouchsafes a sample of her expert and accomplished syncopated slinking ability, finally wiggling herself off the stage, leaving an almost hysterical audience.
>
> It is to be expected that Miss Brice, if properly besought by Miss Bara, will censor herself somewhat. Her impersonation as it stands in these first days of the new *Follies* is veritably an irresistible rib-tickler, but by the same token it is unmitigatedly cruel.

Fanny also had the only solo scene, and Sime Silverman said she "walked off with the comedy hit of the show" with "The Hat" and "The Dying Swan," two new songs by Blanche Merrill. She also sang "Nijinsky" in a scene that featured Williams as the famous ballet dancer.

The show, despite its flaws, provided Fanny with her first Broadway triumph since the *Follies* of 1910. Sime said she "caught the house from her first entrance of the evening," and opined that the *Follies* of 1916 would "place Fannie Brice where she has belonged for a long while since, without the proper recognition, as one of America's real comediennes."

Fanny Brice was now a Broadway favorite, on a par in salary and prestige with the top female performers of the era. Rarely introducing big hit songs, she was nonetheless the theatre's top singing comedienne and a leading candidate for solo starring honors.

She now dressed with an elegance unsurpassed by any other woman in the theatre. Almost twenty-five, she had the slender figure to wear high-fashion clothes and the money to afford them. (White was her favorite color, though she seldom wore it in New York. Kiviette, on Broadway, supplied most of her dresses for the next fifteen years.) Nearly a head taller than most women of her time, Fanny carried herself with an almost regal dignity that gave her a bearing more befitting a socialite than the top comedienne on Broadway.

She remained, however, the same Fanny, albeit with more polished manners and less of the enthusiasm that had marked her teen-aged years. She still liked to cook, still loved smelts and kippered herring, and still had the same earthy humor, fascination with people, and love of a good bargain.

"I am a bargain hunter," she told one interviewer. "I watch the advertisements and when I see a sale advertised, I go and buy, if the things are bargains.

"When my purchases get home I show them to my mother and maybe I say: 'Mother, look at this; a coat that sells for $225, and I got it for $100,' or something like that."

One old story about Fanny had her trying to sell a hat to a chorus girl backstage. "This hat is you, Gladys. And the price is right."

"You're on, Miss Brice."

"Okay. Gladys, wait here."

Fanny went onstage and was her funniest. The laughter reverberated off the roof of the New Amsterdam Theatre, and the audience made her take one curtain call after another. Finally, she got off and came back to Gladys.

"Wonderful, Fanny," said the chorine, her eyes gleaming with excitement.

"That's what I was telling you, Gladys. At twenty-five dollars, you couldn't get a better buy anywhere."

Such was Fanny's lack of all pretension. Her work was simply that— her work—and show biz was her business. She wanted to have quality in everything she did, and often thought in terms that were surprisingly artistic. But the theatre was, essentially, a trade to her, and not something to live for. As the years went on, she lived for it less and less. She always, though, retained the need to be creative—whether through the stage or hobbies like interior decorating and fashion design.

Fanny was known for telling chorus girls to "bring four and a half yards of silk to the theatre tomorrow and I'll make you a dress." The dress would usually be made between changes of costume. While at home, Fan cooked and managed her household affairs. Once, some curtains she had bought turned out to be the wrong color. Fanny redyed them herself, not to save money but because it amused her to do it.

She frequently had friends to the apartment after shows, and often did not get to bed before daybreak. Nick's imprisonment made it hard for her to sleep at night, the beginning of a lifelong battle with insomnia.

Her mornings, then, were usually spent sleeping. (The first thing Fanny did when she got up was make the bed.) Breakfast was, if anything, a cup of coffee and some toast. Lunch was often prepared by her mother, a frequent guest in early afternoon.

Fanny read her mail while en route to the theatre, usually humming a new song she might be learning at the time. Her reading was, at all times, interrupted by long gazes out the window. Broadway was indeed a magic place at that time, with its scores of theatres, swanky restaurants, small shops, and well-dressed, interesting people.

People truly fascinated Fanny, a captivation evident in all of her best stagework. The element of commentary she put into her characterizations was based not so much on contempt as on Fanny's magical absorption with different types of people—Jewish mothers, chorus girls, or con men like Nick Arnstein.

Fanny's new-found status meant a change in her professional lifestyle, and Dell's place in her dressing room was soon augmented by the presence of Roger Davis, a professional "stooge."

"Stooge" in this case means a jester—someone who could make a star like Fanny laugh before she went onstage and thus enable her to give a good performance unaffected by either personal problems or professional pressures. Stooges were quite common in the theatre world prior to the Great Depression, and some stars would not take an assignment without making provision for the employment of their "court clown."

Dave Chasen was the stooge for Joe Cook in the late 'twenties and early 'thirties. "Basil" was valet and stooge to Herb Williams for years and worked in Williams' act. Renowned gate-crasher Tammany Young stooged for W. C. Fields, and Harry Wardell served Al Jolson in a similar capacity for decades. Occasionally, a clown to a great star was a comedian with real talent. Gay, red-haired, and balding Roger Davis fell into this category, if not into a class all by himself.

A promising revue comedian with a principal role in *Our Miss Gibbs* (1910) and featured bits in *The Passing Show* of 1912, Davis had been relegated to the chorus by the time that he met Fanny in the 1916 *Follies*. Had Davis been as funny on the stage as off, he would have rivaled Tinney, Wynn, and Fields. Fanny, who was often bored by famous professional comedians, swore by his talents. Roger nearly always made her laugh.

Davis had no regular routine, no prepared script, and no set "line," but possessed a natural sense of comedy and a genius for mimicry. Ina Claire shared Fanny's admiration for Davis, and once used him in her vaudeville act. It was with Fanny, however, that Roger was identified. He played a part in most of her professional activities over the next thirty-five years, and was portrayed by Roddy McDowell in the movie *Funny Lady*.

Fanny made at least one trip to Sing Sing weekly, bringing Nick her home-cooked food and spending all the time with him the prison would allow. Harry Houdini was on the same train with her on one of those trips upstate in August—trips that Fan looked forward to as much as, or more than, Nick did.

Nick did not tell her that he had similar visits from Carrie Greenthal Arnstein.

The 1916 *Follies* closed at the New Amsterdam Theatre on September 16 and opened a seven-month tour at the Colonial Theatre in Boston the following Monday. Extensive surgery had improved the show considerably since the Broadway opening, and critic E. F. Harkins said that it "was staged . . . more artistically than any *Follies* was ever staged before." The tour continued on through Philadelphia, Pittsburgh, Cleveland, Detroit, Chicago, St. Louis, Cincinnati, Indianapolis, Columbus, Washington, and Baltimore before closing at Harmanus Bleecker Hall in Albany on April 7, 1917. Fanny returned to New York for a brief rest before beginning rehearsals for the new *Follies*.

The *Ziegfeld Follies* of 1917 may or may not have been the greatest edition of that famous annual revue, but it certainly had the most talented group of comedians ever in one show: Fanny Brice, W. C. Fields, Bert Williams, Will Rogers, Walter Catlett, and, in his *Follies* debut, Eddie Cantor.

Cantor, a twenty-five-year-old comedian and singer who had scored a hit in Ziegfeld's *Midnight Frolic* (a cabaret show given on the roof of the New Amsterdam) in October, was a brash young man who had found that nerve was more important to success than talent. Determined to "make good," he was aggressive at rehearsals, pushing for advantage in his scenes and working almost too hard in his songs.

Fanny was less than a year older than Eddie, but far more established, and more aware of the sophistication demanded by Broadway audiences. Cantor remembered her in his autobiography forty years later.

> Her first advice to me was, "Kid, don't push yourself here. You're up against top competition and you don't have to push." She sensed the brashness in me and she didn't want me to get slapped down.
>
> And I quickly saw that what Fanny was giving me was more than lip service. She'd watch me rehearsing with Bert Williams and give me tips. "You don't take bows the way you took 'em in vaudeville, kid. The *Follies* audience is wiser." In vaudeville you'd always have a trick on your bow, something to milk a little extra applause. Here, she showed me, you wanted reserve and poise. "You mustn't have the attitude that you're an interloper; you belong."

Eddie was a somewhat undernourished-looking Jew whom Fanny mothered from the first day of rehearsals. When Cantor told her that he danced, she had Dave Stamper and Gene Buck create a soft-shoe number for them titled "Just You and Me."

Cantor, though, had never danced at all, as Fanny quickly found during rehearsals. ("You bastard, you can't dance!" said Fanny.) Still Cantor's mentor, she had Ned Wayburn teach Eddie some steps, and "You and Me" was ready by the time the *Follies* opened in Atlantic City. As a complement to Cantor, Fan herself "tanned up"—the closest that she ever came to blackface.

Fanny did two new songs by Blanche Merrill in another of her solo spots near the end of the show, and Sime Silverman singled out "Egyptian" as "the real riot of the evening." The story of a Jewish girl who became an Egyptian dancer when she "made some improvements upon her Yiddisher movements," it was the first in a new cycle of Brice songs about young "Yiddisher" women in improbable situations.

The 1917 *Follies* was heralded as the best yet, not just in terms of comedy (Fields did a great "lawn tennis" scene with Catlett), but in looks and cost. "There is so much to see in the show, without watching the performance, that maybe the Ziegfeld scheme is to draw 'em twice, once to watch the scenery and clothes, and the next time the performance. The *Follies* this season is certainly worth double price. It's a 'sight show' of a kind never before shown." Those were Sime's words, but he spoke for the majority. The *Follies* was better than ever.

The show opened at the New Amsterdam on June 12, 1917. Less than five weeks later, Governor Charles S. Whitman pardoned Nick.

Instead of waiting until eight o'clock in the morning, when prisoners were usually released, authorities at Sing Sing let Nick go at 5:10 in the afternoon of July 16, the day the pardon was rushed down from Albany to Sing Sing.

If the waiting had made Fanny tired, it had also given her time to think. She now insisted they be married, and Carrie just as stubbornly would not give a divorce.

Nick travelled with Fanny when the *Follies* went on tour that fall. W. C. Fields did not usually like trains; only "fairies" rode on trains. (In truth, he had been told to ride in open cars to cure a touch of tuberculosis he had contracted in Europe.) During that 1917–18 *Follies* tour, Nick and Fanny often travelled with Eddie Cantor, Bessie Poole (Fields' mistress), and Fields himself in the latter's big open Cadillac. Weather permitting, they would stop and picnic. At other times, they'd dine in the best restaurants along the way. W. C., like Nick, insisted on good food.

Nick was unique: a "ladies' man" who also was a "man's man." He fascinated Fields, who integrated some of Arnstein's more flowery talk into his own comedy routine. "Never give a sucker an even break" was one of Nick's favorite expressions. "Never smarten up a sucker" was another. Fields took both lines and wove them into "Never give a sucker an even break and never smarten up a chump."

Adele Moon travelled with the luggage on the train, but Fanny kept her jewel case in her lap. Once, on a cold day, a man waved their car down and asked for a lift; his car, he said, was stuck two miles up the road. Fields told him to hop on the running board and drove. Without moving his lips, Nick muttered, "This guy's a stick-up man."

"What'll I do with my jewel case?" whispered Fanny.

"Drop it on the floor. Bill, slow down and tell the guy to jump."

Fields slowed down and, swearing, told the man to jump. Nick leaned forward threateningly and the man jumped. "There was no doubt Nick was right," said Cantor. "He knew what he knew about crooks and we never questioned it."

Fanny likewise tried to ask no questions when Nick said that he would see her in New York at the tour's end. He then left Chicago, never mentioning the nature of his "business deal," and becoming taciturn when pressed. One thing, though, was certain: Arnstein's business, in New York or elsewhere, had nothing to do with a divorce from Carrie. Nick's obtaining that divorce was all that concerned Fanny now.

A Midwest blizzard forced Fields and company to abandon their usual scenic route and travel to Cincinnati by train. Fields and Cantor were all set to eat in the train's dining car, but Fanny would not hear of it. "Ridiculous," she said. "We'll be in in an hour. I'll cook your dinner."

The blizzard made the train two hours late. When they finally arrived in Cincinnati, Fanny bought a box of spaghetti, met Dell at the hotel, and started cooking. Cantor remembered her "smelling up the Sinton Hotel (Suite 607–609) with spaghetti sauce, and splashing around expensive perfume to drown the essence of garlic and olive oil. The spaghetti is finally finished, we dive in, and Fields starts foaming at the mouth. Me too, and Fanny. We look like we all have hydrophobia."

Dell, who had a tendency to mix things up, had filled the grated cheese jar with soap powder. Fanny gathered up all the spaghetti, flushed it down the toilet, and then had to pay a plumbing bill to have the bowl unplugged. Dell was promptly fired—and rehired the next day.

The weather was mild enough for Fields to motor to Indianapolis, the show's next point of call, even if it was too cold for Cantor. Fields put the top up when it snowed, but Cantor shivered, his ears red with frostbite. Once they hit a ditch, and Eddie bumped his head against the top. Fanny laughed, and Eddie, who was in pain, hit her. Fanny hit him back, and then they kicked each other.

Fanny and Eddie were not speaking to each other when the car pulled into Indianapolis. That night, onstage at English's Opera House, they sang about how much they liked each other in "Just You and Me." The incongruity of it overcame them in mid-song, and both performers laughed so hard they couldn't get the words out.

So ended Fan and Eddie's one-day feud. They remained friends from then on. One Midwestern architect, attempting to court Fanny, asked Cantor for help. Eddie tried, but it was hopeless; Nick Arnstein was the only man for Fanny.

The tour ended at His Majesty's Theatre in Montreal on April 20, 1918. Fanny did a brief turn in the Ziegfeld *Midnight Frolic* for the last two weeks in May, singing "Becky Is Back in the Ballet" and "Egyptian." Afternoons found her guiding a saddle horse over the bridal paths of Central Park. She also found the time to start a dressmaking establishment on West Seventy-second Street in partnership with Lottie Cantor, a young Jewish modiste from Chicago.

Her second two-year contract with Flo Ziegfeld had expired. Fanny might have re-signed with him, but the prospect of another *Follies* failed to excite her. She felt ready for a starring vehicle, and jumped when A. H. Woods offered her the chance to star in *Why Worry?*, a three-act "melodramatic farce" by Montague Glass and Jules Eckert Goodman.

The play was intended as a female version of *Potash and Perlmutter*, a well-known comedy about two Jewish merchants, with May Boley play-ing opposite Fanny as a supposed German spy who is really an American agent. The Avon Comedy Four (Joe Smith, Charley Dale, Irving Kauf-man, and Harry Goodwin) was also featured.

Why Worry?, which also boasted Fanny in two songs and Roger Davis in the part of a gas bill collector, opened at the Belasco Theatre in Wash-ington, D.C., on Monday evening, July 29, 1918. Roger managed to de-liver a line ("I've got to have that money") that made Fanny almost fall down laughing in the first act, but the audience did not find *Why Worry?* one-half as amusing.

The play ran the following week at the Globe in Atlantic City. "If all the acts were as good as the final," Charles Scheuer wrote in *Variety,* "*Why Worry? . . .* would be in fine shape for its Broadway run. But as presented at the Globe Monday night, after a week in Washington, it proved somewhat short of the ideals which A. H. Woods is usually ex-pected to achieve in that length of time."

They did extensive rewrites, and reopened two weeks later at the Harris Theatre in New York without additional pre-Broadway warm-ups. The result was a near-disaster. "Miss Brice and the Avon Comedy Four de-served happier fate than to worry over *Why Worry?*" said the New York *Herald.* The *Evening Sun* said the "lines have real humor, but as a play it is quite hopeless," and the *Times* was guilty of understatement when it said "the effect was not quite convincing." Fanny was successful with two new songs by Blanche Merrill—"I'm Bad" and "I'm an Indian"— but *The Billboard* said that "Fanny Brice in the stellar role of a produc-tion, did not prove a great success." It was, for Fanny, an experiment in stardom, one that proved a brutal disappointment.

Even the play's weakness was not Fanny's chief concern. Nick, who had found Carrie with another man, now had power to divorce her. The threat led her to sue Fanny for $100,000 (a tremendous sum in those days) for alienation of affections. The suit was filed in July, while *Why Worry?* was still in rehearsal.

On Wednesday, August 21, Nick called his wife and asked her to meet him at Bretton Hall in New York that evening. (Carrie afterwards claimed she "did not care about seeing him, but consented after some rough language.") They drank highballs and then switched to wine, Nick offer-ing to give his wife one thousand dollars and set her up in business if she would withdraw the suit. He was careful to explain that Fanny did not know what he was doing, that he "wanted to do something for Fanny" since she "had been very good to me. She gave me money while I was in jail and also got me out on bail." Carrie later said that she had been "full of liquor" and did not know what took place that evening. In the morning she awoke and found herself with one hundred and fifty dollars.

They met again on the afternoon of the following day at the Hotel Imperial. More highballs were downed, and the matter of the settlement was again broached. Carrie said that while she could hardly do anything with the five hundred dollars Nick now offered, being set up in business appealed to her. Her mention of the name of her attorney, Herman L. Roth, only made Nick angry. Arnstein reiterated that he, and not Fanny, was doing the "fixing."

Nick got paper and envelopes from the front desk and dictated both a release for Carrie to sign and a letter to her attorney. It then required more talk, more explanations, and more veiled threats before Carrie signed the release, which was witnessed by a notary at the Hotel Astor.

Carrie renewed her suit less than three weeks later, charging Nick had gotten her drunk and that she "did not know the purpose of the paper" she had signed. "He said it was just a release. I saw it mentioned Fanny Brice and five hundred dollars." Nick applied more pressure, and the suit was dropped again.

Carrie now agreed to sue Nick for divorce and not name Fanny. Having Nick sue her would have been most unpleasant; adultery, at that time, was an ugly stain for women.

Why Worry? closed on September 14 after only twenty-seven performances in New York, so Jenny Wagner, Fanny's new agent, booked her for seven weeks in New York vaudeville at one thousand dollars a week. (She had gotten seven hundred three years earlier.) But Fanny chose to cancel all these bookings and devote her time to Nick and her new dress shop. She had already re-signed with Flo Ziegfeld.

On December 9, 1918, Fanny opened in the Ziegfeld *Nine O'Clock Revue* and *Midnight Frolic*, two entertainments that provided a total of six hours of relief to the tired millionaire playboy on the roof of the New Amsterdam Theatre. The *New York Times*, reviewing the *Nine O'Clock* show, said that "Fannie Brice, with two numbers, was as hilariously funny as usual, particularly in her burlesque of a vampire." Fanny did "I'm an Indian" in the *Midnight Frolic*, and Sime Silverman reported that "S-sh's could be heard all over the house. The audience did not want to miss the comedy punches of the lines. Miss Brice was a laughing riot. . . ."

At Fanny's own suggestion, the number of her songs was upped from three to six. Ziegfeld readily agreed that the shows needed them, but balked when Fanny followed up by asking for more money.

Ziegfeld gave in after only a few days. "My only worry now," quipped

Fanny, "is that I'll be asked to make a gown at regular rates for Jenny Wagner."

There were, however, other worries. Fanny had discovered she was pregnant, the baby due in August. She had already had one abortion, did not want another, and the weeks preceding Nick's divorce were little short of hell. Fanny, in addition, found the morning sickness horrid, with bitter-tasting bile "the color of orange juice."

Nick himself soon started having stomach cramps. A doctor who examined him found nothing wrong, but when the cramps continued, Arnstein made a second visit. The doctor then decided to make tests—until he spoke to Fanny and she mentioned she was pregnant. Then he laughed and sent the couple home.

Finally, in March, divorce was granted. Nick and Fanny were married in New Jersey on the fifth of April and celebrated with a wedding dinner Fanny cooked herself. The main course was a black sea bass that Fan had bought that morning.

This was not the age of women's liberation, and Fanny Brice saw nothing wrong with taking care of her husband. She took pride in both her cooking and her home, and wanted Nick to be strong and protective. That he was essentially a weak man playing a strong part did not matter to Fanny. "I thought that I could change Nick," she admitted later. Fanny, in fact, was the strong one, but not strong enough to change Nick Arnstein.

But their marriage and the coming baby made Nick want to make at least a show of being a provider. Claiming to have made some money gambling, he bought the residence of Mrs. Emma Allard in Halesite, an exclusive section of Huntington, New York, early that summer. Title was taken in the names of Jules W. Arnold and Fannie B. Arnold.

Nick paid $12,500 for the property, and Fanny later claimed to have spent twenty-five thousand dollars having it remodelled. "Nick had to have stables for his horses," Fanny recalled. "So he lines the stables with mahogany. 'If we can't have it good, we won't have it at all,' he tells me. Well, he builds the mahogany stables, and I never saw a horse in them. Not even horse shit." Fan was also driven to distraction by the insects. She would never like the house.

Fanny now learned Nick's divorce would not be final for three months. She was five months pregnant and, legally, unmarried.

Fanny worked until Ziegfeld shut the *Nine O'Clock Revue* and *Midnight Frolic* in anticipation of the 1919 *Follies*. The advanced state of Fanny's pregnancy precluded her appearing in this edition, usually considered the greatest in the series.

Nick's divorce from Carrie became final on June 11, 1919. Exactly one week later, he and Fanny underwent another wedding ceremony, performed by Deputy City Clerk John F. Quale in Brooklyn. Fanny, seven months pregnant, gave her name as Fanny Borach and her occupation as dressmaker. Nick gave his as "businessman." After more than six and a half years, Fanny was, officially, Mrs. Jules W. Arnstein.

Two months later, on August 12, 1919, Fanny gave birth to a daughter, Frances, in the house in Huntington.

Fran's birth coincided with the actors' strike that shut down New York theatres for six weeks and led to the establishment of Actors' Equity on Broadway. Fanny, who had no more interest in unionism than she had in politics, was only too glad not to be involved. The daughter of a hardnosed businesswoman, she thought most people got what they deserved. Fanny, always willing to help friends of hers in need, had little or no social conscience. She never felt she owed strangers a thing.

In September, after Fanny had recovered, she and Nick moved back into the city, abandoning their old rooms on West Fifty-eighth Street for new quarters on West Eighty-third.

Fanny, in the meantime, went into rehearsal for the ninth edition of the Ziegfeld *Midnight Frolic*. The audience was made up largely of show business professionals, and Fanny proved the hit of the bill with "Spring," a ludicrous burlesque on classical dancing based on Felix Mendelssohn's famous "Spring Song." Fanny had the idea for the song herself.

> I was in a theatre watching a very beautiful ballet performance. Thirteen girls . . . postured and flitted about the stage in the pantomime of Pierrot and Harlequin. The orchestra was playing the Spring Song and through it ran the sweet caroling of birds.
>
> And while I watched I said to myself, "They get up on their toes and chase madly after—nobody. Then they flee where no man pursueth, while the little birds sing. Oh, would I were a bird! Oh, would I were a bird! I would fly in the spring!"
>
> All that night these silly words kept recurring to me. "Oh, would I were a bird! I would fly in the spring. Oh, would I were a flower! I would grow in the spring. Oh, would I were a spring! I would bird in the flower." I fell asleep, still going over them. The next morning they were still with me, so I knew I had a song idea. I called up Blanche Merrill and she arrived at my apartment in the middle of the morning.

Fanny did this number in an oversized ballet costume, the humor coming largely from the sight of an angular and very ethnic woman blissfully unaware of her shortcomings as a ballerina.

Fanny's first appearance in this edition of the *Midnight Frolic* saw her do a travesty Apache song and dance assisted by Eddie Cantor. "This was excruciatingly funny in a burlesque way," said Joshua Lowe, reviewing for *Variety*. "Miss Brice sacrifices all sense of dignity, permitting Cantor to administer kicks upon her posterior."

Fanny introduced one of the most famous songs of her career in this show. The title was "Rose of Washington Square," a song unique in that it was first written—and performed—as a comedy number, then transformed into a ballad. The song was first heard in the *Frolic* after the show opened.

The original lyrics, sung by Fan as "Rose," describe a young Jewish woman from the Bronx who "wanders from there down to Washington Square," meets "Harrison Fisher" (a contemporary artist who depicted beautiful women for magazine covers), and finds work as a nude model. Fanny got a big laugh with the line, "They say my Roman nose—It seems to please . . . artistic people," by turning her profile to the audience and pointing a long finger to her own pronounced proboscis.

The short performance hours left her free to spend a lot of time with Nick and the new baby. Nick, however, was not comfortable in his new role as father. He sometimes came into the baby's room and bent over her crib, fascinated by the child's perfection and marvelling at the miracle of creation. When Fanny saw him, though, he'd stiffen up, embarrassed at his own display of human wonder. He was always Nick the gentleman, *bon vivant* friend of dukes and gangsters—"at ease always," Nicky Arnstein.

His attitude hurt Fanny. It was, however, basically a happy time—almost an ideal.

CHAPTER 7

The Fugitive

Early in the morning of Thursday, February 12, 1920, Fanny returned to the Eight-third Street apartment from her night's work in the *Frolic* to find Nick packing. Purposeful and grim, he asked his wife if she'd been followed, said that he was "innocent," handed her two checks, and told her not to worry as he walked away from the apartment. Usually the most discriminating dresser, he was wearing a black hat Fanny had bought for him in Europe and an old coat. Nick had never liked the hat and had not worn the coat in years.

Fanny went through the next five days in a sort of daze, wondering what Nick had done, where he had gone, when he would be back—and what troubles they would face if the law found he was not "innocent" of whatever he had or had not been doing.

Then, on Tuesday afternoon, February 17, police headquarters phoned and asked if they could search the apartment. "I told them they could search it to their heart's content so long as they didn't wake the baby," Fanny told a reporter from the *New York American*. "They went through the apartment and all my personal papers. It didn't bother me any, as I had nothing to conceal. They then questioned me and I told them all I knew. I then offered to tell my story to the District Attorney and did so, answering a thousand questions."

She also got some answers from the police in the process. Nick had disappeared because of news he had received of a confession by a youth named Joseph Gluck. The events in question went back more than six months, and concerned the thefts of about five million dollars in Wall Street securities—not to mention a beautiful "sting" of more than half a dozen Wall Street messengers.

The story is exceedingly complex, but the gist of it here follows: In

1919, there were almost five hundred thefts from New York brokerage houses and banks in amounts ranging from five hundred dollars to nearly half a million; the total was a little over five million dollars. The thefts, it was discovered, were all inside jobs involving either employees of the brokers in league with the criminals or messengers who would allow themselves to be "held up" in exchange for a promised share of the loot after the stolen securities were negotiated through the "proper" channels.

Police suspected the work of an organized ring, but had no other leads until early February 1920, when David W. Sullivan & Company, a small Wall Street brokerage house, failed to meet a loan of $20,000 from the Riggs National Bank, forcing Riggs to sell $45,000 worth of securities that had been pledged as collateral. When they did, they found the said securities were "hot."

David W. Sullivan, head of the bankrupt brokerage house, had suspected he was receiving stolen goods, having dealt personally with Arnstein, who supplied the securities, and Nick's associate, Isadore (Nick) Cohen. Sullivan and Arnstein met in the bar of a hotel in uptown New York City in October 1919, after Randolph Newman, a lawyer who rented part of his office to Sullivan, said he "knew a man who would lend the firm some stock to help tide it over its difficulties." Arnstein was the man.

Sullivan wore a yellow coat so Arnstein would be able to recognize him. "He (Arnstein) told me I looked all right to him," said Sullivan. "I think he said I looked a little bit like a copper, but he was willing to overlook that; I talked all right." Sullivan met Nick Cohen some time later.

Armed with Sullivan's description and identification of Nick Arnstein from past mug shots, the police intensified both their investigation of the thefts and their interrogations of Wall Street messengers. Joseph Gluck, the messenger who acted as chief liaison between the rest of the messengers and "Big Bill" Furey, one of the conspirators, said he had stolen $600,000 worth of bonds and gotten nine thousand dollars as his share—but that Furey and a man he knew as "Count Carrigan" subsequently posed as United States marshals and took $6,400 of it from him. He said a gang of messenger boys met daily in New Street, in back of the Stock Exchange, and arranged to be "robbed." Gluck subsequently identified Nick Arnstein as one of the conspirators.

Several other messengers told of having accompanied Gluck to the Claridge Hotel in Times Square, where they met Furey, who later introduced them to several alleged politicians who, he said, would aid them in escaping without interference from the local police. Furey also let them see a "banker" who would negotiate the stolen securities for cash. Gluck identified the banker as Nick Arnstein.

In an effort to get hold of the stolen securities, the National Surety Company of 115 Broadway brought bankruptcy proceedings against Arnstein on February 20, 1920. Nick was identified under aliases ranging from "Nick Arnstein," to "Jules W. Arnold," to "Jules W. Ames," to "Julius Arndt Stein," to "Jules W. Adams," the name he used in England. The next day's papers identified Nick Arnstein as the "mastermind" of all the thefts and swindles—an exaggeration, to say the least; Nick had "only" been involved with about $2,300,000, less than half the total stolen. He was undoubtedly, however, one of the chief fixers.

Arnstein claimed that he was innocent until his dying day. His story, which Fanny managed to convince herself was true, was that Bill Furey had told Gluck and another of the messengers that he would negotiate all the stocks and bonds through a banker from Washington. When the messengers asked to meet the banker, Furey said he had refused to deal with them directly, but would be meeting with him, Furey, in a restaurant at Eighty-sixth and Broadway. He then supposedly arranged to have the innocent Nick meet him at the restaurant and be seen by the messengers. When the messengers were caught, they told all about the "banker" and identified Nick Arnstein from police mug shots.

Nick never explained Sullivan's dealings with, and subsequent identification of, him as the man who had arranged the sale of the stolen securities. He only said that he was being framed.

Fanny's statements to the district attorney should have ended matters, as far as she was concerned. But the newspapers' identification of Nick as "mastermind" of all the bank heists had made New York's publicity-sensitive police brass anxious to put him behind bars. First they had to find him, and they thought that they could do that through his wife. Fanny, though, had thus far told them nothing, and they simply were not satisfied with that.

When Fanny came out in the *Midnight Frolic* the night following her talk with the D.A., Detective Grover C. Brown was seated at one of the tables. Fanny soon learned she was being followed.

There was a language spoken by the underworld in those days that has not survived the changing American crime scene. They knew how to spot a cop, a "hop" (i.e., "junkie"), a pickpocket, and a hit man. They knew, moreover, how to deal with them all. And they knew toughness. Making a living in show business, with its heartbreaks, disappointments, and elbows in the clinches, had taught Fanny to be tough in one way.

Nick, however, taught her to stand up to cops, attorneys, government officials, and a host of other people that one never met in show biz. By 1920, Fanny Brice could give and take it—in the theatre and in Nick's world. She could "spot a phony," stand up for her rights, and swear like the proverbial sailor.

Be that as it may, the constant tailing and other harassment made her a nervous wreck by the time she testified before United States Commissioner Gilchrist on Thursday, February 26. Fanny's only defense was bravado—the last resort of any actor.

"Hard to get down so early in the morning, eh?" she laughed on entering the commissioner's room shortly after eleven o'clock. Fanny wore a long sable coat she took off to reveal a plain black meteor frock. She wore no jewelry apart from her engraved wedding ring.

Saul S. Myers, counsel for the National Surety Company, questioned Fanny.

"Where is Arnstein now?"

"I don't know. I saw him last on February 12th in my apartment, No. 1 West Eighty-third Street. I have not laid eyes on him since."

"You have communicated with him since?"

"No."

"Did you confer with Mr. Fallon yesterday?"

Arnstein, aided by several friends, had retained William Fallon, probably the greatest trial lawyer in the country. Fallon's partner, Eugene McGee, had already met with Fanny at the Hotel Commodore, where they "talked about two minutes."

At one point in the hearing, Fanny said it was the first time she'd "ever had an audience standing up and me sitting down."

"Would you rather stand up?"

"No. I'd rather sing a song. If I can't, please get a glass of water for me."

The water appeared, and Fanny told of bank accounts she had in the United States Mortgage and Trust Company—one under the name of Fanny Brice and one as Fanny Arnold. She also said she had an account in the Colonial Bank in the name of Fanny Brice, the three accounts totalling five hundred dollars.

Fan then told about the two checks Nick had given her before he left.

"Did your husband often give you large checks, and did you not wonder where he got the money?"

"Why, I've heard him say he got it gambling. Believe me, sir, I have no intention of concealing anything."

"Hasn't your husband given you many expensive jewels in the last few months?"

"Hah! He hasn't given me any ever, and the ones I have were bought two or three years ago from Rudolph Hamill."

"How were they paid for—cash or check?"

"I don't know."

"You mean you don't know how $27,000 worth of jewelry, bought, as you say, with your own money, was paid for?"

"No. I just know it was my dough. Ask the jeweler how it was paid for and when, if you want to know."

The home in Huntington that Nick had purchased was the subject of Myers' next question. It was finally established that the home was bought for twelve thousand dollars, but Fanny said she could not remember how it had been paid for.

"Why, I tell you I don't know about these business things. And if I tried to tell about them it would just make you laugh. There are just two things I can remember: telephone numbers and the royalties of my songs. I'm such a good businesswoman that I paid gas bills to two companies for three months for the same service without knowing it. Seriously, I have only enough time for my baby and my work."

"W-e-l-l, get your mind off the baby and the work and put it on this Huntington property for a minute."

"I'm telling you where you can find every little detail your heart could desire. Go to the agent. He knows."

"What is your stage income?"

"It is $650 a week. I get more from a little dressmaking shop I run as 'Lottie and Brice.' "

"Who is your partner in that?"

"Oh, that's Lottie Cantor from Chicago. She's a nice leetle Jewish girl," said Fanny, slipping into her stage dialect. Fanny might have told the counsel that her salary was higher when she appeared in the *Follies* and not just the *Midnight Frolic*.

Fanny's lawyer, Alfred Beekman of House, Grossman & Vorhaus, launched a protest when Myers asked to see her bankbooks; but she had nothing to hide. "Sure," said Fanny. "You can have everything I've got. Give him the books, boys. Let him play with 'em for awhile."

While Myers looked them over, Fanny whispered to Beekman. "Schmart boy! Schmart boy!"

Myers resumed his questioning and Fanny her replies. "I have a safe deposit box in the Lincoln Trust company. In it are a gold vanity bag, a gold cigarette case, and a gold mesh bag. I lost the key to it three or four months ago."

"Are you willing to have it opened?"

"Betcha life I am that! Let the receiver open it. And there's another one at the Madison Safe Deposit Company, but I've lost the key to it, too."

"Do you know Sam G-I-O-U-X?"

"Say it."

"You say it. Sounds like 'Gooey' to me."

"Naw, I could never know a man with a name like Gooey."

Fanny admitted knowing Nick Cohen slightly, because he had come to her apartment six weeks earlier to see her husband. She said that she knew Arnold Rothstein well. He was, she maintained, her friend—not her husband's. Once, she and her mother had played poker with him—fifty-cent ante.

The hearing was a waste of time, proving neither Fanny's complicity nor her total innocence. Nick, in the meantime, still had not contacted Fanny.

Late that evening, shortly before midnight, W. C. Fields came into Fanny's dressing room and handed her a note he had received. The envelope was postmarked Akron, Ohio, and the note read:

> You remember the rides in your car with our friend. Tell her I've left the stage and am working in a brassiere shop on Second Avenue.

Fanny understood. From then until Nick finally returned, they spoke at intervals, Fanny waiting for his calls at a downtown brassiere factory owned by the brother of the man Arnstein was hiding with in Cleveland. She dodged the detectives who followed her by going to the ladies' room in Macy's, which led to a back stairway. Fanny had remembered it from years before, when she'd known a girl who worked there.

At one point, Lottie Cantor got the keys to the apartment of one of her customers, a woman going out of town for several weeks. Fanny, tired of her excursions to the brassiere factory, arranged for Nick to call her there one day at 3:00 P.M.

Someone knocked on the door moments after she arrived in the apartment. Moments later, three detectives entered and asked her if she had heard from Nick.

Fanny stood up to them, mindful that her purse contained Nick's latest letter. When the phone rang, she refused to answer, stating that it was a customer's apartment. One of the detectives picked up the receiver, but Nick hung up at the first sound of a man's voice.

Police harassment of Fanny Brice continued for three months, during which time she lost twenty pounds, was unable to sleep without pills, and could keep nothing on her stomach except liquids. When the police were not hounding her, there were the reporters asking her the same unanswerable questions or the photographers wanting her to pose for different pictures. The friend who most sustained her at this point was May Weston, whose own husband, Willie, had died of Hodgkin's disease a few months earlier. (Weston, only thirty-six, was buried by his fellow Masons.) May stayed with Fanny almost constantly, offering endless hours of diverting conversation and trying, rather futilely, to get her to take food. At one point, Fanny's body stiffened and she had to have a massage by an osteopath before she could stand up, much less go on in the *Midnight Frolic*. She went on, and kept the osteopath on weekly retainer for two months.

Nor did she want sympathy. Fanny left explicit instructions with the stage manager of the *Midnight Frolic:* no one was to mention anything about Nick Arnstein.

Fanny hated displays of emotion. "I can't cry in front of anybody and I don't want them to cry in front of me. I could only cry in front of the man I loved." That man was now a fugitive from justice, and the cause of any tears Fanny might shed.

William Fallon wanted Arnstein to give himself up, but Nick, who did not want to go to the Tombs under any circumstances, said he would return to New York only if the courts would guarantee low bail.

Fallon spoke to the district attorney's office, but could get no guarantees. The authorities agreed, however, not to actually arrest Arnstein if he surrendered to them out of town. It was a fine technical point, but one that Fallon thought would stand them in good stead in the contempt proceedings.

Arnstein, it was thought, would now surrender. Detectives Mayer and Brown of the Wall Street squad and Lieutenant Geghan were assigned to accompany Fallon's partner, Eugene McGee, to the Hotel Astor. A telephone call told them to go to Pittsburgh. In that city, after McGee had admitted that the D.A.'s office had not guaranteed low bail, they were told to go to Rochester. From Rochester, they were sent to Utica, and from there to Niagara Falls, New York. Then it was back to Utica, to Syracuse, and back to Pittsburgh. A return trip to Syracuse was next. From there, they went to Albany, and, fed up with what had turned into a wild-goose chase, back to New York.

The farce continued two more months, Arnstein hopping from one city to another but favoring Pittsburgh and Cleveland, where the increasingly cynical New York press maintained he was under the protection of a particularly corrupt civil administration. "I'll bring Arnstein to justice," said one embattled New York detective, "no matter what the public thinks because of Fanny Brice."

Fanny tried to focus on the baby, but she still lost weight. A doctor told her to drink wine, but Fan subsisted on a pint of milk a day. It was all she could keep down.

She was back to working full time, making nightly appearances in a new edition of the Ziegfeld *Nine O'Clock Revue* beginning March 9 and opening in a totally revised *Midnight Frolic* a week later. Alexander Woollcott, reviewing the *Nine O'clock Revue* in the *New York Times,* referred to Fanny as the "imperturbable Fanny Brice, remembering several songs and singing them with infinite relish."

William Fallon told Fanny that the D.A.'s office would set bail at $100,000. There were people she could go to for the money, but Fanny was more than surprised when Ann Pennington came into her dressing room with a handkerchief and laid it on the dressing table. "Fanny, I don't really need these," Penny said. When Fanny looked inside the kerchief, she saw $20,000 in jewelry. Fan turned down Penny's offer, but it strengthened a good friendship that had started four years earlier, in the 1916 *Follies.*

Fanny said that Ann Pennington was another example of the way she "duplicated friendships" throughout life. Just as Polly Moran "duplicated" Hannah Ryan, Fanny's friend in Brooklyn, "Penny" was a "duplicate" of Hattie Levy, her first friend in Newark. Penny would remain Fan's closest friend among her fellow performers.

Penny was in the *Follies* from 1913 to 1918, deserting them to join her boyfriend, George White, in his *Scandals* the following year. She was physically quite unlike Fanny: less than four-foot-ten in her stocking feet to Fanny's five-foot-seven, dainty (less than one hundred pounds and wearing remarkably small 1½ C shoes), pretty, and a girl who welcomed men's attentions. (Penny had a sign above the door of her dressing room that said, "For Men Only.") She rouged her cheeks, her chin, and her famous dimpled knees, and loved practical jokes. When a man she did not fancy telephoned, asking, "Is this Miss Pennington?" she replied, "This ain't me." Her favorite nickname for herself was "Tiny," and "Won't you do that for Tiny?" was her favorite way of asking favors.

She had other nicknames, too—"The Countess," "Pipsy," and "Bananas." In Boston, house detectives burst in on her in bed with George White. Penny, taken by surprise, just cried out, "He's my brother."

Penny was a sweet and sincere soul who, unlike many performers, honestly wished everyone success. She was reportedly engaged, at various times, to White, Jack Dempsey, Brooke Johns, and Buster West, but never married. Fanny thought it was because Penny "wouldn't take anything from anybody." What Fan and Penny had in common were sincerity and heart. Both were generous to friends, personally selfless, and able to stand on their own feet in a theatrical business run by men.

Ziegfeld might have supplied the money, but his business contracts barred him going bond. Fallon said that Nick's own friends should give it, pointedly referring to Arnold Rothstein, who kept Fallon on retainer as his lawyer. Rothstein was now richer than ever, having masterminded and cleaned up on the World Series fix.

Because of their friendship, their similar names, and similar ethnic origins, many thought that Rothstein and not Nick was the real "mastermind" of the Wall Street escapade as well. Fallon soon brought Rothstein to see Fanny in the *Frolic*.

Fanny, who knew Rothstein well, had been reluctant to approach him. Aware of the price men like him set upon their favors, and wishing to remain as aloof from the underworld as possible, she now agreed to talk to Rothstein because time was running out.

Arnold Rothstein, for his part, liked Fanny, appreciated her integrity, and admired her guts. He agreed to put up the one hundred thousand dollars.

It had been exactly ten years since an eighteen-year-old Fanny Brice had stood at the corner of Forty-seventh Street and Broadway showing her new Ziegfeld contract to anyone connected with the theatre. She had been through much in that time—a quick, barely consummated marriage, four editions of the *Follies, Midnight Frolics,* a season for the Shuberts, and a common-law marriage to Nick Arnstein legalized in two civil ceremonies shortly before the birth of her daughter. She had also matured—from an eager, stagestruck girl caught in the thrill of Broadway, to a young woman in love, to a show-wise comedienne who could deal with experienced producers on their own terms. Part of this maturity was due to passing time and her position in an always hard profession. Much of it, however, came from Nick.

She now had "been around" and met famous names ranging from society people like the Harrimans to men like Arnold Rothstein, Nick Cohen, and innumerable other friends of Nick's. Fanny was able to bring each of them up or down to her own level with an amazing sense of personal dignity—of the essential "rightness" of things. It was that sense of self that let her deal so successfully with men like Arnold Rothstein without compromising her integrity. That, not comedy or singing, may indeed have been her greatest talent.

On May 15, 1920, Nick Arnstein, the most famous and most hunted fugitive in North America, was picked up in a car by Fanny and Bill Fallon and driven right through the annual Police Parade to Criminal Courts Building, where he surrendered to Assistant District Attorney Dooling. His three months of wandering, and Fanny's three of wondering, were over.

Nick was examined before the United States Commission under the Bankruptcy Law. Many of the questions had to do with how he'd lived and who had aided him during his three-month sojourn, and Nick refused to answer "on the grounds that to do so might tend to incriminate or degrade" him.

Arnstein later would be cited for contempt. In the meantime, he was a free man—free to see his wife in the new *Follies*.

CHAPTER *8*

What Every Woman Nose

T he Fourteenth Annual Production of the *Ziegfeld Follies* opened at the New Amsterdam Theatre on Tuesday night, June 22, 1920. Advance reports from Atlantic City, where the show had its usual pre-Broadway tryout, said that this particular edition needed much more work than usual—reports that were confirmed when the show reached New York. Sime Silverman said the 1920 *Follies* "was in bad shape in comedy when starting off at the New Amsterdam. It was badly off in all other departments as well, other than production. Ziegfeld never falls down on the producing end. But comedy is sadly missed in a great big long time running show like the *Follies,* especially when there is no decided musical hit, also happening in this season's performance."

Most of New York's critics were of similar opinion: the 1920 *Follies* was a let-down after the great 1919 show, just the way the 1916 edition had failed to live up to the 1915 production; and for the same reason—poor material in the show's book. The best comedy scene was one called "The Little *Follies* Theatre—During Intermission" at the beginning of Act II, featuring W. C. Fields as "Just a Husband" who pays too much attention to a beauty in the first row of the chorus. Fanny played "His Wife" and got the laugh of the evening when she dragged the henpecked Fields from the theatre.

Other potentially funny scenes failed to come off on opening night. Fields wrote and starred in "The Family Ford" (actually an adaptation of Harry Tate's "Motoring," as Broadway wags were quick to point out), with Fanny as his wife and Rae Dooley as their daughter, Baby Rose. A mechanical mishap prevented the scene from receiving its due critical plaudits, although Sime was quick to see it as a "laugh maker." Fanny failed to score as well as expected in Act II, scene 3, "The Dancing School," which featured Charles Winninger as the Master, eighteen-year-old beauty Mary Eaton as the Pupil, and Fanny as "Another Pupil"—comically inept, gleefully unselfconscious, and arching her long eyebrows in ridiculous flirtation.

Fanny had two songs in this edition of the *Follies,* and did well with both. "I Was a Floradora Baby," in the second act, told about a Jewish girl who claimed to be the only one of the original *Floradora* sextette who had married for love. ("Now at home, I'm bringing up a sextette. Five I got, the other one I'll get yet.") But it was with "I'm a Vamp from East Broadway" that she showed to best advantage. For the finish, Fanny held an imaginary conversation with one of her East Side victims, over whom she gloated as he detailed the ruin her vamping had brought him to. As she exited, Fan looked at him and said, "You look terrible, thank God."

Variety even knocked the Ziegfeld girls, claiming they were not up to their predecessors in looks, talent, or charm. Ben Ali Haggin's magnificent posings were their usual hit, but it was acknowledged that the show still needed fixing.

But the *Follies* was the *Follies,* still a national repository of beauty, comedy, and exquisite presentation that had not yet begun to look old-fashioned. The 1920 *Follies,* like its predecessors, ran into the fall.

In September, Nick was cited for contempt for refusing to answer questions in the bankruptcy case. He was taken to the Ludlow Street jail, and Fallon obtained a writ of habeas corpus to test the commitment—a writ that every judge in New York Federal Court refused to sign. Fallon fought—right up to the United States Supreme Court, which reversed federal judge Manton's refusal on November 8. Fallon had won an important legal victory—one that modern defense lawyers take for granted. "Taking the Fifth" was not legally permissible, in the sense now understood, until Bill Fallon made it so for Fanny Brice's husband.

Fanny, now in Boston with the *Follies,* was in constant touch by phone with Nick, but saw nothing of him for the next six months. Arnstein and Fallon stayed at the Willard Hotel in Washington, entertaining people— mostly women—with rare wines made rarer still by Prohibition. The parties went on late; some women stayed much later.

Fan, whose money paid for all these parties, had her own contacts in Washington and soon learned what was going on. Hopelessly in love with Nick, she readily attributed his actions to the strain that he was under and her own absence from Washington. She was, at this point, willing to forgive.

Nick's trial resulted in a hung jury on December 24, a few days after the *Follies* opened its annual engagement in Chicago. A new trial was set for late April.

Arnstein might well have won acquittal—for all his obvious guilt—had he not made the mistake of alienating his attorney. Bill Fallon had become infatuated with musical comedy performer Gertrude Vanderbilt, then appearing in vaudeville in Washington. Nick, who did not approve of Gertrude or his lawyer paying attention to anything except his case, gave Fallon a gorgeous ring, which he, in turn, gave to Miss Vanderbilt. Gertrude then lost it in a taxi, making matters worse.

Nick then overstepped his bounds, insulting both Fallon and Gertrude. Fallon withdrew from the case, leaving McGee, his junior partner, to defend Arnstein.

Fanny had another problem in Chicago. Pregnant since July, she'd had a girdle made allowing her to play the show's demanding scenes with her condition undetected. On Sunday night, February 13, her unborn child having moved, Fanny found herself unable to put on the girdle. ("*You* put it on, she told Ed Rosenbaum, the insistent company manager.) The understudy went on, and Fanny had to withdraw from the show. *Variety,* which was usually more accurate, said "she left the show prematurely after a bitter dispute with the management over a point of backstage discipline." Ziegfeld, at the time, was riding roughshod over performers, with Actor's Equity insisting he rehire a chorine previously fired.

Ziegfeld, in fact, sent Fanny a telegram, as follows: YOU SHOULD HAVE MORE RESPECT FOR YOUR CONTRACT THAN TO ALLOW YOURSELF TO GET IN A POSITION WHERE YOU ARE FORCED TO QUIT ANY TIME YOU SEE FIT

The wire may have been a joke; Fanny was never sure. Ziegfeld had a rather cryptic sense of humor, but Fanny heard that he had forced an abortion on Anna Held in order to produce *Miss Innocence* on schedule.

Fanny's second child, William Jules Arnstein, was born in New York's Stern Sanitarium on April 23, 1921. Unlike Frances, William was a handsome baby, and Fanny had him photographed five hours after birth. She named him William after Fallon, hoping the famed lawyer would make peace with Nick. It never happened.

The second trial of Nick Arnstein and company had already started. In Washington, on May 4, Arnstein, Bowles, Easterday, Cohn, and Sullivan were found guilty. McGee immediately filed a motion for a new trial—the beginning of a three-year fight to keep Nick out of jail.

Later that month, Fanny joined rehearsals for the *Ziegfeld Follies* of 1921. This show would mark her greatest triumph, as well as one of Ziegfeld's.

During the rehearsals, Ziegfeld gave Fanny "My Man," an English-language version of a French song called "Mon Homme," which Mistinguette had introduced in Paris.

Writer Channing Pollock had originally prepared his English lyric as a literal translation of the French. This was the first version sung by Fanny at rehearsals. When it proved unsatisfactory, Pollock prepared an entirely new lyric and presented it to Ziegfeld.

The scene in which Fanny was to sing the song was programmed "By the River Seine." In rehearsal, Fanny made her entrance in a red wig, wearing a black velvet dress, sparkling earrings, and ballroom shoes. Ziegfeld said she looked like a female impersonator.

It was, of course, a vain attempt on Fanny's part to distance herself from a song that touched her life so closely. Flo Ziegfeld would have none of it. Insisting that she muss her hair, he sent Ben Ali Haggan onstage with a pair of scissors. Haggan cut the skirt in half, tore it on the side, ripped up her stockings, and smeared her costume with ashes.

Only then was Ziegfeld satisfied. "Now," he told her, "sing it."

But the musical arrangement was inappropriate to both the song and Fanny's rendition, and "My Man" was not successful when the *Follies* opened in Atlantic City on Tuesday night, June 14, 1921. Another orchestration was prepared by the immortal Victor Herbert.

Fanny never sang "My Man" without her eyes closed, feeling her left arm with her right and thinking of Nick. Her rendition made the song the greatest ballad ever in the *Follies,* but it would be inaccurate to say it stopped the show when the 1921 *Follies* opened at the Globe Theatre on Broadway. Reviews lauded the fifteenth edition of the *Follies* as the great show that it was, and the *Times* called it the best *Follies* of them all. Yet little notice was paid to "My Man." Possibly the critics, very much aware of Arnstein's situation, were striving to avoid comments the increasingly sophisticated 'twenties might have seen as obvious or mawkish. Nick himself objected to the song, especially the line, "He isn't true, he beats me too, what can I do?" Nick, of course, did not beat Fanny. Neither was he "true."

The critics who praised Fanny wrote primarily about her comedy. The *New York Evening Journal* said the 1921 *Follies* "had an unstarred star—no candidate for the Ziegfeld beauty prize, but an archly humorous woman with a gorgeous sense of burlesque. I refer to Miss Fannie Brice. Fannie handed me the laugh of the season with her burlesque of Ethel Barrymore as Camille. She was so much funnier than Ethel that nobody can doubt her burlesque abilities. There she lay on her tuberculosis bed-stead, with Raymond Hitchcock as Armand.

" 'I've been a bad woman,' sighed K'meel—'but such good company.' In her delirium she failed to recognize Hitchi as Armand. 'The face is familiar,' she said, 'but I can't place the body.' " The scene also featured W. C. Fields in a devastating take-off on his friend John Barrymore.

Fanny was also in two other sketches—"The Championship of the World," in which she played French boxer Georges Carpentier to Rae Dooley's amazingly accurate imitation of heavyweight title holder Jack Dempsey; and "Off to the Country," another one of Fields' creations, in which the Flivertons (W. C. and Fanny) take their family to the country via subway. She also did three songs besides "My Man"—Blanche Mer-rill's "I'm a Hieland Lassie" and two numbers by James F. Hanley, "Allay Up," near the end of the show, and "Second Hand Rose," the rather semicomic, almost bittersweet lament of a second hand dealer's daughter who has "never had a thing that ain't been used." The "Hieland Lassie" song, another in the vein of "I'm an Indian," had Fanny as a Jewish girl named Cohen who married "Jock MacPherson one brow brick moon-lick nick" and included snippets of traditional Scottish songs made fa-mous in America by Harry Lauder.

No performer ever was starred in the *Follies*. Fanny, though, com-pletely dominated that year's show, demonstrating a potency and range of talent that made her the season's Toast of Broadway. Jack Lait of *Variety* said Fanny "easily qualified as principal comic, despite the distin-guished competition. . . . It is by far the most conspicuous work this funster has ever offered."

On June 24, three days after the show opened, Eugene McGee's motion for a new trial was denied. Nick was sentenced to two years in prison and a ten-thousand-dollar fine. McGee now used one legal maneuver and appeal after another to keep Arnstein out of jail.

New evidence against Nick was still coming in, evidence that made it more and more inevitable that he would spend at least some time in prison. In August, Nick's connection with a band of Chicago mail rob-bers was established and, in December, after the *Follies* had gone out on tour, W. W. Easterday revealed still more details of the stock robberies. Each week that passed just made things that much more hopeless.

Having kids made Fanny much more avaricious. The mother of a baby and a two-year-old daughter, she was not anxious to go on the road with the 1921 *Follies,* and argued, as she always did, with Ziegfeld over money.

Ziegfeld wanted his shows on the road to be just as good as on Broadway, and was irked by Fanny's demands for a big raise if she simply honored her contract by going on tour. ("She's been with crooks so long that she's becoming one," he said.) But Fanny, as the unbilled star, was far too vital to the show. She got her raise, without making apologies to Ziegfeld.

Fanny, with her mother's healthy respect for the dollar, wanted to save money for her old age and her children. Conscious of the unrecorded nature of her stage art, and the fickle nature of show business, she saw money as a means of eternal celebrity as well as a bulwark against poverty. Her children, and their children, and their children's children, would, she now envisioned, have her money as a mainstay, and revere her as the person who had made it.

Fanny said that people who had failed to save money had no pride. Money, she maintained, could give a feeling of well-being and self-worth long after youth and talent disappeared. Money's absence, on the other hand, could make one's whole life seem a waste, creating doubts about one's basic worth, ability, and talent.

"I've been rich and I've been poor," reported Fanny. "Rich is better."

Fanny had to leave the children with the nurse in New York when she went on the road with the *Follies*. The 1921–22 tour was a success from every viewpoint, and Fanny told Ziegfeld she wanted a book show for the following season. Ziegfeld wanted Fanny for the next edition of the *Follies*, but her current contract had expired, and he planned to star her in a play by Rida Johnson Young when Fanny threatened to spend the 1922–23 season in vaudeville.

The play would not be ready before the fall, so Fan had Jenny Wagner book her into vaudeville in a new act called "Around the World," written by Blanche Merrill and featuring her song hits from the *Follies* and the *Frolics*.

Fanny opened her vaudeville tour at Proctor's Theatre in Mount Vernon, New York on Thursday, May 11, 1922. The act was not in finished form until a few weeks later, but was finely polished by the time she opened at the Palace on June 12.

This was an exceptionally strong Palace bill, boasting the names and talents of Fanny; Lionel Atwill and Company; Kitty, Ted, and Rose Doner; and Harry Jolson; among others. Fanny was the headliner, her next-to-closing spot a strong reminder of her two-thousand-dollar weekly salary. "Miss Brice," wrote Sime, "whanged them for thirty-one minutes with songs and fun. Nearly all of the songs were comics. In the Indian number while lying upon the stage, almost prone, and saying with a Yiddish accent, 'I'm an Indian,' Miss Brice leaned her head down as though detecting a scent (it was a woodland drop in 'one') and said, 'I smell a ham.' The Yiddish may have squared it, but is that nice, Fanny?"

On Tuesday night, the audience demanded she do "Second Hand Rose" before she left the stage, and Fanny, for once in her career, complied. She definitely "played off" her audience—never sure, by her own account, exactly what she would do till she got onstage. She seldom added, though, to her set act. "Once she was through, she was through," said a contemporary. On this occasion, Fanny had the number in reserve; usually, it was a different story. Her tradesman's approach to stagework generally allowed her to go on, establish her rapport with the audience, do her act, and take her leave.

Fanny the performer had a trademark—as much hers as Cantor's rolling "banjo eyes" or Joe Penner's line, "You nasty man!" It was a "salute" to the audience in which she touched her forehead and then flung her arm out to the gallery, her eyes bright, wide, and full of fun, her wide mouth drawn into a sort of twisted grin. The critic Gilbert Seldes said that there was "magic in it, establishing her character at once." It also established a firm bond between Fanny and the audience, who felt they were beginning—or re-establishing—a personal relationship with her.

An article that carried Fanny's by-line says a lot about her feelings for an audience and the way she analyzed both her friends and herself.

There is no thrill more wonderful than that which comes with the feel of a friendly audience, and it is a thrill that comes more than once in a lifetime. It is subconscious but powerful, much like sensing the presence of a friend in the darkness. An audience reflects an actor's attitude as faithfully as a mirror. If he is relaxed and sure of himself his audience gives him its heart. But if he feels fear or works too hard for his effects it strains with him and there is thrown over the house the chill of discomfort.

An artist who goes out on a stage with the query in mind, "I wonder if they will accept me," is beaten before the start.

One must accept oneself. If one can see the picture of the character portrayed, then the audience will have to accept it.

Fanny's weapons on the stage were characterization and satire. "With the utmost economy of means," wrote Seldes, "she creates the original in the very process of destroying it, as in two numbers which are exquisite—her present opening song in vaudeville, with its reiterations of Victor Herbert's 'Kiss Me Again,' and her Spring Dance. The first is pressed far into burlesque, but before she gets there it has fatally destroyed the whole tedious business of polite and sentimental concert-room vocalism; and the second (Fanny in ballet, with her amazingly angular parody of five-position dancing) puts an end forever to that great obsession of ours, classical interpretative dancing."

Fanny's engagement at the Palace lasted four weeks—one of the longest headline engagements in that theatre's history. Her voice had improved since her last appearances in New York vaudeville almost seven years earlier, and Sime Silverman noticed "how a certain plaintiveness gave added force" to "Second Hand Rose." Fanny, in her early thirties, had now peaked as a performer, and her Palace dressing room became a social center. Blanche Merrill, a naturally frequent visitor, encountered guests like:

"Brother Phil with his argument, 'Niblo of the N.V.A.';

"Then there's Miss Moon, when she starts in she never wants to stop.

"And Lottie, who's in business with Fanny, always talking shop."

Fanny once suggested that Blanche go into vaudeville with an act of her own, but the young author had no desire to be a performer. Three years Fanny's junior, she continued to write quality special material for female performers until the Great Depression.

Fanny's brother Lew was on the bill during the final week of her engagement at the Palace, opening the second half of the program with Fanny following in her star turn. "For an encore bit," *Bell* reported in *Variety*, "Miss Brice got into Lew's dress suit and he donned one of her costumes for some likeable clowning. A song, evidently put together by Miss Merrill for the special bit, had Miss Brice kidding Lew about his booking at the Palace, the lyrics giving Fannie and Lew alternate laughs, through the "get-backs" interpolated in rhyme. She says she taught him to sing, and he replies he taught her to dance. It looks as if Fannie got the best of that argument, for the number had her dancing as nimbly as the best of hoofers."

Lew Brice had had his share of stops and starts since 1909, the year he joined the Cohan & Harris Minstrels, starring George "Honey Boy" Evans, and abandoned tap in favor of eccentric dancing at the advice of Jerry Cohan, George M.'s father. Fanny recommended him to Ziegfeld, and Lew replaced a dancing act called the Four Fords in the *Follies* of 1910. When his dancing spot was eliminated, Lew spent the balance of the season doing Bert Williams' material in a burlesque show called *The Queen of Bohemia*.

The season of 1911–12 saw him in Gus Edwards' "School Boys and Girls," an act that had worn out its welcome since Edwards' composition of the classic "School Days" in 1907. Sime Silverman said Lew was "simply wasting his talents" in the Edwards act, and Lew soon left to form a singing and dancing turn with Lillian Gonne, a fellow refugee from Edwards.

Lew Brice was a footloose, irresponsible individual in a profession never known for steadiness. His 1914 marriage to seventeen-year-old Tillie Zick was annulled by the bride's guardian after Lew was jailed for abduction. Lew then married Muriel Worth, with whom he formed an act called "Worth and Brice." They split up after a violent quarrel in 1916, whereupon Brice formed an act with Ellen Kearns, renamed her "Ellen Worth," and continued as "Worth and Brice" until his wife legally restrained him.

Lew enjoyed brief stints in a few Winter Garden shows, including *The Passing Show,* the Shuberts' annual revue at the Winter Garden, and *Maid in America* (1915), but never made a name for himself as a solo. Sime Silverman thought he was an over-confident hoofer who was lost without a partner. Joshua Lowe, who reviewed Brice in 1912, said that he could not speak lines.

Lew produced his own acts, an enterprise his love of gambling made all but impossible without his sister's aid. In 1917, he formed another act with the Barr Twins, two beautiful young women who were approached to replace the Dolly Sisters when that famous pair left *The Bridal Night.* Brice, by that time, had them under contract.

The team of Lew Brice and the Barr Twins ended when he went into the Army. When Lew got out, he formed another act ("Dances and Tunes of 1919") with Adelaide Mason and pianist Rube Beckwith. Lew, however, was soon back at his first love—the races.

Lew's compulsive gambling rivalled that of Chico Marx, whose brothers kept him reasonably solvent until their famous team dissolved. Lew had no one except Fanny, who helped him out with money, which he gambled away, and contacts he failed to use.

Though he was often broke, or in some trouble, nothing could discourage Fanny's brother. He idolized Nick Arnstein and at one point grew a mustache similar to Nick's. And if Lew lacked Nick's charming manners, he more than rivalled him in irresponsibility. A show biz goodtime Charlie, Lew would hustle for survival when the world of vaudeville crumbled.

Fanny followed up her Palace run with weeks in Philadelphia and Brooklyn before taking a rest. She wanted to spend as much time as possible with Nick, never quite sure when he would face jail.

It was now, however, that the cracks began to surface in their marriage. Fanny's nerves had suffered in the last two years, not just from Arnstein's troubles and the police persecution, but from her battles with Ziegfeld and the difficulty of finding a suitable vehicle for her first starring book show.

Most of Fanny's troubles, though, involved Nick Arnstein. She loved elegant dining, and few things infuriated her more than Nick's being late for dinner. One night, he was a half-hour late, and exhibited his usual insouciance in response to his wife's angry questions. Fanny recognized it as the same blasé indifference he had shown to Rosie when they lived in the Albany Apartments. The knowledge that he dealt with her in the same way made Fanny twice as angry.

She looked at him, serenely eating dinner, and grew livid. Suddenly, she pulled up the entire tablecloth, dumping food all over Arnstein, who had just come from his tailor and was wearing a new suit. Nick jumped up and ran into the bathroom.

Fanny went into the bedroom and, still seething, lay down on the chaise. Minutes later, Dell knocked on the door and asked her if she wanted the strawberry shortcake dessert.

"For Chrissakes, Dell," said Fanny in exasperated tones. This had been her first big fight with Nick; it would not be the last.

Fanny now began to react to the reports of Arnstein's sexual exploits in Washington. More and more, she saw his frequent absences as signs of his unfaithfulness, a cynical and selfish stab in the back. She felt laughed at and, above all, "used"—the one humiliation that her ego could not take.

The fights with Nick became more frequent, and more violent on Fanny's part as well. Once, she broke a glass and rammed the jagged edge into his face. Fanny was beginning to see Arnstein as he was—a con man, liar, cheat, and, she now felt, an adulterer.

Considering Fanny's almost mindless love for Nick, the way she had stood by him in his battles with the law, their two children, and the fact that they had been together for more than ten years, one may ask how he could be so callous and ungrateful. Without excusing Nick, some explanations might be offered.

A lot of water had gone over the dam since Nick and Fanny had met back in 1912. Arnstein had served a prison sentence, and had failed—through his own indifference—in at least three legitimate business ventures. Nick and Fanny had endured numerous separations, and Arnstein had undoubtedly availed himself of other women. Arnstein was not a man with much consideration for others, and was quite apathetic towards his children. Above all, however, Fanny herself had changed.

She was no longer the enthusiastic, sweet, and simple funny girl who made Nick laugh all through the night. Fanny's life with Nick had toughened her, while her position in the theatre made her increasingly shrewd. By the middle 'twenties, she was just as tough as Nick was—and demonstrably smarter. She had always been much more successful, and a man with Arnstein's ego did not want a wife like that.

Fanny, with two children and a career based in Manhattan, now wanted a townhouse. In truth, she also hoped a change of residence would somehow give a new start to her troubled marriage. Early in October, she secured a five-story townhouse at 306 West Seventy-sixth Street that had been owned by Gilbert Colgate. Fanny got the Dry Dock Savings Institution to advance a first mortgage of thirty thousand dollars and took a loan of fifteen thousand from the Fabian Bond and Mortgage Corporation.

Fanny's interest in interior decorating, first awakened by Nick's refurnishing of the Albany Apartments, grew as she prepared to buy the townhouse. More and more, she went to auctions, spoke to recognized authorities, and learned about color schemes, balance, and what made each right for different places.

Fanny's immediate plans for the townhouse were settled, not by her, but by Arnold Rothstein. The famous gangster gambler insisted Fanny buy her furnishings from him. He himself, what's more, would make all the selections.

Rothstein was most insistent.

Within a day, the furnishings arrived, together with a bill for fifty thousand dollars. Fanny called in an appraiser, who told her the stuff was worth from ten to thirteen thousand dollars.

Fanny paid Rothstein the fifty thousand dollars and said nothing. But she knew the difference between the payment and value of the furnishings was simply Rothstein's interest on Nick's $100,000 bail money.

Fanny managed the house wisely, taking the first three floors for her own use (including Nick, their two young children, servants, and revolving guests), and making the two top floors into four apartments that she rented out to friends: May Weston, Valeska Suratt, and others.

The dark-haired and exotic Suratt was one of that small group of female vaudeville headliners (Olga Petrova was another) who affected European chic both off the stage and on. Born in Terre Haute, Indiana, Suratt called everybody "dawling" years before the advent of Tallulah Bankhead. While in the townhouse, she suggested that May Weston cut the legs off her piano because they weren't "putting legs on pianos anymore," and put a hammock, suspended from the ceiling, into her own bedroom. Fanny thought Suratt was sweet . . . and crazy.

In the midst of fixing up the townhouse—which soon included very tasteful furnishings, a baby-grand piano, and a beautiful portrait of Fanny and

her children by Saportas, the noted portrait artist—Fanny opened another vaudeville tour with a two-week engagement at the Palace. Her act
was little different from her last one, but *Variety* was quick to note that
"a Belasco could visualize Miss Brice elaborating the character portrayed
in 'My Man' into a serious play that might give the American stage a
female [David] Warfield."

Fanny stayed in vaudeville for nine more months, playing the Keith
and Orpheum circuits and finishing her tour with three weeks at Chicago's Palace Music Hall in July 1923.

The notice in *Variety,* in addition to other critical plaudits she had
gotten from her introduction of "My Man" in the 1921 *Follies,* had made
Fanny conscious of her potential as an actress. The Rida Johnson Young
play had not panned out as expected, and Ziegfeld's failure to find a
starring role for her in musical comedy made that dramatic potential all
the more valuable. Her professional dilemma made Fanny increasingly
conscious of her physical appearance. She had started to look noticeably
older, and Nick's obvious unfaithfulness did not help her self-image.

The science of plastic surgery had made great advances during World
War I. While in Chicago, Fanny talked to an actor who had had his nose
"re-contoured" by Dr. Henry J. Shireson. Fanny subsequently spoke to
Dr. Shireson, and decided to have a similar operation—one that would
give her a "normal" nose.

Arnstein was totally against it, but Fanny went ahead. The nose job
was, in part, a breaking of her old bonds with Nick Arnstein. Fanny
always made substantial changes in her life when she felt things were just
not working. Sometimes it involved auctioning her furniture or buying
a new house. This time, it was getting a new nose.

Dr. Shireson was not licensed in New York, so the operation was
performed in Atlantic City on August 15. Fanny, her nose swathed in
bandages but only slightly changed, said she "would suggest, in the interest of those who must submit to operations, that the surgeons use
rubber tools. For myself, I'd rather a darn sight be cut than hear the
clink of. . . ."

The operation got Fanny more publicity than anything since Nick's
flight from the law. The most quoted pun came from Dorothy Parker:

"Fanny Brice cut off her nose to spite her race."

CHAPTER 9

The Divorce from "My Man"

Neither Ziegfeld nor any other producer could come up with a starring musical comedy for Fanny in the fall of 1923. Charlotte Greenwood's *Letty* shows aside, comediennes like Fanny were not readily saleable as stars of Broadway shows. Beautiful Marilyn Miller, not Fanny Brice, was the top female musical comedy star of the 1920s.

It was a frustrating time for Fanny, made more bearable, at times, by Nick and her two children. With no star vehicle in sight, she went into rehearsals for the *Ziegfeld Follies* of 1923 in September. This was the eighteenth annual edition of the *Follies*, now unblushingly programmed as "The National Institution" and subtitled "Glorifying the American Girl." Like its seventeen predecessors, it starred no one, but none doubted that its biggest name and principal attraction—outside of the gorgeous sets and half-nude showgirls—was Fanny Brice. There was equally little doubt about its being a particularly weak edition in the series—short on good new songs and sketch material. The show did justice to neither Ziegfeld nor Fanny.

Fanny had a solo spot (scene 6) in the first act and introduced a new Blanche Merrill number three scenes later. This one was titled "Russian Art," a commentary on the craze for Russian cultural influence in art that had swept through "chic" moneyed classes following the Red scare of the early 'twenties. Morris Gest's famed *Chauve Souris* was the song's particular target, with Fanny as a Russian-Jewish girl named Luba Rockamonanoffsky who bumped into the eccentric impresario on the "Bronx express" and soon found herself entertaining gullible aristocrats with "Russian" artistry:

"We went like this and we went like that
And the whole darn bunch were talking through their hat.

"Snappy Stories of History" had Fanny as Pocohontas and Queen Isabella. They were not as well received as "Amateur Night," a Gene Buck recreation of an amateur show at Miner's Eighth Avenue Theatre in the early 1900s, with Fanny as one of ten "amachewers."

Opening night ran until 2:03 in the morning, leaving *New York Times* critic John Corbin to observe that when

> the first-night audience streamed out of the theatre into an all-night restaurant, it was commonly agreed that three hours of excellent entertainment were contained in the five and a quarter hours that Mr. Ziegfeld had just revealed.
>
> In styling his premier a "public rehearsal," Mr. Ziegfeld admitted frankly that it was a tentative performance, designed to separate the good from the bad. As a matter of fact, the cutting should not be difficult. The good portions of Saturday night's production were so conspicuously good, and the bad portions so incredibly bad, that almost any number of the first audience could do Mr. Ziegfeld's cutting for him. By tonight, probably—certainly by tomorrow—the *Follies* of 1923 will be a grand revue.

Corbin's review, like most of those the show received, stands as testimony to the indulgence with which Broadway's critics treated musical revues and the impregnable position of Ziegfeld and the *Follies*. Not until Andrew Lloyd Webber would a Broadway personage so hypnotize his critics.

The show was pruned down to two hours and fifty-seven minutes by the Tuesday night performance, but Sid Silverman, Sime's son, found the tightened *Follies* still left "much to be desired." There was still "a deplorable lack of comedy" and the music was "null and void."

It would be Fanny's final show for Ziegfeld.

Fanny's West Seventy-sixth Street townhouse was a social rendezvous throughout the season. Johnny Wanamaker was a very frequent guest, and one of the most welcome. Fanny said Wanamaker "skated into life with some twenty million dollars. That much money does one of two things: either it makes you unbearable or it turns you into a grand human." Johnny remained one of Fanny's favorite people till his death in 1934.

One afternoon, Fanny and May Weston got back from an auction house, "the sort where you poke in dusty corners and handle dirty furniture. I had never felt so untidy and grimy in my life, and I looked it." The baby's nurse was in the house along with "Hobby," the English elevator boy, Fanny's other servants having taken the day off.

Fanny thus answered the door herself when Johnny Wanamaker stopped by with a young man he described as "a great little guy . . .

and you are the one person in America he has to meet." The young man was a blond and slender Englishman who seemed both bored and nervous.

Fanny mixed some highballs for her guests, and then went to the bedroom to remove the dirt she'd picked up in the auction house. It was then that the nurse told her that the young man was the Prince of Wales. Edward Albert had been recognized by Hobby, who had also seen five bodyguards downstairs.

Fanny gave no sign she recognized the prince when she led her guests to the living room. But when the prince admired the upholstered chair he was about to sit in—a chair Fanny had bought at the auction—she said, "Yes, take that chair. And when I come to sell it, I'll get twice as much because you sat in it."

Fan described the future king—and Duke of Windsor—as a "weary, bored young man who wanted to be amused. I never had a more enthusiastic audience." Edward saw the *Follies* from a box the following night, but no one knew, until years later, that he had been Fanny's guest that afternoon.

That 1923–24 season saw the New York debut of another great comedienne, the inimitable Beatrice Lillie.

The Toronto-born Lillie had been convulsing English audiences with her mannered absurdities for years before *Charlot's Revue* opened at the Times Square Theatre on January 9, 1924. Jack Buchanan and Gertrude Lawrence (who sang "Limehouse Blues," the show's big hit) also made their Broadway bows in this show, but it was Bea Lillie, clad as "Britannia" and leading a cadre into helpless chaos in the number "March with Me," whom New York raved about in *Charlot's Revue*. Many called her "England's Fanny Brice."

Fanny caught a special midnight performance of *Charlot's Revue* and saw Bea literally stop the show. The audience was made up mostly of her Broadway colleagues, and Lady Peel, as Bea was known in private life, was forced to make a speech. Fanny was impressed and, meeting Bea in her dressing room after the performance, invited her to tea the following day. Bea also got an invitation for a friend of hers, a journalist named Beatrice Wilson.

Any hoped-for female rivalry between the two greatest comediennes of their generation failed to materialize. Instead of comedy, the women talked about their children. Bea told Fanny of a letter she'd received from her son, Robert, then away at boarding school in England, and the two young women soon shared tears—the beginning of a lifelong friendship. Fanny was once asked who she thought was the greatest comedienne, "present company excepted." "Beatrice Lillie," was her quick response "—present company not excepted!" Bea thus received the ultimate professional compliment.

Fanny introduced her children at this tea: four-year-old Frances in a pink silk dress and looking, to Bea Wilson, "like her mother except for the eyes, which were the most fascinating shape, slanting into a wicked droop over the blue pupils"; and two-and-a-half-year-old Bill, doted on by Fanny. ("Bill, what's the mater with your pants? Why do they hang down below your knees like that? Let me see," said Fanny, like a Jewish mother in her stage routine.) Both children told her they'd learned "nothing" in school that day. ("Bright children, aren't they? Did you ever see such intelligence in two such young children?" asked Fanny.)

Nick made an appearance, and Fan introduced him with "just pride." Bea Wilson described Nick as "tall, handsome, dignified, and with as much magnetism as any man I had ever laid eyes on."

Fan herself still felt the power of Nick's magnetism, but the mystery and, to some extent, the romance, were long over. Their arguments continued in the Colgate mansion, usually occasioned by some "silly" thing like Arnstein's being late for dinner—with no explanation.

It was Fanny and not Nick who yelled, and Fanny who continued to get violent. Once, she picked up her dish, full of food, and sailed it straight at him like a discus. Nick moved his head slightly, and the plate grazed the side of his face as it flew out through the window. He ran up to his bathroom as Fan stared at the window, unbroken except for the slit made by the plate. She marvelled that the hole could be so narrow, and looked out to see a dog enjoying what had been her dinner. When Nick left the bathroom, Fan went in and saw a towel dotted with his blood.

Once she might have wept if Nick had merely cut his finger. Now she just thought it was funny.

The fight, like almost all their arguments, was over very quickly. Fan had spent her anger, and Nick didn't want to fight.

Nick's efforts to avoid a prison term came full-circle during the succeeding months. On February 5, 1924, the D.C. Court of Appeals confirmed the convictions of Jules W. (Nick) Arnstein, Isadore (Nick) Cohn, David W. Sullivan, Norman S. Bowles, and Wilen W. Easterday. Their lawyers immediately requested that the appeals court conduct a rehearing of the original trial.

Nor was the bond case Arnstein's only legal trouble. Two days later, warrants were issued in Youngstown, Ohio, charging Nick, Charles Drucker, and three other men with having obtained $48,300 under false pretenses in July 1922. Police were also investigating a similar operation there in the same year involving a man from Hoboken, New Jersey, who was said to have lost $80,000. Both schemes involved Nick's old standby: wiretapping.

That night, February 5, the Arnsteins drove down to the theater from the townhouse. Traffic was heavy, they were running late, and it was almost eight o'clock—the theatre's sacred "half hour" before curtain—when Fanny parked the car on Seventh Avenue between Fortieth and Forty-first. No sooner had she pulled in than a cop told her she could not park there. Fanny had been parking in that spot for weeks, and had been ordered not to only recently. On this occasion, Nick told her to run ahead to the theatre; he would handle matters.

Nick, who thought intimidation was the best way to handle "coppers," told the cop—Patrolman Fallon; no relation to Nick's former lawyer—he would be "pounding a beat on Staten Island" if he "didn't watch his step." A crowd soon gathered, and Nick continued using what the police officer later described as "loud and boisterous language."

The cop finally hauled Arnstein off to jail. Nick pled his case before Magistrate Francis McQuade in night court.

"Your Honor, this policeman treated me like a common thief and a vagabond. He pulled me out of the automobile by my coat lapel and later shoved me into a cell with a lot of rough fellows. He embarrassed me shamefully before a large crowd there, and dragged me a block through the street.

"Miss Brice had been permitted to park her car there until some strange policemen were assigned to the place about a month ago. This policeman seems to be sore on somebody in the vicinity and he took it out on me tonight." The magistrate dismissed the charge.

On February 19, the District Court of Appeals denied a rehearing in the stolen bond case, but agreed to stay its mandate for thirty days to allow counsel for the defendants to apply to the United States Supreme Court for a writ to transfer the whole proceedings for review. The petition to review, alleging technical defects in the indictment and proceedings in the lower courts, was filed twenty-nine days later.

The case officially came up before the high court on April 8, 1924, when Henry E. Davis and T. Morris Wampler, counsel for Nick and his co-defendants, asked the court to have the Court of Appeals send up the record for review.

They had their answer thirteen days later, when the court refused to review the case. Nick's last chance was now behind him. He had to go to prison.

Wilen W. Easterday was already in jail on a forgery conviction. David W. Sullivan, a former saloonkeeper, and Norman S. Bowles, a Washington lawyer, surrendered themselves to Justice William Hitz in D.C. Criminal Court No. 1 on schedule on May 5. Nick Arnstein and Nick Cohn stayed in New York, forfeiting their appearance bonds of ten thousand dollars each.

Bench warrants were issued, and three days later they surrendered in the D.C. Supreme Court. Arnstein walked in smiling and nattily dressed. He was prepared, he said, to go to prison, but had one request to make. Would Judge Hitz "cooperate" with him by having him sent to Atlanta's federal penitentiary instead of Leavenworth?

The judge said he had no discretion in the matter and advised Arnstein to make his request to the Department of Justice.

Nick nodded, smiled, thanked the judge, and said that he was ready.

The *Follies* closed in New York two nights later, and Fanny went to Washington to say good-bye to Nick the following Monday. Nick and Fanny had about twenty minutes together in the Washington jail before she left for Baltimore en route back to New York.

Before he was taken to Leavenworth, Nick told William B. Leahy, the Special United States District Attorney, who had prosecuted him and Cohn, that he was willing to aid the federal authorities in recovering a batch of the stolen non-negotiable securities. Cohn corroborated Arnstein's statement, and both convicts allegedly said that "a married man in New York had the securities," which had a face value of more than one million dollars. Arnstein and Cohn also said the man would hand over the securities and tell the whole story of the plot as soon as they confronted him in court.

Federal court judge Knox immediately issued an order calling for Arnstein and Cohn to testify before Seaman Miller, referee in the New York bankruptcy proceeding. The two convicts were taken from Leavenworth to New York, housed in the Tombs, and brought to Marshal Hecht's office in the Federal Building shortly after 5:00 P.M. on Wednesday, July 16, 1924. Nick still had indictments pending against him in General Sessions, and thought they would be quashed if he pretended to cooperate.

Nick acted as the spokesman for himself and Cohn. He seemed calm and cooperative when the session began, but when it became evident that

Fanny Brice in her late
teens.

Fanny, ca. 1915, when she
played the leading role in
Nobody Home.

Fanny at the peak of her great stage career, the early 1920s, at the time she introduced the song "My Man."

Fanny at the time of her divorce from Julius W. (Nick) Arnstein.

ABOVE: Fanny and the chorus in a costume number in the film *My Man.*
(Warner Bros. publicity still, from the collection of Chip Deffaa) BELOW: Fanny
and musicians in *My Man.*

ABOVE: Fanny in *Be Yourself!* (United Artists, 1930). ABOVE LEFT: Wedding photograph of Billy Rose and Fanny (1929). Miss Brice was eight years Billy's senior; the mustache was a try at looking older. BELOW LEFT: Fanny at the time she played a featured role in *Fioretta,* Earl Carroll's vehicle for Dorothy Knapp.

ABOVE: Fanny in the 1930s. ABOVE LEFT: Fanny, Harry Green, and Robert Armstrong in *Be Yourself!* BELOW LEFT: Fanny in *Sweet and Low,* the show that made her husband, Billy, a producer.

"I'm Soul-Saving Sadie from Avenue A, preachin' salvation, and makin' it pay." Fanny as an East Side Aimee Semple McPherson in the *Ziegfeld Follies of 1934*.

At Jenny Dolly's home in Chicago while touring in the *Follies* in the fall of '34. LEFT TO RIGHT: Jenny, Willie Howard, Sophie Tucker, Fanny, and Rosie Dolly. *(Courtesy of Klari Marby)*

Fanny and her good friend Ann Pennington, ca. 1935.

ABOVE: Fanny as "Baby Snooks," ca. 1937. ABOVE LEFT: Fanny in *The Great Ziegfeld* (M-G-M, 1936). BELOW LEFT: Miss Brice at her make-up table during the run of the *Ziegfeld Follies of 1936*.

Fanny as Olga, the maid, in *Everybody Sing* (M-G-M, 1938).

On *Good News* of 1938: Fanny, Hanley Stafford, Allan Jones, Mary Martin, and Dick Powell.

Fanny Brice as "Baby Snooks" with Hanley Stafford as "Daddy."

ABOVE: One of the numerous "gag" publicity shots taken of Miss Brice as "Baby Snooks." (*From the collection of Chip Deffaa*) ABOVE RIGHT: Fanny with Hume Cronyn in the "Sweepstakes Ticket" sequence in the film *Ziegfeld Follies* (M-G-M, 1946). BELOW RIGHT: The private Fanny of the 1940s.

Fanny as "Snooks" on her return to radio on N.B.C. in 1949.

he was merely sparring for more time, the lawyers became angry and more relentless in their questions.

For another half an hour, Nick acted unperturbed. Then he lost his temper and "almost shrieked his answers." He frequently shouted "That was bunk!" when pressed to reveal the name of the man he said had stolen securities. "There never was such a man, and we never said there was."

Saul S. Myers, special counsel for some of the surety companies that had sustained heavy losses through the conspiracy, told Nick it was his "last chance" as he and Cohn were being led out of the marshal's office. "If you don't tell us about that man and the location of those securities, you'll be taken [back] to Leavenworth right away."

"Do you want to put others in the place where I'm going?" replied Arnstein. He and Cohn were taken back to the Tombs, and back to Leavenworth the following morning.

Ziegfeld was ostensibly still searching for a book show to star Fanny, but too much time had passed, and other top producers made her offers. Fanny said "$2,500 a week" when Sam H. Harris asked her how much she wanted to appear in the fourth annual *Music Box Revue,* and was surprised when Harris countered with $2,000—more than Ziegfeld would have paid. It just confirmed what Fanny had long known: when they want you, they want you; and money is a secondary consideration. Increasingly, she tried to overprice herself—a strategy that very seldom failed. Fanny remained one of the highest-paid women in show business for the rest of her career.

Negotiations with Sam Harris, underway when Fanny opened at the Palace Theatre in Milwaukee on June 29, were finally concluded, via telegraph, on August 23, when she was in San Francisco. The outcome was entirely in Fanny's favor: a run-of-the-play contract at $2,500 a week, to go to $2,750 if the show was still in New York in October 1925.

Harris' weekly operating expenses would exceed $15,000—a huge sum for the mid-1920s. Star salaries were his biggest expense. Besides Fanny's $2,500, there was Bobby Clark and Paul McCullough at $2,000, and young Grace Moore at $1,000. Fanny, though, soon made another request.

In late September, while playing the Orpheum Theatre in Kansas City, Fanny went to see Arnstein in Leavenworth. The district attorney's office, angered at Nick's antics in the bankruptcy proceeding, had persuaded prison authorities to give Arnstein "the works" on his return to Leavenworth. Nick was shovelling coal when Fanny got there.

Fanny offered to perform, but the warden felt it was bad policy for a prisoner's wife to appear before the other inmates. Fanny, in the meantime, coached Chief Officer Lee's eighteen-year-old stepdaughter, Lucilla, who starred in the prison show.

Before the week was over, Fanny had promised Chief Officer Lee that Lucilla would be in the upcoming *Music Box Revue,* providing Nick was taken from the coal pile and made Lee's messenger—probably the best job in the prison. Mrs. Lee, moreover, would prepare Nick's meals.

All parties kept their word. Lucilla Lee was placed in the *Revue*—but only until Nick got out of prison.

The fourth *Music Box Revue,* like its predecessors, had lyrics and music by Irving Berlin, Fanny's comedy godfather, Harris' partner in the Music Box Theatre and, at thirty-six, a Tin Pan Alley legend. Berlin, who wrote two songs for Fanny in this show—"Don't Send Me Back to Petrograd," and "I Want to Be a Ballet Dancer," took on most of the producing chores when Harris became ill during rehearsals. That left him little energy for writing songs; *Variety* dubbed the show the "weakling" of the *Music Box Revue* series, and said the songs were among the weakest parts. John Murray Anderson's staging was lauded, but the absence of good comedy material was apparent to astute reviewers. Fanny played Eve to Bobby Clark's club-wielding Adam in the only memorable scene. Another sketch saw Fan as Madame Pompadour, but Grace Moore and Oscar Shaw received the best notices, and the show was another comedown after Fanny's great success in the *Follies* of 1921.

Her only other bright spot in the show was a new song by Blanche Merrill called "Poor Little Moving Picture Baby," in which she was a "little star what doesn't shine." The song was aimed at "Baby Peggy," a silent-screen Shirley Temple who always seemed to wear pink or blue dresses. Fanny thought she looked "like an ice cream soda."

Fanny was not sentimental and, her own two kids excepted, did not care that much for children. She found most child actors obnoxious, and swore her kids would not be like the brats she met backstage—"kids I could have killed—every one of them."

Not that Fanny was a martinet. As she told Ethel E. Sanders of *Opinion: A Journal of Jewish Life and Letters* in 1932:

> I want my children to like me, and I think they do. I want them to like me because I'm a nice person—not because I'm their mother. This business of bringing them up with the idea that they must love their mother is a big mistake. You can't force people to love you, for whatever reason, good or bad. And whereas love is a natural sequence of liking another, you cannot possibly love a person you don't like. When

my children grow up, they can go where they like, be what they like, do what they like. I won't interfere, and I won't make them slaves to my whims and preferences. But if they get into trouble, I'll be right there, and I'll never force them to hate me by saying, "I told you so."

Fanny wanted Fran and Bill unspoiled but well-mannered. To that end, she hired a French governess to teach and supervise them. The children and, indeed, all Fanny's friends and relatives, knew her by no other name than "Mademoiselle." Mae Clarke said the children spoke more French than English. "Fanny would spend time with them, but if Mademoiselle saw she was exhausted, she would tell the children, 'Shoo, shoo. Your mother is tired.' Mademoiselle was with them all the time."

Frances went to private school until she "objected to playing with a little girl because her dress was soiled. I didn't plan to raise my child to be a snob," said Fanny, "so I snatched her right out of that fancy school, and sent her to public school. Her cure was miraculous."

While the *Music Box Revue* was still running on Broadway, Jenny Wagner told Fan of a play about a fighter and his manager called *Is Zat So?* Written by James Gleason and Richard Taber, the play starred Gleason as the manager and Robert Armstrong as the fighter. Fanny liked what she saw and became one of seven investors before the middle of January. Before the end of March, however, she disposed of all her stock, losing out in what became one of the smash hit plays of the 'twenties.

The *Music Box Revue* ran a profitable 186 performances—largely because its producers owned the theatre. Fanny liked Sam H. Harris, and made a pact with him similar to that she'd made with Vera Maxwell in 1911— each agreeing to support the other in case of poverty. Harris died a millionaire in 1941.

Shortly before the show closed on May 9, the theatre world was startled to learn that Fanny Brice had signed a contract with David Belasco, the clerical-collared "Bishop of Broadway," famed for his great stagings of dramatic plays. The idea that a comedienne like Fanny could play "drama" was an odd one to theatre habitués of 1925, who considered musical comedy more in the league of vaudeville than serious theatre. No vehicle had been selected, but rehearsals were already set for the following spring.

Wanting to make up for her bad judgement about *Is Zat So?*, Fanny spent the summer of 1925 producing *The Brown Derby*, a new musical comedy starring Bert and Betty Wheeler.

Fan had met the Wheelers, a comedy song-and-dance team, in the

1923 *Follies*. Fanny's hard work on their behalf went for nothing, as the show closed during tryouts, and stardom eluded Bert Wheeler until he teamed with Robert Woolsey three years later.

Fanny, in the meantime, had her own career, opening a tour in the *Music Box Revue* at Werba's Brooklyn Theatre on September 28, 1925. The show was in Milwaukee on December 22, the day that Nick got out of jail.

"Now I believe in Santa Claus" was how Fanny described her feelings to the press. Rather than meet Nick at the train station, Fanny wired him the name of the hotel where she was staying with the children. Six-year-old Frances and four-year-old Bill were waiting there with her when Nick arrived. There were gifts under the Christmas tree, and after Mademoiselle put the children to bed, Fanny and Nick were together again, with a bottle of champagne, for the first time in over nineteen months.

One of Frances' most vivid memories is of an actor making a snowman for her and Bill that Christmas, and then fainting from exhaustion. Fanny's happiness was almost as short-lived. The day after Christmas, Nick was up to his old games. "Big Tim" Murphy, a gangster he had met in Leavenworth, was in Chicago, and the two men made a deal to open a gambling casino in the exclusive North Side of the city under the cover of legitimate business. Fanny begged Nick not to do it. He could become her agent, she said, and have big names beating on his door in no time. Nick, however, would have none of it. He was "Nick Arnstein," and did not want to seem like he was living off his wife.

Some women marry men like Nick because they find the "con man" type romantic, believing, with some vanity, that they can reform him. Fanny was like that. "I always felt I could change Nick," she later admitted. But Nick's self-image was too strong for that.

Fanny soon agreed to loan Nick money to open up the gambling casino with Tim Murphy. She knew he would have gotten it from Rothstein—or some other, equally threatening source—had she refused.

Nick now agreed to return East with Fran, Bill, and Mademoiselle. The children were due back in school, and Nick, for his part, wanted to see "businessmen" in New York—men like Frank Costello and Lucky Luciano, rising gangsters and good friends of Arnold Rothstein.

Fanny continued on tour with the *Music Box Revue*. In Kansas City, she met Tish Lee, a sixteen-year-old girl who had arrived from Texas with a letter of introduction from her father, a prominent architect. Through her father, Tish had met Fanny's brother, Lew.

"I remember Fanny's first words to me," Tish recalled in 1989. "She said, 'Does your mother know where you are?'

"I loved theatre people, but I idolized Fanny Brice. Going to Kansas City to see her in the *Music Box Revue* was the birthday present I had begged my father for.

"I stayed close to Fanny while the show was in that city, and someone with the show told Fan that it would be great publicity for her to kind of take me on as a sort of protegé.

"Fanny told them that she didn't think it was a good idea. She said she wasn't sure what some of Nick's friends might try if certain things happened. She was afraid that they might kidnap me or something.

"I wouldn't say Fanny was an especially open or warm person, but she could let her hair down rather easily with people on all levels. With me, she was a star, an older person (she was thirty-four; I was sixteen), manicured, well mannered, but a little distant, almost like a parent. She didn't wear emotions on her sleeve.

"I saw Fanny in New York a few times later, but we were never really that close. She was a great performer, and shrewd, smart by the time I first met her in Kansas City. She had obviously got a little hardened."

Fanny had indeed been hardened. The final stage occurred when Arnstein was in Leavenworth and she got a further feeling of independence, a feeling she no longer needed Nick—or anybody except Fanny. She still loved Nick, however, and looked forward to his settling down and becoming a good, solid, faithful husband who cared about her and the kids.

On a deeper level, though, she knew it would not happen.

Fanny rejoined Nick in New York when the *Music Box* tour ended, and went into rehearsals for *Fanny*, the play David Belasco had obtained for her first starring role on Broadway.

David Belasco was then sixty-six years old, the deified, if increasingly passé "Bishop of Broadway," who had woven a career as, successively, actor, playwright, and director and producer, beginning in San Francisco in 1871. He had opened the first Belasco Theatre in New York in 1902, built the Stuyvesant Theatre (later the Belasco) in 1907, and written plays like *Men and Women, Darling of the Gods, The Girl of the Golden West, The Auctioneer,* and *Zaza.* He had directed E. H. Sothern, David Warfield, and Leo Ditrichstein, among others, and made a star of Lenore Ulrich. The ultimate father figure, he would greet his actors with the phrase "Hello, children" upon entering the theatre. "His theatre was like a shrine" remembered John J. Cameron. "Then again, there had sometimes been a crap game there last night."

There was considerable hypocrisy in Belasco's puritanical stance and clerical garb. Belasco had his female stars show their appreciation in two ways: to pull him onstage when they took their bows and to enter a small bedroom in his office. Jeanne Eagels refused to pull him onstage when she took her bows; Laurette Taylor refused to enter the bedroom.

The great Belasco, though, had no designs like that on Fanny. His interests in her were artistic, commercial, and somewhat born of vanity as well. Belasco had made a dramatic star out of Ina Claire, theretofore a mimic and musical comedy star; and young Jeanne Eagels was called the "fourth jewel in the diadem" of Belasco's brilliant leading ladies when she scored a hit in the Bishop's production of *Daddies*. Frances Starr, Lenore Ulrich (his chief leading lady of the 'twenties), and Ina Claire were the other three, and Belasco, prodded by reviews that linked his name with Fanny's after she first sang "My Man," saw Miss Brice as the fifth jewel in the crown.

There were two big problems in the project. The first one was the play. *Fanny,* by Willard Mack (and Belasco, who listed himself as co-author after doctoring the play), was a "melodramatic comedy" in three acts that had Brice as "Fanny Fiebaum," a Jewish girl who serves the wealthy, philanthropic "Leah Mendoza" (Jane Ellison) as companion and friend. When they go to Arizona for Mendoza's health, the clever Fanny foils a robbery by a notorious Western gang. The chief robber later finds $60,000 Leah's brother had hidden on his ranch before dying, but Fanny Yiddisher-vamps him out of his money belt and recovers the money. It was claptrap, but Belasco claptrap, and therefore confused with Art.

The other problem was Fanny, who had failed to learn anything about acting during her brief and dubious apprenticeship to Rachel Lewis in 1907. Belasco himself could not believe Fanny's ineptitude. She had rather naïve and distorted notions about acting, and "declaimed" her lines, listening to herself in the manner of an untrained singer hearing his voice hum against his ear. It took coaching from John Cromwell (later a top-flight director), who played Gradyear, the villain, before she could make any progress.

Belasco had no intention of opening *Fanny* on Broadway until the fall, but he had to know what rewrites were in order. After four weeks of rehearsals, the play opened in Atlantic City on May 31, 1926, to horrible reviews. Extensive work was done in the next few weeks, but no amount of rewriting could help *Fanny.*

Fanny, in the meantime, started to rehearse a new vaudeville act written for her by Ballard MacDonald, a sketch writer and lyricist as well known in the business for his drinking as for his songs. Much of the rehearsing was done in Huntington, leaving Fanny time to spend with Nick, the kids, and friends.

The Arnsteins entertained and lived the good life apart from Nick's professed need for long "drives." He never took Fanny or the children.

One Sunday, they had more than ten guests due, and Fanny suggested hiring a boat to take them fishing after lunch. Nick immediately insisted on going to the dock himself to rent the boat.

The dock was only about a hundred yards away, but Nick did not return that day. Fanny entertained the guests herself and sent them to the station in their other car. Then she waited, sleeplessly, for Arnstein to return. He finally came in at 2:00 A.M.

Nick said very little, but enough to convince Fanny that there was another woman. His blasé manner made it even worse.

Fanny had been angered by Nick's cheating; this admission hurt much more. She hired a detective agency to keep Nick under surveilance, took the children with her, and left to play vaudeville dates in California. Brice opened at the Orpheum in San Francisco on Saturday, July 3, 1926, billed as "David Belasco's New Star . . . The Infinite in Comedy and Song."

MacDonald had done his job well. The act was not all new, as Fanny did Blanche Merrill's "Spring" and sang "My Man" and "I'm an Indian" for encores. But it was elaborate and clever—performed by a great artist at her pinnacle.

She opened with a number telling how much trouble it was to prepare a new act, and followed with "the Last of the Sextette of Lucia," the "Spring" song, and a burlesque on the visit of the Queen of Sheba to King Solomon with veteran vaudevillian Sam Sidman as Solomon and Roger Davis as their son. A serious number, "A Crime as Old as the World," in which Fanny pleaded the cause of a fallen woman before a jury, finished the act. George C. Warren of the *San Francisco Chronicle* called it "an affecting thing and brilliantly played, all the more remarkable because of the broad fun of the Queen of Sheba number just preceding it." It was, in short, an act well worthy of Miss Brice's talents, spotlighting her abilities as singer, comedienne, and, to some extent, dramatic actress.

In contrast to some stars, who hid their children to maintain a public image of eternal youth and beauty, Fanny was unashamedly proud of Fran and Bill. A framed portrait of the kids was on her dressing room wall, and interviewers who called them "beautiful children" were seconded by the comedienne.

"And so smart!" she'd add. Fanny told a reporter for the *Chronicle* about a new car she had bought and taken Frances for a ride in. " 'Mother,' she asked, 'How much did it cost?' Fourteen thousand five hundred and ninety-five dollars,' I told her. 'Yes,' she said, 'that was the price, but what did you pay for it?' Smart, eh?"

Frances also knew that her mother, who lived well despite her concern for the dollar, had a charge account "in every good store in the country." When the children were in school, and Fanny could not take them with her, she sent gifts from cities like Detroit, Cleveland, and Chicago. These are, of course, the run-down, problem-ridden, decayed cities of the present. At the time, however, they were vibrant centers of the nation's culture, important stops on the chief vaudeville circuits and the proud possessors of the nation's major sports teams long before the term "expansion" had significance in baseball. And while Fan made sure that Fran and Bill had "normal" educations, they were privileged in seeing, not just cities, but show business at its zenith.

Fanny played a total of three weeks in San Francisco. She added new material the second week and the "Amateur Night Twenty Years Ago" sketch from the 1923 *Follies* was put in for the final week of the engagement. A similar booking at the Orpheum in Los Angeles followed. The money was excellent, and Fanny knew when she had a good act. But she missed her children, and it was almost time to start the new rehearsals with Belasco.

Fanny was returning to her husband with mixed feelings. She had already received a report from the detective agency hired to keep tabs on Nick: his "drives" were to a rendezvous with a woman on the Manhattan side of the Queensboro Bridge. They would then drive, in her car, to someplace on Long Island, stay there for two hours, go for a ride in the country, and return to the Manhattan side of the bridge.

Fanny took no action, hoping against hope that the affair would run its course. But she knew there would be others.

The atmosphere in Huntington was far from happy, but Fanny tried to shield the kids from her troubles with Nick. Rehearsals for the revised *Fanny* started on August 10, and Fanny tried to lose herself under Belasco's demanding direction. It was not easy, since she was still untrained as an actress. Nick, moreover, sniffed at the Belasco project.

After tryout dates in Washington and Baltimore, *Fanny* opened at the Lyceum in New York on Monday night, September 21, 1926. Fanny kissed Belasco at the end of the second act, and the *Evening Post*'s John Anderson said he hoped "it was on his producing cheek. . . . His tongue probably was in the other one."

The rest of the reviews were of a similar tone. Gilbert W. Gabriel of the *New York Sun* called it "a stagnant, highly stupid, sometimes malodorous piece of playmaking. When a wheezy old cowboy gets down on his hands and knees the better to watch a girl climb into a flivver, somebody ought to shake the drama's fountain pen dry." Alexander Woollcott, writing for the *World*, said it was "a rubbishy play which, upon inspection, turned out to be just a rather inferior musical comedy libretto without any songs except one lullaby which Miss Brice croons at the end of the first act. . . . It was written by Willard Mack and Mr. Belasco and they both ought to be ashamed of themselves and of each other." The consensus was that *Fanny* was a shallow attempt to transfer Fanny's mugging, bowlegged comedy to the legitimate arena, and that the only hope lay in making the third act into a comedy sketch with Bobby Clark and Willie Collier in the parts played by Warren William and John Cromwell.

"Fanny's Worst Play," as one wit called it, ran for eight weeks at the Lyceum.

Fanny toured the "subway circuit" when its Broadway run was over. This comprised theatres in the Bronx, upper Manhattan and Brooklyn, where Belasco's people hoped to find Jewish audiences for Fanny Fiebaum and Leah Mendoza. The play breathed its last on January 8, 1927, following a two-week stay at the Broad Street Theatre in Philadelphia.

Fanny spent the next two weeks at home with Nick in Huntington. He still disappeared for "drives," however, and on one occasion he stayed out all night. In the morning, Fanny went into New York to see her agent, Jenny Wagner. When she returned to Huntington at dinner time, Nick called to say he was in Manhattan and would be spending that night in their townhouse on West Seventy-sixth Street. Fanny had the chauffeur drive her back into the city.

Nick was alone, but this time Fanny would not let things rest. They slept in separate bedrooms when Nick refused to say where he had been the previous night.

Fanny called "the other woman" in the morning and invited her out to the house in Huntington. The purpose? "I'd like to ask you to please keep your hands off my husband." The woman hung up the receiver.

All pretense was abandoned. Fanny put her foot down, and Nick, who wanted to avoid all conflict, said that he was going to Chicago to help Murphy run their gambling casino. The news pleased Fanny, since it meant a lull in the affair. It also meant Nick would be away from home, which, at this point, seemed almost a blessing.

Fanny never mentioned who the "other woman" was, and the memories of those close to her fail to recall the name. The most that Fanny did was to describe her for the *New York Daily News:* "She's about twelve years older than I am and a good deal fatter. . . . That woman knew that all I had was Nick. She knew all I had gone through."

There is no reason to suspect Fan made up her description; no sane woman would say her husband left her for an "older, fatter" woman unless it was true. But why would Nick, a handsome, charming man who might have had his pick of beauties, leave his wife, a famous stage performer, for a woman presumably less attractive?

Fanny sometimes blamed her nose job for the trouble; Nick once blamed the song "My Man." Fanny even blamed herself for having women friends around too much, as if she should have concentrated only on Nick Arnstein.

None of this, however, had much bearing on the matter. The truth was that their marriage was a victim of Nick's male ego. The whole world knew that Fanny had stood up for and protected him, and that they lived off of her money. Readers of the nation's most prestigious daily papers knew that Nick, in fact, had bought her almost nothing.

Arnstein, people knew, was just an unsuccessful con man—a loser who had failed at everything from running a shirt hospital to manufacturing fire extinguishers.

Nick no longer felt like the dashing, handsome man Fanny had pursued in 1912. A man of pride if nothing else, he felt the need to prove himself; and independence was the way to do it. There were other, wealthy women who would want Nick Arnstein—women without Fanny's talent, brains, or fame. And the uglier the woman, the more she would appreciate a handsome, suave, and urbane man like him. Such, in part, had been the case with Fanny years before.

Others might have called Arnstein a gigolo. Nick just thought he was being a man.

Performers of that era seldom remained idle long, and Fanny, with her children, high lifestyle, and quest for personal security, had to keep the money flowing. In January, then, she signed to star in Louis O. Macloon's *Hollywood Music Box Revue,* supported by Roger Davis, Ted Doner, Don Barclay, and close to a hundred other actors, singers, dancers, and showgirls.

The *Revue,* which opened February 2, suffered from both lack of preparation and an absence of new material. Embarrassing stage waits abounded, and Fanny's burlesque of *Camille,* so uproarious on Broadway with W. C. Fields and Raymond Hitchcock, fell flat in Macloon's show.

Fanny sang two songs in this show, hurriedly written for her by Blanche Merrill: "Make 'Em Laugh," which she performed in the first act, and "I'm a Little Butterfly," her latest dance lampoon. The *Hollywood Music Box Revue* closed after nine weeks, a near-financial-bust. Fanny, however, had been seen by Hollywood producers, and the Film Booking Office offered her $1,500 a week to play opposite George Sidney in *Clancy's Kosher Wedding,* a cheap imitation of Anne Nichols' famous stage hit, *Abie's Irish Rose.* Fanny turned it down since it was not a starring role, but listened when United Artists offered her the lead in a film based on an original story by former Chicago newspaperman Wallace Smith.

United Artists failed to reach terms with Fanny's agents, Ahser, Small

& Rogers. Finally, in May, she signed a contract to appear in three films about the life of a young East Side woman for First National. Fanny then departed for New York, stopping in Chicago to see Nick along the way.

He met Fanny at the station and took her back to his hotel. Nick was his charming, smiling self, and everything seemed fine until Fanny answered a long-distance phone call from New York. She heard a woman ask for "Jules."

When Arnstein had no explanation, Fanny left and went on to New York. Shortly after midnight on June 3, she sailed for France on the *Majestic* with her friend, film actress Norma Talmadge. Fanny had arranged to have the children sail there on June 24, immediately after the school year.

In France, that haven of divorce in the sophisticated 1920s, Fanny made up her mind to divorce Nick. She even tried for a Parisian divorce, but learned it was not possible without Nick's presence. Then, when she returned to the United States in August, she found Arnstein in trouble once again.

On Wednesday, August 17, Chicago police raided Nick and Big Tim's gambling casino. Nineteen people were ordered to leave the lavishly furnished resort, and four roulette wheels and other gambling devices were confiscated. Murphy, as it turned out, did not have Al Capone's protection.

Nick was angry, in no mood to hear Fanny's lawyer tell him he had "better give" her a divorce. Women, he cynically observed on numerous occasions, were "a dime a dozen," and giving in to one was not "Nick Arnstein."

But Arnstein was still facing wiretapping charges in Ohio, and a judge in New York ruled that the addition of certain new evidence meant he could be tried for the 1920 bond thefts in a New York court without being put in double jeopardy. All in all, it behooved Nick to give Fanny her freedom.

And he did so, even after Fanny told him he would never see the children.

On September 20, 1927, Nick checked into the Berkshire Hotel in Chicago with someone identified only as "a certain lewd woman"—really a paid corespondent—the then-accepted way to give a wife grounds for divorce without involving the real "other woman." Divorce was granted several days later.

Fanny and Nick were finished. Their relationship had lasted almost fifteen years.

Nick called Fanny after the divorce and asked to see her. Fanny knew enough about divorce law not to see Arnstein alone, but agreed to meet him at the house of Dr. Sheridan, a family friend. When she walked in, Nick was sitting on the couch.

"Well, you wanted a divorce," he began, "didn't you? I gave it to you, didn't I? I gave it to you so fast it made your head swim." He looked at her intently. "If you ever loved me, you never would have divorced me."

Fanny looked him back. "If you ever loved me," she said, "you never would have given it to me."

The unexpected words stung Nick, who went to pieces. The warning he "would never see the kids" had been, not a taunt, but Fanny's way of testing Nick, to see if he loved Fran and Bill enough to fight for them. Arnstein, though, had never understood.

Gone at once was his demeanor, the firm elegance and studied poise. He wept, became hysterical, and said that he would prove himself to Fanny. Nick went on and on for several minutes until Sheridan gave him a shot to calm him down.

Fanny was relieved that Nick still loved her, but she had to get away, and she declined Arnstein's offer to escort her to the depot. She took a train to New York, making a gabardine skirt en route, and was met by a platoon of reporters upon her arrival in Grand Central Station.

Fanny talked of suing the unnamed but wealthy "other woman" for $250,000 for alienation of affections. "And I'll give every nickel I win to the Jewish Actors' Guild—or something like that."

"Will you get married again, Fanny?"

"Now isn't that a stupid question to ask me. How do I know?"

She thought—or hoped—that Nick would call her and propose that they remarry. But two weeks passed, and she heard he was in California. It was only then she realized her life with him was over.

She wept, almost nightly, for the next five years.

CHAPTER *10*

The Short-Stemmed Rose

Fanny felt the need for an entirely new start. The West Side townhouse had reminders of Nick everywhere, and Fanny now decided to move out.

First, she told May Weston and Valeska Suratt that she planned to sell the building. Next, she auctioned everything she owned—including some of Nick's old suits—sparing only personal mementos. Every stick of furniture went under the auctioneer's hammer in the next few weeks. She was like a refugee fleeing the holocaust with nothing but the clothes on her back. The difference was that Fanny was a Broadway "name" with talent, fame, and money.

The auction, though, was not the only thing that kept her active. She felt the need to work—as much for her sanity as for the money. The new season was already under way when she contacted Ballard MacDonald.

Fanny wanted him to streamline the act he'd written for her several months earlier. It needed a smarter opening, more elaborate settings, and a finished bridge between the numbers. In the meantime, Fanny had Jenny Wagner contact the Keith Vaudeville Exchange and book her for an Eastern tour that included the Palace.

MacDonald readily agreed to do the job, but his talents were also wanted by a young songwriter working on the lyrics for a new Broadway show called *Harry Delmar's Revels*. The young song lyricist in question never worked alone—leaving many with sharp questions about his talents.

When MacDonald tried to beg off, citing his agreement with Fanny, the writer suggested they collaborate on both the Brice act and the show. MacDonald, who needed a co-worker for entirely different reasons—as well as extra money to pay off his massive bar tabs—soon arranged to have the writer come to the Brice home.

The songwriter in question was an undersized young genius known as Billy Rose.

Time has not been kind to Rose. Several of his songs—"I Found a Million Dollar Baby," "That Old Gang of Mine," "Barney Google," "Me and My Shadow," "Paper Moon," and "There's a Rainbow 'Round My Shoulder" among them—have become pop standards, but few if any writers on the subject have considered him a giant of American songwriting. Nor has his great fame as a producer and showman echoed through the decades as has Ziegfeld's.

He was famous in his own day, although never held in awe as either writer or producer by those in the entertainment business. He was known as the "Bantam Barnum" and the "Napoleon of American Show Business"—a little (5' 3") man who wanted everything he did to be the biggest and (as almost a secondary consideration) the best. He might well be described as a somewhat less mean-spirited Sammy Glick with the location switched from Hollywood to Broadway. Rose did not generally ruin people's lives. It's also true that he used people—right and left—to make himself successful.

He was an intelligent man who spoke the language of the streets, a charming man on numerous occasions, but most of all a smart one. He was probably much nicer than he should have been, considering his size and tough fights for survival on the streets of Old New York.

Born William Samuel Rosenberg on September 4, 1899, he quickly learned to fight a little bit and run fast quite a lot against the tough, larger, anti-Semitic kids he found at school. Billy became a scholastic track star before long, and then learned shorthand. Before Rose left his teens, he won the national quick shorthand contest and became personal stenographer to Bernard Baruch, Wall Street's economic genius.

Rose had little artistic inclination, and showed no interest in songwriting until a trip across the country changed his life for good. On the boat home from New Orleans, a young woman named Sylvia piqued Rose's curiosity about the world of show biz. Arriving in New York, she took Billy to Wolpin's and introduced him to several songwriters he had never heard of.

"I wasn't at all impressed by those people," Rose recalled. "I saw they were unimportant, shoddy, second-rate compared to the men I had worked for." But Billy was impressed when he heard that these "second-raters" made as much as $75,000 a year, and he decided to make a close study of the songwriting field.

At twenty-one, Rose left Baruch's employ and lived on five dollars a week while he studied songwriting by poring over every copy of sheet music in the collection of the New York Public Library. He kept company with other young songwriters and contributed rough outlines they would polish into publishable ditties with titles like "If You'll Be My Lolly, I Will Be Your Pop," Rose's first known song—written in collaboration with Howard Johnson and Irving M. Bibo, and published by Leo Feist on March 27, 1921. That same year, he found another good collaborator in Benny Ryan, a fellow lyricist who planned to marry a young dancer named Gracie Allen. Rose and Ryan, in collaboration with composer Bibo, turned out "I Hold Her Hand and She Holds Mine" and "Ain't Nature Grand?" a minor hit that (Gus) Van and (Joe) Schenck sang in the *Ziegfeld Follies*. Billy saw that show, and knew he'd seen a great performer when he heard Fanny Brice sing "My Man." "She was thunder in the mountains," he said later. "I heard her sing 'My Man' a thousand times, but I never heard her sing it the way she sang it that night at the Globe."

Rose's many "collaborations" with other lyricists were a source of frequent comment along Tin Pan Alley. Many pros regarded him as a good "title man" and salesman who lived off the talents of legitimate lyricists. Few would give him credit for more than a small part of "That Old Gang of Mine," but Rose's status increased considerably with "Barney Google (With the Goo-Goo-Googley Eyes)," of which he was sole lyricist.

Speakeasies were a source of considerable profit in the 1920s, and the always-enterprising and pragmatic Rose put part of his ever-growing wealth into the Backstage Club, located over a garage on West Fifty-sixth Street and, a little later, the posher Fifth Avenue Club. It was at the Backstage Club, in 1925, that he met Fanny.

Rose remembered the Backstage Club as a "joint so small that—so the joke went—when a busboy leaned over, we threw a tablecloth over him and put four chairs around him. . . . One 2:00 A.M., La Brice swept in with a party of society toffs." Helen Morgan, still two years away from great success in *Show Boat,* sang a song of Billy's called "Tonight You Belong to Me" on that occasion.

Fanny thought the song was beautiful, especially the line, "In the middle of a moment, you and I forgot what 'no' meant." When told the song was written by the owner of the club, she asked if she could meet him.

Billy Rose was far from handsome, an almost dwarfish man with a big head and chalky face. Rose's personal grooming also left much to be desired. His fingernails were invariably dirty, he always seemed to need a haircut, and the jacket of his suit was littered with thick dandruff. Fanny said hello and quickly turned back to her drink.

" 'I'm sorry you're disappointed,' [Rose] said. 'I guess you thought I'd look like Valentino.'

"Fanny looked up and grinned. 'It's a lovely song,' she said. 'It's nice to meet the kid who wrote it.' "

That was Billy's only meeting with Miss Brice until Ballard MacDonald and he taxied to Fanny's new apartment at 15 East Sixtieth Street in the fall of 1927. Rose was one of perhaps forty major popular songwriters in the business, but there was a marked difference between Tin Pan Alley and the world that Fanny lived in. Rose remembered this new meeting with Fanny as his "first how-do-you-do with elegance. . . . A butler, who was fascinated by the belt on the back of my coat, ushered us in."

Billy was impressed by Fanny's pine-paneled living room, simulated Chippendale furniture, and silver plates—but not enough to work for the small money Fanny offered. Fanny objected to a song that Billy outlined titled "Riverside Rose," claiming it was in bad taste and, unlike her other songs, offensive to the Jews. "When I did a song about a Jewish girl, I was that person. I could never do a song where I was standing outside of the race poking fun."

Rose talked more than Fanny or MacDonald, his comments barbed and stinging. A cigarette dangled from his mouth as he spoke, the ashes spilling onto Fanny's tablecloth. The meeting ended early.

Fanny called MacDonald the next day and asked him not to bring "that dirty goose" to her again.

Ballard MacDonald worked on both the *Revels* and Fanny's act, completing three songs for the *Revels* before falling off the wagon. Rose, seeking to better his position, called up Fanny, who asked him to come back to the apartment.

The news about MacDonald stung and angered Fanny, who paced back in front of Billy, cursing out bootleggers, unreliable songwriters, and the world in general.

"I open in two weeks. Where am I going to get an act in two weeks? And then if I get it, how can I learn it so fast? And if I learn it so fast it won't be a goddam fucking bit of good." Fanny was still reeling from the divorce from Arnstein, and MacDonald's weakness seemed to her another man's betrayal. Her angry panic, and the language she employed, effectively destroyed the gulf that had made Rose defensively obnoxious. There and then, the two began to bond.

Fanny rang for dinner, a meal interrupted when Billy suffered the first and only nosebleed of his life. One hour later, after several cold compresses, Fanny fixed him a plate of eggs and onions. Grateful for her tact, sympathetic to her plight, and probably weakened by the loss of blood, Rose promised to write her an act in record time—for reasonable money.

Billy returned the following afternoon with a new song all written. It was "Sascha, The Passion of the Pasha," a number Fanny did in Arab costume, her lips pursed outlandishly as she delightfully described herself as the star of the Pasha's harem. "Then," said Fanny, "do I sit up and think he is a smart little guy."

Rose now took the act MacDonald had written several months earlier, got composer Jesse Greer to write new music, and prepared the new act in a week—spending every night with Fanny in her new apartment, at theatres, at Lindy's, or any number of all-night delicatessens. They went over concepts, lines, and bits of business; Billy stimulating Fanny with his ideas and clever reworkings of older material, Fanny responding with suggestions on how things could be improved and her first-hand knowledge of what worked on stage. When they weren't working on the act, Rose talked about his parents, Bernard Baruch, and other songwriters; Fanny told him stories about Ziegfeld. "There was never a shade of emotion between us," Fanny recalled; "never a thought or a word of love. But we enjoyed being together. We spoke the same language and loved the same language. We were friends—I thought."

Five weeks of tryouts followed, Billy travelling with Fanny to do rewrites and tightening. By the time she opened at the Palace on November 21, 1927, Fanny had the best and strongest act of her career.

It was an expensive act; Fanny carried her own special conductor (Vincent Collings) and used Roger Davis as a "prop" butler. It was a clever act as well, utilizing almost the full stage for an opening that showed Fanny talking to "Mr. [Edward] Albee" on the telephone—protesting her inability to do anything in vaudeville, but then saying she can open right away when he mentions a salary of $3,700 a week.

A new Cole Porter ballad, "Weren't We Fooled?" provided for a sly swipe at Nick Arnstein. Rose wrote the remainder of the songs, including "Sascha," (with its line, "speakin' of the art of sheikin', a sultan's wife is a wonderful life, providin' you do not weaken)." the socially conscious "Song of the Sewing Machine," and "Is Something the Matter with Otto Kahn (Or Is Something the Matter with Me)?" in which Fanny, as an aspiring diva, wonders why the celebrated impresario will not give her a chance. Rose also provided "Mrs. Cohen at the Beach," a comedy monologue Fanny would make continued use of till her whole career became consumed by Baby Snooks. Its thrust is the earthy but good-humored practicality of Mrs. Cohen as she shepherds her children—and, to some extent, her husband—on a trip to Coney Island.

While Fanny Brice was doubtless not the first comedienne to do a Jewish mother, it is nonetheless significant that "The Rise of the Gold-bergs," Gertrude Berg's first "Goldberg" story and the vehicle that launched her on a long career, was written shortly after Fanny repeated this mono-logue in her first motion picture. The same enthusiasm, naïveté, and zest for living that marked "Mrs. Cohen" are visible in Molly Goldberg, and Fanny's line, "Hello, Mrs. Bloom," was later reprised—many times—in Molly's famous "Yoo-hoo, Mrs. Bloom."

The new act proved to be one of the best-produced in vaudeville. "Miss Brice," wrote Abel Green, "was the iridescent Tiffany in a Palace setting rich, for once, with talent, impressing the more despite the wor-thy supporting show."

The season, which had started out so dismally with the divorce from Nick Arnstein and the death of Fanny's brother, Phil, from asthma at the age of forty, had been turned into a triumph by the act and its young author, Billy Rose—now identified as Fanny Brice's boyfriend. Fan had not yet sold the townhouse, and she used the empty top floor as a tryst-ing place with Billy, naming it "Goose Heaven."

Fanny played the Palace for three weeks before opening a tour of the Orpheum Circuit with a two-week engagement at Chicago's Palace Mu-sic Hall. Her brother Lew showed up again at this time, introducing his new bride, the seventeen-year-old Mae Clarke.

Lew had seen Mae dancing in George White's *Manhattan Mary,* an Ed Wynn vehicle, on Broadway earlier that season. She was an attractive girl whose father was a movie theatre organist. Mae wanted a home life, but loved the stage as well. Fanny was the perfect sister-in-law.

"When I first met Fanny, she said, 'Now I'll tell you what I'm gonna do for you two kids. You're both hams. You gotta work. I'm gonna buy you a really handsome act that can close a bill, and you'll be on the second half of every house you play. I'll get you the best writers.' And she did! Billy Rose and Ballard MacDonald wrote the act, and it was a honey!

"I was a Brice! Fanny took me right into the family, and our mothers, Rosie and Violet, got very close and tried to outdo each other in their kitchens.

"Fanny used to take me shopping. On certain afternoons, I'd get a call from her and she'd say, 'Mae, they have a sale on at'—whatever the store was—and we'd go there. She always wore old, beat up looking clothes to go to sales so she'd get a better price—especially if she was shopping for somebody else. She was usually the best dressed woman in New York, because nobody had taste like Fanny."

Lew, at thirty-four, was twice the age of his new bride. What made their marriage difficult, however, was his asthma. It kept them both from getting a night's sleep and made Lew drink as much as, or more than, his late father, Charlie.

Show business was changing. Broadway had tightened up in 1924, as Equity established a union shop, and composers, backed by the American Society of Composers, Authors and Publishers (ASCAP), won the right to control scores, limiting interpolations and paving the way for the "modern" American musical of the next forty years. Vaudeville's popularity was waning, and "the road" of one-night stands practically disappeared in the early 'twenties, as motion pictures reached the hinterlands and the widespread use of the automobile enabled people in small towns to travel to large cities within hours. But perhaps the most far-reaching changes came in 1927–28. Warner Brothers made and released *The Jazz Singer,* paving the way for the acceptance of talking films, and Joseph P. Kennedy's Radio Pictures acquired the Keith-Orpheum theatres, forming RKO (Radio Keith Orpheum) and phasing out vaudeville.

Warner's, having acquired their own theatres and First National Pictures, went ahead with plans for two more talking pictures, films that would launch the sound era once and for all.

The first would be *The Singing Fool,* a vehicle for Jolson; the second picture would star Fanny. Her contract with First National, now owned by Warner Bros., was renegotiated, and a screenplay, called *My Man,* was hurriedly outlined and written.

Fanny was in Kansas City when she heard about the deal. Conscious of her bad teeth and the camera's eye, she heard about a local dentist who specialized in porcelain caps—still uncommon at the time. Fanny, Lew and Mae (then playing the Main Street Theatre as "Mr. and Mrs. Lew Brice") and Roger Davis all had their teeth capped within the week.

"We spent that whole week laughing," recalls Mae. "I was the kid of the family, and in on the jokes, in a loving way. But the dentist had used a word, 'gutta-percha,' which was a material they used to put in the caps, and Lew and Fanny seemed to think not having heard of it before showed they were ignorant. They were always making fun of their lack of a formal education. They had the equivalent of *cum laude* degrees in experience, and they travelled in high circles, but they loved to kid each other about their lack of schooling when they didn't know a word."

Fanny's next appearance was in the Bronx Coliseum. Her first two songs went smoothly, but when Fanny started to do "Mrs. Cohen at the Beach," she found the caps made her Yiddish accent sound more English than Jewish. She got through the performance and immediately asked the stage manager if there was a dentist near the theatre. Told that there was one around the corner, she ran to his office frantically and asked him to file down her capped teeth. He took them down a little and then handed her a mirror, but Fanny just excused herself, went to a corner of the room and tried her Jewish accent. ("Hold on to Mama's dress, Sadie, you shouldn't fall.") After two more fillings, the dialect was perfect once again. It was only then that Fanny looked into the mirror, and found her teeth were shorter than they were before the capping.

The Fox Film Corporation, well aware of Fanny's contract with the Warners, had someone scout her brother Lew in vaudeville. But the scout was more impressed with Mae than Lew, and offered the young girl a screen test. Mae was still a bride, however, and reluctant about Hollywood.

"I loved being on the stage, and in the act, and didn't want to go out West and perform for a camera," she confesses. "And I felt I wasn't all that pretty—or, perhaps, talented. I told it all to Fanny, but she said, 'Look, you can't afford not to take this. And you won't be alone, 'cause I'll be out there, and then Lew, once he's there with you, will get something too. So you're doing it; that's final.' And I said, 'Yes, mom,' and that was it.

"Fanny coached me for the screen test, telling me to do one scene, one ballad as a singer, and one fast number to sing and dance to. She even gave me one of her own gowns to wear, but she was so tall we had to pin it up." Mae passed the screen test, and went on to a notable career in films. Best remembered as the gal who took a grapefruit in the face from Jimmy Cagney, she did her finest work in the 1931 version of *Waterloo Bridge*.

Billy Rose went to Hollywood ahead of Fanny to write numbers for Metro-Goldwyn-Mayer, a studio that used few theme songs and whose entry into musicals would wait until *The Broadway Melody* the following season. Rose's contract said that he could sell whatever songs he wrote that Metro did not want; a clause he took advantage of with "There's a Rainbow 'Round My Shoulder," introduced by Jolson in his Warner film, *The Singing Fool*. Billy, Jolson, William Perlberg, and several Warner executives met Fanny at the train when she arrived in early June to start *My Man*.

My Man was about a worker in a theatrical costume house (Fanny as "Fannie Brand") engaged to a young man (Guinn "Big Boy" Williams as "Joe Halsey") who earns his living demonstrating an elastic exerciser in a drugstore window. Fannie's sister, Edna (Edna Murphy) makes a play for Joe, but Fannie wins him back after scoring a predictable success on Broadway. The film's chief merit was the chance it gave Fan to immortalize her famous numbers: "I'm an Indian," "Second Hand Rose," "Spring," "My Man," "I Was a Floradora Baby," and the monologue, "Mrs. Cohen at the Beach." Rose, who had left Metro, contributed two new songs, "If You Want the Rainbow (You Must Have the Rain)" and "I'd Rather Be Blue Over You (Than Be Happy with Somebody Else)."

Billy did much more than write the songs. Fanny had agreed to do *My Man* for $25,000, a figure that he told her was insulting. "All right," Fanny told him. "See if you can get me fifty thousand." Billy, pointing out that Fanny would be seen in ten thousand movie theatres charging two dollars a ticket, reportedly asked Warner Brothers for $250,000 and wound up getting $125,000. Fanny already knew Billy was smart; now she thought he was a genius.

My Man was one-third silent, giving Fanny a unique experience in picture-making that unfortunately served her little stead in later life. (Fanny filled in her spare moments making dresses for film stars like her friend Norma Talmadge, and the beautiful Dolores Costello.) She returned east with Billy when the film was finished, claiming she had been in Hollywood for "eight months, worked five weeks, and got paid for three years." It seemed that way to Fanny.

"We saw all the shows together," Billy later wrote. "She was the warmest and wittiest lady I had ever met, and for reasons that neither I nor her best friends could understand, she took a shine to me. It may not have been love in the classic tradition, but it quickly grew into something that was easy to confuse with love." Rose was certainly flattered by Fanny's attention; she was, indeed, one of the biggest names on Broadway in an era in which Broadway was, to some extent, the center of the world. But Billy "knew she would never have given me a tumble had I not caught her on the rebound after the split-up with Nicky Arnstein."

The fall of 1928 saw Fanny back in vaudeville with a two-week stint at the Palace and one-week engagements at the New York Coliseum and the Memorial in Boston. She could have had a full route for the season, but producer Earl Carroll made Fanny a lucrative offer to play a featured role in *Fioretta,* a costume vehicle for his beautiful paramour, Dorothy Knapp. The plot concerned a wicked Duke of Venice who plans to marry Fioretta (Knapp) to the outlawed Count Di Rovani, slay Rovani, and have the girl for himself.

The show's music was undistinguished, the book slow and pompous. Carroll hired Fanny and Leon Erroll to play, respectively, the Marchesa Vera Di Livio and Julio Pepolo, in a futile bid to give the show some life; but the parts failed to do justice to the players or the production.

That Fanny, the first woman to star in a sound motion picture, returned to Broadway in a featured character part says as much about the status of comediennes as it does about the position of live theatre in that era.

My Man opened at the New York Warner Theatre in December while the Carroll show was in rehearsal. The reviews were disastrous, most critics focusing on the inane story and the fact that Fanny was a far from beautiful woman, well into her thirties, playing a young girl.

My Man was Fanny's greatest chance at solo stardom, and its failure was a bitter disappointment. Fanny was now thirty-seven in a day in which many women were considered too old for leads at thirty. And the fact that she was playing an old dowager in *Fioretta* did not help her professional self-image.

Nor was the show well received when it opened out of town in Baltimore. Fanny felt helpless at her inability to score in scene after scene, and asked Billy (or "Putsy," her new nickname for him) to come down from New York for an opinion. This was a great compliment to Billy, and he did not let her down. Brushing aside Earl Carroll's protests, he insisted she perform her role in Yiddish dialect. "What he says goes," Fanny told Carroll, "or I walk." The dialect went in and helped, not only Fanny's part, but the entire show.

A couple of nights later, Billy and Fanny were alone in her dressing room at Ford's Opera House. Fan was taking off her make-up when Rose suddenly said that they were "good for each other" and suggested they get married.

Fanny, who felt very close to Billy and was deeply touched, was nevertheless cautious and defensive. Pretending not to take him seriously, she told him they would talk about it "some other time" and leaned over to put on a shoe.

"I've always figured," Rose said later, "that when a man asks a girl to marry him, he's entitled to a civil answer." Angry and insulted, he kicked Fanny in the backside.

Fanny straightened up, much more surprised than hurt. "If it means that much to you, Bill," she said, her eyes brimming with tears, "of course we'll get married."

Fanny used to say she married Frank White, the barber, because "he smelled so good," Nick because "he looked so good," and Billy Rose because "he thought so good." Writers, including both Billy and Fanny, have tended to describe their lives together as a combination of professional alliance and platonic marriage of convenience. Neither was quite true, though Fanny still loved Nick and found making a joke out of her marriage to a five-foot-three songwriter an effective way of dealing with disapproving friends. Fanny may have been one of the most honest people in show business, but she was also a comedienne—and, like all successful performers, something of an expert in public relations. The incongruity of their appearance—Fanny, in the heels and high women's hats of the late 'twenties, simply towered over her young husband—made good newspaper copy. But their marriage was a marriage; both liked sex too much for anything else.

People often bond because of things they share. Billy and Fanny had similar ethnic backgrounds, intelligence, ambition, and a mutual interest in show business. Rose had grown to, in his fashion, love the theatre. He saw every show, and venerated Fanny as a great performer.

Some men are especially receptive to the charms of women in the theatre. In the 'twenties, more than now, such women had a charm, a vivacity, that other women—even models, with all their physical beauty— simply lacked. Fanny had that charm, plus keen intelligence, obvious talent, and a position in show business that carried its own glamour. Billy Rose, the Tin Pan Alley songster who worshipped stars like Jolson, Eddie Cantor, and Harry Richman, was hooked.

Fanny later said she saw Rose as "the right one for me now. . . . We can be pals. I don't want to be alone. A woman without a man is not right for herself. Then I pulled a good one. I said to myself, 'and he can never hurt me.' " Billy Rose could not have been more unlike Nick Arnstein if he'd been bred for the purpose. He was short; Arnstein was tall. He was homely; Nick was handsome. Billy was a "doer," Nick a dreamer. Rose, in short, was a good antidote for Nick. And Fanny loved him—more, at least, than she had loved Frank White.

Fanny and Billy were married on February 9, 1929, four days after *Fior-etta* opened at the Earl Carroll Theatre. Fanny rode to City Hall together with her friend Jay Brennan, who played "Caponetti" in the show. (Brennan was the former straight man of Bert Savoy, the outrageously camp female impersonator struck dead by lightning on June 26, 1923.) Throughout the ride downtown, at every traffic stop, Brennan struck his head out of the car and yelled, "She's getting married!" Fanny, who had started the day nervous, was all smiles by the time she faced the photographers at City Hall.

The civil ceremony was performed by James J. Walker, New York's famous playboy mayor, and movie cameras recorded the event for posterity. Humorist Bugs Baer was Rose's best man, and Jay Brennan gave Fanny away. Fanny's mother, Rosie, was there, too, looking older than her sixty-one years.

A reporter from the *New York Evening Graphic* interviewed Fanny backstage at the Earl Carroll Theatre the day following the wedding. Asked how she liked married life, Fan said, "It's better with your shoes off."

Billy's mother—also named Fanny—was delighted that her far-from-orthodox son had married a Jewess—even one eight years older and four inches taller than he was. The wedding, however, was no big hit with Fan's children; "Mademoiselle" had poisoned their minds against their new stepfather, claiming "Mr. Rose" was not a "gentleman" like their own father, Mr. Arnstein. Frances even locked herself in her bedroom to avoid attending the reception.

Fanny did her best to bring her new spouse up to standards, taking him to Broadway tailor Earl Benham for new suits; Sulka's for ties, socks, and shirts; and Whyte's for three new pairs of shoes. The overhaul made Rose into a sharp dresser, but did little to endear him to the kids.

Fioretta was almost as unpopular with Broadway's critics as Fan's new husband was with Fran and Bill. Brice and Erroll came in for the only praise; Percy Hammond of the *New York Herald Tribune* saying Fanny "sang and jested intimately in the role of a Venetian noblewoman with a ghetto accent and a ghetto sense of burlesque. . . . When she cracked a Krafft-Ebing joke about a fairy and a red necktie she was rewarded by an ovation that almost stopped the show." St. John Ervine of the *New York World* said:

> Mr. Errol was reduced to falling over things, which he did extremely well . . . while Miss Brice, a lady with a singularly expressive counte-nance, was compelled to add bountifully to her "lines" and songs from her store of rich, insinuating leers and grimaces. "The Wicked Old Willage of Wenice" would have left us all yawning had Miss Brice not been one of the trio who sang it.
>
> Merely to watch her humorous eyes lighting up as she feels some-thing funny coming into her head is a joy, and her comic lower east-side voice makes the baldest assertion seem slyly amusing. Miss Brice is a brilliant comedienne and a very handsome woman. She can do things with her mouth and nose that are extraordinarily ludicrous, yet they never rob her of her attractive looks. We do not see enough of her work in this piece.

Brice and Erroll might have kept *Fioretta* running longer than the 111 performances it managed, had not Carroll had a fight with his chief backer, a rich aunt of one of the composers. Fanny and Billy took a belated honeymoon after the show closed and then went to Hollywood, where United Artists president Joseph M. Schenck wanted to star Fanny in a new film vehicle. Schenck had recently signed Jolson, and despite the poor reception given to her first film, he thought Fanny would be effective opposite an offbeat leading man like Robert Armstrong. The money was again in the six-figure bracket, and the picture, based on a story called *The Champ*, was finally released as *Be Yourself!*

The plot, in which nightclub entertainer "Fanny Field" guides boxer Jerry Moore (Armstrong, who had also played a fighter in the Broadway play *Is Zat So?* and is now remembered chiefly for his role as Carl Denham in the film *King Kong*) to the heavyweight championship, loses him to the bright lights of Broadway, and subsequently gets him back, was simply a reworking of Fanny's first picture. Billy wrote three new songs for *Be Yourself!*—"Cooking Breakfast for the One I Love," "When a Woman Loves a Man," and a production number called "Kicking a Hole in the Sky"—all of which were sung by Fanny.

My Man is a lost film; no known print survives. But *Be Yourself!* exists, and, though an antique—made at the tail end of that uncomfortable period when the art of moviemaking took a temporary backward leap in order to assimilate the new techniques of sound—it serves as a good window on Miss Brice's charm and talent. Her sense of fun, of parodying pretense, shines through in scene after scene, and "Cooking Breakfast for the One I Love," in which Fanny sings the first chorus "straight" and the second one in Yiddish dialect, involves what film historian Miles Kreuger has called "several quick silver changes of mood." The song contrasts a woman's love for the sweet "married" life with the comedienne's self-parodying, divorced perspective, echoing the two Brice viewpoints—Fanny the romantic and Fanny the cynic.

Singing "When a Woman Loves a Man," without the false vibrato that characterized the average torch singer, Fanny conveys the deep feeling of a woman desperately in love with the same conviction seen in Jolson's best film work. Fanny sings this song with her eyes shut, her right hand caressing her left elbow as she thinks of being touched by the great love of her life. It was the same way she had sung "My Man" more than two hundred times before, and the only way she could sing any number like it.

"When a Woman Loves a Man" has, if anything, a better, more sophisticated lyric than "My Man": "Mountains toss their fingers at care since this old world began. But they're nothing compared to the mountains she'll climb when a gal yearns for a man." Where the popularity of "My Man" had as much to do with Arnstein's troubles as it did with Brice's great rendition, "When a Woman Loves a Man" serves more as a testament to Fanny's depth of feeling as a woman and an artist. She sings the number in a torchy black gown; the poetic lyrics given a clear, heartfelt treatment that keeps clear of the maudlin and leaves listeners, to this day, spellbound.

Fanny's rendition of "When a Woman Loves a Man" was filmed, ironically, just when her "man," Arnstein, left her life forever. On October 18, 1929, Nick married heiress Irene Matlack McCullough in Quebec.

Shortly after he married Irene, the charges against Nick in New York on the old bond-theft scheme were finally, miraculously, dropped. Fan herself fixed the swindling charges in Ohio by promising to "reimburse" the man that Nick had swindled. (She never did, and Nathan Weiss sued her estate.)

Nick, who had met Irene at a Chicago party thrown in Fanny's honor, was set, seemingly, for life. He was fifty years old, but a young, handsome, vibrant fifty—"straight as an arrow" and self-confident as ever. From Arnstein's point of view, it was a marriage of convenience, giving him both money and a high social position. For Nick, with his fine tastes and solid ego, things could not have worked out better.

He claimed, in later years, that he had married Irene to spite Fanny. His marriage, like Fan's own to Billy Rose, was really two parts marriage of convenience, one part marriage of revenge.

Fanny was playing a special two-week vaudeville engagement at the Orpheum Theatre in Los Angeles when Mae had her first big trouble with Lew. "I'd come home after a day at the studio, and he'd say, 'Who the hell have you been flirting with today?' And that was so unfair, because I'd spent the day working like crazy trying to learn lines before I stepped before a camera. It was awful. Besides, I didn't want to flirt. I wanted to be married.

"Lew hadn't gotten anywhere in pictures, and he'd started to complain about being known as 'Mae Clarke's husband' after years of being known as 'Fanny Brice's brother.' (Fanny often told him that he'd be 'Lew Brice' if only he'd learn business, get new suits, and work on his material instead of spending all that time at the race track.) He punched me in the nose one day, and I called Fanny at the Roosevelt Hotel. You might have expected her to say, 'Well, he's my brother," but she listened to my side and said, 'Well, that's intolerable.' She let me stay with her that night." The Brices were divorced in 1930.

Fan and Billy returned to New York in December, settled into a new floor-through apartment at 32 East Sixty-Fourth Street, and hosted several parties between Christmas and their first wedding anniversary on

February 9. The guests regarded Fanny as the hostess; Billy Rose was just her husband.

The floor-through always seemed to be filled with celebrities, many of whom stayed all night and were still singing, playing, or talking when the children were taken to school in the morning. There were the greats of Broadway—Ziegfeld, George M. Cohan, Beatrice Lillie, Noël Coward, Cole Porter, the cream of society, and, on other occasions, people Fanny had met through Nick Arnstein—"Large Face the Safecracker," "English Bob the Nose-Biter," "Charles 'Chink' Sherman," and others not yet imprisoned for life or killed in the great gang wars of the era.

Rose remembered Large Face as "a man with the largest, the squarest, and the grayest face" he had ever seen on a human being. Billy watched in amazement as Fanny lent Large Face a thousand dollars because he was "the best safecracker in the business" and would pay as soon as he was able. Large Face repaid Fanny in Chicago some time later, counting out ten hundred-dollar bills and asking her not to negotiate them for a few weeks.

"I'd be fancying it up," Rose later wrote, "if I said that the big names and the wags and wacks around Fanny ever got me down. Actually, they intrigued and delighted me. What did get me down was the loss of my second name. Single-O, I had been Billy Rose, a successful songwriter and nightclub owner. As Fanny's husband, I was either Mr. Brice or Billy Who?"

Fanny pulled the ultimate *faux pas* when she forgot Billy's name while introducing him to guests. She apologized, but Billy was insulted when she did it again several minutes later. At other times, she introduced him with lines like: "This is my husband, Billy Rose. He's just a little shrimp, but mentally he's Gary Cooper." Billy had a sense of humor, but his ego was continually ruffled by his lack of professional—and physical—stature.

Actors were persona non grata in society before World War II, and if the Vanderbilts liked Fanny, it was despite, not because of, her position in the theatre. Many socialites were entertained by her no-nonsense behavior, even if she saw right through them and occasionally put them in their places. But the very rich were simply amused by show people, and looked up to them no more than they looked up to a fine chef.

Songwriters were, if anything, considerably below performers on the social ladder. The names of Tin Pan Alley tunesmiths were not familiar to most people, and only Irving Berlin, the multitalented George M. Cohan, Jerome Kern, and George Gershwin had anything approaching real fame. Billy, a co-lyricist with more than twenty hit songs to his credit, was little more than a nodding curiosity at Fanny's parties.

In his own crowd, Rose had been successful—a go-getter and a man respected, if not truly admired, by his colleagues. When he married Fanny, though, he moved into a world of bigger names. She was a star; he was a songwriter. The difference was like that between a princess and a knight.

Rose was also younger than his wife, which meant there were few people he could mix with at Fan's parties. One of them, however, was a man he looked up to, a man of his own age, ethnicity, and intellect whose great accomplishments, huge ego, and ideas set Billy on a new career.

The man in question was Jed Harris, Broadway's boy wonder producer of the late 'twenties (*Broadway, The Royal Family, The Front Page,* etc.) and one of the most arrogant, disliked men in the theatre. A genius at envisioning how scripts would work on stage, casting, staging, and lighting, Harris found in Rose a willing listener for his frequent discourses on the drama.

Rose now looked at George M. Cohan and Irving Berlin, two songwriters turned producers, and began to see himself in the same mold on Broadway. And just as he had built a songwriting career by studying hundreds of pop tunes, he now began to study the art and business of producing under Harris' exclusive tutelage.

Jed, with customary arrogance, told Billy that dramatic plays required more ability than novices like him could handle. Harris suggested that Rose start with a revue, since, as a songwriter, he had all the needed talent.

The "needed talent" turned out to be Fanny.

CHAPTER *II*

Baby Snooks at Last

Fanny was playing the Albee Theatre in Brooklyn when *Be Your-self!* premiered at the Rialto on Friday evening, March 6, 1930. The criticism once more focused on her age. "Miss Brice, of all persons, appears as the ingenue," observed the caustic *New York World*. *Be Yourself!* lost so much money that Joe Schenck declined to make the second film on Fanny's contract. Fan, who had a guarantee, sued Schenck's Art Cinema Corporation for $125,000.

Her hopes for a career in films now dashed, Fanny spent most of the summer in a house on Fire Island, a long, narrow, sandy spit of land off the southern coast of central Long Island. Billy stayed in Manhattan making plans for his new show, but visited his wife there in July. "Boy, did those greenies sting," he wrote. "Seemed like they had mouths full of needles. Tried to rest on the beach after dodging countless hunks of broken glass. No good. First the flies bit right through the bathing suit and then Fanny's kibitzers made merry very loudly." Rose hated everything about Fire Island, and left after an argument with Fanny. They made up via telephone, and Billy soon returned. He still, however, hated Fire Island.

Rose selected *Corned Beef and Roses* as the title for his show, made Jed Harris his partner for $25,000, and signed Broadway star Hal Skelly in addition to Fanny. In August, Billy also signed George Jessel, who had given up the idea of starring in *The Wonder Bar,* a Morris Gest importation from Europe, following a disagreement with Jake Shubert.

Rose, who knew comparatively little of the various intricacies involved in pulling together a Broadway musical, studied what little had been written on the subject and talked, endlessly, with Jed and older heads like Cohan and Sam Harris. Fanny, who rejoined Billy from Fire Island in late August, helped him with her knowledge of fine furnishings and fabrics. Billy had what Fanny called a "seven-track mind" that enabled him to do several things at one time. He soaked up what Fanny taught him while attending to other business, and never forgot anything he learned.

Rose got young David Freedman to write the libretto for *Corned Beef and Roses*. Freedman, the son of an editorial writer for the *Jewish Daily Forward,* had been Eddie Cantor's ghostwriter for several years following the publication of his first novel, *Mendel Marantz,* in 1926. With Rose giving him ideas and worrying about everything from the cost of sets to songs, Freedman wrote what then was called an "intimate revue."

Intimate revues, which held their own on Broadway in the early to mid-'thirties, were termed "intimate" because they lacked the grand opulence of the great shows of the 1920s. To make up for their lack of splendor, intimate revues emphasized sophistication, cleverness, and, especially in Rose's first revue, what many then considered "dirt."

Rehearsals started in September and spread to two additional theatres before the end of the first week. Rose had budgeted his show at fifty thousand dollars, failing to figure on the extra drapes, platforms, and side wings that crept in during rehearsals. There were additional scenes, new scenery, and a general realignment of the whole production before rehearsals ended in the middle of October.

When Rose showed up in Philadelphia on Sunday, October 12, 1930, to ready his production for its opening, he found the alley in the rear of the theatre littered with scenery. Asking when the stagehands would remove "this other show," he was informed it was the scenic overflow of his own production.

Early worries about paucity of material dwindled when the first act ran five hours at the dress rehearsal. And the opening, while not as comically inept as the one pictured in the movie *Funny Lady,* was a torturous affair because the original stage manager walked out on Rose at the last minute.

But *Corned Beef and Roses* had its strong points, and *Variety* said it "looked like the smartest, most original, up-to-the-minute revue" of the era at the intermission. "After that, it faded fast, and had to depend on smut, of which there was plenty. In fact, it is generally agreed in Philly that *Corned Beef and Roses* is the dirtiest show ever witnessed here."

Act II started with an "Angel Ballet," conceived by Tamara Geva, and followed with George Jessel as a lecturer with a series of "stereopticon slides' of what turned out to be a woman's body. *Variety* called it the "dirtiest bit in the show. . . . This wasn't just off color; it was lower-class, stag-smoker stuff and many a blasé theatregoer was hard put to it to keep from blushing. Even Jessel was intensely embarrassed."

Fanny put most of the blame on Harris, who had usurped the duties of director. Jed had little feeling for musical comedy, and lit her comic scenes with low-key blues instead of the bright whites her mugging needed. After the reviews came out in Philadelphia, Rose told his partner there was "too damned much genius around this show." Harris took the hint and went back to New York.

After two weeks of tryouts, Rose petitioned Equity to allow him to go back into rehearsals for one week. The request was granted, largely due to the departure of Hal Skelly and the signing of James Barton, a brilliant entertainer best known for his "Mad Dog" specialty.

Almost everyone he asked told him that *Corned Beef and Roses* was a bad title, but Billy failed to see the light until the end of the first tryouts. With the show back in rehearsal, its name was changed to *Sweet and Low*.

Barton, Brice, and Jessel got together for a new song titled "Dancing with Tears in Their Eyes," and Fanny did a number with Barton ("Chinese White") near the end of the second act. Barton also got a solo spot in the first act, but it was "Babykins," the forerunner of "Baby Snooks," that soon became the high point of the show.

"Babykins," surprisingly, was Rose's own idea. Impressed with Fanny's wont of speaking in a child's lisping voice when something had displeased her, he had Freedman write a sketch in which she played a baby. Fanny had done children in three songs, "If We Could Only Take Their World" (1915), "Rockaway Baby" (1919), and "Poor Little Moving Picture Baby" (1924), and her hesitancy to portray one in a sketch was doubtless partly due to the success of comedienne Rae Dooley's "Baby Rose" characterization in the *Follies*. It took Billy to persuade Fanny to overcome her fears. Rose was no artistic genius, but he had a certain showman's instinct for what worked onstage—an instinct Fanny had now come to value.

The first Babykins sketch, written by the young Moss Hart, had been tossed out by Harris at rehearsals. David Freedman's version had Fanny as the baby, Arthur Treacher as the doctor, Peggy Andre as the mother, Lucile Osborne as the nurse, and Roger Davis as the father, making him the first in a short line of "Daddies" that would end with Hanley Stafford.

The sophisticated 'thirties approach to the revue form was typified in "Strictly Unmentionable," a take-off on the play *Strictly Unbearable*, with Fanny and George Jessel. Fanny also sang two songs, "I Knew Him Before He Was Spanish" and "Overnight." Another number, Jessel's "When a Pansy Was a Flower," came in for some comment, but the hits were "Cheerful Little Earful," sung by pretty Hannah Williams and Jerry Norris, and "Would You Like to Take a Walk?" performed by Williams, Hal Thompson, and the chorines—exceptionally beautiful and widely exploited in several semi-nude photographs.

Sweet and Low played a week at the Majestic Theatre in Brooklyn before opening at Chainin's Forty-sixth Street Theatre on Broadway on Monday night, November 17, 1930. The reviews were good, with some reservations about the remaining "blue" material, and Rose was gratified until he saw the audiences at matinees.

That 1930–31 season was the worst in Broadway history. Despite its three top name performers, *Sweet and Low* was rarely sold out, and Rose again asked older, more experienced producers for advice. Cohan and Sam H. Harris both told him to close the show, but Rose refused to admit failure. "If I closed it," he said after Fanny died, "I went back to being Fanny's husband again, and I was a mite tired of that." After two months of dwindling attendance and high rent, he moved *Sweet and Low* to the Forty-fourth Street Theatre, where it bounced back nicely before closing in late April.

Sweet and Low closed slightly in the red, but Rose was far from finished. Barton and Jessel went their separate ways, but Billy took the bulk of the remaining cast, put them in rehearsals for four weeks, and opened an ostensibly new show called *Crazy Quilt* on May 18. Fanny was still his ace in the hole and, in place of Barton and Jessel, Rose signed Ted Healy and his "Stooges" (Moe Howard, Larry Fine, and Shemp Howard) and accordionist Phil Baker, all of whom had been in Shubert Winter Garden shows. New material was written—cleaner than for *Sweet and Low*—as well as fine new songs, including "I Found a Million Dollar Baby in a Five-and-Ten Cent Store," which Healy, Brice, and Baker performed as a trio in top hat, white tie, and tails.

Fanny also had a new "Rose" number, "Rest Room Rose," by Richard Rodgers and Lorenz Hart. *Crazy Quilt* got good reviews, but only ran in New York for eight weeks, closing with unbearably hot weather on July 25. Fanny appeared on the fifteen-minute *International Shoe Company Program* on WABC with Rich's Orchestra on Wednesday night, August 12, and spent the balance of the summer on Fire Island.

Crazy Quilt was slated for another incarnation. Ned Alvord, a tall press agent who looked and dressed like a nineteenth-century undertaker, had alerted Rose to waiting profits on the road. Many small towns that had not seen shows since before the war were undergoing a theatrical revival as established "show towns" of the 'twenties found themselves unable to support touring productions. *Crazy Quilt* was accordingly booked for a heavily publicized tour, much of the publicity focusing on the risqué elements in the show.

Alvord's prophecies of profits were proved true throughout the tour. Opening in Pittsburgh on September 28, 1931, *Crazy Quilt* played an eleven-week engagement at the Apollo Theatre in Chicago, where the gross was never below $28,000. A one-night stand in Memphis brought in $14,000. Two-week engagements in Los Angeles and San Francisco were almost equally successful. Only in Duluth was there a problem; reformers there claimed the show was "indecent," and Rose had to cancel. For the most part, though, the show's small element of risqué humor—exaggerated in Alvord's advance publicity— helped rather than hindered.

Rose asked his stars—including Fanny—to take temporary two-thirds cuts in salary at the beginning of the tour, cuts that were restored after nine weeks. Healy was, if anything, more mercenary than Fanny. He even disliked paper money, preferring to obtain gold bullion that, he said, would survive all depressions. Fanny, who loved practical jokes, tricked him into buying a "gold brick" in Billings, Montana, a joke enjoyed by Baker and the Stooges, who resented Healy's highhanded ways as much as they respected his talent as a comic.

When the tour ended at the end of April, Rose was $240,000 ahead of all investments since planning *Corned Beef and Roses* almost two years earlier.

Billy Rose was "Mr. Brice" no longer. Fanny had been his principal star, but Billy's own pragmatism, intelligence, and business acumen had allowed him to turn failure into distinct success. Despite his lack of stature, Rose seemed almost ten feet tall to many along Broadway.

His ego was becoming even larger.

Billy and Fanny were together throughout the tour, their accommodations ranging from the fashionable Ambassador East Hotel in Chicago to compartments in Pullmans. The situation changed, however, when they returned to New York, and Rose rented the penthouse of the Wurlitzer Building. He read script after script, and finally decided to produce *The Great Magoo,* a play about a Coney Island barker and his girlfriend, by Ben Hecht and Gene Fowler. Rose now spent his days away from Fanny, who was glad to have a husband who at least "did something" besides dream.

Fanny, who hated public displays of emotion, still wept every night and morning, just as she had done since the divorce from Nick. The situation changed, however, when she got a call from Roger Davis.

Nick was moving to California with Irene, and wanted to say good-bye to Fanny at Davis' apartment. Fanny went, and they had dinner. As the minutes wore on, she found that she was looking at Nick almost from a distance. The studied charm, proud lies, and empty boasts were now bared by time and absence; Fanny quickly realized she did not love Nick any longer.

Fanny left Roger's apartment as early as she could.

The magic was gone, and Fanny never wept again. She was not happy, only curiously empty—sorry she had ever met Nick Arnstein.

She missed being in love. "With Nick," she once said, "I was happily miserable. With Billy, I was miserably happy." Her feelings toward Billy also underwent a change. She loved him neither more nor less, but a sort of emptiness, a malaise, came into their marriage. Fan had married Billy largely because he was the opposite of Nick. As such, he had served as a surrogate for Arnstein. Now that Nick was really out of Fanny's life, Billy found her very unresponsive.

Fanny filled the new void in her life with additional friends, entertaining eight or ten for dinner every night. But where Fan's parties had sometimes humiliated Rose, her dinners made him downright angry. More and more of Fanny's friends were male homosexuals, many of them met through Roger Davis, all of whom just worshipped at her feet. Fanny was among the first "Gay Goddesses" of show biz, a strong woman of great talent who had undergone a fair amount of grief. Billy, while aware of the great contributions made to theatre by homosexuals, found their fawning over Fanny disconcerting, their mannerisms irritating, and their condescension toward heterosexual males—like him—maddening. "She's up to her ass in nances," Billy told his sister Polly—not intending any pun.

Increasingly, he dined at Lindy's, usually with columnists like Mark Hellinger, Walter Winchell, Jimmy Cannon, and Sidney Skolsky. More and more, the only times Fan saw him was at 4:00 A.M., when they would discuss show business over fried egg sandwiches and coffee.

In May 1932, soon after finishing her tour in *Crazy Quilt,* Fanny made two guest appearances on *Ziegfeld Follies of the Air,* a weekly radio show hosted by the now-fabled producer, whose health had been crushed by the market crash, several flop shows, Monte Carlo (where he was a major plunger), and sciatica, a painful neuritis of the sciatic nerve. The sums he spent on his productions also led to his ruination, as costs rose to where the *Follies* could no longer make a profit. Changing tastes were yet another factor; his great shows looked out of fashion as the nation fell into the Great Depression. While radio and talking pictures flourished, the live theatre lost its hold as the chief form of amusement, and a new, "sophisticated" theatregoer replaced the old. Ziegfeld was through.

Bernard Sobel, Ziegfeld's press agent during the late stages of his long career, quietly called Fanny at one point for needed money. Fanny sent a check, then worked out a plan whereby she deposited five hundred dollars in Ziegfeld's account at the City National Bank each month without Flo's knowledge. Ziegfeld, an untidy businessman in his best days, died in July, never knowing he had received help from Fanny.

May 22 marked Fanny's last appearance on the program. On June 4, she sailed on the *Île de France* with Frances, now almost thirteen; eleven-year-old Bill; and Bea Lillie, who shared Fanny's interests in fine furnishings and clothes. The comediennes stocked up on smart buys around Paris, and, in Cannes, more than a score of people moved into their hotel after word somehow got out that they were registered. Fanny got the rates reduced when she found out.

When they returned to New York two months later, Fanny began work on a new act for picture theaters. The old show business—including "two-a-day" big-time vaudeville—was dead, and only major picture houses could afford to pay huge salaries to big-name entertainers.

Fanny opened her picture-house tour at the Paramount in New York on September 16, "running the gamut from her sumptuous spoof in the 'Dying Swan' ballet, which is the last word in low comedy clowning, to her identifying 'My Man' number at the other end of her artistic scale and making a grand bit of trouping of the whole business." Fanny and Phil Baker, who served as master of ceremonies, reprised their bedroom tapestry, "Strictly Unmentionable," from *Crazy Quilt*, and reviewers called it "the backbone of the entertainment."

In October, Fanny left New York to play film houses in the Midwest. She opened a week's engagement at the Oriental Theatre in Chicago on Armistice Day, her material including "Babykins."

(Jesse) Block and (Eve) Sully were on the bill at the Oriental. Eve recalled that, at one performance, Fanny "was late coming down after our act, so I got into the crib. When she got there, she didn't know I was in it. The curtain went up and the audience knew it was me. They were hysterical. But she couldn't ad lib. She couldn't say anything. I handed her a lollipop and said, 'Take the paper off and eat it.' She said, 'What?' So I said, 'You're supposed to take the paper off and throw the lollipop away.' It was a joke that we did years ago but she couldn't ad lib, unless it was written for her."

The Great Magoo, the new play Billy was producing, opened at the

Selwyn Theatre while Fanny played a return engagement at the Paramount in New York in December. The cast included Paul Kelly, Claire Carleton, Harry Green, and, in a supporting role, Charlotte Greenwood. George Abbott directed, but *The Great Magoo* closed after eleven performances, its only saving grace a song Rose wrote for one scene, one that might well sum up his philosophy of life: "It's a Barnum and Bailey world. It's as phoney as it can be. But it wouldn't be make believe if you believed in me." It is, however, doubtful that Rose believed in romantic love. "There was no passion in our life," Fanny told author Maurice Zolotow in March, 1946. "He never kissed me with any real passion. I don't think he is capable of passion. He isn't an emotional sort of person, altogether, unless maybe he's engaged in a big deal. He might get emotional about that."

Rose, who lost about $25,000 on *The Great Magoo,* simply bided his time selecting the right vehicle for his next production. He had no intention of returning to his role as "Mr. Brice."

Neither Fan nor Billy was very active in the following three months. Rose made plans to send a tabloid version of *Crazy Quilt* on tour with Ann Pennington, Charles King, Smith & Dale, and Anita Page. Fanny followed Beatrice Lillie as guest artist on the second of Rex Evans' Thursday nights at the Algonquin Supper Club on March 2 after doing "Poor Little Popular Song," a "whimsy," on the "Rudy Vallee *Fleischman Hour*" of January 15. Interest in radio was at an all-time high among Broadway performers. Eddie Cantor, the first established name to have his own network radio show, had started the ball rolling with the *Chase & Sanborn Hour* on September 13, 1931.

Fanny was not sure that her material and modus operandi—clowning and mugging—would score in the new medium, but agreed to sign when the Royal Gelatine Company, impressed with her success on Vallee's program, offered her a contract to replace Ken Murray on *Royal Vagabonds* with George Olsen and his orchestra.

Fanny's worst fears were confirmed when her usual repertoire of comedy songs did not go over. "Missing was the Brice skill at visual burlesque," said the *Variety* reviewer. "As air comedy it couldn't have been productive of anything but an occasional giggle, even to those familiar with the comedienne's style." Fanny's songs on the first show included "Second Hand Rose," "Egyptian," and the "Poor Little Popular Song" whimsy she had done—as "Babykins"—on the Vallee show two months before. That last-named routine proved the most successful.

Fanny was becoming more aware of the great possibilities in "Babykins." Broadway was becoming less and less consistent in its output of

revues, and radio did not suit her old brand of comedy. She was, moreover, over forty, and too realistic to delude herself about the approaching
years. It did not take long to realized that Babykins, who was ageless and
could make use of material that might be deemed risqué if done by an
adult character, was well suited to her needs.

While Fanny was singing over the radio—from the roof of the New
Amsterdam, the theatre she had scored so many triumphs in for Ziegfeld—Billie Burke, Flo's redheaded actress widow, was trying to pay off
the massive debts her husband's death had left her. While Billie's professional ambitions pointed towards Broadway, she found playing silly, bird-
brained women in the movies far more lucrative. Yet even the considerable cash she earned in pictures like *Dinner at Eight* did not begin to pay
off Ziegfeld's debts.

Billie had already written a letter to Lee Shubert, probably Ziegfeld's
greatest professional enemy, proposing that the Shuberts produce a new
Follies using Ziegfeld's name—a show in which she, as Ziegfeld's widow,
would share in the profits. "It would keep Flo's name alive," she wrote.
"I trust you to do the show as you would have done it with Flo, if things
had been different."

Lee Shubert hated Ziegfeld because of an old breach of contract, but
the idea of producing the *Ziegfeld Follies* tickled his theatrical ego. He
concluded a deal whereby he would produce the *Follies* under Billie's
name: "Mrs. Florenz Ziegfeld, Jr., presents the *Ziegfeld Follies*." The contract between Billie Burke Ziegfeld, Saul J. Baron (as temporary admin-
istrator of the estate of Abraham L. Erlanger), and the Producing Association, Inc. (i.e., the Shuberts) was dated May 16, 1933.

The cost of using most of the old Ziegfeld stars would be prohibitive.
Eddie Cantor, wiped out by the stock market crash, had found that radio
and films were more effective ways of replenishing his bank account than
stage work. W. C. Fields was in Hollywood, Bert Williams had died in
1922, and Will Rogers was tied up with films, radio work, and newspaper
columns. Only Fanny, of all Ziegfeld's comedy stars, was readily available. She had developed a nostalgic affection for Ziegfeld far beyond the
sometimes strained professional relationship they had maintained during
the producer's life. Like other women who had worked for Ziegfeld,
Fanny was appreciative of his striving for professional excellence, exquisite taste, and obvious obsession with "Glorifying the American Girl."
Following several weeks of negotiations, Fanny signed a contract with
the Select Theatres Corporation on Wednesday, September 27, 1933.

Fan and Billy, both of them still avid theatregoers, attended a performance of *Ah, Wilderness!* starring George M. Cohan, a few nights later.
They sat first-row center, and Fanny, bored to tears, fell asleep in half an

hour. Cohan, whom the critics had applauded for his acting in the piece, became aware of Fanny's heavy breathing and glared down in her direction. For the rest of the performance, George M. concentrated more on Fanny's sleeping than he did on the problems of his character, Nat Miller. Billy tried to rouse his wife with elbows in the ribs, but Fanny just described the play as "talk, talk, talk," and went right back to sleep. Rose took her home before the final act.

Fanny had gotten her revenge on the man who fired her in 1907.

Lee Shubert was a businessman, a Jewish immigrant whose lack of education was derided by theatrical contemporaries and later biographers. But Shubert appreciated quality and hired the best talent available for his *Follies*—Bobby Connolly to stage, E. Y. Harburg for the lyrics, Vernon Duke and Samuel Pokrass for the music.

Billy Rose wrote Fanny's two solo songs, "Soul Saving Sadie" and "Countess Dubinsky." The former was a takeoff on evangelist Aimee Semple MacPherson, then still active as the priestess of her Hollywood temple, while the latter ("Countess Dubinsky, now she strips for Minsky") was the story of a Russian aristocrat forced to work in burlesque after losing all her money in the Russian Revolution.

The show opened at the Shubert Theatre in Boston on Thursday night, November 2, 1933, "not," in the words of one contemporary critic, "as a Ziegfeld-like show, but as [an] entertaining and variegated revue in 1933. Only at the end, in a retrospective glance at earlier *Follies* is there any regard for the Ziegfeld tradition. The current sketches are more pithy and pointed than was Ziegfeld's way with them. On the other hand, the present chorus would hardly have passed muster for what he used to call 'Pulchritude.'

"Bobby Connolly, who has really had a free hand, is busier with the making of 'an all-'round good show' than with any glorifying of the American girl. So far, Fannie Brice dominates, plying her broadest humors, as often as not upon the broadest possible topics." Vilma and Buddy Ebsen and the veteran Willie Howard were also in the cast.

Howard, at least five years Fanny's senior, had been one of the top comedy stars on the American stage for more than twenty years, "the greatest of the revue comics, bar none," according to George Jessel. His best-known routine was probably his "French Taught in a Hurry," in which he actually taught Yiddish.

The diminutive Howard's only scene with Fanny was a parody of the bedroom scene from *Sailor, Beware* (titled "Sailor, Behave") in Act II. David Freedman, who wrote the sketch, was surprised that Howard, a major name in his own right, offered no complaints when Fanny got the laughs—and notices—in Boston. Willie seemed to underplay—the wrong strategy for his part and the scene. Howard's "strategy" continued all through Boston, Philadelphia, Washington, Pittsburgh, and Newark.

The *New York Times'* Brooks Atkinson found Howard "painfully comic" in his first appearance as the President of Cuba in a sketch by H. I. Phillips when the *Ziegfeld Follies* of 1934 opened at the Winter Garden on January 4. But it was in "Sailor, Behave" that Willie surprised Freedman, Shubert, and the company—not to mention Fanny. With the money on the line, he pulled the stops out, waiting until Fanny had her back turned to the audience and letting go with rolling eyes and arms as he delivered a key line. Fanny, caught completely by surprise, found herself played out of position for the balance of the sketch. She did not get one laugh in the scene.

Fanny was roaring mad when they got offstage. Picking up a chair with murderous intent, she chased the small man out the stage door and halfway up the block. Willie's next scene in the show was ironically titled "The Man Who Came Back."

"Sailor, Behave," Fanny's last scene in the show, was actually an anticlimax, since she had already walked off with the honors of the evening. Her greatest—and most lasting—triumph came in the first act in a new "baby" sketch by Freedman.

"Babykins" now had a name, one that would pass into the pop lexicon within the next few years and provide Fanny with a new career. Beginning with this Shubert *Ziegfeld Follies,* "Babykins" would be called "Baby Snooks."

"Snooks" had been a baby-talk endearment years before Irving Berlin wrote "Snooky Ookums" in 1912. May Weston's second husband, a wealthy man she married after years as Fanny's tenant, called her Snooks. Fanny liked the name, and gave it to her baby as a tribute to her friend.

The first Snooks sketch had Victor Morley as Snooks' father and young Eve Arden as her mother. The skit concerned Snooks' listening to "Daddy" tell the story of George Washington, and then lying to her father without any sense of shame.

The Snooks sketch marked the first time Fanny's baby exhibited the precocious quality that marked Snooks' later career and gave the character its bite and truth. Snooks saw the fallibility and hypocrisy of adults— but, as a baby, lacked fear and the compassion needed to respect them. Her precocious worldly wisdom and uninhibited selfishness would have been obnoxious in an adolescent or a young adult. In a baby, as portrayed by Fanny, they were innocent, if knowing—and hilarious.

Fanny liked Eve Arden, who did an imitation of her doing "Mrs. Cohen at the Beach" and had, in Fanny's own words, "a good Jewish accent for a goy!" Fan took Eve to Klein's Department Store for bargains in clothes, but her closest friend at this point was Bea Lillie. Bea would often sit in the front row and watch the *Follies,* then go backstage, wait for Fanny to dress, and go off with her to join a party at Elsa Maxwell's new club on top of the Winter Garden. Fanny would arrive home around 4:00 A.M. and chat with Billy for about a half an hour before going to sleep.

They had what was, at this point, practically an open marriage. Fanny had her life and friends, and Billy Rose had his life, friends, and girls. None of his affairs was very serious, and an occasionally raised eyebrow was the closest Fanny came to an objection. Billy once told her a joke he had heard from a showgirl. "Did you fall out of bed when you heard that one?" Fanny asked.

CHAPTER *12*

"Rewolt!"

The Billy Rose the world knew best—the fabulous showman, the "mighty mite" of American entertainment, was born in May of 1933—three months after the Twenty-second Amendment, repealing Prohibition, was proposed in Congress.

That was when Rose was approached by a man who said he represented several "gentlemen" who wanted to rent the Fortune Gallo Theatre at 254 West Fifty-fourth Street, dark for seven years, and install a cabaret on the premises. They were "very fine businessmen," he maintained, adding that "the owners of King's Beer" had an interest. They wanted Billy to stage the shows, become a partner, and lend the enterprise his increasingly famous name.

Rose, who knew that King's Beer was owned by Lucky Luciano, declined to be a partner, but agreed to stage the shows and lend his name to the new enterprise if the money was right. He was then introduced to Luciano lieutenant Willie Galuppo, Meyer Lansky–Bugsy Siegel worker "Nocky" Schwartz, and a representative of the Lepke-Gurrah interests. Billy demanded a salary of $1,000 a week for as long as the show ran and used his name.

So was born the famed Casino de Paree, which opened its doors to the public on December 30, 1933, twenty-five days after the repeal amendment was ratified. Rose produced a superb floor show with comedian Jimmy Savo, Cardini the magician, tap dancer Eleanor Powell, torch singer Gertrude Niesen, and a good-looking, well-trained chorus. Two shows were given nightly, one at 8:30 and one at 12:30.

Rose began to hit his stride. He was a showman, not an artist like Flo Ziegfeld, and realized the 1920s glory days of Broadway were long gone. The rich playboys, town wits, and society gallants who had been the audience for shows and night spots in the past had given way to a medium-income group that had respect for money and wanted quality entertainment at affordable prices. Rose built the Casino's bill for them.

There was no cover charge, and for a minimum bill of $2.50, one received an eight-course dinner and a ninety-minute show. This made it possible for a couple to spend an entire evening dining, dancing, seeing entertainment, and having several drinks for a total tap of ten or twelve dollars, including tips. Billy thought his "new audience" would make the Casino a big moneymaker and start a new, post-Prohibition nightclub era.

Rose was proven right. The Casino's 1,200 seating capacity was doubled every night because of the two shows, and the first week's gross of $40,000 yielded a profit of $15,000—$2,800 of it from the bar, which featured a nude Girl-in-the-Fish-Bowl visible through special lenses. Walter Winchell made the Casino de Paree his unofficial late night headquarters, and promoted the Casino in column after column.

Billy's success was somewhat tarnished by an ugly scene involving one hundred and fifty strikers who picketed the Casino on February 5, 1934. All the doors and plate-glass windows were smashed when the picketers became infuriated at what union leaders described as a barrage of whisky bottles from the place's upper floor. Rose was not involved, but the fact remains that, while he paid good money to established entertainers, he was cynical and cheap with dispensable personnel. "He could be a bastard if he felt he didn't need you," said one old-time actor.

Be that as it may, his backers—Luciano and associates—were pleased with the Casino and eager to open up a second spot under the Rose name and personal direction. Rose suggested leasing the Hammerstein Theatre, at 1697 Broadway near Fifty-third Street, and turning it into a popular-priced restaurant with variety entertainment "for the fellow out for a nice evening with his girl." The result was Billy Rose's Music Hall, staffed with one hundred and twenty Gay Nineties–style singing waiters, one hundred pretty girls in tight black satin dresses called the Lonely Hearts Club, and forty seedy vaudeville acts entitled the Small-Time Cavalcade. "I want the real corn," said Rose. "I don't care how stupid or silly the acts are. I want actors who look like they slept in dollar-a-night hotels all their life and played theatres in spots that even Rand McNally wouldn't print."

Rose may not have invented "camp," but he certainly made it profitable with the Music Hall. "BILLY ROSE'S MUSIC HALL" was spelled out in enormous electric letters on the outside of the building. Shortly after the opening, Rose stood outside and overheard two out-of-towners talk about the sign.

" 'Billy Rose.' Who's Billy Rose?"

"That's Fanny Brice's husband."

Billy was intelligent enough to see the humor. Out-of-towners notwithstanding, Rose's backers, who now included such "luminaries" as Yermie Stern, Sam Rosoff, and John Steinberg, were delighted with the Music Hall and seemed ready to invest in yet another Rose night spot. In July, Billy announced plans for a "Broadway Circus" presented in a huge main tent seating eight thousand people. Late that month, he left for Europe to sign up the needed talent.

Fanny did not go along. More and more, their marriage fell apart, as Rose's new successes further swelled his ego and exposed him to the charms of beautiful women younger and more eager than his famous wife. His hours at both the Casino and the Music Hall were irregular at best, and even his 4:00 A.M. meetings with Fanny over fried egg sandwiches became infrequent by the time the *Ziegfeld Follies* closed on Broadway on June 9, 1934.

Having renewed her contract with the Shuberts on May 30 ("in accordance with our recent conversation and in consideration of $1.00 and other valuable considerations paid by you to me"), Fanny went on the road with the *Follies* in the fall. The tour opened at Chicago's Grand Opera House on September 4, 1934, and Fanny, Willie Howard, and Sophie Tucker were frequent dinner guests at Yansci Dolly's home. One night was well recalled by Yansci's daughter, Klari.

"Fanny had her little pet dog with her, a tiny little thing; I don't know what the breed was. It was so small that she could put it in her pocketbook, and she carried it everywhere.

"She even had it on her lap at dinner. The dog was never fed dogfood; she simply took little tidbits from her plate and put them down on her napkin for him. The conversation was rather quiet for awhile. Then she looked down at the dog on her lap and suddenly said 'Eat, ya rat!' "

Eve Arden always remembered Fanny, all in black, the little dog peering from her muff, preparing to debark from the train after an all-night poker session with the crew, and stating, in her inimitable way, "It took the Shuberts to invent a new way to kill the Jews!"

The tour was mostly pleasant, Fanny having long forgiven Willie Howard for his tactical upstaging of her on opening night at the Winter Garden. After nine weeks in Chicago, the show moved on to St. Louis, Cincinnati, and Cleveland, where Fan hypnotized a young man at a party. She had been introduced to mesmerism in New York, but had never practiced it until then. It would remain a passion, trotted out from time to time at gatherings of friends.

"I think Fanny really loved touring," Eve recalled. "It was a lonely life, though, away from her children, and she often asked me to have dinner with her in her dressing room between performances. In those moments she would tell me of her life with Nicky Arnstein and her final disillusionment with him. She had a certain toughness and was capable of occasional small cruelties, but in those moments of confiding in me I felt great empathy with her."

In Kansas City during Christmas–New Year's week, Fan waited at the station for the train on which Mademoiselle was due with Fran and Bill. When the train pulled in, Fanny embraced both her children, failing to note that Billy Rose and not the governess had brought them from New York.

Rose had brought not just the children, but the presents, time, and spirit to make 1934 the greatest Christmas Fran and Bill had ever spent. If Mademoiselle had truly poisoned the kids' minds against their stepfather (whom they called "Mr. Rose," not "Billy," and never anything like "Father"), she had not stopped them from enjoying the train ride to Kansas City. Billy could indeed be charming on occasion, and his ideas made the trip great fun for Fran and Bill. The good times continued in Kansas City, and Fanny was very sad when Billy took the kids back to New York at the end of the week.

Billy had returned from Paris in September to find there had been no checks from the Luciano-Stern syndicate, which now owed him sixteen thousand dollars. Rose attended both the Music Hall and the Casino that same evening, and was shocked to find cheap acts, cheap service, and cheap food at the Casino. He also learned an organizer from the American Federation of Actors who had gone backstage to unionize performers at the Music Hall had been beaten by two thugs in the control of Luciano.

Rose demanded all the money due him, the removal of his name from both establishments, and the return of the scenery and costumes from *Crazy Quilt* he had loaned Stern for a summer show at the Casino. When they threatened to get tough, he called his old employer Bernard Baruch, who contacted J. Edgar Hoover through Attorney General Homer Cummings. There was no trouble, and Billy was able to swear out a writ of replevin and secure his scenery and costumes. Rose never received the sixteen thousand dollars owed him, but he had the satisfaction of seeing both clubs go into bankruptcy within three months.

The end of the partnership brought a temporary halt to Billy's proposed "Broadway Circus," but Rose was huddling with wealthy backers like Jock Whitney within weeks of his return from Kansas City. His revised idea called for a big musical extravaganza centering around a circus, to be produced at the Hippodrome and titled *Jumbo*. This show was destined to epitomize Billy Rose, a five-foot-three, low-grade genius with built-in needs for great success and even greater size.

While Billy planned his monuments, Fanny played one-nighters. At one point, in late February, she, her mother, and her daughter were involved in a triple automobile crash near Lancaster, Pennsylvania. Fan escaped unhurt, but Rosie, Frances, and three occupants in the other cars were slightly injured. In the hospital, a semiconscious Rosie reached, as if by instinct, for her jewels.

The *Ziegfeld Follies* closed in New Haven on March 16, 1935. Following the last performance, which was taped in its entirety, some two hundred Yale students tried to crash the stage door and get at the showgirls. A tough stage crew held them off until a riot squad appeared. Five college boys were finally arrested.

So ended the first *Follies* without Ziegfeld.

Back in New York, Fanny could be found most nights at Lindy's, swapping gossip with performers, agents, and songwriters. Harry Warren, composer of five songs in *Crazy Quilt,* introduced Fanny to Gary Stevens, an eighteen-year-old college student Fanny labelled "smart, precocious, and knowledgeable," unaware that Gary had been in show business for five years. "She took a liking to me," recalled Stevens. "Bernie Sobel had informed me about her helping Ziegfeld in the months before his death, and I told her what a wonderful thing she had done. She only said, 'Please, I don't want to discuss it.'

"She took me and a group of people out to Fire Island that summer, hiring some cars that took us out to Bayshore, and a boat that took us to the island. We got there around noon, and got back about midnight after we'd been Fanny's guests at a big, lavish dinner."

Fanny spent that summer on Fire Island playing hostess to scores of friends, including Mildred Harris (Jed's sister), Ann Pennington, and a Clifford Odetts contingent of left-wing theatre people. Jimmy Durante was there frequently, entertaining Fanny's other guests at the piano while his wife, Jeanne, sat quietly in a corner.

George Gershwin was another guest, and Frances, who had been treated to first playings of the songs in *Sweet and Low* and *Crazy Quilt,* now heard the score of *Porgy and Bess* played, by its composer, months before it opened.

And there was Fanny's husband, Billy. "When I first met Billy," Mildred Harris recalled, "he seemed devoted to Fanny. But when I saw them at Fire Island, I didn't see that devotion. He was kind of sullen, not enthusiastic with his arm around her like he'd been a few years before.

"Bea Lillie was there very often. They had a big card game on Saturday night, and Bea was so funny because she didn't play very good poker. Billy Rose used to get very impatient with her and tell her, 'Hurry up and bid.' She got very angry one time, threw the cards down, and stormed out saying, 'It's my money. I can do what I want with it.' "

Fanny had full houses on the weekends, but entertained small groups of friends practically every night. She invited Mildred's friends, Ruth and Jerry Goode, one evening, and prepared a menu specially for Jerry, then on a strict diet.

Fanny would do anything for—and sometimes to—her friends. She was able to hypnotize every guest she had on Fire Island except Ben Hecht—who *wanted* to be hypnotized. The sessions frightened Dell, who sometimes wondered whether "Miss Fanny" was supernatural.

Fanny had indulged her son Bill's obvious artistic talent—first publicly displayed on sidewalks near the West Side townhouse—by allowing him to study art with Henry Bodkin, cousin of the Gershwins. As if to underscore Bill's efforts, Fanny also took up painting, her first extensive attempts at art since childhood. Hating to do anything alone, she bought an extra paint set and had Herman, her German cook, paint along beside her near the beach. She gradually acquired skill, and painting soon ranked number four on Fanny's hobby list—behind interior decorating, card playing, and (for now) hypnosis.

Billie Burke, still trying to pay off her husband's massive debts, had already sold the film rights to the Ziegfeld story to Universal, which in turn sold them to M-G-M. As was the case with Shubert's *Ziegfeld Follies,* Ziggy's other stars were either dead, not available, or wanted too much money to be in the proposed film. Fanny alone, of all of Flo's great stars, would play herself in *The Great Ziegfeld.*

The Great Ziegfeld was the first of Hollywood's musical tributes to the names of Broadway's Golden Age. It portrayed Ziegfeld as a passionate, sincere, and polished genius who yearned for "more steps" to glorify the beauty of women and the theatre of his era. The less endearing aspects of his life and person were ignored, as they would be in film bios of such other greats as Cohan, Jolson, Tanguay, Bayes, and Cantor.

Fanny substituted for Ginger Rogers on Al Jolson's *Shell Chateau* program on September 14 before leaving for Hollywood. Her segment in the film depicted her "discovery" by Ziegfeld (there is no intermediary) and introduction of the song "My Man," re-creating—faithfully, to some extent—the master's inspiration for her torn and shabby costume. Fanny's total time on screen was under ten minutes.

On the sixteenth of November, just before rehearsals for the second Shubert *Ziegfeld Follies* started, Fanny accompanied her husband to the opening of *Jumbo* at the Hippodrome. It was easily the biggest success of Rose's life, and enthroned him as, in all probability, the most important show-man in the country. Critics, who gave plaudits to the show, called Rose "the Bantam Barnum." Billy was too proud to be offended.

Jumbo, or "Billy Rose's *Jumbo,*" as all billing read, was easily the big-gest show on Broadway since the 'twenties, with a cast including twenty principals, Paul Whiteman and his orchestra, nine showgirls, sixteen dancers, seventeen "Allan K. Foster Girls," and thirty members of Hen-derson's Singing Razorbacks, not to mention a huge elephant, "Big Rosie," in the title role. Jimmy Durante as "Claudius B. Bowers" was the only "name" in the production, and the book about the love affair between the children of rival circus owners named Considine and Mulligan, bore more resemblance to the love affair between the children of rival vaude-ville magnates John W. Considine and Alexander Pantages than to Shakespeare's Romeo and Juliet. Ben Hecht and Charles MacArthur wrote the libretto, and the show's score, which included "The Most Beautiful Girl in the World," "Little Girl Blue," and "Over and Over Again," was by Richard Rodgers and Lorenz Hart.

Percy Hammond of the *New York Herald Tribune* called *Jumbo* "a sane and exciting compound of opera, animal show, folk drama, harle-quinade, carnival, circus, extravaganza and spectacle," while Robert Gar-land of the *World-Telegram,* seldom shy of using accolades, said it was "a happy, haphazard harlequinade . . . something different, something ex-citing that even a city slicker can enjoy." Most of the other critics wrote along similar lines, with a few reservations about the plot being "fool's fodder for dullwits," as John Anderson called it in the *New York Journal.* Frank Norris of *Time* may have been closest to the truth when he called *Jumbo* "a megalomaniac medley of musicomedy and circus, with the cir-cus gaining a shade the advantage."

The megalomania was that of Billy Rose, now at least as big a name in show business as Fanny. "The Mighty Mite" had arrived and found his niche—a New York hybrid of Ziegfeld and Barnum.

The new Shubert *Ziegfeld Follies* arrived, too—though later than ex-pected.

The show opened out of town at the Boston Opera House on Mon-day night, December 30, 1935, and while Lee Shubert was later criticized for making this *Follies* "more Shubert and less Ziegfeld" than the pre-vious edition, he did not skimp on either sets or costumes. Young Vincente Minnelli, who designed the sets, was lauded for repeating "on an even more elaborate and costly scale the success that he had with the backgrounds of *At Home Abroad*," and Raoul Péne Du Bois did the costumes, which included clothing the renowned "no clothes" horse, Josephine Baker.

There were almost as many people in the *Ziegfeld Follies* of 1936 as Billy had in *Jumbo*, and several programmed numbers were omitted at the opening in Boston due to lack of preparation. Fanny's insomnia grew worse under the tension, and a doctor gave her a liquid sedative to ease her nerves. He warned her not to exceed the dosage of two teaspoonfuls at any given time, but Fanny felt especially uncomfortable one night, and took an extra nip before the show. During the performance, she took other nips, and finally, near the end of the number titled "Modernistic Moe," she slipped down to the floor and fell asleep. The curtain fell, and irate patrons, under the impression Fanny had been drunk, besieged the box office for refunds.

John Murray Anderson, who staged the show, had his hands full getting the production ready to open at the Winter Garden on Thursday night, January 30, 1936. Anderson, however, was an experienced professional who could, and did, save many a doomed show. This *Follies* would prove no exception.

The 1936 edition of the *Ziegfeld Follies* had, in fact, one of the greatest talent line-ups seen on Broadway since the *Follies* of the war years. Fanny got first billing—solo spotted right below the title—followed by Bob Hope, Gertrude Niesen, Hugh O'Connell, Harriet Hoctor, Eve Arden, Judy Canova, Cherry and June Preisser, and John Hoysradt. The great Nicholas Brothers were billed further down, along with Duke McHale, Rodney McLennan, Stan Kavanagh, Ben Yost's Varsity Eight, George Church, "and Josephine Baker."

The material again reeked of that "sophistication" so familiar in 'thirties revues on Broadway. Fanny sang a satire on torch songs called "He Hasn't a Thing Except Me" in the first act. But in "The Sweepstakes Ticket," a return to earlier comedy forms, she mugged and displayed her strong flair for physical comedy as Norma Shaffer, a woman who wins the Great Sweepstakes only to find that her husband, Monty (Hugh O'Connell) has lost the ticket.

Fanny carried the show. Brooks Atkinson lauded the "coarse elegance she contrived for the upper-class English of Ira Gershwin's 'Fancy Free,' " and Fanny and Bob Hope anticipated *Dames at Sea* by more than thirty years in "The Gazooka," a "Super-Special Musical Photoplay" starring

"Ruby Blondell and Bing Powell with a Large Supporting Cast of Featured Players" in four scenes.

The comparatively short Act II saw Fanny play "Myrtle Oppenshaw" in "Amateur Night," with Hugh O'Connell as "Major Bones," Judy Canova as "Elvira Mackintosh," and Eve Arden as "Lady DeVere." But it was in "Modernistic Moe," a devastating satire on Martha Graham's modern dance movement, that she scored her greatest triumph of the evening. Fanny played this scene with her hair down—a rarity for her at that time—sticking out her thighs and twisting her thin body and mobile face in an outrageous parody of Graham's theories and performance. This grotesque burlesque was capped when, inspired by the left-wing intellectuals she'd entertained on Fire Island, Fanny shouted "Rewolt!" with her eyes crossed. The loudest laughs came from the leftists. Brooks Atkinson called it "Fanny in top form."

There was also a new Snooks routine called "Baby Snooks in Hollywood," with Eve Arden repeating her role as Snooks' mother (now programmed as "Mrs. Higgins"), and young Bob Hope, fresh from his roles in *Roberta* and *Say When,* as a director driven to distraction by Snooks' impossible demands and temper-tantrums.

The show was a triumph for all concerned, though Josie Baker's singing and dancing were called disappointing by some critics. Anderson was lauded for the way he pulled the show together, while Fanny and Bob Hope walked away with the performing honors.

The *Ziegfeld Follies* of 1936 looked like it would be among the longest-running shows of the decade. Fanny, however, came down with the flu a few days after the show opened and was forced to withdraw from the cast. She had to miss the premiere broadcast of the new *Ziegfeld Follies of the Air* on February 22 (Minerva Pious, "Mrs. Nussbaum" of Fred Allen's "Allen's Alley," subbed), and Robert J. Landry said she was "in poor scoring trim" on her first appearance a week later. "She was a comedienne without comedy," he wrote.

> Her material left her fighting a losing battle. In the studio she seemed to get a few snickers on mugging. But on the loudspeaker, cold and callous, this didn't register. It was pretty plaintive humor all the way.
>
> Came up first with a string of wisecracks that lacked glitter and were unbecoming to a woman. Later did her Snooks. This was mildly diverting. Still later did a satire that wasn't satirical on a female platform-demon discussing international affairs. Finally she sang "I'm an Indian," with most of the lines either brushed up for radio or shorn of

most of their force when divorced from the mimicry that makes this performer stand out behind the footlights. It was a disappointment.

Fanny, who rejoined the *Follies* at the Winter Garden, was still not in the best of health, and had to clear her throat in her Snooks scene with Hope. "That's my cold clearing up," she ad-libbed at one point.

"I thought you were just oversexed," was Bob Hope's quick reply. The line stayed in.

Fanny's first real health problems surfaced in the spring, forcing her to withdraw from the cast on May 9, 1936. This time, Lee Shubert did not bother to put in a replacement; he simply closed the show after 113 Broadway performances.

Dr. Joseph S. Diamond diagnosed Fanny's trouble as radiculitis—neuritis of the spine. "Fanny Brice is a sick woman," said the *New York Evening Journal*. "Much sicker than people know. It is said she may never appear on the stage again. Most of us who appreciate her for the great artist she is hope that isn't so."

Fan's condition was extremely complicated if not very serious. Having already lost most of her teeth to decay, she decided to have the remaining ones extracted that summer after being told that it would help her other health problems. Fanny soon had three complete sets of false teeth—one for eating, one for work on stage, and one to wear when she went out. One set, reportedly costing $7,500, was made of platinum.

By June, she had recovered, and was seen at nightclub after nightclub, "sitting around at ringside tables until three o'clock in the morning," as she told the *New York World-Telegram*. When not at nightclubs—which she often claimed not to like—Fanny stayed on Fire Island going over material for the *Follies* with Bobby Clark—who would replace Hope when the show reopened in September.

That 1935–36 season saw the Rose–Brice marriage go from cool to almost frigid. Billy, as producer of the monumental *Jumbo*, no longer looked on Fanny as the high goddess of show biz. Nor had he any further need for Fanny's fame or talent. Rose now craved the kind of feminine companionship, sans Fanny's intelligence and caustic comments, that would feed his growing ego and Napoleonic complex. There were plenty of ambitious, sweet young ladies eager to oblige.

Fanny, for her part, was not about to change. That summer, as she recuperated from radiculitis, Billy went to Fort Worth, where the Centennial Committee had asked him to stage their Frontier Exposition. Billy planned a Wild West show called the "Frontier Fiesta," an 1870 "Honky-

Tonk Cabaret called the "Pioneer Palace," a mammoth outdoor café called the "Casa Mañana," and a revival of *Jumbo.*

In Fort Worth, Rose bought himself a cowboy outfit, and was filmed for the newsreels as he sat astride a horse, waving his hat in the air and shouting, "I'll make Texas the biggest state in the union."

Fanny saw the pictures and sent Rose a wire: ONE JEW COMIC IN THE FAMILY IS ENOUGH.

Fanny went to Fort Worth for the opening a short time later. Eddie Foy, Jr., was playing Durante's part in *Jumbo,* but the role, along with most of the plot, was eliminated shortly after the Exposition opened on July 18. Rose was paid one hundred thousand dollars for his role as grand producer, thus becoming one of America's first major non-profit show-men—thirty years ahead of Joseph Papp.

Fanny, in the meantime, went back to New York and to rehearsals for the new edition of the 1936 *Ziegfeld Follies.* It was a cheaper show than that of nine months earlier, due to the departures of Bob Hope, Eve Arden, Gertrude Niesen, and several other increasingly expensive names. Gypsy Rose Lee was added to the cast—accepting a small fraction of her burlesque salary in order to gain prestige far above that she earned at Minsky's. Bobby Clark, complete with leer and painted-on glasses, was now principal comedian—his first engagement since the death of his partner, Paul McCullough, by suicide months earlier.

Clark took over most of Bob Hope's role. One new sketch was added, called "Dr. Fradler's Dilemma," in which he did a classic nutty-doctor routine with Gypsy Rose Lee as a sexy nurse and Fanny as "Mrs. Phoebe Schwartz," a suffering Jewish patient.

Fanny also returned to radio as the star of *Revue de Paree,* a half-hour weekly show sponsored by the R. L. Watkins Company (makers of Dr. Lyons' Tooth Powder) over the National Broadcasting Company's Blue Network. "Baby Snooks" provided most of Fanny's material, and she found the perfect actor to play Lancelot "Daddy" Higgins, Snooks' ex-asperated father.

He was Hanley Stafford, a thirty-seven-year-old stage and radio actor who had left his native England as a boy, appeared in Broadway plays like *Double Dummy,* and landed a bit part in *The Great Ziegfeld.* "As soon as the second one began to read, I knew he was the one," remembered Fanny twelve years later. " 'But there are thirty-eight more waiting to be heard,' I was told. 'He's the man,' I said, and he was." Stafford's perfor-mance as the irritated "Daddy," forced to answer endless queries of "Why?" from Snooks, made him one of the most popular second bananas in the history of radio.

Fanny's life increasingly revolved around her children. Frances, having overcome a stammer, was now an attractive girl of seventeen who idolized her mother and took part in school productions of *Everyman, The Devil's Disciple,* and *The Ivory Door* at Dalton. A young woman of considerable achievement, she was also a fine equestriene, winning several cups in junior competitions held in Madison Square Garden; she even nursed ambitions for the opera. Bill was fifteen, smitten with a young girl in the *Follies* and interested in scenic design as well as painting.

On Saturday, October 17, 1936, Fran made her Broadway debut as a showgirl in the *Follies* with two lines to speak. Nick, then living on the West Coast with Irene, came back to New York to see her play the same part the following weekend.

A reporter from the *New York World–Telegram* interviewed Fanny and her children at this time. Fanny did not see why the subject of Nick Arnstein had to be brought up.

"The children have not seen their father since the divorce in 1927," explained Fanny, "but occasionally they exchange letters and photographs."

Frances did not wish to discuss him, but Bill's response to the reporter's question, "What do you remember of your father?" may have summed up both the children's attitudes toward Nick. A look of puzzlement came over the boy's face.

"He was very tall, wasn't he?" he asked, looking to his mother. Fanny nodded.

CHAPTER *13*

Divorced Again: "That Rat"

T he revived *Ziegfeld Follies* of 1936 racked up 112 continuous performances at the Winter Garden before taking to the road on Christmas day. Fanny and Billy had abandoned Sixtieth Street in favor of a fourteen-room apartment at 1212 Park Avenue. "Unless I'm broke," Billy confided at this time, "I'll never let Fanny go out on the road again. It's terrible to come home to fifty-six bare walls." Not that Rose was lonely very often.

Fanny was again a frequent dinner guest at Yansci Dolly's home during the show's ten-week engagement in Chicago. "One time," recalled Klari Marbi, "the adults were at the table, on the subject of the children having to get braces for their teeth, and in a rather unexpected way, being very, very demonstrative, Fanny simply remarked, 'Teeth, teeth. My teeth. No good, no good. Had them all out.' As if to prove the point, she took out both her plates and put them on the table.

"My mother had been approached to put some entertainment together for a local charity. Roger Pryor and his orchestra were appearing at the College Inn at the Sherman Hotel, and the benefit was held there. It turned into a bit of a fiasco, though, because their Shubert contracts prohibited Fanny and Gypsy Rose Lee from performing under any circumstances. They could be interviewed, but not perform.

"The audience was terribly disappointed, so Ann Pennington was called upon to dance. Penny was not under contract to anybody, but she was not in costume and had not had a rehearsal. She simply went up to the orchestra conductor, Roger Pryor, told him what to play, and went into a wild . . . shimmy, or call it what you will.

"In those days, we didn't have panty hose. Women had garter belts, and Penny's skirt was flying. It didn't look particularly attractive, and every now and then I heard Fanny let out a roar, 'Keep your skoit down!' Ann, however, either didn't hear or just ignored her. She was caught up in her dancing."

Penny, who had danced as "Little Egypt" in Billy's Fort Worth "Casa Mañana," travelled with the Follies as Fan's guest. Only two years Fanny's junior, she had come across as remarkably young in a screen test and was signed to play herself in *The Great Ziegfeld*. As show business changed, as work became less plentiful and Penny herself aged, she lived, increasingly, with Fanny—never asking for a dime, yet graciously accepting Fanny's lodging and free meals.

Penny had been one of the highest-paid performers on Broadway in the early 1920s. Changing career fortunes, the stock market crash, Penny's own generosity, and her love of race track betting had now left her destitute, but cheerful. "The way I look at it," said Penny, "I started in this town with nothing, and I've got nothing today." Fanny, who liked strength, admired her friend's attitude. Fan, however, knew and valued money far too highly to wind up in that position.

The *Follies* had played most of the major cities in the East and middle West by the time it closed on Wednesday night, May 26. Fanny immediately went to Cleveland for the opening of *Billy Rose's Aquacade*, a water spectacular he was producing for the Great Lakes Exposition. The *Aquacade* had everything that Rose thought was important—prestige, size, and, this time, water, anticipating the spectaculars M-G-M would later mount for Esther Williams.

But Billy Rose's original *Aquacade* had its own swimming Venus—a former Olympic champion named Eleanor Holm.

Eleanor Holm was one of the small handful of female sports stars who transcended their importance as athletes prior to the television era. The youngest of six children, born in Brooklyn, she was the only one not "scared to death of the water" and took to swimming at the age of ten in 1924, when the family was summering in Long Beach.

In 1927, after only six months' formal training, Eleanor won the national junior outdoor medley title and gained her first senior crown. One year later, she placed fifth in the Olympic Games in Amsterdam. By mid-1931, when she graduated from Erasmus Hall High School in Brooklyn, the seventeen-year-old Miss Holm held at least twenty-eight national marks, many of them virtually world's standards—more credited records than any other female swimmer in the world. She won the 100-meter backstroke in the 1932 Olympics, held in Los Angeles, and was signed to a contract by Warner's.

Eleanor's desire to retain her amateur status and participate in the 1936 Olympics in Berlin forced Warner's to avoid casting her in aquatic roles, a situation that kept her from becoming a film swim star ten years before Esther Williams. Eleanor was given a six-month course in dramatic training to prepare her for "conventional parts."

There would be no "conventional parts" for Eleanor, however, who did not display much aptitude for acting. She posed for loads of photographs (usually in swimsuits, as she had a stunning figure) swam, collected her paychecks, and went out with actors and musicians. On September 2, 1933, the nineteen-year-old Holm married Arthur L. Jarrett, a West Coast crooner and bandleader, in the Church of the Good Shepherd in Beverly Hills.

On September 8, 1934, Eleanor Holm set new records for the 50-and 100-yard backstrokes. She planned to turn professional after the '36 Olympics, though her amateur status was even then being questioned by the Amateur Athletic Union. On May 30, 1936, Eleanor started her Olympic comeback by setting a new American mark for the 200-yard backstroke, winning the Metropolitan A.A.U. women's 220-yard backstroke championship a little over three weeks later and the national title in the same event just one week after that. In July, she sailed for Hamburg with the rest of the Olympic team on board the SS *Manhattan,* Artie Jarrett having stayed in California.

Eleanor had publicly stated that she "trained on champagne and caviar," a statement that embarrassed the American Olympic Committee and the A.A.U. But Eleanor was simply being honest; she was a natural swimmer who swam in the ocean nearly every day in summer and went into the pool two or three times in the winter. Before serious competitions, she trained hard for a short time and was in top condition. Otherwise, she liked good times.

On Friday night, July 17, 1936, on board the *Manhattan* in the Atlantic Ocean, she attended an all-night party and refused to heed hints that she return to the athletes' quarters until well into the morning. Eleanor drank champagne at this party, stating she was "free, white, and twenty-two" when bartenders and waiters were reluctant to serve her.

Statements by the official chaperones caused Eleanor to be issued a stern warning and given one more chance. Eleanor was reported as "the hardest working athlete on the boat" from that day on, but Avery Brundage, head of the American Olympic Committee, was one of those embarrassed by her publicity, her thinly veiled contempt for starch-white "amateurism," and her movie contract. Another minor "offense" was the excuse he used to drop her from the team.

Eleanor Holm attended the 1936 Olympic Games as a reporter for

American newspapers. Artie Jarrett joined his wife at this point, and even considered taking action against the A.O.C. The situation did not cool until the Amateur Athletic Union, of which Brundage was also president, "asked" Eleanor to turn in her amateur card.

Eleanor tried to regain her amateur status in the fall, but hopes of that soon faded, and, on February 23, 1937, she signed a $30,000 contract to appear in *Billy Rose's Aquacade* at the Great Lakes Exposition in Cleveland. "I'd have given up this offer in a minute if the A.A.U. had voluntarily reinstated me," she told the Associated Press, "but I know they won't. If I'd apply for reinstatement, it would just mean slinging that Olympic mud all over again.

"I've had all kinds of offers, thanks to Avery Brundage and the other A.A.U. officials, and I've turned them all down, but I read in the papers the other day that even the metropolitan district committeemen are against me, so I decided to cash in."

Billy Rose later said he fell in love with Eleanor the first time he saw her dive into the water in the *Aquacade*. In fact, he had been smitten the first time Eleanor's agent, Louis (Blinky) Irwin, brought her to his office in the Wurlitzer Building. She was young, vibrant, had a dazzling smile, and radiated good health. Billy, still a miser with non-star performers, willingly signed her at $750 a week.

He started having "business" lunches with her once they were in Cleveland. They dined together after a few days, and were almost constant companions by the time the *Aquacade* opened on May 29, 1937.

If Fanny saw a look of fascination on her husband's face that night, she failed to note it at the time. Eleanor was an alluring woman, but alluring women were a staple of the show world Billy had been part of for seventeen years.

The Rose–Holm romance blossomed after Fanny returned to New York. He found her both vivacious and intelligent, yet uncritical—girlishly excited by his plans without the knowing cynicism that made Fanny often difficult to bear. Eleanor was also slightly shorter than Billy, meaning she looked up to him both mentally and physically. Fanny was incapable of either.

Eleanor was also more than twenty years younger than Fanny, and, while not photogenically beautiful by Hollywood standards, was vibrantly attractive and magnetic. She had a firm, sun-browned, perfectly proportioned body, grayish blue eyes that twinkled mischievously, and, like Fanny, she was a good listener. Billy Rose appreciated that.

The only thing that kept Rose from giving Eleanor his complete attention was the reopening of the Frontier Exposition in Fort Worth. Fanny, who would play a featured role in *Swing Fever*, an M-G-M musical with Allan Jones, Billie Burke, and teen-aged Judy Garland, showed up for the June 26 opening on her way out to Hollywood.

"At that time," remembered Billy, "I was living in a small room at the Fort Worth Athletic Club and not liking it much.

" 'This marriage is only good for the telephone company,' I told Fanny. 'I wish you could stay here. It gets mighty lonely on the pampas.' " Fanny's answer was to try to talk Billy into becoming a producer for M-G-M, where she was now under contract. Billy, who was making more per year than almost anyone at M-G-M save Mayer, Irving Thalberg, and Greta Garbo, gave the matter little thought before Fanny left for Hollywood.

Fan had tended to compare any possible romance between Billy and Eleanor to Rose's frequent flings with chorines in New York. But Billy's words on this occasion sounded strange, and when a friend told Fanny she had seen Billy going into Eleanor's room in Cleveland's Lakeshore Hotel, Fanny phoned, told Eleanor she was "Mrs. Rose looking for Mr. Rose," and promptly hung up the receiver.

The call just served to move the situation forward. At 5:30 A.M. on Sunday, July 18, Eleanor phoned her husband, then appearing at the Pan-American Exposition in Dallas, and said she wanted a divorce.

Two days later, Eleanor made public her request. "But maybe there won't be a divorce if we are lucky enough to get together somewhere," she told the press. Jarrett refused to see interviewers, but friends said he was heartbroken. Eleanor, careful to protect herself and Billy, said that she was "burned up" that her name had been linked in gossip with that of "Mr. Rose."

Billy had returned, albeit briefly, to New York. "I know nothing about it except as the producer of the show in which she is the star," he said. "I am married to Miss Brice and I intend to stay so." Questioned in Beverly Hills, where she had rented the estate of the Countess di Frasso, Fanny said she didn't "know a thing about it. . . . I certainly would feel unflattered if just a swimmer got him. Probably she can beat me in the water—but that's all."

Fanny kept her doubts and questions to herself. Allan Jones remembered her as "private but not aloof" on the set of *Swing Fever* (now retitled *Everybody Sing*). "She spent most of the time in her dressing room when she wasn't working."

Everybody Sing was a forerunner of the "Let's-Put-On-a-Show" films Judy Garland later co-starred in with Mickey Rooney. The Bellaire family is a nutty theatrical clan with more ego than talent; the exception is young Judy, who gets herself thrown out of one exclusive private boarding school after another. Judy finally teams up with Ricky Saboni (Jones), the family's cook, and puts on a new musical producion that keeps the Bellaires' fortunes from becoming theatrical history.

Fanny played Olga Chekaloff, a Russian-Jewish maid, while Reginald Owen and Billie Burke played Mr. and Mrs. Bellaire. Fanny's finest moments were in songs, "Quainty, Dainty Me," another one of her self-mocking ballet parodies, and "Why? Because!" a duet with young Garland that saw Fan as Baby Snooks.

While Fanny worked in Hollywood, Rose worked and played and travelled between Cleveland, Fort Worth, and New York. Eleanor stayed in Cleveland in the *Aquacade* until late August, when she left for Hollywood to play Jane in Sol Lesser's *Tarzan's Revenge* at Twentieth Century–Fox.

In October, Arthur Jarrett instructed his attorney, Martin Wifrey, to file suit for divorce the following February, when his legal residence of one year in Texas was completed. "Eleanor asked me four months ago for a divorce," he told a reporter from the Associated Press, "but so far has done nothing about it. I am seeking one of my own free will. I think it best for my own career and for hers that we go our respective ways alone."

Fanny had regarded Billy's affair with Eleanor as another of his show biz dalliances. But these statements, quickly relayed to her out in California, gave her pause. She had always told Billy their marriage would last "until you fall in love." If he had, why did she have to hear it second-hand? More bewildered at this point than injured, Fanny buried herself in her work.

Fanny did not go to out to Fort Worth for the opening of *Show of Shows*, Rose's latest production, at the Municipal Auditorium on November 5. Eleanor was there, having flown out from Los Angeles to be on Billy's arm. They no longer made a secret of their romance, and left for San Francisco a few days later, stopping off in Denver on November 12. It was there, pacing the floor of a luxurious suite at the Brown Palace Hotel, that Billy told the press he wanted a divorce. He said he had not seen Fanny for "about six or eight weeks, and then only for two days" when he was visiting on the West Coast. He claimed he had not told her that he wanted a divorce.

"But the writing's been on the wall for some time," he said. "It's no fun being married to an electric light. Miss Brice is one of the brightest and cleverest stars the stage or screen has ever had, but our careers clash. I have to travel a lot and I want my wife by my side.

"No one has been ousted in this case. It's just an instance of four bull-headed careers clashing. Miss Brice wants her career. Arthur Jarrett wants his. Miss Holm is willing to give up hers for me. I don't know why, but she is, and that's that."

Rose admitted that he and Eleanor had been "mumbling about getting married, and it was hard to get our plan in the open because we've gone the eternal triangle one better and our difficulties run into the quadrangle stage.

"I want you to get this straight and make it clear that there are no hard feelings among any of us involved. If I know Fanny Brice, she will simply say: 'Good luck, kids,' and go right ahead and get a divorce. We're all going to go on being friends. That is, all except Miss Holm and I— we love each other."

Fanny seemed amazed, but almost flip, when queried by reporters. "It's a fine way for two people to be gallivanting around the country together. I'm not used to that sort of thing. I guess it's what you call modern. I haven't talked to Mr. Rose or to a lawyer. Bea Lillie is here as my house guest, and I guess I'll talk to her."

Privately, she felt abandoned and betrayed. "Right up to the morning when I read the news in the papers, the news that he wanted a divorce, I thought we were friends. The first I knew that this had happened, the first hint I had, was that story in the papers. I hadn't had the slightest idea that there was anyone else. Why, if he had come to me and told me I would have said, 'Look, if that comes into your life, go right out and grab it.' It wasn't what he did that hurt me—more, yes, even more than Nicky—it was the way he did it. I knew then what Flo [Ziegfeld] had meant those years ago when he kept saying [*re* Lillian Lorraine's elopement with Fred Gresheimer], 'While I was away, she married him.' It was the 'while I was away' part that poisoned the wound. I didn't lose Billy Rose's love. I'd never had it. He'd never had mine. We both knew that. There was never anything between us but friendship and honesty."

With candor that was rare even for her, she complained that men liked women who were demonstrative in bed—whether they enjoyed the sex or not. At times, she blamed her own reserve—in evidence since the last time she had seen Nick in Roger Davis' apartment—for having crimped her second marriage. Over forty-five with two teen-aged children and a less-than-certain future in show business, she leaned, increasingly, on money and friendships as the mainstays of her life. "I found out I got great joy from my friends, because of the lack of emotion. When this thing [love] doesn't go on in your life, you're through in a way, because while it is there it's like a motor that's going, you have such vitality." At the age of forty-six, Fan lost that vitality for good.

She could not help feeling, with considerable justification, that her two husbands had used her. But where she saw Nick as weak, a fool despite his never-ending confidence attempts, she now regarded Billy as a "low down, no good louse." Gary Stevens, now a young agent, said she "spoke in a very derogatory manner about Billy" and rued the day they were married, saying that her friend, James J. Walker, would never have married them if he knew anything about "that rat." "Fanny said Billy was 'a little son of a bitch' in my presence," Stevens later recalled. "Then she looked at me, laughed, apologized, and told me to forget the 'little.'

"I thought Fanny was a very interesting, talented woman who never realized her potential. She seemed to have seven toes on the ground. She always seemed to doubt herself, to fear not being accepted. She looked upon herself as an awkward, unattractive woman."

And that is why Billy's desertion of her—in a cold, perfunctory, no-bones-about-it manner, hurt Fanny so deeply. Little Billy Rose had made her 'men will use me and then leave me" negative prophecy come true.

She flatly told the press she would not marry a fourth time. Fanny, unlike many famous women, kept her word.

M-G-M, impressed with her fine work in *Everybody Sing,* thought it might star Fanny in the years to come. But roles for Yiddish dialect comediennes were in short supply, particularly those that justified the use of high-priced stars like Fanny. The only two-reel comedies being cranked out were those started before 1935—Leon Errol, Edgar Kennedy, the Three Stooges, Our Gang, and a few others. There was no room or demand for a series of two-reelers starring a middle-aged Jewess. Nor was Fanny particularly interested in doing them.

But if movies had no place for Fanny, radio still beckoned. M-G-M had signed an agreement with General Foods that Robert J. Landry called of "historic significance. . . . For on November 4, 1937, a film studio boldly embraced as brother its erstwhile box office foe, radio. And, simultaneously, the sales technique of modern branded-article merchandising frankly went the whole distance, unabashed, into the deep mesa of theatricalism.

"Louis B. Mayer, the showman, symbolically presented C. M. Chester, the super-grocer, with a master key to the front gate of the M-G-M lot."

General Foods paid M-G-M $25,000 a broadcast for whatever stars Mayer could spare and were useful for promotions of new pictures. The weekly show, titled *Good News of 1938,* was slotted from nine to ten o'clock every Thursday night on N.B.C.'s Red Network. Fanny, playing "Baby

Snooks," with Hanley Stafford as "Daddy," first appeared on the fourth program in the series.

The first three broadcasts received short shrift from the critics, who recognized them for the well-produced, pretentious pastiches that they were. Baby Snooks put *Good News* on the hit list and started Fanny on the radio career she would continue for the rest of her short life.

Landry described Fanny's debut on the *Good News* program of November 25, 1937, as "one of the funniest of her radio-familiar Baby Snooks routines" and lauded her for "whamming a nice tally of guffaws." Fanny appeared as Snooks on all but one of the remaining *Good News* shows that season. Hanley Stafford was always Daddy but initially received no credit.

"We rehearsed at the El Capitan Theatre [later the Paramount] in Hollywood," remembered Jerry Hausner, who did trick voices on the show and was a friend of Stafford's. "One day, we worked all morning, and then broke for lunch. I asked Hanley if he wanted to grab a sandwich, and he said, 'Yeah, but wait until this place clears out.' When the theatre was empty, Hanley walked to the piano, where Robert Taylor, the m.c., had laid his script. Hanley had already done the part on *Good News* a few times. He was only getting thirty-five dollars a week and that was through the William Morris Agency. Fanny, who was getting thousands, didn't give a goddam who played that part. She was only wrapped up in herself, and didn't think it mattered who played 'Daddy.'

"The script read, 'Maxwell House presents *Good News of 1938* starring Tom Patricola, George Jessel, George White, Frank Morgan, and Fanny Brice as Baby Snooks.' Hanley took out his pencil and added ". . . with Hanley Stafford as Daddy.' Now other changes had been pencilled in by the script girl in Robert Taylor's absence, so Taylor just assumed it was another change and read it at the dress rehearsal. Nobody questioned it, so that's the way the broadcast was done. That's the way that Hanley got his billing, and it stayed the same for every broadcast."

On January 18, 1938, while Fanny was establishing a new career in radio, *Everybody Sing* was previewed at the Village Theatre in Westwood, California. Ads for the picture, which premiered in New York at the Capitol a couple of months later, called Fanny "The Baby Snooks of the Radio," leading Walter Winchell to ask, "Since when did Fannie Brice need any other introduction but Fannie Brice?" in his column in the *New York Mirror*. Reviews for the film called it "a swell show of its variety," and only the *World-Telegram* denounced it as "a rather commonplace and conventional musical comedy with a fine set of performances wasted on its machine-made plot mechanics.

"The film has a number of catchy tunes and several hilarious scenes, thanks to the efforts of Fannie Brice and Billie Burke, but for the most part the story it tells is stereotyped and the manner in which it tells it is wooden and uninspired. . . . The total effect is definitely disappointing."

Fanny, who did not attend the New York premiere, arrived there on the fifth of April to fight a lawsuit filed by theatrical agent Edgar Allen, who claimed she owed him $34,000 in commissions for his work on the Shubert *Ziegfeld Follies*. Billy, who was in New York with Eleanor, said that he was ready to aid Fanny.

"Allen was hired merely to set a deal and at no time acted as a booking agent for Miss Brice," Billy explained. Fanny simply called Allen "a rat," apparently projecting anger felt towards Rose onto the agent. Reporters greeting her in New York, naturally more interested in the Rose-Brice-Holm-Jarrett love quadrangle than in Fanny's response to Allen's lawsuit, asked her whether she would say that Billy Rose had left her bed and board.

Fanny raised her eyebrows. "Anyway," she quipped, "he left me bored."

Allen lost his case, and Fanny returned to Los Angeles for the remainder of the 1937–38 radio season. When *Good News* left the air on June 30, she spent the summer moving from the Countess' estate to a new place of her own at 312 North Faring Road in Holmby Hills. She was altering her life again—and for the final time.

Fanny had three other homes in California over the next dozen years: 14134 Riverside Drive in North Hollywood, 424 Comstock Avenue in Westwood, and a beach house down in Malibu. The Holmby Hills house, though, remained her mainstay. Soon after she bought it, Fanny sent for all her New York furniture and proceeded to redecorate. At the end, she had old furniture left over, so she built a guest house. Her daughter, Frances, thought this was extravagant. In later years, however, she was glad Fanny had done it. For a time, the guest house served as an art studio for Fan's son, Bill. During World War II, Fran lived there—with her own phone—while her husband, Ray, served in the Navy.

On October 1, 1938, Fanny filed a divorce complaint against Billy Rose in Los Angeles Superior Court, charging he had deserted her on June 10, 1937, and that for some time prior to their separation had fallen into the habit of quarrelling with her over trivial matters and of absenting himself from their home without offering explanation. The suit, filed by attorney Martin Gang under the names of Fanny and William Rosenberg, made no mention of Eleanor Holm.

Billy starred Eleanor in his 1939 and 1940 *Aquacades* at the New York

World's Fair. He opened Billy Rose's Diamond Horseshoe in New York, produced a few plays, and continued to make money from his seat in the upper reaches of the Ziegfeld Theatre he bought in the 1930s. When in California, he saw Fanny, and they looked to any neutral observer like two friends who had shared great old times. Fanny might have been brutally honest, but she had too much pride to let her hurt show, too much self-respect to let Rose or any other person think she had been left with scars.

But in fact the scars were there, whether or not Fanny let them show. In 1945, on a rare visit to New York, she and a friend passed the Ziegfeld Theatre. Pointing up to what she knew was Billy's office, Fanny said: "Right up there lurks the most evil man I've ever known."

Rose was faithful to Eleanor Holm only to a point; she found him in a "love nest" and finally divorced him. Billy then wed Milton Berle's ex-wife, showgirl Joyce Matthews, who divorced, remarried, and divorced him. Billy, notwithstanding a deep love for his own mother, regarded women as mere playthings. His marriage to Fanny lasted more than nine years legally, but was really over after three.

Fanny never liked Billy after their divorce, but she respected him—much the same way she respected Arnold Rothstein, English Bob the Nose-Biter, Large Face the Safecracker, and others she had met through Nick.

Billy Rose retreated from show business as the changing tax laws made theatre profits an increasingly rare commodity and changing tastes found him too weary and too rich—he never lost his interest in the stock market—to keep up with the times. The last fifteen years of his life saw him overseeing his by then-considerable wealth, collecting art, travelling, and living "the good life."

After Fanny's death, he became one of her staunchest supporters, telling all and sundry she was "Thunder in the Mountains" as a stage performer. He openly admitted, with no visible remorse, that he owed Fanny quite a bit, had used her contacts to create his legend, and betrayed her in return.

Rose, in retrospect, was showman rather than producer, businessman rather than songwriter, and more of a hustler than anything else. It was as a hustler, in fact, that Billy had his closest links with Nick and Fanny's father, Charlie Borach. All three men, in that respect, touched Fanny's need for romance—a need that seemed to lessen as she aged.

CHAPTER *14*

Life Without Roses

Fanny's whole life changed when she moved out to California. "Back in New York," she told one interviewer, "I get up at noon, maybe one o'clock. Out here I get up at 8 A.M. Back east I never ate breakfast. Since I've been in pictures I've had my first bowl of oatmeal in a third of a century."

Instead of spending her afternoons shopping and the nighttime, after a performance, with her friends, she now spent her days either working or decorating and her evenings painting. At ten o'clock, she went to bed—whether her insomnia would let her sleep or not.

"That's how Hollywood hits a Broadwayite. It makes a farmer out of him. I've got no desire to go out. Back east, I was prodded all day long by a sort of feverish flittering here and there.

"Back east, I couldn't wait until I got out of my apartment. Out here I don't want to stir from the set. Out here I can do nothing else all day long—and yet the day doesn't drag. I keep working.

"In New York, I'm always dressed up. Out here I don't get dressed unless I have to—and I don't have to. I lounge around in slacks.

"It's semi-tropical. It's like a resort. It's like being on a vacation."

Fanny, though, was basically a transplanted New Yorker, and she claimed the L.A. climate made her sleepy. "Hollywood," she once said, "is not good for the brain. It's only good for the body. The longer you're here, the stronger you grow—and the dumber."

Adele Moon was a casualty of the move westward. Remaining in New York, Dell worked for one well-to-do family after another, telling each one in succession that "Miss Fanny never did it this way," and losing every job she got until Fanny wrote her a letter: "Look kid, if you want to keep your job, don't mention Miss Fanny's name."

Fanny now had much more time for things like painting, and finished a rather nice canvas portrait of Gypsy Rose Lee before completing work on *Everybody Sing*. She became, in her own words, "a pretty good painter," after she improved her technique with a one-year course at the Chouinard Art Institute in Los Angeles.

Fanny looked at her career without illusion or the ego that clouds judgment in performers. She could not see herself in major roles on Broadway in that era, and a career in nightclubs was out of the question for people who, like Fanny, valued comfort.

Fan, as Baby Snooks, had found a home in radio, a medium that spelled easy money for performers who had earned their spurs in years of stage work. After three marriages, two kids, and more than a quarter of a century as a top-line performer, Fanny had decided to quit trooping; she was tired.

Fanny's health was yet another factor. The radiculitis, the loss of her teeth, and the recurring colds and assorted ailments that caused her to take aspirin in large amounts, made sunny southern California a welcome climate. She was also through with New York winters.

The end of her marriage to Billy Rose was the icing on the cake. Rose's presence in New York, the site of their all-night delicatessen courtship and romance, made the remoteness of L.A. much more inviting. Fanny Brice had cast her bread on the Pacific.

For a while, she had visions of more film work. In the fall of 1938, M-G-M announced that Fanny would play a fashion expert in *A New York Cinderella,* co-starring Spencer Tracy and Hedy Lamarr. The project suffered several postponements, though, and Fanny's part was written out by the time filming started, M-G-M finally released the picture as *I Take This Woman* in January 1940.

With film work nonexistent after *Everybody Sing* and radio demanding comparatively little of her time, Fanny found herself in need of a second career. Her interest in clothing lessened in the casual climate of Los Angeles, but her fascination with interior decorating fit in just as well there as back East—more so, considering New Yorkers spent so little time in their apartments.

Fanny though of charging for her efforts, and asked bit actress Barbara Barondess, also an interior decorator, about reasonable rates. "If you're a consultant," Barbara told her, "you charge by the hour. If you are buying and financing and selling the furniture, you figure what you think you're worth an hour, but tell them what you're going to charge them. Or, you're going to buy it wholesale and sell it retail; you know what the markup is. If you have a shop, employees, and an overhead, you have to charge the set wholesale and retail price, which is usually double, otherwise you cut down a little. And if you have a reputation . . . ." Fanny soon decided to do all her work for free.

It was in Hollywood, then, in the late 1930s, that Fanny Brice became the ultimate interior decorator—the official unofficial decorator to the stars—or, more properly, those stars she numbered as her friends—Katharine Hepburn, Ira Gershwin, Eddie Cantor, Dinah Shore, and a coterie of actors, agents, writers, and producers whom she took an interest in. Fanny's real hobby, in a sense, was people.

"Fanny," Ben Hecht wrote in *A Child of the Century,* "lived her life among people—a thing so rare as to make her seem off another planet. Like some fanatic at an easel, she was interested only in the sitter's face before her—the face of another human being. Into this face she stared with all her art and mysticism. On it she smiled. At it she cursed. Her love and hate were for the human face only. What went on behind such a face was Fanny's idea of the world."

Fanny was a humanist in the most basic sense; abstract concepts like existentialism and political philosophy simply held no interest for her. In October 1939, she, along with Beatrice Lillie and Joan Marsh, signed a Loyalty Pledge in accordance with Loyalty Days, endorsing the campaign against "irreligion, crime and other factors which suggest un-Americanism." Some may be disappointed, but Fanny saw it as nothing more significant than reciting the Pledge of Allegiance. She had virtually no politics, and little awareness of it, either.

Fanny met Franklin D. Roosevelt at a Gridiron Dinner, and came away with doubts about the President's sincerity. His manner, or, more pointedly, his smile, left her with the feeling that a con man lurked beneath the surface. But, encouraged by her friend, Frank Murphy, and by Dorothy Thompson's speech, Fanny donated two thousand dollars to the F.D.R. campaign fund in 1940. She thought it was tax deductible.

In the early thirties, just as Hitler was rising to power in Germany, a wave of anti-Semitism ran through Eastern Europe, and Hungary refused Molly Picon entry during her tour of Europe. When told of this—and more violent atrocities against the Jewish people—Fanny said, "I don't expect to be stopped in Hungary or Roumania or anywhere else I want to go. I'd like to see them try it—and as for this Hitler, a good, old fashioned Bronx cheer ought to put him in his place. Of course, when I do read or hear of prejudice against Jews, it burns me up. I don't want to read about it. I'd rather be ignorant. I guess there's nothing Jews can do about it beyond showing contempt for those indulging in it. Curiously enough, I've met with very little of it. I think I can honestly say it was never an obstacle in the path of my career." Fanny, in a sense, lived in an isolated world. She knew all kinds of people and was streetwise, but her life was really bordered by her family, show business, and a few selected interests such as painting, decorating, reading poetry (she knew an entire volume of Paul Geraldy by heart), and, sometimes, the occult. On certain evenings, she would hypnotize her friends or perform tricks of yoga. Sometimes, like the wise old gypsy that she partly was, Fanny would read palms and tell the future. "That Hungarian part of her was overwhelming," said her great-niece, Judy Altman. "She had this instinctive knowledge."

Bill and Frances went to Temple Emanuel, and Bill learned to read a little Hebrew. The woman whose career—at least to 1937—had been built on Jewish dialect was not at all religious and still spoke only a hundred words of Yiddish. Fan was Jewish, if you asked her, but not much more Jewish, ethnically, than Hungarian, American, or French. Her religion, in a real sense, was people. Her ethnicity might best be described as "New York."

Her practicality could verge on the eccentric. None of Fanny's friends knew where she hid her jewelry till an equally eccentric burglar found them wrapped in bathroom tissue in a window box containing potted plants. When the police caught the burglar, Fanny looked at him in wonder, said he was "a smart kid," and wanted him to tell her how he'd found them.

Good News of 1939 was on the air for forty-four weeks beginning September 1, 1938. Meredith Wilson was its musical conductor, projecting rural humor between waves of his baton and giving just a hint of the gentle genius that would surface in *The Music Man*—the show that took him years to write and years to get produced.

Robert Young returned as emcee, and Frank Morgan (in character as the world's biggest liar), Fanny, and Hanley Stafford were now established regulars. The hour-long show continued with M-G-M stars as guests, usually in excerpts from their up-and-coming pictures. Allan Jones, Tony Martin, and Connie Boswell alternated as semi-regular vocalists, and the theme song, "Always and Always," sung by a large mixed-voice chorus, was the acme of Euro-American "class." In the world of radio, to M-G-M, to General Foods, and to listeners, the *Good News* program was a prestige show worth much more than its ratings.

Fanny Brice was now known as Baby Snooks. It almost seemed as if her Broadway triumphs had never occurred, as if the brilliant comedienne and torch singer named Fanny Brice had been merely a prelude to her life as a mischievous tot who drove her father wild with questions and outrageous misbehavior.

Baby Snooks even marched in the Annual Hollywood Parade. Fanny, in her costume, had her chauffeur park a block from the parade, instructing him to wait there until she returned.

That year's parade was ruined by a thunderstorm erupting just as Fanny and her colleagues had completed half the march. Fanny ran back to the parking spot, but the chauffeur and car were gone.

About an hour later, Fanny's maid answered the door in Holmby Hills. There stood angry Fanny, still in her Snooks costume, soaked right to the skin.

"Where the hell," asked Fanny, "is that fucking chauffeur?"

That season saw the making and release of *Rose of Washington Square,* a Twentieth Century–Fox motion picture starring Alice Faye and Tyrone Powers in roles that looked suspiciously like Fanny and Nick Arnstein—especially when Alice, as "Rose Sargent," sang "My Man." Fanny saw the film, which featured Al Jolson in a supporting role, and promptly sued Twentieth Century–Fox, Alice Faye, Tyrone Power, and (she had never liked him) Jolson, for $100,000.

Fanny settled out of court, receiving $40,000. Nick, who filed a similar suit, got $25,000.

Fanny spent countless hours with Ida, Eddie Cantor's wife, that summer, decorating Cantor's home with her fine color sense, good taste, economy, and absolute intolerance of any interference.

Shortly after finishing the Cantor home, Fanny dropped by for a visit and, needing another seat, Eddie pulled the Chippendale desk chair toward the center of the playroom. Fan immediately yelled at him to put the chair back because he was "spoiling the whole balance of the room." Eddie was amazed, but she was serious. "Her taste was exquisite," Cantor later said.

Fanny was an astute shopper and knew the durable values of all kinds of antique furniture. A regular at Jack Earle's shop on Cahuenga Boulevard as well as several other similar establishments, she always fought for bargains for her "clients."

She was a woman of her generation—dominant in her own sphere but possessing little urge to go beyond it. That sphere included show business, and she brooked no bilge from anybody in it.

In 1934, while in Chicago, she, Sophie Tucker, and the Dolly Sisters played poker with two agents, Irving and Johnny Simon. The Simons won every hand until Fanny, who had played with men like Arnold Rothstein, got suspicious. Seeing how one agent palmed a card off to the other, Fanny grabbed both of their hands. "If I don't get my eight hundred dollars in ten minutes," she informed them, "I'm going to call Albee." Fanny got her money.

Good News of 1940 premiered on September 7, 1939, with guest star Gladys George, Frank Morgan, vocalist Connie Boswell, announcer Warren Hull, Walter Huston, Roland Young, Fanny, and Hanley Stafford. General Foods' contract with M-G-M having expired, the title of the show was changed to *Maxwell House Coffee Time* in October.

Stafford married for the second time that year. His new bride was a young, New York-born actress named Vyola Vonn. "I broke into the business when I was six years old as 'The Little Wild Rose of KHJ' doing cartwheels over the air; there was no visual. There were a lot of people from that group who went on to other big things. I went on to dancing and studied tap with the Mosconi Brothers and did a lot of vaudeville—never any dramatic stuff, but I did a lot of singing, dancing, and comedy. I was on some of Bob Hope's tours and sang with Bing Crosby on a couple of occasions.

"I met Hanley through Joe E. Brown. Hanley was a 'real killer.' He had just gotten done with one divorce and was then living in a bachelor pad near Pickfair. I was singing at the Beverly Wilshire Hotel at the time, and I met Fanny some time after I met Hanley—months before she attended our wedding."

Vyola remembers Fanny as "a wonderful woman. . . . She called everybody 'Kid,' as you know, and she could belch in front of anybody. Nobody would care. Anytime anybody went to Fanny, they would go up to the bedroom and find her in bed—belching. She liked to hold court in bed."

That fall saw the twenty-one-year-old Frances put her equestrian medals aside and marry Raymond Stark, a twenty-five-year-old Rutgers dropout, former vacuum-cleaner salesman, and rising star in the Warner Brothers publicity department.

When Frances first asked Fanny what she thought of Ray, Fan said he looked "like a rabbit."

The "rabbit," who had come to Hollywood in his mid-teens by sharing the driving and expenses with a middle-aged woman, soon became the West Coast entertainment editor for Fawcett Publications. Shortly after World War II, he became a literary agent, selling *Red Ryder* radio scripts written by his former Shakespeare professor at Rutgers. Using

Fanny as a contact, he corralled names like Ben Hecht, Raymond Chandler, and J. P. Marquand. Later, he joined the Famous Artists Agency and expanded his horizons to include actors—representing such top stars as William Holden, Kirk Douglas, Lana Turner, and Richard Burton. By the 1950s, he was one of the top agents in the business.

As Ray and Frances were married, Fan herself began a love affair with John Conte, a handsome singer, actor, and announcer more than twenty years her junior.

Fanny, a year older than John's mother, was painfully conscious of the difference in their ages. All her life, she'd disliked older women who went out with younger men. Now she found that she was doing it herself, and cringed at what she thought people were saying.

Part of John's appeal was the way that he made Fanny feel young. They would go fishing, and do other things that Fanny, born and bred in cities, experienced for the first time. John was fun, Fan told her friends, and really a nice guy. Sex, as such, was not the only issue.

Gary Stevens, who had come out to the West Coast as agent for singer Virginia Verrill, described John's relationship with Fanny as "a mutual arrangement. He gave her the escort and whatever other services he supplied, and she moved him into circles that he never would have been in. John was a very suave, charming 'professional hello man' who made it his business to know and gladhand everybody. He was in the business, doing lots of things, when he met Fanny. She put him in the big leagues." John ended an affair with beautiful, young Alice Faye shortly before Fanny got him the job as announcer on *Maxwell House Coffee Time*.

Fan was almost fifty, but if Conte's ambitions as a singer and actor made her a valuable career tool, she was still a fascinating woman. A young, enthusiastic, naïve Fanny had been good enough for polished handsome Nick Arnstein in 1912. An older Fanny, with the glamor of a star, was good enough for young, handsome John Conte twenty-eight years later.

The January 2, 1941, broadcast, in which Conte replaced Don Wilson as announcer, also marked a major turn in the program's evolution. Minus M-G-M guest stars and singers, the show was transformed from a big, expensive musical production to a comparatively modest comedy program split into two fifteen-minute segments: (1) Frank Morgan as the world's biggest liar, with Meredith Wilson and Conte as foils, and (2) Fanny and Hanley Stafford as Baby Snooks and Daddy.

The cast of "Baby Snooks" was expanded past the roles of Snooks and Daddy to include Robspierre, Snooks' baby brother. The actor who played him was Jerry Hausner.

"I was on a radio show out here and they needed the voice of a baby crying. They were set to use an old sound effects record, but it was all scratchy, and I told them I could do a baby crying. I did it, and word spread. Finally, I got a call from Jess Oppenheimer to do it on *Maxwell House Coffee Time,* and that's how I got to work with Fanny.

"They had had a couple of girls doing it from time to time, but Oppenheimer figured it would have more comedy value in front of a studio audience if a man did the voice instead of a woman. And he was right. We got very big laughs.

"Fanny did not seem like a very sensitive person. Actually, she must have been, but outwardly, she was kind of loud and bold—raucous, very assertive, and not too friendly. I'm sure she never knew my name, and didn't care. She called everybody 'kid,' but then so did a lot of those big stars; they were so wrapped up in themselves.

"The closest I ever got to her is when we started to work out this idea, and I don't remember at this point whose idea it was. Up to this time in radio, a baby's voice was just a sound effect, indicated in the script as the sound of a baby crying or a baby gurgling, or whatever it was doing. But somehow, we evolved a system where whenever Robspierre would formulate a sound or incomprehensible words, Snooks, and Snooks alone, would understand what he was saying. And then Robspierre became like a human being for the first time, and that made it very funny and very successful—Fanny, as Baby Snooks, understanding Robspierre and translating as he spoke. It added a dimension to the show, and was a great source of humor. I thought that was the most important thing that came out of that show—for me, anyway.

"When performing, she was brilliant. Her timing was impeccable, and she had a great sense of comedy like Lucille Ball and those other geniuses that are not the nicest people in the world.

"Abrasive? Yes. Watching her eat was really an experience. She ate fast and in a hurry, like it was a necessary evil. She would eat sandwiches and things like that backstage." Hausner, in all fairness, never saw Fan at a banquet.

"She was like a machine. She was gonna do what she was gonna do, and it had nothing to do with anybody else. You never got inside of her. I don't remember ever having a conversation; there was no reason for her to have a conversation with me or with anybody else.

"If Fanny thought something was wrong with the script, she'd voice her opinion at the microphone during rehearsals, something like, 'I don't like this; it's a piece of shit.' And the script would then be changed to please her."

The early 1940s were a turning point for Fanny, who had given up hopes of a film career and satisfied herself with life as a radio star and part-time unpaid interior decorator. The death of Frank White, her first husband, in February 1940, brought back memories of her years in burlesque, and Fran's marriage to Ray Stark was a bittersweet reminder of the passing years. A real loss, and sadness, was the death of Fanny's mother, Rosie, who succumbed to a heart ailment on April 30, 1941.

Many people soften as they age. Fanny was the opposite. After the divorce from Billy Rose, she hardened. She had come up in "a man's world," been hurt by men for years, and looked on the world with increasingly less sentiment. Fanny, who had always been ambivalent about her mother, shed no tears at Rosie's death, and threatened to walk out if her own sister, Carrie, wept during the funeral.

She had become as hard as Rosie had when she walked out on Charlie.

General Foods, endeavoring to save twelve thousand dollars in talent costs for the month of September, did not feature Fanny on the first four broadcasts of the 1941–42 season. Hanley Stafford made several appearances on those shows, saying Snooks had "run away" and trying, unsuccessfully, to find her. "Morgan," wrote Ben Bodec in *Variety*, "is still sputtering Baron Munchausens, John Conte is still interrupting him with insulting badinage, and Meredith Wilson, when not batoning the orchestra in what the program terms 'chiffon' arrangements, is still contributing his hayseed character to the dialogue. Also included in the opening stagline was Allan Jones. He talked more than he sang." Fanny returned in October.

The Pearl Harbor bombing changed Fan's life in one respect: she cancelled her subscriptions to all newspapers and magazines. She knew what side she was on when the war came, and that, to Fanny, was enough.

Ray, Fran's husband, joined the Navy during World War II. Fan's son, Bill, a tall (6' 4½") young man who looked like his father, graduated from the Chouinard Art Institute in 1942 and married Shirley Ann Bardeen on August 23 of that year. (Bill and his new fiancée had gone to school together, and Fanny herself gave Shirley the engagement ring.) A 1943 stint in the Army Air Force found Bill in the same unit as Jerry Hausner.

"That was at Gardner Field in Taft, California," recalled Hausner. "As luck would have it, the commanding officer was a theatrical agent I had known before the war named Amery Eckley. He introduced me to Bill Brice and put us in charge of the recreation hall—which was great for Bill, who wanted time to paint. Nobody had the keys to the place but us, and we would go there to 'hide out' whenever we could.

"I had studied art in Cleveland, so Bill and I had that to talk about. He was a tall, thin, very aesthetic, very sensitive kind of a guy, which was surprising to me, because his mother was, outwardly at least, not much like that at all.

"Strangely enough, when I was transferred out, we said 'good-bye' and 'I'll see you,' and to this day I've never seen him again."

Fanny's guests for the length of the war included Lew, her brother; Fran, her daughter; Shirley, her son Bill's wife; and Harry Pilcer.

Pilcer, a familiar figure on the Parisian nightclub scene after Gaby Deslys' death in 1920, had escaped to London just before the Nazi invasion of 1940. Fanny's home in California was just the sort of retreat from the war, and other pressures, Pilcer wanted. He would return to Paris after the war's end.

Fanny stayed on *Maxwell House Coffee Time* through June 15, 1944, missing only two broadcasts and shouldering the show alone, with Stafford and guest stars, whenever Frank Morgan was busy with film work. *Variety* reviewer Hobe Morrison commented on the "borderline nature of some of the comedy material," but the show retained a high place in the weekly Hooper Ratings. (Many thought that Fanny's sponsor gave her extra allotments of coffee during the war. That, however, was not true; "Baby Snooks" got as many ration stamps as anybody else.)

The unabated popularity of "Baby Snooks" led General Foods to give Fanny her own show for 1944–45. *Toasties Time,* in the 6:30 to 7:00 P.M. time slot over the Columbia Broadcasting System on Sunday evenings, marked her first solo starring effort since *Be Yourself!* fifteen years earlier. It was, however, without Conte, who stayed on *Maxwell House Coffee Time* as Morgan's foil and announcer.

Conte's relationship with Fanny ended when he met blonde beauty Marilyn Maxwell on the set of the film *Lost in a Harem.* John and Marilyn were married on September 17 but eventually divorced. His subsequent marriage to Ruth Collins produced a son, John Charles Conte.

Fanny took the end of her affair with Conte stoically. She talked about it once, with Harry in his bedroom, until the sensitive Pilcer started weeping. Fanny thereupon slapped Harry in the face and walked out of the room. Neither of them mentioned John again.

That same year saw Fanny do two sketches for the M-G-M film revue *Ziegfeld Follies.* Once again, she was the only one of Ziegfeld's long-time stars to appear in a major show or film that bore his name.

Like *Rhapsody in Blue* and several other musicals released in the mid-'forties, *Ziegfeld Follies* was in production for almost a year—and held back for six months prior to its New York premiere and release. The scenes Fanny would do were "A Sweepstakes Ticket" and "Baby Snooks Traps a Burglar."

"Hanley called me one night," remembered Jerry Hausner, "and said 'What do you think? I just picked up the paper and I see that Fanny has been signed to do Baby Snooks in the new *Ziegfeld Follies* movie for fifty thousand dollars. Now the sketch is one we've done on the radio. Wouldn't you think that Fanny would call me and tell me that the studio would want me? But I haven't gotten a call from her or from the studio. I have no idea who they're gonna do it with.'

"I told him, 'She wouldn't do it with anybody else.' He said, 'The hell she wouldn't. She doesn't give a goddamn who does it; she feels that it doesn't make any difference.' I said, 'You mean she doesn't appreciate how good you are?' He said, 'She doesn't even know I'm there. She's never fought for me before. It's damned annoying.'

"Anyway, a day went by, and he called me again, and said, 'Well, I just got a call from Metro and they want me to be in the picture. They said it was just a small sketch, and there wouldn't be that much to do, and that there wouldn't be an awful lot of money. I said, well, Fanny's getting fifty thousand dollars. I want three thousand dollars.'

"They raised hell about it. They simply didn't want to pay him three thousand dollars. Finally, Hanley said, 'Look, if I'm not worth three thousand dollars to you people, get somebody else. So he hung up on them.

"They called him a couple of days later, and said, 'Okay, you'll get the three thousand dollars. But we won't forget this. We'll hold this against you for the rest of your life, and you'll never work again.' All those kinds of threats.

"They went into rehearsal, working in a hall-barn where there was no set. The scene was to be in Baby Snooks' bedroom, and had to do with B. S. Pulley as a burglar who has broken into the house and hides under the bed.

"They rehearsed for three weeks. Hanley said he was glad he was getting the three thousand because he wasn't sure when they were going to 'shoot the damned thing . . . I'm working every God damned day. . . . It's all right for her to get fifty thousand; she's a big star, but. . . .'

"The following week, they were taken over to the soundstage at Metro. The set, however, wasn't built yet, so they rehearsed another week. Then they started to build the set; another week went by before the thing was ready. Then they started to stage the thing, and Fanny suddenly spoke up: 'Wait, this set is backwards. It's all wrong. I can't work on this set.'

"The director got the set designer and they asked Fanny what was wrong. 'There's only one door on this set,' said Fanny, 'and it's on the wrong side. If I come out there, the audience will see my bad side.' That was because of the old nose job.

"Then they had to rebuild the set, which took two more weeks. Then they rehearsed, got everything all set, and filmed the sequence.

"Hanley called me shortly afterwards. 'Well,' he told me, 'it's all filmed. And I got thirty thousand dollars.' I asked him how.

"He said, 'When we were arguing about the money, I was talking about three thousand dollars as a complete fee. They were talking about three thousand dollars a week. The sequence took ten weeks, and I just got a check for thirty thousand.' "

The capper to this story was not supplied until later, when the film's nineteen scenes clocked in at 273 minutes and the "Snooks" sequence was cut from United States release prints.

Fanny, young Hume Cronyn, and William Frawley appeared in "A Sweepstakes Ticket," the David Freedman skit she had done with two other actors in the 1936 *Follies*. Fanny pulled out all the stops, using her mobile face, angular body, and flawless timing to drive home (a bit too forcefully, perhaps) the comic desperation of a woman whose husband has given their winning Irish Sweepstakes ticket to the landlord. The scene, directed by Roy Del Ruth, is shot with neither cuts nor closeups, and although Fanny's takes are funny, her Yiddish accent does seem out of place against the background of Hume Cronyn's perfect namby-pamby English. Frawley is all wrong for the part of the landlord, and Cronyn, though a fine young actor, was out of his element in sketch comedy. Fanny gave Cronyn a Bill Brice painting at the end of filming, probably his only happy moment in the project.

Ziegfeld Follies, reduced to thirteen scenes running one hundred minutes, previewed in Boston on August 10, 1945, and opened at the Capitol in New York on March 22, 1946, to generally favorable reviews that overlooked its comic misfires and overall plasticity. Budgeted at three million dollars, the film grossed over five and was another feather in the caps of Arthur Freed, Vincente Minnelli, and Metro-Goldwyn-Mayer.

Toasties Time premiered on September 17 with Fanny in two fifteen-minute sketches—"Irma Potts" and "Baby Snooks." Irma was a trustful shopgirl with a protruding lower lip and a slight lisp. "If we could record what we say all day long," said Fanny, "and it was played back to us at night, we'd hate ourselves. We mean ten percent of what we say. Irma is different. She says a hundred percent what she thinks and is always in trouble."

The first "Irma Potts" skit had her leave her boss's drugstore unattended to rush out and help a man kicked by a horse. In her absence, the cash register is robbed. Irma's stabs at finding nice young men were equally pathetic:

Irma: The only reason I ask is 'cause I'm a total stranger in town. Not that I would mind meeting some nice young feller to go out with. Separate checks, of course.

Man: Why don't you try the Canteen? I'm sure the servicemen would welcome you.

Irma: Do you think so?

Man: Certainly. Those fellows haven't passed anything since their physical.

Irma had a boyfriend, "Jerry Dingle, the Postman," by the end of that first broadcast. "Jerry" was played by Danny Thomas, a new young comic foisted on Fanny by Abe Lastfogel, head of the William Morris Agency and a friend for years. Fanny had never seen Thomas work, but liked his material—the way it was performed by Abe's wife, Frances.

Thrilled at working with a big name after years of heartbreak, Thomas told Fanny it was a thrill to meet her.

"Don't give me that crap, kid," Fanny told him. "You'd just better be funny."

In order to show Fanny and the writers how he worked, he did his act in the famous Hollywood Canteen for soldiers, sailors, and Marines. Thomas performed his best routines, including the celebrated "Jack Story" he would never do on national television.

Fan was unimpressed. "Abe's wife, Fran," she said, "does the stuff better."

Toasties Time was opposite tough competition: *The Great Gildersleeve* on N.B.C. "Irma Potts" was neither a critical nor a popular success, and plans were made to drop it for the following season. This led some to believe Fanny would be leaving radio—a rumor that looked credible in April, when she visited New York for the first time in years.

Many thought that Fanny would be coming back to Broadway. "It ain't so," she told Irving Spiegel of the *New York Times*. "Me, I love California, nothing but slacks all day, such wonderful slacks—$150 a pair. My friends say: 'Fanny, where dicha buy them? I tell them. Only they don't get them; they're super special slacks, only for Fanny.

"I miss the theatre," she continued, "but I won't come back unless someone comes along with material that would be startlingly new; not an imitation of 'My Man.' . . . It has to be very, very good."

Lack of material was not the only reason she did not return to Broadway. Her health, never quite the same since 1936, declined still further in the months ahead.

CHAPTER *15*

Closing Number

T oasties Time left the air after thirty-nine broadcasts, leaving Fanny more time to spend before her easel. Her paintings—mostly pastoral—showed improved technique, but further progress was cut short by a sudden heart attack that sent her to Cedars of Lebanon Hospital for the balance of the summer.

Those around her tried to keep things secret, but it was a major heart attack, and Fanny spent a few days in an oxygen tent. Her many friends in Hollywood—Katharine Hepburn, Spencer Tracy, George Cukor, and Constance Collier, among others—paid visit after visit. Tracy heard Fanny moan slightly as he sat down on the bed and held her hand.

"What is it, Fanny?" Tracy asked.

"Too many first nights," Fanny replied. ". . . And taking all that sonofabitch aspirin didn't help, either."

Fanny spent the bulk of her hospital stay studying the racing form and placing bets with George Jessel's bookie, a fellow patient. She felt capable of driving down to her beach house in Malibu upon her release from Cedars, but her doctor sent her home in an ambulance. "When the men were carrying me to the house in a stretcher," Fanny said a short time later, "I saw a small boy who lived next door. I later heard that he ran to his mother and said, 'Fanny Brice is coming home. I guess she just had a baby.' Well, that was so cute, because you know I'm a grandmother now." Fran had given birth to her first child, Peter Stark, the previous year.

Fanny was still convalescing when *The Baby Snooks Show,* sponsored by Sanka, premiered on September 16, 1945. Eddie Cantor, who with his wife Ida and their daughters had been up to see Fan frequently at Cedars, was the guest star, playing himself as a "family friend" enlisted in a hunt for the missing Snooks. *Variety* reported that he "swapped gags with Daddy Higgins, had some amusing repartee about his own daughters and their problems, engaged in a match with Daddy in diapering babies, and finished off with a very funny imitation of Baby Snooks herself." Robert Benchley and Kay Kyser appeared on the following two broadcasts.

Fanny finally appeared, as Snooks, on the fourth broadcast of the season. The script had Snooks claim that she'd had amnesia for three weeks. Fan herself had something worse. No doctor could explain it, but she started to get surging headaches several times weekly.

Fanny's health was the main problem of her later years. An ear infection affected her equilibrium, a low blood-count caused her to take liver injections three times weekly, and the unexplained headaches always left her limp. Fanny never became an "intellectual," but her abiding fascination with people, natural curiosity, and all-night chats with highly educated friends now got her interested in psychology. She even began to think her headaches had a psychosomatic origin. In the fall of 1946, after *Baby Snooks* returned from a hiatus of three months, she and Ida Cantor took a course of sixteen lectures on the theories of psychosomatic medicine. Fanny thought the lectures interesting, but found nothing in them to explain her headaches.

Fanny got to know Ida Cantor quite well in these later years, and grew much closer to her than she'd ever been to Eddie. The Cantors' daughters were all friends of hers—especially Edna, another painter—and Fanny dropped by their house every day to chat and raid the icebox. She would often stay all night, handling her insomnia by talking to the Cantors over coffee in their kitchen until 5:00 A.M. Cantor said Fanny "couldn't bear loneliness. The phone would ring at 1, 2, 3, a.m. and Fanny'd say, 'Whatcha doin', Eddie?'

" 'Nothing,' I'd lie, and pulling pants over my pajamas, I'd waken Ida, and off we'd go to yak with Fanny."

The success of *Yankee Doodle Dandy,* Warner's film biography of George M. Cohan, led Hollywood studios to consider similar projects on other titans of the pre-Depression show world. Fanny was among the names considered, and had no problem when asked who would play her. "There's one dame who could play me," Fanny said: "Joan Davis."

Joan was then among the country's most celebrated comediennes, having played supporting roles in films since the mid-'thirties. She was tall and angular with a rubbery face she used to great advantage with her mugging. Whether she had Fanny's versatility or depth—or the acting talent to play her convincingly—was quite another matter. Studio heads also doubted whether America could embrace the story of a Yiddish dialect comedienne who became "Baby Snooks." No film biography of Fanny, therefore, advanced past the talking stage.

Fanny's life during the 1946–47 and 1947–48 radio seasons fell into a pattern. Interior decorating had become her main activity, and she usually spent two weekday afternoons a week at Rennick's Antique Shop on Sunset Boulevard, Jack Earle's, or one of the other shops. Returning home at six, she generally had about four fingers of straight bourbon before dinner. ("I get no mileage out of anything I drink at my age," she once quipped.) Fanny ate mostly at home. When dining out, she preferred Chinese food. Don the Beachcomber's was another of her favorite places.

The cast of *Baby Snooks* grew over the years: Arlene Harris as Snooks' mother, Vera Higgins, various character actors (including Hans Conreid and Ben Alexander, among others), and Leone Ledoux as "Robspierre," Snooks' baby brother and occasional innocent victim. (One skit had Snooks cutting all the fur off of her mother's coat, gluing it to Robspierre, and trying to sell him to the kid down the block as a pet monkey.)

The process of assembling the weekly Friday show started at 1:30 every Wednesday. Fanny usually wore black wedgies, slacks, and a blouse on arriving for the reading of the script in Studio Two of the CBS Building in Hollywood. The reading would be followed by two rehearsals the same day, Fanny whispering her way as she felt through the script. Further conferences and run-throughs were held Thursday, the cast gathering in Fanny's dressing room at noon on Fridays for possible last-minute changes in the script. Two more rehearsals would then follow, the second one a dress at half past three.

Fanny gave dispirited readings at rehearsals, worrying Everett Freeman, now the show's head writer. But Fanny knew how to rehearse, and gradually assumed the character of Snooks before air time on Friday. After dress rehearsal, she would go back to her dressing room for a light meal—usually a chicken sandwich with tea—and an hour's rest. The show went on the air at 5:00 P.M. Pacific Coast Time.

She would, by then, have become Baby Snooks. Author Maurice Zolotow said that something outside of Fanny seemed "to dominate her," her face changing and screwing itself into that of a child. "The large mouth puckers, bending upward at the corners like a scimitar blade. Her knees knock together. She shrinks fifty years out of her life. The performance, as always, is polished and bright, with perfect timing." Fanny invariably felt she had been "terribly dull" after every broadcast. She also thought the writers, striving for sure laughs and growing increasingly short of material, were making "Schnooks" (as she called the character) too vicious. "You'll maybe get laughs on this gag," she would tell them, "but you're murdering the character. I tell you, Schnooks is a sweet kid at heart."

Variety's Hobe Morrison agreed with Fan when he reviewed the broadcast of September 5, 1947.

> As written by Phil Rapp, "Baby Snooks" was more than simply a comedy show with an occasional laugh. It was pleasant listening and its characters were essentially likable people. Snooks was a mischievous moppet, with an incurable knack for turning a quiet household into turmoil and shaking the sanity of her parents, but she was not a brat. She was not nasty or mean, spiteful or sadistic. She was at heart a nice kid. Similarly, Daddy, as played by Hanley Stafford, was harried and desperate, and occasionally was driven to spanking his impish daughter at the sigh-off. But Daddy wasn't ill-tempered or unkind with the kid. He wasn't a crab. And the show was amusing and enjoyable. It was fun, without offending good taste or anyone's sensibilities. Any listener could safely hear it in his home, whether the company included strangers or children.
>
> At other times, and last week's episode seemed a step in that direction, the plotting was forced and the characters became unattractive. Snooks was not merely mischievous, but became mean and vengeful. She did nasty things to her baby brother, Robspierre, such as coating his head with green paint, or deliberately burning down a neighbor's garage, or willfully jeopardizing the father's job. Daddy, in turn, became a chronic grouch, and his quarreling with Mommy Higgins was a listener's ordeal. All of which seems incomprehensible when it should be apparent to anyone that the basic quality of all comedy or drama, in fact any successful story-telling, is sympathy for the principal characters. Maybe that "Terrible Tot" subtitle, which was obviously adopted merely because it's alliterative, is the evil influence.

Even scripts were not Fanny's biggest professional headache. Television proved itself during the 1947–48 season, and General Foods, wanting to phase out of radio, demanded that Fanny take a major slash in salary. Many other stars agreed to similar cuts, and Fanny's weekly paycheck was one of the largest in radio.

Fanny, though, would not accept a pay cut. "Oh, no," she said, "not Fanny." *The Baby Snooks Show* had had a $12,500 weekly talent budget since its inception, and Fanny saw no reason to cut any part of it—least of all her five-grand weekly paycheck. Her agents argued with her, pointing out the other actors' plights, their own commissions, and the people who loved "Snooks."

Nothing, however, would move Fanny. She knew TV would displace radio, and did not see Snooks—or Brice—in the new medium. "It wouldn't work," she said. "The character, it wouldn't be believable in the same way on that screen." Doing a Snooks sketch in a revue on Broadway was one thing; a weekly Snooks show on TV was quite another.

These fears were confirmed when Fanny appeared on *The Popsicle Parade of Stars,* a fifteen-minute CBS TV show seen in California. Performing a Snooks sketch that had played brilliantly on radio, Fanny looked too old for Snooks, too tall (it was mostly undirected, and she stood too close to Stafford), and uncomfortable. She had not worked in the theatre for ten years, and the radio timing she and Stafford now employed was too slow for television.

Fanny had been in show business for over forty years, had "done everything but marry a property man," and had no further worlds to conquer. Television, she believed, was her worst enemy—one she could not beat. "Look at me," she'd say to Ida Cantor. "Wrinkles. . . . I'm getting old."

She now labeled show biz "too much work"—despite the fact that radio took less than three days weekly. Fanny claimed to be much happier decorating friends' houses for free. Now in her mid-fifties, she no longer needed to perform.

Baby Snooks, as a result, was off the air for the entire season of 1948–49 after eleven consecutive years on the air. Fanny had aged, from forty-six to fifty-seven, in the interval, though kind observers, misled by her buoyant energy, said she looked much younger than her years. Baby Snooks, far less prone to the ravages of time than her creator, had merely gone from four to six.

Fanny still had not retired, and took part in a *Screen Guild Theatre* radio presentation of *Pinocchio* at Christmastime. Basically, however, she concerned herself with family, her parties, and her houses. Fanny now had two grandchildren, Frances having given birth to a daughter, Wendy, in 1947. ("Whoever's amounted to anything who's been named Wendy?" Fanny had asked Fran.)

Fanny's son, Bill, worked in the M-G-M art department for ten months, quitting when he realized that "working for effect" would threaten his more serious painting. With Fanny's help, he embarked on a four-year career as a freelance artist, giving one-man shows at the Santa Barbara Museum of Art and the Downtown Gallery in New York City. Fanny went to all his shows, convinced that Bill would become a great modern painter—after years of effort. "She was very difficult," Bill said in 1990. "She prided herself with not being prey to the seductions of maternal sentiment. . . . She said she liked some things and didn't like others." Bill became an instructor at the Jedson Art Institute in Los Angeles in 1948.

Fanny still liked cooking. Her dinner parties were always famous in Hollywood, as varied in their guests as in their food. Once she had as house guests a producer and an actress known to be living together. When they asked for separate bedrooms (with an air of seeming innocence), Fanny told them not to "shit an old-timer."

She went to others' parties under pressure, and considered most Hollywood actors "schmendriks." Fanny was once introduced to the great modern Austrian composer, Arnold Schoenberg, at a friend's house. Never having heard of him before, but hearing the word "composer," Fanny went up to him after dinner. "Okay, kid," Fanny told him, "now you can sit down and play some of your tunes."

Fanny was still happiest with her old friends from burlesque, vaudeville, and Broadway—Eddie Cantor and his family, Trixie Wilson, Polly Moran, and others who spoke the language of "old show business"— pre-Depression, pre-commercial radio, and pre-"Hollywood." These were the people who knew what it was like to rehearse for a show, to break it in amidst a batch of rewrites, to play vaudeville with different people every week and know countless numbers of other hardworking performers, booking agents, and theatre managers. Fanny understood and liked these people; she was one of them herself.

Her closest friends at this point were Bea Lillie, Constance Collier, Ann Pennington, and Polly Moran. One or more would stay with her at any given time.

Penny had remained that show-biz rarity: a performer with no ego, but enormous pride. During World War II, Billy Rose wanted Penny for his Diamond Horseshoe in New York. Fanny took the message over the phone, tried unsuccessfully to locate Penny, and then bought her a train ticket through the William Morris office.

When Penny, who'd been at the races, finally returned and got the news from Fanny, she was angry. The Morris office knew that Fan had bought the ticket, and, Penny imagined, probably felt happy that "poor washed up Ann Pennington" was working. It made her feel small, and she got into an argument with Fanny.

Penny was once forced to ask for a small loan from Harry Pilcer. "And damn it," she told Pilcer, "don't tell Fanny." Penny wound up living in a cheap hotel in New York after Fanny died.

Constance Collier, thirteen years older than Fanny, was an English-born actress who had appeared in innumerable plays with stars like Wilson Barrett and John Barrymore, and had a short career in silent films. Constance had all but retired to teach acting, and Fanny found her a remarkably stimulating conversationalist. Constance, a born artist, found Fanny's need to analyze depressing, and said it was like "dusting off a flower." But Fanny's curiosity—about people, if not institutions—simply grew.

"To stay with Fanny was usually good for your soul," said Beatrice Lillie. "She could build you up if you needed building up, and knock you down, too, if that is what she thought the prescription called for. Making movies was hard work, lasting sometimes until seven or eight in the evening, then starting in again bright and early before dawn the next day." Bea once intended staying at the Beverly Hills Hotel, but Fanny wouldn't hear of it.

" 'Ah, the best of legs must part. I've never been so insulted. You come and stay with me. I insist.' "

Bea had a peculiar allergy to garlic, an allergy Fanny claimed was psychosomatic. To prove her point, Fan served her friend a dish with garlic in it, and then watched as Lady Peel threw up over her, the table, and the carpet. It was one of the few times Fanny was wrong on any subject, and she said so, sarcastically naming Bea "The Lotus Flower of the Far East" at the same time.

Fanny had no Hollywood ambitions, no illusions of a film career or more fame than she'd known as Baby Snooks. The economic strain of keeping on a full-time secretary (Kaye Brewer, an efficient and attractive woman with silver hair who also acted as Fan's nurse, chauffeur, injector of liver extract, and general confidante) and a household staff of three made immediate retirement inadvisable, but Fanny thought that she had earned her rest, and had no problems with semi-retirement.

Entertaining friends, not radio audiences, now gave Fanny her greatest satisfaction. One of her parties at "Pelican Park" (Fanny's nickname for the house in Holmby) was a black-tie dinner in honor of Mr. and Mrs. William Rhinelander Stewart. Cobina Wright, George Cukor, Laurence Olivier, Lionel Atwill, Frank Orsatti, and the other guests were treated to the sight of Polly Moran, incognito as a maid, sans teeth but painted with what seemed like jars of rouge. Polly served the guests that night, spilling a good portion of a plate of soup on Atwill, and playing the part of a rough, familiar, drunken servant to perfection. When Fanny led her guests into the barroom for coffee and liqueurs, Polly came in with a broom and dustpan and told everyone, in turn, to raise their feet. Told by Fanny that she could leave, Polly finally re-entered with a raised half-glass of brandy and began to sing "God Bless America!"

Fanny finally brought "the maid" back and introduced her to the guests as Polly Moran, great screen comedienne and friend of hers for over forty years. It was the last large formal party Fanny ever threw.

Fanny's letters tended to be three-line scrawls; Kaye typed all her correspondence. Fanny hated writing, but loved telephones. New York, Chicago, and Miami—in that order—were the three locales she called most often, and she tended to call people at odd hours. (Three in the morning was not too late to get a call from Fanny if you lived in New York City. She sometimes forgot—or pretended to forget—about the three-hour time difference between coasts.) Sometimes, at equally odd hours, she would call up friends and ask them to immediately "come over." And they usually came.

Insomnia still plagued her—the result of loneliness and a lifetime of sleeping patterns interrupted by the varied routines of *Midnight Frolics* and late-night after-theatre parties.

Fanny never let herself get maudlin, never let her loneliness and innate sensitivity destroy her self-respect. Unlike her male show-business contemporaries, she never shed a tear in front of people. In that, she was like many Jewish women—emotionally harder than their male counterparts. She, like they, saw toughness as a bulwark—a hard power she did not want to relinquish.

That spring, after almost a full season of leisure in which most of her "work" involved the use of decorators' color schemes rather than scripts, Fan made up her mind to write her memoirs. With Kaye Brewer taking notes, she reminisced about her parents, of her girlhood days in Newark, and of breaking in on amateur night at Keeney's Theatre on Fulton Street in Brooklyn. Fanny was far more candid than she had been for commercial interviewers; and, ever the analyst, tried vainly to see why she had behaved the way she had throughout her life—especially with Nick.

Fanny soon began to feel like she'd said it all. In fact, she had said little—leaving glaring questions about her marriage to Frank White, her father, and Billy Rose, about whom she said nothing that conveyed the fierce resentment that her friends and even acquaintances had seen from time to time. Billy, for the public, would remain almost a comic interlude in Fanny's life, an incongruous joke like her earlier marriage to Frank White.

Goddard Leiberson, originator of "Original Cast Recording" LP records, was brought in to stimulate Fanny with questions, but the project went slowly, and was interrupted when her other life—as Baby Snooks—revived.

Fanny had received a great deal of mail from Snooks fans who wanted to know when the "Terrible Tot" would reappear on network radio. Fanny was still vibrant, still just fifty-seven; and a few conferences with her financial brokers convinced her that a couple more years of work would make her financially comfortable for the rest of her life.

In September 1949, the National Broadcasting Company sold *The Baby Snooks Show* to Tums through the Lewis-Howe Agency at $6,500 a week— a figure that represented salaries for Fanny, Stafford, Arlene Harris, Leone Ledoux, Ken Christy, Hans Conried, Doris Singleton, announcer Don Wilson, producer Al Kabakere, director and writer Artie Stander, and writer Robert Fisher. Fanny had agreed to a considerable cut from what she had received at CBS, making it quite clear that this two-season contract would be the end of her career.

Phil Weltmann, Fanny's agent at the Morris office, engineered and handled the *Return of Baby Snooks*. "Maybe she will come back with a little freshness for the audience," Fan told Zuma Palmer of the *Hollywood Citizen News*. "It seemed to me the programs which had only been off for the summer were just the same thing."

The Baby Snooks Show went on the air at 5:30 P.M. (8:30 Eastern Standard Time) on Tuesday, November 8, 1949, opposite *Milton Berle's Texico Star Theater* television show. It was a losing battle, and George Rosen of *Variety* said that the "projection of the old-hat 'Snooks' formula, which is practically as old as radio itself, accentuates anew the plight of radio personalities resurrecting ancient formats and characterizations. Even on the non-TV fringe belt, 'Baby Snooks,' as revealed anew on last Tuesday's 'premiere,' was strictly dated material, with a none too inspiring script, which found Miss Brice, Hanley Stafford and the rest trying valiantly to make it all sound fresh." Artie Stander was a veteran comedy writer who gradually got into the Snooks character by working closely with Bob Fisher, his assistant. Their early scripts, however, left a lot to be desired.

Everett Freeman had found that honesty about scripts was the best policy with Fanny. If the script that he submitted was a weak one, he would tell her so and ask that she do her best. Fanny, as a trouper, then would reassure him. If, however, he said that a script was good and Fanny found it "stunk," she let him know it—in words that Snooks was not supposed to use.

Nick's wife, Irene, died in Los Angeles on New Year's Day. Two months later, he called Fanny, asking that she see him.

Fanny tried to remain calm, but spent the days before the visit calling her close friends and talking about Nick. At 3:00 A.M., she called up

Eddie Cantor and asked him to come over "right away." Cantor, who had fears for Fanny's health, pulled his pants over his pajamas, sped to her house, and nearly fainted when he found out she just wanted to talk.

Nick arrived on the appointed day and spoke, sincerely, of the loneliness he had known prior to his first marriage, and of how he could not be alone again.

It was probably more truth than line. Nick was seventy—a young, fit seventy, but nonetheless too old to be a playboy. His twenty-year marriage to Isabelle had gotten him accustomed to a more sedate and secure home life than he had known in younger days. He now needed a wife.

The Arnstein Fanny now saw had been humbled. There were still the studied manners and the same old polished act. But the confident and masculine *bon vivant* was long gone. Fanny saw through all the charm and missed the confident masculinity. If Nick had changed, it was in the wrong way.

The interview ended rather amicably. Fanny felt little emotion, and expressed even less.

Ten days later, Nick called her and made a date. He took her to a restaurant, and tried to talk to Fanny about marrying again.

It was too predictable for Fanny. "Love," she once said, "is like a card trick. After you see it done once, it loses all its mystery." Arnstein was now just a faded version of the magnetic, handsome man she had met years ago.

Fanny was not fifty-eight, and she had seen all the card tricks men could offer. She looked at Arnstein now through the eyes of "the mother" in her—her own mother, Rosie.

Nick phoned again the following morning, but Fan refused to take the call. "From now on," she told her maid, "I'm not in when he calls."

She never saw Arnstein again.

The Baby Snooks Show left the air on May 2, 1950, returning for the first of thirty-nine additional broadcasts on October 10. The scripts took on a new and more humane direction, and Bril of *Variety* said that Fanny "after all these years . . . still pleases with her stock characterization. The stanza remains in the familiar groove and audiences know what to expect from Snooks in the way of pranks. Yet the variations are amusing even if the theme is old, and the impish moppet has a lasting appeal similar to her Katzenjammer Kids prototypes."

Leone Ledoux was back as "Robspierre," Snooks' little baby brother. Leone always wore tight overalls or trousers when the show was broadcast, unlike Fanny, who performed in her own stylish street clothes. "Wearing a costume is okay if you're doing Schnooks on a stage in a sketch," she said. "But it would just look silly in front of a microphone when I'm being 'Schnooks.' "

The *Snooks* scripts that last season saw an element of reform introduced in the spirit of *Dr. Spock's Baby and Child Care.* "There was a period," wrote *Bril,*

> when Snooks' scripters went too heavy on sadism, trying to milk humor from unnecessarily vicious and destructive tricks. Now, however, her antics are more mischievous than mean. A typical stunt mentioned on the initialer Tuesday was her cutting the neighbor's roses and selling them to him in a bouquet.
>
> Her unruliness poses a script problem, in that her wrong-doing can't be condoned. Situation last week revolved around her playing hookey from school by feigning a case of the mumps, using a pair of rubber balls to puff out her cheeks. After Daddy (nicely played by Hanley Stafford) gave her a "lying doesn't pay" lecture, it developed he himself was staying home from work with a phoney illness, and when the boss dropped in he had to pretend he had the mumps. Payoff was his swallowing a ball and really needing the doctor. Fact that Daddy is a cutup himself and loses his temper gives Snooks' badgering of him some justification.
>
> There was some good comedic writing, and the scene in which Snooks pulled a switch and examined the medico was tops. Brief segment in which the doc gave Stafford some psychological pointers explaining Snooks' malingering and suggesting a calm approach was nicely handled and important for giving the airer [show] a realistic touch.

Fanny and Stafford had recorded six sides for a Capitol record album that summer, with the titles "Crossing Streets," "Truthfulness," "Cleanliness," "Kindness to Animals," "Table Manners," and "Good and Bad." The preachy approach typified the *Snooks* show during its last season. Whether it would keep the show on the air any longer was entirely academic, since Fanny had decided 1950–51 would be her last season as Snooks. TV was now established, Fanny would be sixty the following October, and it seemed, therefore, the right time to retire.

Bill and Shirley had a son, John, in November, and Fanny now looked forward to a happy retirement with her three grandchildren. She found Peter, Ray and Frances' son, "a little on the fresh side." She'd found he had, at the age of two, a penchant for breaking ashtrays and pulling flowers off stems. "I don't know," she said. "Maybe it's these new ideas of bringin' kids up or something. Progressive methods. All these mothers of today are studying books. I didn't study books to bring up my two children. I took them on the road with me when I trouped in vaudeville or a *Follies*. We traveled with a governess. She didn't read child psychology books either. I cooked their meals for them in a hotel room. Once, I was frying some fish in the room and the house detective reported I was stinking up the joint so I took the frying pan to the theatre and finished cooking in the dressing room. The two kids read parts with me when I was rehearsing a sketch for a new show. We had fun. It's all these crazy books, child psychology."

Interior decorating, painting, and entertaining were the pastimes Fanny envisioned for herself as Snooks went off the air for good early that summer. (She also loved cards, but had a reputation as the slowest gin rummy player in the world. Eddie Cantor once had his bags packed for a trip to New York, but Fanny begged him to play just one game, and Eddie acquiesced. Fanny, though, could not decide just how to play her hand. Cantor finally excused himself, drove to the station, caught his train, and sent a wire two days later from Chicago: "Well?")

With *Baby Snooks* and Fanny both headed for permanent retirement at the end of the 1950–51 season, Fanny now looked forward to returning to her memoirs and turning out a published book with the help of a professional author. Fanny was very selective about ghostwriters.

Stark set up a number of appointments, and Fanny looked like she would choose Norman Katkov, a former feature writer for the *New York World-Telegram* and frequent *Saturday Evening Post* short story contributor with two novels published by Doubleday. Katkov had also done several Hollywood assignments at Warner's and RKO.

Time was not essential, though, since Fanny would not start work with a writer until *Snooks* went off the air. Then there would be nothing but time—for the parties, paintings, grandchildren, and homes. The only problem Fanny had was keeping up her health. She still had headaches, but had ceased to take large quantities of aspirin, convinced—modern medical opinions to the contrary—it had brought on her heart attack.

It came without much warning. On Thursday morning, May 24, 1951, Fanny suffered a severe cerebral hemorrhage at her home in Westwood. Dr. Myron Prizmetal was called and rushed her to Cedars of Lebanon Hospital.

Fran and Ray, Bill and Shirley maintained a vigil while Fanny remained in a coma. At N.B.C. and the homes of the cast, there was the agony of waiting. The fact that only six shows remained on the contract seemed irrelevant at this point. Across the country, people wondered whether Fanny would pull through. No one wanted Baby Snooks to depart radio via death.

Those close to the situation sensed there was no hope. "The waiting was the hard thing," said Vyola Vonn. "Not knowing. . . . The hospital reports were so few and far between. And then the final news. . . ."

Fanny died on Tuesday morning, May 29, 1951. Her family was nearby when the final moment came.

The Legacy

An estimated 1,300 people attended Fanny Brice's funeral in Temple Israel on Thursday, May 31. More than a hundred floral pieces were banked against the pulpit in memory of Fanny, whose body lay in a simple silver-gray casket covered with carnations.

A massive ring of orchids came from Billy Rose.

Rabbi Max Nussbaum performed the ceremony and delivered a brief eulogy. "The heart ennobles any calling," he said, quoting from the Talmud. "A jester may be first in the kingdom of heaven because he has diminished the sadness of human life." He spoke of Fanny's Jewish heritage, and of the Jew's capacity for weeping and laughing.

"Fanny Brice inherited from our tradition not only the capacity of moving people to laughter and to tears, but also she inherited the heart that ennobled her calling.

"She has diminished the sadness of human lives and brought joy into human hearts. We are proud that she was one of us. We feel honored that she came from us and gave years of happiness to the whole world."

George Jessel then delivered another eulogy, a eulogy "for the men and women in the theatrical business: the gang on Forty-second Street and Broadway; for the crowds in front of Henrici's in the Loop in Chicago; for the bunch on the corners of Hollywood and Vine. . . .

"I shall not think," said Jessel, 'Here lies Fanny Brice, stilled into silence from violent illness.' I shall say over and over in my mind that Fanny Brice, a fine American Jewess, a great artist and devoted mother has gone up the road to her fathers—and I shall say to my little girl-child, 'Baby Snooks has gone to sleep.' "

Fanny's will, filed for probate in Los Angeles Superior Court on June 19, bequeathed most of her two-million dollar estate to her children, Frances and William. One thousand dollars was left to Fanny's New York secretary, Marion Altenberg. The rest was put in trust for Fanny's brother, sister, children (with their spouses), and grandchildren.

Fanny's furniture and effects went under the auctioneer's hammer at the Ames Art Galleries, 8725 Wilshire Boulevard, from Saturday night, November 13, 1951, to Wednesday evening of the following week. Included were the modern paintings Fanny had collected. Two weeks later, Fanny's home at 424 Comstock Avenue in Westwood was sold to Mr. and Mrs. Jacob S. Potts for $65,000 at a probate court auction.

With Fanny's estate liquidated, Ray, Fran, Bill, and Shirley turned their attention to her memoirs. Remembering his mother-in-law's comments on the various authors she had interviewed, Ray Stark contacted Norman Katkov. A contract was soon drawn up between the Brice heirs, Katkov, and Alfred A. Knopf, one of the world's leading publishers.

Katkov was supplied with more than three hundred pages of Fanny's notes and given access to the influential people in her life by Ray and Fran. He proceeded to interview Fan's brother, Lew, her sister Carolyn, Nick Arnstein, Billy Rose, Phil Rapp, Eddie and Ida Cantor, Trixie Wilson, Ann Pennington, John Cromswell, Ben Hecht, Everett Freeman, Katharine Hepburn, and George Cukor, who, like Kate, had known Fanny socially in Hollywood.

The economic arrangements did not favor long, hard work by Katkov. He was given sole authorship credit, but had to be content with a comparatively modest percentage of the royalties. The Starks and Bill and Shirley got the rest.

Katkov named most of the chapters after his various interviewees, but relied on Fanny's memoirs for most of his information. The manuscript was finished and delivered to the publisher in April, and plans were made to serialize it in a major magazine prior to its appearance in book form. The *Ladies' Home Journal,* which published *The Fabulous Fanny* in four installments, kicked off a big promotional drive with a cocktail party at Toots Shor's New York restaurant on October 28, 1952.

The book was well reviewed in the indulgent fashion reserved for theatrical biographies in that period, and Knopf did an excellent job of marketing. Katkov looked forward to fine royalties until Fran Stark had a sudden change of heart.

Frances now said the book did not capture her mother; objecting, pointedly, to Katkov's depiction of Fanny as a childhood thief—a depiction drawn from Fanny's own notes, plus interviews with Lew and Carrie.

Katkov bitterly responded, mentioning the harsh financial arrangement he had made with Stark and complaining of the way the family had blue-pencilled much of the material before publication.

Stark then settled matters in the best way he knew how—paying Knopf $50,000 to take *The Fabulous Fanny* off the market. The Brice heirs made no further direct mention of the Katkov book, and Ray Stark turned his attention away from his late mother-in-law for the next eight years.

Bill Brice left his post at the Jedson Art Institute and joined the faculty of UCLA in 1952, eventually becoming a full professor. He continued to show his paintings in various group shows at the Whitney Museum and enjoyed domestic life with his wife, Shirley, and son, John. Bill Brice lived for art, leaving show biz to his increasingly powerful brother-in-law, Ray Stark.

Stark was never satisfied with being an agent and getting only ten percent of what his clients made. Shortly after Fanny died, he made the move to being a producer, resigning his executive position with the Famous Artists Agency to form an independent production company with Eliot Hyman that became Seven Arts Productions. Stark was both smart and aggressive, acquiring a fine array of books and Broadway plays for filming. Included were such properties as *West Side Story, The Nun's Story, Anatomy of a Murder,* and *By Love Possessed.*

Stark supervised over fifty feature productions at Seven Arts, and personally produced two films directed by John Huston: *Night of the Iguana* with Richard Burton (his former client), Ava Gardner, and Deborah Kerr (1964), and *Reflections in a Golden Eye* with Elizabeth Taylor and Marlon Brando (1967).

After *The World of Suzie Wong* was released in 1961, Stark turned his attention back to Fanny, commissioning Isabel Lennart to write a screenplay of her life. Lennart wrote a treatment, the reading of which caused several to say the subject would be better treated as a Broadway musical. Stark agreed, and Lennart then wrote *Funny Girl,* her first Broadway libretto.

Broadway musicals could still be financed for calculable sums, and Stark had the acumen, contacts, and initial capitalization to get all the big investments he needed. Never one to tread where he was unsure of his footing, he entered into an agreement with Broadway producer David Merrick, then at the peak of his powers, to co-produce a show based on the life of Fanny Brice.

The problem then became who would play Fanny. The Starks, still thinking in terms of a movie or a straight play, wanted Anne Bancroft, who had leaped to the forefront as a fine dramatic actress with her portrayal of Annie Sullivan in *The Miracle Worker*. Another strong contender was Carol Burnett, then among the hottest young talents on television. That Burnett could shoulder a Broadway musical was evident from her great work in *Once Upon a Mattress*. The role of Fanny, though, called for someone who worked well with ethnic humor, and Carol did not see herself as that type of performer.

Merrick then withdrew from the entire project, citing difficulty with the book as well as the obvious problem with finding an actress who could portray Fanny Brice—and sing. Among those not unhappy with this decision was Billy Rose. "I have no desire to see a hand-me-down Brice played by some girl who couldn't carry her pocketbook," he wrote. "Nor do I want to sit through a cardboard-and-canvas memorial to one of the few performers who have rated the adjective 'great.' "

Stark decided to pursue the project without Merrick, making up with hard work, money, and street savvy what he lacked in first-hand Broadway expertise. The big remaining problem was still whom to star as Fanny. Ray and Fran still wanted Bancroft, but Jule Styne, like all composers, wanted his songs sung by someone who was principally a singer. Styne knew who he wanted after seeing Barbra Streisand as "Miss Marmelstein" in a show called *I Can Get It for You Wholesale*.

The Brooklyn-born Streisand had made her theatrical debut in an Off-Broadway flop called *Another Evening with Harry Stoones* before opening in *Wholesale* one month before her twentieth birthday in 1962. Appearances on *The Jack Parr Show* and a Columbia LP *(The First Barbra Streisand Album)* made her a "name" performer over the next year. By the fall of 1963, Barbra Streisand was big enough to star in a full-scale Broadway show.

Fran, who always pictured her mother as a fashionable lady with impeccable manners, wanted Bancroft more than ever after meeting Streisand, who showed up for the appointment in the beatnik clothes that marked her style before superstardom turned her avant-garde. "There is no way she will play my mother," Frances vowed. Stark, however, was pragmatic, and enough of a professional to see Styne's points about the show and Streisand's rising star. Barbra got the role, if not Fran Stark's approval. "No character could be quite like Mother," she told Eugenia Sheppard of the *New York Herald Tribune* a few days before the show opened on Broadway. "Mother was a comic, but she was never a nut."

The politicking, false starts, severed partnerships, and shifting alliances that finally put *Funny Girl* onstage were shadowed by an eighty-four-year-old man in New York while the show was in rehearsals. The old man's name was Julius Wilford Arnstein.

Money had again rolled through Nick's long, slim fingers. He was living in Los Angeles with Fanny's brother Lew in 1963, but returned to New York as the guest of his son-in-law, who wished to avoid a possible lawsuit over the coming show. Nick appeared to put the touch on his rich son-in-law on several occasions. One time, Stark, beset by problems with his hoped-for Broadway triumph, loudly turned him down. "Hell, no," he said. "I gave you a grand just last week!"

Nick went back to California and did not attend the opening. "I don't want to see what they will make me into" was his only comment. The script, in truth, made Arnstein more of an embittered failure getting into trouble in an effort to prove his independence than the habitual con man Nick had been. As such, it portrayed Nick as Fanny herself saw him— "just a fool" who "couldn't mastermind an electric lightbulb into a socket." Arnstein passed away October 2, 1965, at the age of eighty-six. Lew Brice, who had remained his closest friend for years, died the following June.

Funny Girl made Streisand the non–rock 'n' roll performer of the decade, and the show rivalled *Hello Dolly!* as the most successful Broadway musical of 1963–64. It did not, however, revive interest in its subject.

Fanny had been dead for less than thirteen years when *Funny Girl* opened at the Winter Garden on March 26, 1964. But she had not appeared on Broadway since 1936, and there were not enough filmed tributes to her greatness to make her more than a vague name to those born after 1920. If young people knew Fanny at all, it was as Baby Snooks— not the young Yiddish comedienne and singer Streisand breathed new life into in 1964.

All of which just helped the show's success. Impressionist and show-business historian Will Jordan has observed that the "only way for a show about a performer to be successful is for its star to make the audience forget about the star she is portraying." Ethel Merman's performance as Mama Rose in *Gypsy* was so riveting that only a few devotees remained marginally aware that the show was about *three* real people— "Mama Rose" Hovick, June Havoc, and Gypsy Rose Lee. *Funny Girl* succeeded because Streisand turned it into a tour de force for her own talents. Had the audience spent the night thinking about Fanny Brice, the show would not have run more than a week.

Streisand simply played a young Jewess growing up in New York in the early 1900s with a burning desire to be a performer. She succeeds, despite not being "pretty like a Miss Atlantic City"; finds (and later loses) the love of a handsome playboy named Nick, and resolves to carry on courageously with her life as the curtain falls.

The facts of Fanny's life are necessarily abridged, although the story is quite accurate in spirit. The naïveté and energy of Fanny in her youth are well portrayed, and certain songs evoke the satirical elements of Fan's best numbers ("Sadie, Sadie, Married Lady"), the opulence and fun of Broadway in the 'teens and 'twenties ("Rat-Tat-Tat-Tat" with Fanny as "Private Schwarts vim Rockavay"), and Fan's own peculiar viewpoint ("People").

It was her unique interest in people—an interest common to many far-less-talented Jewish women—that made Fanny so well loved and special to her friends. If Fanny was a hybrid of a nice, wise Jewish lady and a tough broad from show business, then "People" captures perfectly the first side. It's a tribute to Jule Styne and Streisand that the song described the character, worked well within the show, and became a popular hit into the bargain.

It is ironic that, despite all that she had in common with Fanny Brice— the New York background, the Jewish ethnicity, the fierce ambition to succeed in show business, the talents for comedy and singing, and—perhaps most interesting of all—the loss of a father at an early age (Barbra's father died when she was fifteen months old), Streisand became totally unlike Fanny after the success of *Funny Girl*. Where Fanny remained her earthy self, acquiring culture and polish without changing her completely honest, "What's with this Miss Brice?" persona, Streisand became more and more self-absorbed and megalomaniacal after she became "The Greatest Star."

Streisand's personal isolationism and supreme ego (which would dwarf Al Jolson's) are as much the products of her show-biz era and position as they are of any quirks of personality or reaction to past injuries. The show business of the past twenty-five years is not the chummy, intimate profession it was in the early years of the twentieth century, when little except salary and billing separated stars and other players, and years of touring, in Fanny's own words, "gave you an interesting background, made a *mensch* out of you." It is a world in which, thanks to the mass media, an unimaginably wide gulf separates performers who make it and those who don't, in which stars make megabucks and non-stars do not make a living, in which a star lives on a level different from that of mere mortals, becoming a role model and a god. It is a world quite different from the one that Fanny knew in 1910.

The success of *Funny Girl* as show and movie made Ray Stark richer and more powerful than ever. It did not, however, prevent tragedy from striking him and Fran. In February 1970, their only son, Peter, left his apartment-office to mail a letter at around 6:30 in the morning. He then came back, wrote a note to his secretary telling her to take the day off, and stuck it to the door. Then he opened a window and jumped sixteen stories to his death. What drove the twenty-five-year-old Stark, who was becoming a producer under his father's wing and was heir to a considerable fortune, to take his life will probably remain as much a mystery as the combination of thoughts that drove the talented Freddie Prinze to commit suicide at the age of twenty-one.

Funny Lady, Ray Stark's film sequel to *Funny Girl,* was released in 1975. It "covered" Fanny's life from the time she and Nick divorced until, conceivably, just before her death in 1951. James Caan played Billy Rose as more of a Peter Falk character than the highly intelligent hustler Rose really was. A critical mediocrity, the film was nonetheless commercially successful.

Thanks to the two Streisand vehicles—for such they ultimately were—Fanny Brice became a "role" that thousands of would-be Streisands, Broadway singers, and comediennes in drama schools throughout the country aspired to play, the more serious of whom hoped to bring to the role something of the "real Brice" that Streisand had not captured.

There are a handful of female performers, attempting to make a living in the ever-shrinking world of show biz, who perform Fanny's original songs, some of them with flairs for farce and mimicry. They ultimately fail, though, to capture the uninhibited joy that Fanny brought to her best work—a kind of fun and madness that was part of Fanny but belonged, in a much larger sense, to Brice's era. It is a sense of fun not easily acquired—or retained—in this complex, neurotic, and compulsively idealistic world than in the one that spawned and nurtured Fanny.

If Fanny had no feelings for the "instant stars" and starlets of the 1930s and 'forties, she might have found the stars of the 'seventies and 'eighties, if not quite so vacuous, at least phoney, pseudo-intellectual, and self-absorbed. They are as unlike Fanny as "Miss Atlantic City," and we are the poorer for it.

Fanny was a woman for all seasons, but uniquely of her own time, too—both as a performer and as a person. In later years, she complemented her own liberation as a "show biz gal" with the real liberation born of age and distance. Those last years, though, were lonely ones—despite her independence, or because of it.

Fanny was, indeed, one of those "people who need people." As she grew disillusioned in her love live, she lost the great capacity for personal joy that marked her early years. Her later life was filled with friends and satisfaction, but devoid of that great happiness that marked her early years with Arnstein.

She ultimately became a polished version of her mother (a literal "Second Hand Rose"), the same practical, cynical, and unromantic person she had rejected in early life. It is that capitulation that makes Fanny Brice's life less than a triumph.

Bibliography

While this biography leans heavily on scattered items in daily newspapers, the following books and by-lined articles (many of them interviews with Fanny), were of help.

Books

Arden, Eve. *Three Phases of Eve*. New York: St. Martin's Press, 1985.

Bordman, Gerald. *American Musical Theatre: A Chronicle*. New York: Oxford University Press, 1978.

Burns, George, and David Fisher. *All My Best Friends*. New York: G. P. Putnam's sons, 1989.

Cahn, William. *A Pictorial History of the Great Comedians*. New York: Grosset & Dunlap, 1970.

Cantor, Eddie. *Take My Life*. Garden City, N.Y.: Doubleday & Co., 1957.

Dunning, John. *Tune In Yesterday*. Englewood Cliffs, N.J.: Prentice Hall, 1976.

Gardiner, James. *Gaby Deslys: A Fatal Attraction*. London: Sidgwick & Jackson, 1986.

Green, Stanley. *The Great Clowns of Broadway*. New York: Oxford University Press, 1984.

Harmon, Jim. *The Great Radio Comedians*. Garden City, N.Y.: Doubleday & Co., 1970.

Hecht, Ben. *A Child of the Century*. New York: Simon and Schuster, 1954.

Jessel, George. *This Way, Miss*. New York: Henry Holt & Co., 1955.

Katkov, Norman. *The Fabulous Fanny*. New York: Alfred A. Knopf, 1952.

Levant, Oscar. *The Memoirs of an Amnesiac*. New York: G. P. Putnam's Sons, 1965.

Lillie, Beatrice. *Every Other Inch a Lady*. Garden City, N.Y.: Doubleday & Co., 1972.

Martin, Linda, and Kerry Segrave. *Women in Comedy*. Secaucus, N.J.: Citadel Press, 1986.

Skolsky, Sidney. *Times Square Tintypes*. New York: Ives Washburn, 1930.

Smith, William. *The Vaudevillians.* New York: Macmillan Publishing Co., 1976.
Tucker, Sophie. *Some of These Days.* Garden City, N.Y.: Doubleday & Co., 1945.

Magazine Articles

Bernstein, Eve. "Fannie Brice Tells Her Story." *Jewish Tribune,* December 28, 1928.
Brice, Fannie. "The Feel of the Audience." *Saturday Evening Post,* November 21, 1925.
———, as told to Palma Wayne. "Fannie of the Follies." *Hearst's International-Cosmopolitan,* three installments, Feb., March, April, 1936.
———. "My Life." *Modern Romances,* 1938.
Busch, Niven, Jr. "Fire Sign." *The New Yorker,* April 20, 1929.
Cattell, Hettie Jithian. "Fanny Brice—Her Own Story." *Panorama,* three installments, October 1,6,13, 1928.
Kutner, Nanette. "If You Were Daughter to Baby Snooks." *Good Housekeeping,* March 1943.
Rose, Billy. "A Girl Named Fanny." *McCall's,* September 1963.
Seldes, Gilbert. "The Daemonic in the American Theatre." *The Dial,* September 1923.
Sanders, Ethel E. "Semitic Silhouettes." *Opinion: A Journal of Jewish Life and Letters,* December 1932.
Shugrue, Thomas. "Little Jumbo." *American Magazine,* January 1937.
Wilson, Beatrice. "Fannie and Her English Rival." *Classic,* June 1924.
Zolotow, Maurice. "Baby Snooks." *Cosmopolitan,* two installments, September, October, 1946.
———. "The Fabulous Billy Rose." *Collier's,* four installments, February 15–March 8, 1947.

City Directories

Manhattan (1886–1913)
Newark (1895–1903)
Brooklyn (1902–1908)

Unpublished Manuscripts

Brice, Fanny. "Don't Pick Your Money Up Until You're Finished Singing."
Zolotow, Maurice. "Billy Rose of Broadway."

Newspaper Articles

Bent, Silas. "Nicky Keeps His Four-Million Dollar Secret." *New York Times,* July 27, 1924.
Black, Karen. "Those Lessons Paid Off for Fanny's Kid." Interview with William Brice.
Darnton, Charles. "Fannie Brice Gives an Audience." *New York Herald Tribune,* August 14, 1938.
Heffernan, Harold. "Follies Being Filmed as Ziegfeld Staged Them." *Dallas Morning News,* August 8, 1944.

Reynolds, Ruth. "Fanny Brice ('One-Man Woman')." *New York Sunday News,* December 12, 1927.
Sheppard, Eugenia. "Life with Mother." *New York Herald-Tribune,* Sunday, March 22, 1964. Interview with Mrs. Ray Stark.
Spiegel, Irving. "Having to Do with Baby Snooks." *New York Times,* April 22, 1945.

Trade Newspapers

The Billboard (1906–1917)
The New York Clipper (1906–1917)
Variety (1906–1951)

New York Review (1910)
New York Dramatic Mirror (1906–1917)

Stageography

A MILLIONAIRE'S REVENGE

A Melodrama in Four Acts, by Hal Reid. Produced by the Mittenthal Brothers Amusement Co.

Cast

Harold Daw	BRINSLEY SHAW
Stanford Black	LOUIS E. MILLER
Benjamin Franklin	MASTER MARTIN
Billy Brown	WALFRED WILSON
Thomas Meade	JAMES BURROWS
Jack Watson	JOHN HENDERSON
Henry Matson	WILLIAM CAMPBELL
Joshua Dingle	HARRY J. LANE
J. Henderson Smith	BOBBY NOLAN
Winston Russell	RALPH SANFORD
Timothy Darrell	FRED COOPER
Charles Blackburn	WILLIAM ABBOTT
Benjamin Dustin	JOHN ROSE
Martin	CHARLES GOODWIN
John Murphy	ROBERT KEITH
Dan McGlone	C. SPARKS
Walter	EDDIE MACK
Kate McElroy	LOUISE MITCHELL
Eloise Daw	ALICE SEYMOUR
Mrs. Wilson Daw	BERTINE ROBISON
Samantha Dingle	MAY E. MCKAY
Alice Walton	JENNY WATERS *
Myrtle Stone	GRACE SMITH
Mabel Keats	MAYSIE HARRISON
Annie Wilson	KATHRYN FLYNN
Emeline Hudspeth Daw	JOSEPHINE THERESE THILL

*Also known as Fanny Borach, later Brice. Fanny was replaced by Alice Seymour (who retained her other role as "Eloise Daw") in Pittsburgh.

1906	Sept. 13	Fulton Opera House	Lancaster, Pa.
	14	York Opera House	York, Pa.
	17–22	Bijou	Pittsburgh, Pa.

A Millionaire's Revenge continued on tour, playing, among numerous engagements, one week at the West End Theatre in Harlem, N.Y., October 1–6, 1906.

THE TRANS-ATLANTIC BURLESQUERS

PRINCIPALS: John W. Quinn, Eddie Fitzgerald, Lizzie Freligh, Eddie Nugent, James Whitely, Clay Smith, Val Raynor, Eddie Convey, Georgia and Dolores DeGraff, Norma Bell, Norma Brown.

CHORUS: Minnie Gordon, Loretta Leroy, Rosita Lawrence, Fannie Borach, Kitty May, Bessie Galard, Mabel Leslie, Florence Chadwick, Jean Athos, May Whiteley, Marie Sheldon, Elsie Ardell, Marie Harvey, Annie Whitney, Clara Sauter, Babe Raymond.

FIRST PART: "The Flubb-Dubb Conspiracy"
"My Irish Rosie"
"In the Land of the Buffalo"
"When the Moon Plays 'Peek-A-Boo' with You"
"Tomorrow"
"I'm Happy When the Band Plays 'Dixie' "

OLIO: Sisters DeGraff (up-to-date songs), Eddie Fitzgerald and John W. Quinn, Kalinowski Brothers (European acrobats), Norma Bell (operatic selections, assisted by her musical ponies), Clay Smith and Eddie Convey (talking and singing act), Val Raynor, James Whitely, and Eddie Nugent (trio).

BURLESQUE: "The Gay Modiste"
"Smile on Me"
"Don't Be Angry"

1907	Nov. 25–30	Olympic	Brooklyn, N.Y.
	Dec. 2–7	Murray Hill	New York, N.Y.
	9–14	Casino	Philadelphia, Pa.
	16–18	Bijou	Reading, Pa.
	19–21	Columbia	Scranton, Pa.
	23–28	Waldmann's	Newark, N.J.
Dec. 30, 1907–Jan. 4, 1908		Hurtig & Seamon's	Harlem, N.Y.
1908	Jan. 6–11	Westminster	Providence, R.I.
	13–18	Palace	Boston, Mass.
	20–22	Gilmore	Springfield, Mass.
	23–25	Empire	Albany, N.Y.
	Jan. 27–Feb. 1	Star	Brooklyn, N.Y.
	Feb. 3–8	Gayety	Brooklyn, N.Y.
	10–12	Columbia	Scranton, Pa.
	13–15	Bijou	Reading, Pa.
	17–22	Gayety	Philadelphia, Pa.

24–29	Gayety	Baltimore, Md.
March 2–7	Gayety	Washington, D.C.
9–14	Gayety	Pittsburgh, Pa.
16–21	Gayety	Columbus, Ohio
22–28	Standard	Cincinnati, Ohio
March 30–April 4	———†	Birmingham, Ala.
19–25	Majestic	Kansas City, Mo.
April 26–May 2	Gayety	St. Louis, Mo.
May 3–9	Star and Garter	Chicago, Ill.
10–16	Gayety	Milwaukee, Wisc.

THE GIRLS FROM HAPPYLAND

PRINCIPALS: Billy W. Watson, Lizzie Freligh, Harry Kohler, Charles Brown, Ed Rogers, Florence Belmont, Nellie Watson, Minnie Gordon, Margie Austin, Loretta LeRoy, Mabel Leslie, Fanny Brice.

CHORUS: May Brown, Lottie Crompton, Vera Domnie, Ruby Fairfax, Pink Reynolds, Jessie Riker, Carrie Franklin, Blanche Mann, Gertrude Blake, Ollie B. Hoyt, Helen Neilson, Harriet Murray, Elsie Ashton, Daisy Belmont.

FIRST PART: "Two Hot Knights"
"Oh, Mr. Greenberg!"
"Down in Lovers' Lane"
"Jane, Jane, Jane"
"Dinah Do"
"I Lova-a Rosa"
"Pansy, My Honey Bee"

OLIO: Margie Austin (singing and dancing soubrette), Billy W. Watson and Co. (in "The Man from Tiffany"), Harry Kohler, (Hebrew comedian), Ed Rogers and Co. (presenting "Cotton Blossoms"), Monarch Comedy Four, Verdi Musical Four.

BURLESQUE: "The Gay Modiste"
"A Pussy Cat"
"Jump in My Taxi Cab, Girlie"

1908	Aug. 30–Sept. 5	———	Birmingham, Ala.
	Sept. 6–12	Greenwall	New Orleans, La.
	14–19	———	Memphis, Tenn.
	21–26	Majestic	Kansas City, Mo.
	Sept. 28–Oct. 3	Gayety	St. Louis, Mo.
	Oct. 4–10	Miaco's Trocadero	Chicago, Ill.
	11–17	Gayety	Milwaukee, Wisc.
	18–24	Euson's	Chicago, Ill.
	26–31	Empire	Cleveland, Ohio
	Nov. 2–7	Garden	Buffalo, N.Y.

†Dash indicates that the information is unavailable for this time period.

9–14	Corinthian	Rochester, N.Y.
16–21	Gayety	Toronto, Ont.
23–28	Princess	Montreal, Que.
Nov. 30–Dec. 2	Empire	Albany, N.Y.
Dec. 3–5	Empire	Holyoke, Mass.
7–12	Palace	Boston, Mass.
14–19	Olympic	Brooklyn, N.Y.
21–26	Murray Hill	New York, N.Y.
Dec. 28, 1908–Jan. 2, 1909	Casino	Philadelphia, Pa.
1909 Jan. 4–9	Waldmann's	Newark, N.J.
11–16	Gayety	Hoboken, N.J.
18–23	Hurtig & Seamon's	New York, N.Y.
25–30	Westminster	Providence, R.I.
Feb. 1–6	Gaiety	Boston, Mass.
8–13	Empire	Springfield, Mass.
15–20	Olympic	New York, N.Y.
22–27	Star	Brooklyn, N.Y.
March 1–6	Gayety	Brooklyn, N.Y.
8–13	Gayety	Philadelphia, Pa.
15–20	Gayety	Baltimore, Md.
22–27	Gayety	Washington, D.C.
March 29–April 3	Gayety	Pittsburgh, Pa.
April 5–10	Gayety	Columbus, Ohio
11–17	Empire	Toledo, Ohio
19–24	Gayety	Detroit, Mich.
April 26–May 1	Star & Garter	Chicago, Ill.
May 3–8	Standard	Cincinnati, Ohio
10–15	Hurtig & Seamon's	New York, N.Y.
17–22	Star	Brooklyn, N.Y.
24–29	Gayety	Brooklyn, N.Y.
May 31–June 5	Murray Hill	New York, N.Y.

THE COLLEGE GIRLS ("At Home and Abroad")

PRINCIPALS: Willie Weston, Andrew Toombes, Grace Childres, Fanny Brice, May Florine Linden, George Scanlon, Joe Fields, R. M. Knowles, Edith Parfray, Joe Peltier, Florence Barry.

SHOWGIRLS: Louise Lloyd, Margaret Primrose, Florence Ross, Eleanor Kershaw, Nellie Yeo, Margaret Arionette, Helen Watson, Lillian Newall, Jeannette Daley, Mabel Schiller.

CHORUS: Sadie Fein, Marion Grant, Mildred Irving, Gladys Morrison, Imogene Carter, May Palmer, May Keating, Bertha Baker, Marie Bryant, Madeline Cohan, Gertrude Ackerman, Fanny Fein, Regina Clark, May Guion, Mazie Small, May Daley.

"Love Thy Neighbor"
"College Boy"
"Memories"

*"Music Man"
*"O.I.C."
"I Love to Waltz with You"
"I'm the Popular Boy"
"La, La, La"
"If a Girl Led the Boys in Blue"
*"The Girl with the Diamond Dress"
"The Tale of the Whale"
* Specialties

1909 Aug. 21–28	Gayety	Brooklyn, N.Y.
Aug. 30–Sept. 4	Casino	Philadelphia, Pa.
Sept. 6–11	Gayety	Baltimore, Md.
13–18	Gayety	Washington, D.C.
20–22	Apollo	Wheeling, W. Va.
23–25	Gayety	Columbus, Ohio
Sept. 27–Oct. 2	Empire	Toledo, Ohio
Oct. 4–9	Gayety	Detroit, Mich.
11–16	Star & Garter	Chicago, Ill.
18–23	Standard	Cincinnati, Ohio
25–30	Gayety	Louisville, Ky.
Nov. 1–6	Gayety	St. Louis, Mo.
8–13	Majestic	Kansas City, Mo.
15–20	Empire	Des Moines, Iowa
22–27	Gayety	Minneapolis, Minn.
Nov. 29–Dec. 4	Gayety	Milwaukee, Wisc.
Dec. 6–11	Alhambra	Chicago, Ill.
13–18	Euson's	Chicago, Ill.
20–25	Empire	Cleveland, Ohio
27–29	Gayety	Columbus, Ohio
Dec. 30, 1909–Jan. 1, 1910	Apollo	Wheeling, W. Va.
1910 Jan. 3–8	Gayety	Pittsburgh, Pa.
10–15	Garden	Buffalo, N.Y.
17–22	Gayety	Toronto, Ont.
24–29	Corinthian	Rochester, N.Y. ˙
Jan. 31–Feb. 2	Mohawk	Schenectady, N.Y.
Feb. 3–5	Empire	Albany, N.Y.
7–12	Casino	Boston, Mass.
14–16	Gilmore	Springfield, Mass.
17–19	Empire	Holyoke, Mass.
21–26	Murray Hill	New York, N.Y.
Feb. 28–March 5	Gayety	Philadelphia, Pa.
March 7–12	Waldmann's	Newark, N.J.
14–19	Gayety	Hoboken, N.J.
21–26	Hurtig & Seamon's	New York, N.Y.
March 28–April 2	Westminster	Providence, R.I.
April 4–9	Gaiety	Boston, Mass.
11–16	Columbia	New York, N.Y.

* Performed by Brice.

THE ZIEGFELD FOLLIES OF 1910

A Musical Revue in Three Acts and Fourteen Scenes. Book and Lyrics by Harry B. Smith. Music by Gus Edwards. Staged by Julian Mitchell.

ACT I

Scene One—"Dress Rehearsal of the *Follies*"

Stage Manager Mitchell	HARRY WATSON, JR
Musical Director Levi	GEORGE BICKEL
Stage Doorkeeper	JEROME VAN NORDEN
Miss Pansy Perkins	FANNY BRICE
Mazie Muggs	ROSIE GREEN
Sadie Spooner	VONNIE HOYE
Flossie Frost	VERA MAXWELL
Flossie's Mother	ALINE BOLEY
Iona Carr	GRACE TYSON
Towne Duer	JOHN REINHARDT
A Waiter	CLIFFORD SAUM

Scene Two—"Office of the Get-Poor-Quick Syndicate"
Scene Three—"The Lakes of Killarney"
Scene Four—"A Street in Reno"
Scene Five—"Behind the Curtains"
Scene Six—"The Apple Blossom Grove"

ACT II

Scene Seven—"Cafe de L'Opera"
Scene Eight—"Reminiscent Ragtime Revue"

"Yankiana Rag" from *Miss Innocence*	SHIRLEY KELLOGG
"Temptation Rag"	LILLIAN LORRAINE
"Fandango Rag" from *Follies of 1909*	MINDEL KINGSTON
"Wild Cherry Rag"	FANNY BRICE
"Italian Rag"	BOBBY NORTH
"Ma Blushin' Rosie" from *Fiddle Dee Dee*	LILLIAN ST. CLAIR
"Rosalie" from *The Wizard of Oz*	LILLIAN LORRAINE
"Franco-American Rag"	MINDEL KINGSTON
	MARGARET MORRIS
"A Woman's Dream"	LILLIAN ST. CLAIR

Scene Nine—"A Band Rehearsal, Metropolitan Tower"
Scene Ten—"The Swings"

ACT III

Scene Eleven—"Office of a Music Publisher"

Frank Steel, songwriter	GEORGE BICKEL
Nibbsie Hooligan, piano mover	HARRY WATSON, JR.

Smiley, a publisher	ARTHUR MCWATERS
Steele, a composer	ARTHUR NICKERSON
The Dotty Sisters	FANNY BRICE
	ALINE BOLEY
Rosie Blow	GRACE TYSON
Frank Bluff	JACQUES KRUGER

Scene Twelve—"Model Hennery"
Scene Thirteen—"The Comet and the Earth"
Scene Fourteen—"The Return of Roosevelt"

FINALE

Score

*"Good-Bye, Becky Cohen" (Irving Berlin)
"Look Me Over Carefully" (Edwards–Smith)
"Nix on the Concertina, Lena" (McDonald)
"Sweet Kitty Bellairs" (Edwards–Smith)
"Kidland" (Gus Edwards–Harry B. Smith)
"The Pensacola Mooch" (Dabney–Cook)
"Swing Me High, Swing Me Low" (Victor Hollaender–Ballard MacDonald)
"Don't Take a Girl Down to Coney" (Edwards–Smith)
*"Lovey Joe" (Joe Jordan–Will Marion Cook)
"The Cock of the Walk" (Edwards–Smith)
"I'll Get You Yet" (Von Tilzer–Burkhart)
"Mr. Earth and His Comet Love" (Edwards)
"The Waltzing Lieutenant" (Gus Edwards)

1910	June 13–18	Nixon's Apollo	Atlantic City, N.J.
	June 20–Sept. 3	Jardin de Paris	New York, N.Y.
	Sept. 5–Oct 8	Colonial	Chicago, Ill.
	Oct. 9–15	Olympic	St. Louis, Mo.
	17–22	Grand Opera House	Cincinnati, Ohio
	24–29	English's Opera House	Indianapolis, Ind.
	Oct. 31–Nov. 5	Detroit Opera House	Detroit, Mich.
	Nov. 7–12	Euclid Ave. Opera House	Cleveland, Ohio
	14–19	Nixon	Pittsburgh, Pa.
	Nov. 21–Dec. 17	Chestnut Street O.H.	Philadelphia, Pa.
	Dec. 19–24	Grand Opera House	New York, N.Y.
	26–31	National	Washington, D.C.
1911	Jan. 2–7	Teller's Broadway	Brooklyn, N.Y.
	Jan. 9–March 4	Tremont	Boston, Mass.
	March 6–11	Montauk	Brooklyn, N.Y.
	13–18	Ford's Opera House	Baltimore, Md.
	20–25	Empire	Syracuse, N.Y.
	27–29	Lyceum	Rochester, N.Y.
	30	Valentine	Toledo, Ohio
	31	Grand Opera House	Davenport, Iowa
	April 1	Foster's Opera House	Des Moines, Iowa

2–8	Willis Wood	Kansas City, Mo.
9–15	(Holy Week Lay-Off)	
16–29	Columbia	San Francisco, Calif.
May 1–2	MacDonough	Oakland, Calif.
3, 4	——	
5	Barton	Fresno, Calif.
7–13	Mason Opera House	Los Angeles, Calif.
15–17	Salt Lake	Salt Lake City, Utah
18	——	Pueblo, Colo.
19–20	Grand Opera House	Colorado Springs, Colo.
21–27	Broadway	Denver, Colo.
29–30	Oliver	Lincoln, Neb.
31	——	Sioux City, Iowa
†June 1–3	Brandeis	Omaha, Neb.

† Several principals left for New York after the first performance.

THE ZIEGFELD FOLLIES OF 1911

A Musical Revue in Two Acts and Fourteen Scenes. Book and Lyrics by George V. Hobart. Music by Maurice Levi and Raymond Hubbell. Staged by Julian Mitchell. Musical Numbers Arranged by Gus Sohlke and Jack Mason.

ACT I

Scene One—"The Customs"
Scene Two—*"Jardin de Paris"*
Scene Three—"A California Poppy Field"
Scene Four—*Everywife* (A Symbolical Play in Four Scenes)

> First Scene—"The Home"
> Second Scene—"The Stage Door" A month elapses.
> Third Scene—"Everyhusband's Club" Other months elapse.
> Fourth Scene—"The Home"

Scene Eight—"The Poppy Field"
Scene Nine—"New Year's Eve on the Barbary Coast—A San Francisco Cabaret"
Fanny Brice, Vera Maxwell, Harry Watson Jr., Leon Errol, Rosie & Yansci Dolly, Stella Chatelaine, Brown & Blyler

ACT II

Scene One—"H.M.S. Vaudeveel"

Sir Glassuf Pilsener, K.E.G.	HARRY WATSON, JR.
Captain Head-Liner	WALTER PERCIVAL
Ralph Hustlestraw	CHAS. HESSONG
Dick Deadeye, imported from Leipsic	CHAS. A. MASON
Bill Bobstay	PETER SWIFT
Gasolene, the Captain's cheeild	CLARA PALMER
Hebe, Sir Glassuf's quaint cousin	LEON ERROL
Rachel Rosenstein	FANNY BRICE

Sailors, Marines, Midshipmites, Chickens, Broilers, and Squab

Scene Two—"Tad's Daffydils"
Scene Three—"New York Central Depot" (Bert Williams and Leon Errol)
Scene Four—"Exterior, New York Central Depot' (Songs by Bert Williams)
Scene Five—"A Fifteen Minute Peep at *The Pink Lady*"

FINALE
Score
"New York (You're the Best Town in Europe)" (R. Hubbell–Raymond Peck)
"The Widow Wood" (Maurice Levi–Channing Pollock–Rennold Wolf)
"Bumble Bee" (James Blyler–Jean Havez–Donnelly)
*"Dog Gone That Chilly Man" (Irving Berlin)
*"Ephraham Played Upon the Piano" (Berlin)
"Woodman, Spare That Tree" (Berlin)
"Whippoorwill (Never Again for Me)" (Blyler–Fagan)
"How Would You Like to Be My Pony?" (Hubbell–Hobart)
"The Girl in Pink" (Hubbell–George V. Hobart)
"I'm a Crazy Daffydil" (Jerome Kern–Bessie McCoy)
"Cakewalk" (Hubbell)
"It Was Me" (Seymour Furth–George W. Day)
"Take Care, Little Girl, Take Care" (Hubbell–Hobart)
"My Beautiful Lady"

1911	June 20–24	Nixon's Apollo	Atlantic City, N.J.
	June 26–Sept. 2	Jardin de Paris	New York, N.Y.
	Sept. 4–Oct. 28	Colonial	Chicago, Ill.
	Oct. 30–Nov. 4	English's Opera House	Indianapolis, Ind.
	Nov. 5–11	Olympic	St. Louis, Mo.
	13–18	Grand Opera House	Cincinnati, Ohio
	20–25	Nixon	Pittsburgh, Pa.
	Nov. 27–Dec. 2	Euclid Ave. Opera House	Cleveland, Ohio
	Dec. 4–9	Detroit Opera House	Detroit, Mich.
Dec. 11, 1911–Jan. 6, 1912		Chestnut St. Opera House	Philadelphia, Pa.
1912	Jan. 8–Feb. 10	Tremont	Boston, Mass.
	Feb. 12–14	Empire	Providence, R.I.
	15		
	16–17	Jefferson	Portland, Me.
	19–20		Worcester, Mass.
	21–22	Court Square	Springfield, Mass.
	23–24	Parsons'	Hartford, Conn.
	Feb. 26–March 2	National	Washington, D.C.
	March 4–9	Ford's Opera House	Baltimore, Md.
	11–13	Empire	Syracuse, N.Y.
	14–16	Lyceum	Rochester, N.Y.
	18–23	Princess	Toronto, Ont.
	25–27	Star	Buffalo, N.Y.
	28	———	Ithaca, N.Y.
	29	Lyceum	Elmira, N.Y.
	30	———	

FANNY BRICE
UBO Vaudeville

1912	April 22–27	Hammerstein's Victoria	New York, N.Y.
	April 29–May 4	Colonial	New York, N.Y.
	May 6–June 1	———	
	June 3–8	Hammerstein's Roof	New York, N.Y.
	10–29	———	
	July 1–6	New Brighton	Brooklyn, N.Y.
	8–13	———	
	15–20	Keith's Union Square	New York, N.Y.
	22–27	———	
	July 29–Aug. 3	Morrison's	Rockaway, N.Y.
	Aug. 5–10	Fifth Avenue	New York, N.Y.
	12–17	Proctor's	Newark, N.J.

THE WHIRL OF SOCIETY

Book by George Bronson-Howard and Harold Atteridge. Music by Louis A. Hirsch. Lyrics by Harold Atteridge. Entire Production staged by Ned Wayburn. Presented by the Messrs. Shubert.

Cast

Miss Vandercrief	FLORENCE CABLE
Mrs. Thatcher-Raypen	CLAUDIA CARLSTEDT
Sadie, a maid	FANNY BRICE
Mrs. J. Hemmingway Deane	ADA LEWIS
Angela Deane	LAURA HAMILTON
Gus, a butler at Deane's	AL JOLSON
Baron von Shine	WILLIE WESTON
Franklyn Copeland	OSCAR SCHWARTZ
J. Hemmingway Deane	CLARENCE HARVEY
A footman	HENRY DETTLOFF
Harry Courtfield	MELVILLE ELLIS
Earl of Pawtucket	LAWRENCE D'ORSAY
Countess of Pawtucket	BESSIE FREWEN

FLORENCE & FAY COURTNEY
FLORENCE WALTON & MAURICE

ACT I—Scene 1—Drawing Room at Deane's.
　　　　Scene 2—"A Night with the Pierrots"
ACT II—Ball Room at Mrs. Deane's.

Score

"Meet Me in Peacock Alley"
*"Fol de Rol Dol Doi" (Schwartz–Madden)
"My Sumurun Girl" (Hirsch–Jolson)
"Ragtime Soldier Man" (Irving Berlin)

*"How Do You Know?"
"Lead Me to That Beautiful Band"
"Row, Row, Row" (Monaco–Jerome)
"Cinderella Waltz"
"Society Bear" (Irving Berlin)
*"Here Comes the Bride"
"Hitchy-Koo" (Muir–Abrahams–Gilbert)
"Ghost of the Violin" (Snyder–Kalmar)

1912	Sept. 1–28	Lyric	Chicago, Ill.
	Sept. 29–Oct. 5	Sam S. Shubert	Kansas City, Mo.
	Oct. 6–12	Sam S. Shubert	St. Louis, Mo.
	13–19	Lyric	Cincinnati, Ohio
	21	Lexington Opera House	Lexington, Ky.
	22–23	Masonic Temple	Louisville, Ky.
	24–26	Murat	Indianapolis, Ind.
	Oct. 28–Nov. 2	Garrick	Detroit, Mich.
	Nov. 4–9	Colonial	Cleveland, Ohio
	11–16	Alvin	Pittsburgh, Pa.
	18–20	Auditorium	Baltimore, Md.
	21–23	Belasco	Washington, D.C.
	Nov. 25–Dec. 28	Lyric	Philadelphia, Pa.
Dec. 30, 1912–Jan. 4, 1913		Princess	Montreal, Que.
1913	Jan. 6–11	Royal Alexandra	Toronto, Ont.
	13–15	Teck	Buffalo, N.Y.
	16	Majestic	Utica, N.Y.
	17	Van Curler Opera House	Schenectady, N.Y.
	18	Harmanus Bleecker Hall	Albany, N.Y.
	20–25	Majestic	Brooklyn, N.Y.

THE HONEYMOON EXPRESS

A Spectacular Farce with Music in Two Acts and Six Scenes. Book by Joseph W. Herbert. Lyrics by Harold Atteridge. Music by Jean Schwartz. Staged by Ned Wayburn. Presented by the Messrs. Shubert.

Cast

Henri Dubonet	ERNEST GLENDINNING
Pierre, his friend	HARRY FOX
Baudry, a lawyer	HARRY PILCER
Gardonne, hotel keeper at Arignon	LOU ANGER
Gus, butler at Dubonet's	AL JOLSON
Doctor D'Zuvray	MELVILLE ELLIS
Achille	FRANK HOLMES
Eduard	ROBERT HASTINGS
Gautier	GERALD MCDONALD
Constant	JACK CARLETON
Paul	HENRY DYER
Guillaume	CLINT RUSSELL

Felix, a gateman	HARRY WARDELL
Alfonse	HARLAND DIXON
Gaston	JAMES DOYLE
Maurice, a poster painter	F. OWEN BAXTER
Yvonne, wife of Henri	GABY DESLYS
Mme. De Bressie, Yvonne's aunt	ADA LEWIS
Marguerite, Gardonne's daughter	YANSCI DOLLY
Marcelle, a domestic	FANNY BRICE
Marcus, a waiter	GILBERT WILSON
Noelie, a maid	MARJORIE LANE

Score

"That Is the Life for Me"
"When the Honeymoon Stops Shining"
* "Syncopatia Land"
"You'll Call the Next Love the First"
"I Want the Strolling Good"
"The Ragtime Express"
"That Gal of Mine"
"Give Me the Hudson Shore"
* "My Coca-Cola Belle"
"You Are the Someone"
"I Want a Toy Soldier Man"
"Our Little Cabaret Up Home"
"Bring Back Your Love"
* "My Raggyadore"
"My Yellow Jacket Girl"
"When Gaby Did the Gaby Glide"

ACT I—Scene 1—Grounds of Cercle du Sport, at rear of Dubonet's Villa.
　　　　Scene 2—Railway Station at Etretat.
　　　　Scene 3—The Junction at Rouen.
ACT II—Scene 1—Henri's Apartments, Paris.
　　　　Scene 2—Corridor Leading to Henri's Apartments.
　　　　Scene 3—Lobby of the Grand Opera House, Paris.

1913	Feb. 3–4	Hyperion	New Haven, Conn.
	Feb. 6–April 26	Winter Garden	New York, N.Y.

FANNY BRICE
UBO Vaudeville

1913	June 9–14	Shea's	Buffalo, N.Y.
	16–21	———	
	23–28	Fifth Avenue	New York, N.Y.
	June 30–July 5	———	
	July 7–12	Brighton Music Hall	Brooklyn, N.Y.

COME OVER HERE

1913	Aug. 4–23	London Opera House	London, Eng.

À LA CARTE

1913	Oct. 27–Nov. 8	Victoria Palace	London, Eng.

HULLO, RAGTIME!

1913	Dec. 1–6	Palladium	London, Eng.
	Dec. 8–Jan. 10	———	
1914	Jan. 12–17	Empire	Bristol, Eng.

FANNY BRICE
UBO Vaudeville

1914	Feb. 23–28	Palace	New York, N.Y.
	March 2–7	Colonial	New York, N.Y.
	9–14	Hammerstein's	New York, N.Y.
	16–21	Grand	Pittsburgh, Pa.
	23–28	Maryland	Baltimore, Md.
	March 30–April 4	Alhambra	New York, N.Y.
	April 6–11	(Travel)	
	13–18	Temple	Detroit, Mich.
	20–25	Temple	Rochester, N.Y.
	April 27–May 2	Keith's	Washington, D.C.
	May 4–9	Colonial	New York, N.Y.
	11–16	Orpheum	Brooklyn, N.Y.
	18–23	Keith's	Philadelphia, Pa.
	25–30	Keith's	Boston, Mass.
	June 1–6	———	
	8–13	Shea's	Buffalo, N.Y.
	15–20	Majestic	Chicago, Ill.
	June 22–July 4	(Travel)	
	July 6–11	Hammerstein's	New York, N.Y.
	Aug. 31–Sept. 5	Orpheum	Brooklyn, N.Y.
	Sept. 7–12	Colonial	New York, N.Y.
	14–19	Bushwick	Brooklyn, N.Y.
	21–26	Alhambra	New York, N.Y.
	Sept. 28–Oct. 10	(layoff; illness)	
	Oct. 12–17	Royal	New York, N.Y.
	19–24	Palace	New York, N.Y.
	Oct. 26–Nov. 21	———	
	Nov. 23–28	Keith's	Louisville, Ky.
	Nov. 30–Dec. 5	Colonial	New York, N.Y.
	Dec. 7–12		
	14–19	Prospect	Brooklyn, N.Y.
	21–26	———	

Dec. 28, 1914–Jan. 2, 1915	Alhambra	New York, N.Y.
1915 Jan. 4–9	Orpheum	Brooklyn, N.Y.
11–16	Grand	Pittsburgh, Pa.
18–23	Maryland	Baltimore, Md.
25–30	Royal	New York, N.Y.
Feb. 1–6	————	
8–13	Keith's	Providence, R.I.
15–20	Temple	Detroit, Mich.
22–27	Temple	Rochester, N.Y.
March 1–6	Keith's	Philadelphia, Pa.
8–13	Orpheum	Montreal, Quebec
15–20	Shea's	Buffalo, N.Y.
22–27	Shea's	Toronto, Ont.
March 29–April 3	Palace Music Hall	Chicago, Ill.
April 5–10	Majestic	Milwaukee, Wisc.
12–17	Majestic	Chicago, Ill.
19–24	Columbia	St. Louis, Mo.
April 26–May 1	Orpheum	Memphis, Tenn.
May 3–8	Orpheum	New Orleans, La.
10–15	————	
17–22	Forsythe	Atlanta, Ga.

HANDS UP

A Summer Revue in Two Acts. Book by Edgar Smith. Lyrics by E. Ray Goetz and William Daly. Music by E. Ray Goetz. Presented by Lew Fields. Staged by William H. Post and Frank Smithson.
CAST: Lew Fields, Maurice and (Florence) Walton, Fanny Brice, Lew Brice, Adelaide Mason, and others.

1915 June 7–12	Sam S. Shubert	New Haven, Conn.
14–16	Harmanus Bleecker Hall	Albany, N.Y.

FANNY BRICE
UBO Vaudeville

July 19–24	New Brighton	Brooklyn, N.Y.
26–Aug. 14	————	
Aug. 16–21	Keith's	Far Rockaway, N.Y.
23–28	New Brighton	Brooklyn, N.Y.
Aug. 30–Sept. 4	————	
Sept. 6–11	Palace	New York, N.Y.
13–18	Colonial	New York, N.Y.

HANDS UP

A Musical Revue in Two Acts and Twelve Scenes. Book by Edgar Smith. Lyrics by E. Ray Goetz. Music by E. Ray Goetz and Sigmund Romberg. Presented by the Messrs. Shubert.

Strong Arm Steve	GEORGE HASSELL
Helene Fudge	HAZEL KIRKE

Percy Bonehead	ARTIE MEHLINGER
Mlle. Marcelle	ADELE JASON
Obediah Fudge	CHARLES H. PRINCE
Waltz King	MAURICE WALTON
La Belle Claire	FLORENCE WALTON
Ingersoll	ALFRED LATELL
Simp Watson	BOBBY NORTH
Fake Kennedy	WILLARD SIMMS
Violet Lavender	IRENE FRANKLIN

Fanny Brice replaced Irene Franklin on October 12, 1915.

ACT I—The Orange Grove (Painted by Mark Lawson)
ACT II—Thé Dansant at Sing Sing (Painted by H. R. Law)

1915 Oct. 11–23	Lyric	Philadelphia, Pa.

NOBODY HOME

A Musical Comedy in Two Acts. Book by Guy Bolton and Paul Rubens. Music by Jerome Kern. Presented by Elisabeth Marbury and F. Ray Comstock.

Cast

Maurice, asst. mgr., Hotel Blitz	THOMAS GRAVES
Bellboy, at the Blitz	QUENTIN TOD
Rolando D'Amorini, the artful husband	CHARLES JUDELS
Mrs. D'Amorini, his wife	MAUDE ODELL
Vernon Popple, a society dancer	NIGEL BARRIE
Violet Brinton, Mrs. D'Amorini's niece	MIGNON MCGIBENY
Barmaid, at the Blitz	CONSTANCE HUNTINGTON
Miss Pippin, a showgirl	ELIZABETH MORE
Lucille, Tony Miller's personal mgr.	CORALIE BLYTHE
Jack Kenyon, a jealous admirer of Tony	GEORGE LYDECKER
Miss "Tony" Miller, prima donna at the Winter Garden	FANNY BRICE
Dolly Dip, a dancer	HELEN CLARKE
Sally Trip, a dancer	ALISON MCBAIN
Freddy Popple, of Ippleton, England	LAWRENCE GROSSMITH
Platt, an ex-groom, Freddy's servant	CARL LYLE
An Interior Decorator	THOMAS GRAVES
Havelock Page	QUENTIN TOD
Veronica Vandelier	HELENE WALLACE
Edna Esmelton	ADELE FRENCH
Madge Fandango	RENA MANNING
Beatrice Beresford	ANNE KELLY
Patricia Parkington	FAUN CONWAY
Violet Vivienne	HATTIE SPENCER
Clarice Carrington	MAE MANNING

(Havelock Page through Clarice Carrington bracketed as: Guests at the Blitz Hotel)

ACT I—Entrance lounge, Hotel Blitz, New York. Evening.
ACT II—"Tony" Miller's apartment, Central Park West. Afternoon of the next day.

Score

"You Don't Take a Sandwich to a Banquet" (David–Long)
"You Know and I Know" (Jerome Kern–Schuyler Greene)
"Keep Moving"
"In Arcady" (Kern–Herbert Reynolds)
*The Magic Melody" (Kern–Greene)
"Nobody Home Cake Walk" (Otto Motzan)
"Beautiful, Beautiful Bed" (Murphy–Lipton)
"Another Little Girl" (Kern–Reynolds)
*"Any Old Night" (Kern–Motzan)
*"At That San Francisco Fair" (Europe–Dabney–Kern)

1915	Nov. 8–13	Academy of Music	Baltimore, Md.
	15–20	Alvin	Pittsburgh, Pa.
	22–27	Colonial	Cleveland, Ohio
Nov. 28–Jan. 8, 1916		Princess	Chicago, Ill.

FANNY BRICE
Orpheum Circuit

1916	Feb. 20–26	Orpheum	Omaha, Nebr.
	Feb. 28–March 4	Orpheum	Kansas City, Mo.
	March 6–11	(Travel)	
	13–18	Grand	Calgary, Alb.
	20–25	Orpheum	Seattle, Wash.
	March 27–April 1	Orpheum	Portland, Ore.
	April 2–8	(Travel)	
	9–15	Orpheum	Oakland, Calif.
	16–29	Orpheum	San Francisco, Calif.
	May 1–2	Orpheum	Sacramento, Calif.
	3–4	Orpheum	Stockton, Calif.
	8–20	Orpheum	Los Angeles, Calif.

ZIEGFELD FOLLIES OF 1916

A Musical Revue in Two Acts and Twenty-One Scenes. Book by George V. Hobart and Gene Buck. Music by Louis A. Hirsch, Jerome D. Kern, and David Stamper. Scenery by Joseph Urban. Staged by Ned Wayburn.

ACT I

Prologue—"The Birth of Elation"
Scene One—"In the Park of Phantasy"
Scene Two—"The Street of Masks and Faces"
Scene Three—"The Forum in Rome"
Scene Four—"In the Golden Corridor"
Scene Five—Travesty of *Romeo and Juliet*
Scene Six—"Escaping the Movies"
Scene Seven—Travesty of *Othello*

Scene Eight—Song (Ina Claire)
Scene Nine—"On the Banks of the Nile"
Scene Ten—"Unpreparedness"
Scene Eleven—"Somewhere in the North Sea"
Scene Twelve—"Recruiting on Broadway"
Scene Thirteen—"In Far Hawaii"

ACT II

Scene One—"The Blushing Ballet"
"The Ante-Room of the Harem"

Dance by Emma Haig and "Sylphides" Girls
A Suggestion of "La Spectre de la Rose" with Carl Randall as "Nijinski"

Travesty of *Scheherazade*

The Sultan	SAM B. HARDY
O. Shaw	W. C. FIELDS
Zobeide	DON BARCLAY
Eunuch	NORMAN BLUME
Nijinski	BERT WILLIAMS
Song, "Nijinski"	FANNY BRICE and Male Chorus

Scene Two—Interlude
Scene Three—"In a Bachelor's Quarters"
Scene Four—"Puck's Pictorial Palace"

Mustardseed	HAZEL LEWIS
Josephus Daniels	W. C. FIELDS
Jane Cowl	INA CLAIRE
William Jennings Bryan	DON BARCLAY
Mary Pickford	ANN PENNINGTON
Lou-Tellegen	SAM B. HARDY
Geraldine Farrar	INA CLAIRE
Theodore Roosevelt	W. C. FIELDS
John D. Rockefeller	WILLIAM ROCK
Theda Bara	FANNY BRICE
Villa	BERT WILLIAMS
Billie Burke	INA CLAIRE

Scene Five—"A Croquet Game" (W. C. Fields)
Scene Six—"Fifth Avenue"
Scene Seven—"The Island of Girls"
Scene Eight—Songs (Fanny Brice)
Scene Nine—"Ziegfeld *Danse de Follies*"

FINALE

Note: A parody of Shakespeare's *Hamlet*, with W. C. Fields as Hamlet and Fanny Brice as Ophelia, was cut during tryouts in Atlantic City.

Score

"There's Ragtime in the Air" (Dave Stamper–Gene Buck)
"The Six Little Wives of the King"
"I've Saved All My Loving for You" (Stamper–Buck)'
"Have a Heart" (Jerome Kern–Buck)
"Somnambulistic Tune" (Stamper–Buck)
"When the Lights Are Low" (Kern–Buck)
"My Lady of the Nile" (Kern–Buck)
"I Left Her on the Beach at Honolulu" (Louis A. Hirsch–Buck)
*"Nijinski" (Stamper–Buck)
"Ain't It Funny What a Difference Just a Few Drinks Make?" (Kern–Buck)
"Bachelor Days" (Hirsch–Buck)
"I Want That Star" (Hirsch–George V. Hobart)
"Stop and Go"
"Beautiful Island of Girls"
"I've Said Good-Bye to Broadway" (Stamper–Buck)
*"The Hat" (Leo Edwards–Blanche Merrill)
*"The Dying Swan" (Edwards–Merrill)
"The *Midnight Frolic* Rag"

1916 June 6–10	Nixon's Apollo	Atlantic City, N.J.
June 12–Sept. 16	New Amsterdam	New York, N.Y.
Sept. 18–Oct. 28	Colonial	Boston, Mass.
Oct. 30–Nov. 25	Forrest	Philadelphia, Pa.
Nov. 27–Dec. 2,	Nixon	Pittsburgh, Pa.
Dec. 4–9	Euclid Ave. Opera House	Cleveland, Ohio
11–23	Detroit Opera House	Detroit, Mich.
Dec. 24, 1916–Feb. 17, 1917	Illinois	Chicago, Ill.
1917 February 18–24	Jefferson	St. Louis, Mo.
Feb. 26–March 3	Grand Opera House	Cincinnati, Ohio
March 5–10	English's Opera House	Indianapolis, Ind.
12–17	Hartman	Columbus, Ohio
19–24	National	Washington, D.C.
26–31	Academy of Music	Baltimore, Md.
April 2–4	———	
5–7	Harmanus Bleecker Hall	Albany, N.Y.

ZIEGFELD FOLLIES OF 1917

A Musical Revue in Two Acts and Nineteen Scenes. Book and Lyrics by Gene Buck and George V. Hobart. Music by Raymond Hubbell and Dave Stamper. Patriotic Finale by Victor Herbert. Scenery by Joseph Urban. Staged by Ned Wayburn. Produced under the Personal Direction of Florenz Ziegfeld, Jr.

ACT I

Scene One—"The Episode of an Arabian Night in New York"
Scene Two—"The Episode of the Purse"
Scene Three—"The Episode of the Garden of Girls"
Scene Four—"The Episode of the Dog"

Scene Five—"The Episode of the Tennis Match"
Scene Six—"The Episode of the *Ziegfeld Follies* Rag"
(Fanny Brice and *Follies* Dancers)
Scene Seven—"The Episode of the Information Bureau"
Scene Eight—"The Episode of the Telephone Wires"
Scene Nine—"The Episode of the Eddiecantor"
Scene Ten—"The Episode of Patriotism"
Scene Eleven—"The Episode of the American Eagle"

ACT II

Scene One—"The Episode of the Wedding Morning"
Scene Two—"The Episode of Williamswarbles"
Scene Three—"The Episode of the Mississippi Levee"
Song—"Just You and Me" (Fanny Brice and Eddie Cantor; dance by Hans Wilson)
The Ante-Bellum Girls—The Misses Braham, M. Boulais, R. Boulais, Rosewood, S. Howard, H. Lloyd, Heil, Gill, and E. Young.
The Dandies of 1859—Messrs. Cavanaugh, Simms, Evans, Baker, Nevins, Burggraf, Newsome, Mathews, and Barrett.
Scene Four—"The Episode of New York Streets and Subway"
Scene Five—"The Episode of the Fannybriceisms"
Scene Six—"The Episode of the Chinese Lacquer"
Scene Seven—"The Episode of the Willrogersayings"
Scene Eight—"The Episode of an Arabian Night (three hours later)"

FINALE
Score

"My Arabian Maid" (Raymond Hubbell–Gene Buck)
"The Arabian Fox Trot"
"Beautiful Garden of Girls" (Hubbell–Buck)
* *"Ziegfeld Follies* Rag" (Dave Stamper–Buck)
"The Potato Bug"
"Hello, My Dearie!" (Stamper–Buck)
"The Modern Maiden's Prayer" (James F. Hanley–Ballard MacDonald)
"That's the Kind of a Baby for Me" (J. C. Egan–Alfred Harriman)
"Can't You Hear Your Country Calling?" (Herbert)
"Because You Are Just You"
"Same Old Moon" (Stamper–Buck)
"Home, Sweet Home" (Ring W. Lardner)
"Unhappy" (Henry Creamer–J. Turner Layton)
* "Just You and Me" (Stamper–Buck)
* "Egyptian" (Leo Edwards–Blanche Merrill)
"Chu-Chin-Chow" (Stamper–Buck)

1917	June 4–9	Nixon's Apollo	Atlantic City, N.J.
	June 12–Sept. 15	New Amsterdam	New York, N.Y.
	Sept. 17–Oct. 27	Colonial	Boston, Mass.
	Oct. 29–Nov. 10	Forrest	Philadelphia, Pa.
	Nov. 12–17	Academy of Music	Baltimore, Md.

19–24	National	Washington, D.C.
Nov. 26–Dec. 1	Nixon	Pittsburgh, Pa.
Dec. 3–8	Euclid Ave. Opera House	Cleveland, Ohio
10–22	Detroit Opera House	Detroit, Mich.
Dec. 23, 1917–March 2, 1918	Illinois	Chicago, Ill.
1918 March 3–9	American	St. Louis, Mo.
11–16	Grand Opera House	Cincinnati, Ohio
18–23	English's Opera House	Indianapolis, Ind.
25–30	Hartman	Columbus, Ohio
April 1–6	Majestic	Buffalo, N.Y.
8–13	Princess	Toronto, Ont.
15–20	His Majesty's	Montreal, Que.

MIDNIGHT FROLIC

1918 May 20–June 1	New Amsterdam Roof	New York, N.Y.

Miss Brice's Songs: "Becky Is Back in the Ballet" (Edwards–Merrill)
"Egyptian" (Edwards–Merrill)

Note: Miss Brice was only in this edition of the Ziegfeld *Midnight Frolic,* a midnight cabaret show presented on the roof of the New Amsterdam, for the two-week period shown.

WHY WORRY?

A Melodramatic Farce by Montague Glass and Jules Eckert Goodman. Staged by George Marion. Presented by A. H. Woods.

Cast

Dora	FANNY BRICE
Stella	MAY BOLEY
Mrs. Harris	VERA GORDON
Shapiro	EZRA C. WALCK
Felix Noblestone	GEORGE SIDNEY
Louis	CARL DIETZ
Steffens	EDWIN MAXWELL
Wolter	HARRY DUMONT
David Meyer	CHAS. TROWBRIDGE
Devlin	JACK SHARKEY
Thorpe	JOHN WALLACE
Dan	RALF BELMONT
A Lady	FRANCESCA ROTOLI
A Gentleman	TRUE S. JAMES
Rashkind	JOE SMITH
Margolius	IRVING KAUFMAN
Dubin	HARRY GOLDWIN
November	CHARLES DALE
Flo	FRANCES RICHARDS

Frost	KALMAN MATUS
Bedell	JAMES CHERRY

Guests, etc.

ACT I—Fischbein & Blintz's Ideal Restaurant and Lunch Room, Harris & Joseph, Successors, Second Avenue, New York.
ACT II—The Ivy Leaf Inn, Boston Post Road, Larchmont. One week later.
ACT III—Same as Act II. Evening of same day.
Note: Miss Brice introduced "I'm Bad" and "I'm an Indian," two new songs by Leo Edwards and Blanche Merrill, in this non-musical play.

1918	July 29–Aug. 3	Belasco	Washington, D.C.
	Aug. 5–10	Globe	Atlantic City, N.J.
	Aug. 23–Sept. 14	Harris	New York, N.Y.

ZIEGFELD NINE O'CLOCK REVUE and MIDNIGHT FROLIC

Dec. 9, 1918–May 24, 1919   New Amsterdam Roof   New York, N.Y.

MIDNIGHT FROLIC

Oct. 3, 1919–Feb. 29, 1920   New Amsterdam Roof   New York, N.Y.

ZIEGFELD NINE O'CLOCK REVUE and MIDNIGHT FROLIC

1920   *March 8–June 5   New Amsterdam Roof   New York, N.Y.
Midnight Frolic opened March 16.

ZIEGFELD FOLLIES OF 1920

A Musical Revue in Two Acts and Twenty-Five Scenes. Book and Lyrics by Gene Buck. Music by Dave Stamper. Additional Lyrics and Music by Irving Berlin. Special Music by Victor Herbert. Scenery by Joseph Urban. Staged by Edward Royce. Produced Under the Personal Direction of Florenz Ziegfeld, Jr.

ACT I

Scene One—Opening
Scene Two—"Creation"
Scent Three—Song—"So Hard to Keep Them When They're Beautiful"
Scene Four—"A Room at Mount Vernon"
Scene Five—"Chiffon Fantasie"
Scene Six—"In the Park"
Scene Seven—Song—"I'm a Vamp from East Broadway." Sung by Fanny Brice
Scene Eight—"In the Clouds"
Scene Nine—Specialty (Moran and Mack)
Scene Ten—"Truly Rural"
(a) Song—"Any Place Would be Wonderful with You" (Bernard Granville and Doris Eaton)

(b) Song—"Mary and Doug" (Mary Eaton and Carl Randall)
(c) Song—"Where Do Mosquitoes Go?" (Gus Van and Joe Schenck)
(d) Dance (Jack Donahue)
(e) "The Family Ford" (Conceived, Written and Staged by W. C. Fields)

George Fliverton	W. C. FIELDS
Baby Rose Fliverton	RAY DOOLEY
Mrs. Fliverton	FANNY BRICE
Elsie May	JESSIE REED
Henry Steel	WM. BLANCHE
James Cunningham	JACK MAHAN
Miss Rose	BABE MARLOW
Jack Rose	MISS ROLPH
Adele Smith	MISS GRADY
Dick Burns	ADDIE YOUNG

Scene Eleven—Specialty (Jerome and Herbert)
Scene Twelve—"The Land of Bells"

FINALE

ACT II

Scene One—"The Little Follies Theatre—During Intermission"
(a) "In the Lobby"

The First Nighter	BERNARD GRANVILLE
Between the Actors	THE FOLLIES BOYS

(b) "In the Theatre"

The Tired Businessman	CARL RANDALL
The Lady With Him	DELYLE ALDA
The Water Girls	SIX LITTLE FOLLIES GIRLS
Just A Husband	W. C. FIELDS
His Wife	FANNY BRICE
A Critic	CHARLES WINNINGER
A Fellow Who Paid to Get In	JACK DONAHUE
A Lover	JOHN STEEL
His Sweetheart	MARY EATON

Scene Two—"The *Follies'* Curtains" (Van and Schenck)
Scene Three—"The Dancing School—Her First Lesson"

The Pupil	MARY EATON
The Master	CHARLES WINNINGER
Another Pupil	FANNY BRICE

Scene Four—Song—"The Legs of Nations"
Scene Five—"On Fifth Avenue—The Ziegfeld Sextette"
The Ziegfeld Follies Girls—Betty Morton, Alta King, Margaret Irving, Jessie
  Reed, Charlotte Wakefield, Ethel Hallor.

Sextette Boys. The Rolls Royce Chauffeurs.

Song—"I Was a Floradora Baby" Sung by Fanny Brice

Scene Six—"Chinese Fantasy"

Scene Seven—Chappie Dance (Bernard Granville and Doris Eaton)

Scene Eight—"The Gypsy Trail"

Scene Nine—Dance (Lillian Broderick and Carl Randall)

Scene Ten—"The Golden Gates"

Scene Eleven—"The Love Boat"

Scene Twelve—? ? ?

Scene Thirteen—"The Midnight Frolic"

FINALE
Score

"So Hard to Keep When They're Beautiful" (Harry Tierney–Joseph McCarthy)

"Sunshine and Shadows" (Dave Stamper–Gene Buck)

"When the Right One Comes Along" (Victor Herbert–Buck)

*"I'm a Vamp from East Broadway" (Irving Berlin–Ruby–Kalmar)

"The Girls of My Dreams" (Berlin)

"Any Place Would Be Wonderful with You" (Stamper–Buck)

"Mary and Doug" (Stamper–Buck)

"Where Do Mosquitoes Go?" (Tierney–McCarthy)

"Bells" (Berlin)

"The Legs of Nations" (Berlin)

*"I Was a Floradora Baby" (Harry Carroll–Ballard MacDonald)

"Chinese Firecrackers" (Berlin)

"Tell Me, Little Gypsy" (Berlin)

"The Syncopated Vamp" (Berlin)

1920	June 15–19	Nixon's Apollo	Atlantic City, N.J.
	June 22–Oct. 16	New Amsterdam	New York, N.Y.
	Oct. 18–Nov. 13	Colonial	Boston, Mass.
	Nov. 15–20	National	Washington, D.C.
	22–27	Nixon	Pittsburgh, Pa.
	Nov. 29–Dec. 4	Euclid Ave. Opera House	Cleveland, Ohio
	Dec. 5–18	New Detroit	Detroit, Mich.
Dec. 19, 1920–March 5, 1921		Colonial	Chicago, Ill.
1921	March 6–12	American	St. Louis, Mo.
	14–19	English's Opera House	Indianapolis, Ind.
	21–26	Grand Opera House	Cincinnati, Ohio
	March 28–April 2	Hartman	Columbus, Ohio
	April 4–23	Forrest	Philadelphia, Pa.
	25–30	Academy of Music	Baltimore, Md.

ZIEGFELD FOLLIES OF 1921

A Musical Revue in Two Acts and Twenty-Seven Scenes. Book and Lyrics by Gene Buck, Channing Pollock, Willard Mack, Ralph Spence, and Bud DeSylva. Music by Dave Stamper, Rudolf Friml, and Victor Herbert. Costumes by James Reynolds. Scenery by Joseph Urban. Dialogue Rehearsed by George Marion.

Staged by Edward Royce. Produced under the Supervision of Florenz Ziegfeld, Jr.

ACT I

Scene One—"The Statue of Liberty"
Scene Two—*"Follies* Mirror" (Ben Ali Haggin tableaux)
Scene Three—"Mr. Ziegfeld's Idea of Chorus Men"
Scene Four—"The Professor"
Scene Five—Song—"Strut Miss Lizzie" (Van and Schenck)
Scene Six—"The Legend of the Cyclamen Tree"
Scene Seven—Song—"Second Hand Rose" (Fanny Brice)
Scene Eight—"The Piano Tuner"
Scene Nine—"The Rose Bower"
Scene Ten—Song—"Plymouth Rock" (Raymond Hitchcock)
Scene Eleven—"The Harem"
Scene Twelve—Song—"I'm a Hieland Lassie" (Fanny Brice)
Scene Thirteen—"The Stage Door"
Scene Fourteen—"Lionel, Ethel and Jack in *Camille*"

Lionel   RAYMOND HITCHCOCK
Ethel   FANNY BRICE
Jack   W. C. FIELDS

Scene Fifteen—Song—"Our Home Town" (Van Schenck)
Scene Sixteen—"The Championship of the World"

Georges Carpentier   FANNY BRICE
Jack Dempsey   RAE DOOLEY
The Announcer   RAYMOND HITCHCOCK
The Referee   W. C. FIELDS
The Fight Fans   THE FOLLIES GIRLS
Trainers, Seconds, Etc.

FINALE

ACT II

Scene One—"The Birthday of the Dauphin"
Scene Two—The Innez Brothers
Scene Three—"The Bridge on the Seine"
Song—"My Man" (Fanny Brice)
Burlesque Apache Dance (Ray Dooley and Chas. O'Donnell)
Scene Four—Song—"Four Little Girls with a Future and Four Little Girls with a Past"
Scene Five—"The Subway" ("Off to the Country" by W. C. Fields)

Mr. Fliverton   W. C. FIELDS
Mrs. Fliverton   FANNY BRICE
Sammy Sap Fliverton   RAYMOND HITCHCOCK
Rae Tut Fliverton   RAE DOOLEY
A Ticket Chopper   FRANK INNEZ

White Wings   PHIL DWYER
Passengers, Etc.

Scene Six—Song—"Some Day the Sun Will Shine" (Mary Milburn)
Scene Seven—Song—"Now I Know" (Mary Eaton and Herbert Hoey)
Scene Eight—"Passion's Altar" (Ben Ali Haggin tableaux)
Scene Nine—Song—"Allay Up" (Fanny Brice)
Scene Ten—Songs (Van and Schenck)
Scene Eleven—"The Blue Lagoon"

FINALE

Score

"Strut, Miss Lizzie" (Henry Creamer–J. Turner Layton)
"Princess of My Dreams" (Victor Herbert–Gene Buck)
"The Legend" (Herbert–Buck)
*"Second Hand Rose" (James F. Hanley–Grant Clarke)
"Bring Back My Blushing Rose" (Rudolf Friml–Buck)
"Plymouth Rock" (Dave Stamper–Channing Pollock)
*"I'm a Hieland Lassie" (Leo Edwards–Blanche Merrill)
"Raggedy Rag" (Stamper–Buck)
"Sally, Won't You Come Back?" (Stamper–Buck)
"Our Home Town" (Harry Carroll–Ballard MacDonald)
*"My Man" (Maurice Yvain–Pollock)
"Four Little Girls with a Future" (Friml–DeSylva)
"Some Day the Sun Will Shine"
*"Allay! Up" (Hanley–MacDonald)
"Now I Know" (James V. Monaco–Clarke)
"Every Time I Hear a Band Play" (Rudolf Friml–Gene Buck)

1921 June 16–18	Nixon's Apollo	Atlantic City, N.J.
June 21–Oct. 1	Globe	New York, N.Y.
Oct. 3–Nov. 5	Colonial	Boston, Mass.
Nov. 7–19	Forrest	Philadelphia, Pa.
21–26	Nixon	Pittsburgh, Pa.
Nov. 28–Dec. 10	Ohio	Cleveland, Ohio
Dec. 11–24	New Detroit	Detroit, Mich.
Dec. 25, 1921–Feb. 18, 1922	Colonial	Chicago, Ill.
1922 Feb. 19–25	American	St. Louis, Mo.
Feb. 27–March 4	Grand Opera House	Cincinnati, Ohio
March 5–11	Victory	Dayton, Ohio
12–18	Davidson	Milwaukee, Wisc.
20–25	English's Opera House	Indianapolis, Ind.
March 27–April 1	Hartman	Columbus, Ohio
April 3–8	Ford's Opera House	Baltimore, Md.
9–15	National	Washington, D.C.

FANNY BRICE
UBO Vaudeville

1922	May 11–13	Proctor's	Mt. Vernon, N.Y.
	15–20	Hippodrome	Cleveland, Ohio
	22–27	Davis	Pittsburgh, Pa.
	May 29–June 3	Orpheum	Brooklyn, N.Y.
	June 5–10	Keith's	Washington, D.C.
	June 12–July 8	Palace	New York, N.Y.
	July 10–15	Keith's	Philadelphia, Pa.
	17–22	Brighton	Brooklyn, N.Y.
	Oct. 30–Nov. 11	Palace	New York, N.Y.
	Nov. 13–18	Orpheum	Brooklyn, N.Y.
	20–25	Riverside	New York, N.Y.
	Nov. 27–Dec. 2	Keith's	Boston, Mass.
	Dec. 4–9	Orpheum	Brooklyn, N.Y.
	11–16	Maryland	Baltimore, Md.
	18–30	Keith's Palace	Cleveland, Ohio
1923	Jan. 1–6		
	8–13	Palace	New York, N.Y.
	15–20	Keith's	Washington, D.C.
	22–27	Alhambra	New York, N.Y.
	Jan. 29–Feb. 3	Colonial	New York, N.Y.
	Feb. 5–10	Royal	New York, N.Y.
	12–17	Albee	Providence, R.I.
	19–24	Riverside	New York, N.Y.
	Feb. 26–March 3	Palace	New York, N.Y.
	March 5–10	Bushwick	Brooklyn, N.Y.

Orpheum Circuit

1923	March 26–31	Orpheum	Kansas City, Mo.
	April 2–14	Palace Music Hall	Chicago, Ill.
	16–21	Orpheum	St. Louis, Mo.
	23–28	Palace	Milwaukee, Wisc.
	April 30–May 5	Hennepin	Minneapolis, Minn.
	May 6–12	(Travel)	
	May 13–June 2	Orpheum	San Francisco, Calif.
	June 4–30	Orpheum	Los Angeles, Calif.
	July 1–7	(Travel)	
	8–28	Palace Music Hall	Chicago, Ill.

ZIEGFELD FOLLIES OF 1923

A Musical Revue in Two Acts and Thirty-Three Scenes. Book and Lyrics by Gene Buck. Music by Dave Stamper, Rudolf Friml, and Victor Herbert. Scenery by Joseph Urban. Staged by Ned Wayburn.

ACT I

Scene One—Song—"Glorifying the Girls"
Scene Two—Song—"Old Fashioned Garden" (Olga Steck)

Scene Three—Linda
Scene Four—Song—"Take Those Lips Away" (Brooke Johns)
Scene Five—Jack Norton and James J. Corbett in "The Sap"
Scene Six—Fanny Brice
Scene Seven—Spanish Study (Dance by Mlle. Paulette Duval)
Scene Eight—Original Dance (Harland Dixon)
Scene Nine—A Russian Number, Danced by Alexander Yakovileff and the *"Follies* Chorus"
Scene Ten—Song—"Russian Art" (Fanny Brice)
Scene Eleven—"Shadowgraph" (Optical Illusion)
Scene Twelve—"Snappy Stories of History" (by Eddie Cantor)

Girl	HILDA FERGUSON
Boy	ROY CROPPER
Pocohontas	FANNY BRICE
Captain John Smith	HARRY SHORT
Servant	BILLY REVEL
Queen Isabella	FANNY BRICE
Christopher Columbus	WILLIAM ROSELLE

Scene Thirteen—"Back to Nature Art Studies" (*Follies* Models)
Scene Fourteen—Song—"Broadway Indians"
Scene Fifteen—"Trying to Get Into the *Follies*"
Scene Sixteen—First Act Finale—Song—"Shake Your Feet" (Brooke Johns and *"Follies* Chorus)

ACT II

Scene One—"La Marquise" (Ben Ali Haggin Picture and Pantomime)
Scene Two—Fanny Brice
Scene Three—Solo Dance by Linda
Scene Four—"Harlequin's Doll"
Scene Five—"Legends of the Drums"
Scene Six—Song—"Little Old New York" (Edna Leedom)
Scene Seven—"Webbing" (Arranged by Gertrude Hoffman)
Scene Eight—Ann Pennington and Brooke Johns
Scene Nine—"In the Slums"
Scene Ten—"The Covered Wagon"
Scene Eleven—Song—"I'd Love to Waltz Through Life with You" (Olga Steck and Roy Cropper)
Scene Twelve—"Ballet" (Alexander Yakovileff, Florentine Gosnova, Catherine Gallimore, and the *Follies* Corps de Ballet)
Scene Thirteen—Paul Whiteman and His Orchestra
Scene Fourteen—Dance by the "Empire Girls" (Presented by Lawrence Tiller)
Scene Fifteen—Song—"Swanee River Blues" (Brooke Johns and Olga Steck)
Scene Sixteen—"Amateur Night (At Miner's Eighth Avenue Theatre Twenty Years Ago)"

The Announcer	WILLIAM ROSELLE
The "Gallery God"	ARTHUR WEST

"Amachewers" ROY CROPPER
HARLAND DIXON
OLGA STECK
EDNA LEEDOM
BROOKE JOHNS
JAMES J. CORBETT
HILDA FERGUSON
HARRY SHORT
LEW HEARN
FANNY BRICE

Scene Seventeen—"Good-Night Finale" (Entire Company)

Score

"Glorifying the Girls" (Dave Stamper–Gene Buck)
"Old Fashioned Garden" (Victor Herbert–Buck)
"Take Those Lips Away" (Harry Tierney–Joseph McCarthy)
*"Russian Art" (Leo Edwards–Blanche Merrill)
"Broadway Indians" (Stamper–Buck)
"I Wonder How They Get That Way?" (Stamper–Buck)
"What Thrills Can There Be?" (Stamper–Harry Ruskin)
"Shake Your Feet" (Stamper–Buck)
"Lady Fair"
"Little Old New York" (Herbert–Buck)
"I'm Bugs Over You" (Stamper–Buck)
"I'd Love to Waltz Through Life With You" (Herbert–Buck)
"Swanee River Blues" (Stamper–Buck)

Oct. 20, 1923–May 10, 1924   New Amsterdam   New York, N.Y.

FANNY BRICE
Orpheum Circuit

1924	June 29–July 5	Palace	Milwaukee, Wisc.
	July 6–26	Palace Music Hall	Chicago, Ill.
	July 27–Aug. 2	(Travel)	
	Aug. 3–23	Orpheum	San Francisco, Calif.
	Aug. 25–Sept. 13	Orpheum	Los Angeles, Calif.
	Sept. 14–20	(Travel)	
	21–27	Orpheum	Denver, Colo.
	Sept. 28–Oct. 4	Orpheum	Kansas City, Mo.
	Oct. 5–11	Orpheum	St. Louis, Mo.

Irving Berlin's Fourth Annual
MUSIC BOX REVUE

A Musical Revue in Two Acts and Twenty Scenes. Sketches by Bert Kalmar and
Harry Ruby. Music and Lyrics by Irving Berlin. Settings by Clark Robinson.

Costumes by James Reynolds. Dances by Carl Randall and Madame Serova. Staged by John Murray Anderson. Produced by Sam H. Harris.

ACT I

Scene One—Opening
  (a) "The Catskills"
  (b) "Times Square"
  (c) "Little Old New York"
Scene Two—In Front of the Curtains (Carl Randall and Girls)
Scene Three—"At Home" ("The Motive" by Kalmar and Ruby)
Scene Four—In Front of the Curtains *(Rigoletto a la Danse)*
Scene Five—"In Tokyo"
Scene Six—In Front of the Curtains (Clark and McCullough)
Scene Seven—"New York Harbor"
The Immigrant (Fanny Brice)
Scene Eight—"Ballet Dancers at Home"
Scene Nine—"The Garden Club" ("The Kid's First and Last Fight")
Scene Ten—In Front of the Curtains (Oscar Shaw)
Scene Eleven—In Front of the Curtains ("Poor Little Moving Picture Baby" sung by Fanny Brice)
Scene Twelve—"Springtime"
Scene Thirteen—"Seeing Is Believing" by Ralph Bunker
Scene Fourteen—In Front of the Curtains (Brox Sisters)
Scene Fifteen—"At the Window" (Grace Moore and Oscar Shaw)
Scene Sixteen—"A Salon of Louis' Palace" ("The King's Gal" by Ned Joyce Heaney)

La Pompadour	FANNY BRICE
Her gentleman-in-waiting	JACK PEARSON
Louis XV	BOBBY CLARK

Scene Seventeen—In Front of the Curtains (Hal Sherman)
Scene Eighteen—In Front of the Tableaux Curtain
  (a) Song—"The Call of the South" (Oscar Shaw and Grace Moore)
  (b) "The Levee"
      Song—"Bandanna Ball" (Fanny Brice and Company)

PART II

Scene One—"Alice in Wonderland"
Scene Two—"A Living Room"
Scene Three—In Front of the Curtains Song—"I Want to Be a Ballet Dancer" Sung by Fanny Brice, Aided by Bobby Clark and Corps de Ballet
Scene Four—"A Lullaby"
Scene Five—"At the Circus" ("Fools Rush In" by Clark and McCullough)
Scene Six—In Front of the Curtains (Carl Randall and Claire Luce)
Scene Seven—"The Battery" ("Another Good Girl Gone Wrong" by Gilbert Clark)

The Girl	FANNY BRICE
The Man	OSCAR SHAW

Scene Eight—In Front of the Curtains (Brox Sisters)
Scene Nine—"The Trees"
Scene Ten—"The Garden of Eden" ("Adam and Eve" by Kalmar and Ruby)

Eve	FANNY BRICE
Adam	BOBBY CLARK
Cain	HAROLD BOYD
Abel	JACK PEARSON

Scene Eleven—The Runaway Four
Scene Twelve—"The Banquet"

FINALE
Score

"Where Is My Little Old New York?"
"Sixteen, Sweet Sixteen"
"Tokyo Blues"
"A Couple of Senseless Censors"
*"Don't Send Me Back to Petrograd"
"Unlucky in Love"
*"Poor Little Moving Picture Baby" (Edwards–Merrill)
"Tell Her in the Springtime"
"Who?"
"Listening"
"The Call of the South"
*"Bandanna Ball"
"Come Along with Alice"
*"I Want to Be a Ballet Dancer"
"Rock-A-Bye Baby"
"Wild Cats"
"In the Shade of a Sheltering Tree"

1924	Nov. 24–29	Nixon	Pittsburgh, Pa.
Dec. 1, 1924–May 9, 1925		Music Box	New York, N.Y.
1925	Sept. 28–Oct. 3	Werba's	Brooklyn, N.Y.
	Oct. 5–10		
	12–17	Ford's Opera House	Baltimore, Md.
	19–24	National	Washington, D.C.
	26–31	Nixon	Pittsburgh, Pa.
	Nov. 2–7	Ohio	Cleveland, Ohio
	Nov. 8–Dec. 19	Illinois	Chicago, Ill.
	Dec. 20–26	Davidson	Milwaukee, Wisc.
Dec. 28, 1925–Jan. 2, 1926		English's Opera House	Indianapolis, Ind.
1926	Jan. 3–9	American	St. Louis, Mo.
	10–16	Sam S. Shubert	Kansas City, Mo.
	18–23	Grand Opera House	Cincinnati, Ohio
	25–30	———	
	Feb. 1–6	New Detroit	Detroit, Mich.

	8–20	Colonial	Boston, Mass.
Feb. 22–March 6		Forrest	Philadelphia, Pa.

FANNY

A Melodramatic Comedy in Three Acts by Willard Mack and David Belasco.
Produced and Staged by David Belasco.

ACT I—The Living Room of David Mendoza, Late Proprietor of the XY Ranch,
   near Horse Blanket, Arizona.
ACT II—The Same.
ACT III—The Same.

Cast

"Doggie" Davis	FRANCIS PIERLOT
"Humpty" Riggs	SPENCER CHARTERS
"Slim" Hawkins	LOUIS MASON
Joe White	WARREN WILLIAM
"Gyp" Gradyear	JOHN CROMWELL
High Low	SAMUEL S. LEE
"Hollywood" Haswell	GEORGE SHERWOOD
Nora Cassell	RUTH DAYTON
Miss Leah Mendoza	JANE ELLISON
Fanny Fiebaum	FANNY BRICE

| 1926 | May 31–June 5 | Nixon's Apollo | Atlantic City, N.J. |
| | June 7–12 | Broadway | Long Branch, N.J. |

FANNY BRICE
Orpheum Vaudeville

| 1926 | July 3–23 | Orpheum | San Francisco, Calif. |
| | July 25–Aug. 14 | Orpheum | Los Angeles, Calif. |

FANNY

1926	Sept. 6–12	Belasco	Washington, D.C.
	14–19	Ford's Opera House	Baltimore, Md.
Sept. 21–Nov. 13		Lyceum	New York, N.Y.
Nov. 15–20		Shubert-Riviera	New York, N.Y.
	22–27	Broad Street	Newark, N.J.
Nov. 29–Dec. 4		Teller's Shubert	Brooklyn, N.Y.
Dec. 6–11		Werba's Brooklyn	Brooklyn, N.Y.
	13–18	Bronx Opera House	Bronx, New York
	20–25	———	
Dec. 27, 1926–Jan. 8, 1927		Broad Street	Philadelphia, Pa.

HOLLYWOOD MUSIC BOX REVUE

A Musical Revue in Two Acts and Twenty-Six Scenes. Staged by Lillian Albertson. Dances by George Cunningham. Costumes by Howard Greer. Produced by Louis O. Macloon.

ACT I

Scene One—Opening ("We Don't Know Why—But")
Scene Two—Charles Howard meets Don Barclay
Scene Three—Song—"You Smile at Me" (Marie Callahan and Billy Hanson)
Scene Four—Sketch—"The Last Customer"
Scene Five—Song—"Make 'Em Laugh" (Fanny Brice)
Scene Six—Turner and Gray
Scene Seven—Song—"Whose Who Are You?" (Ted Doner and Edythe Maye)
Scene Eight—a. Song—"Hold Me in Your Arms" (Sam Ash and Elsie Lee)
     b. Myrtle Pierce as Columbine, Nellie Hanson as Harlequin, and
      the Music Box Ballet Girls
Scene Nine—Sketch—"Window Cleaners" (Barclay and Howard)
Scene Ten—Sketch—"Miss Brice Will Try and Get Her Little Girl into the
 Movies" (Written and Staged by Miss Brice)

Director	TED DONER
Cameraman	ROGER DAVIS
The Child	MIRIAM BYRON

Scene Eleven—a. Song—"Quack, Quack" (Callahan and Hanson)
     b. "At the Beach Club"
Scene Twelve—"A Little Mind Reading" (Barclay and Howard)
Scene Thirteen—Song—"All Alone Monday" (Doner and Maye)
Scene Fourteen—Miss Brice's Interpretation of *Madame Pompadour*

Madame Pompadour	FANNY BRICE
Lady in Waiting	ROGER DAVIS
King Louis XV	CHARLES HOWARD
Captain of the Guard	SAM ASH

Scene Fifteen—Song and Dance—"She Won't Charleston"
     (Marie Callahan and Chorus)

ACT II

Scene One—"Rose of Arizona" ("A Traditional American Musical Comedy")
Scene Two—Song—"I'm a Little Butterfly" (Fanny Brice)
Scene Three—Song—"Spring in Autumn" (Sam Ash and Elsie Lee)
Scene Four—Third Act from *Camille* (Fanny Brice and Don Barclay)
Scene Five—Roger Davis and Charles Howard Will Tell You a Story
Scene Six—a. "Phantom of the Adagio"
    b. "The Hussar Dance"
Scene Seven—Song—"Loose Ankles" (Marie Callahan)

Scene Eight—"Black Eyes"—A Russian Nocturne
                Interpreted by Fanny Brice
                Assisted by Gregory Dniestroff
Scene Nine—Song—"A Hollywood Relief" (Don Barclay)
Scene Ten—"Now Boss" (Played by Sam Baker)
Scene Eleven—Song—"A Little Bit of Spain in California" (Mr. Ash and Miss
Lee, assisted by the Entire Company)

Score

"We Don't Know Why—But" (Arthur Freed–Robert Lord)
"You Smiled at Me" (Harry Ruby–Bert Kalmar)
*"Make 'Em Laugh" (Edwin Weber–Blanche Merrill)
"Whose Who with You?" (Arthur Freed)
"Hold Me in Your Arms" (Freed)
"Quack, Quack" (Freed–Merrill)
"All Alone Monday" (Ruby–Kalmar)
"She Won't Charleston" (Ruby–Kalmar)
"Rose of Arizona" (Richard Rodgers–Lorenz Hart)
*"I'm a Little Butterfly" (Weber–Merrill)
"Spring in Autumn" (William Ortmann)
"Loose Ankles" (Freed–Merrill)
"A Hollywood Relief" (Freed–Leonard Levinson-Robert Lord)
"A Little Bit of Spain in California" (Freed)

| 1927 | Feb. 2–March 22 | Hollywood Music Box | Hollywood, Calif. |
| | March 25–April 7 | Biltmore | Los Angeles, Calif. |

FANNY BRICE
UBO Vaudeville

1927	Oct. 17–22	Proctor's	New Rochelle, N.Y.
	24–29	Keith's	Boston, Mass.
	Oct. 31–Nov. 5	Maryland	Baltimore, Md.
	Nov. 7–12	Keith's	Washington, D.C.
	14–19	Keith's	Philadelphia, Pa.
	Nov. 21–Dec. 10	Palace	New York, N.Y.

Orpheum Circuit

1927	Dec. 19–31	Palace Music Hall	Chicago, Ill.
1928	Jan. 1–6	(Travel)	
	7–20	Orpheum	San Francisco, Calif.
	21–27	Orpheum	Oakland, Calif.
	Jan. 29–Feb. 11	Orpheum	Los Angeles, Calif.
	Feb. 12–19	(Travel)	
	20–25	Orpheum	Denver, Colo.
	Feb. 27–March 3	Orpheum	Omaha, Nebr.
	March 5–10	Palace Music Hall	Chicago, Ill.

11–17	(Travel)	
19–24	Majestic	Milwaukee, Wisc.
26–31	Orpheum	Kansas City, Mo.

UBO Vaudeville

1928	April 9–14	Coliseum	New York, N.Y.
	16–28	————	
	April 30–May 5	Palace	New York, N.Y.
	Oct. 29–Nov. 10	Palace	New York, N.Y.
	Nov. 12–17	Coliseum	New York, N.Y.
	19–24	Memorial	Boston, Mass.

FIORETTA

A Romantic Venetian Operetta in Two Acts and Fourteen Scenes. Book by Earl Carroll and Carlton Andrews. Lyrics by Grace Henry. Music by George Bagby and G. Romilli. Orchestral Scoring by Domenico Savino. Book Staged by Clifford Brooke. Dancing Ensembles by LeRoy Prinz. Presented by Earl Carroll.

Cast

The Duke of Venice	THEO. KARLE
The Duchess of Venice	ETHEL JUNE WALKER
A Jester	CLEMENT TAYLOR
A Sergeant	MARTIN SHEPPARD
Count Matteo Di Brozzo	LIONEL ATWILL
Julio Pepoli	LEON ERROL
Fioretta Pepoli, his daughter	DOROTHY KNAPP
Orsino D'Andrea, Count di Rovani	GEORGE HOUSTON
Marchesa Vera Di Livio	FANNY BRICE
Caponetti, her cicisbeo	JAY BRENNAN
Marquis Filippo Di Livio	CHARLES HOWARD
Captain of the Guard	G. DAVISON CLARK
A Harlequin	NELSON SNOW
Another Harlequin	CHARLES COLUMBUS
Luigi, a gondolier	GIOVANNI GUERRERI
Giacomo	FRANK CULLEN
Rosamonda	LILLIAN BOND
Lucetta	LOUISE BROOKS
Beatrice	ELSIE CONNOR
Spanish Ambassador's daughter	CAROL KINGSBURY
Lady from Milan	MARGARET MANNERS
Dancer from Paris	EVELYN CROWELL
Giuseppa	RITA CRANE

ACT I

Scene One—The Great Square.
Scene Two—The Prison.
Scene Three—The Bridge of Sighs.
Scene Four—The Silver Gondola.

Scene Five—The Park.
Scene Six—The Wine Cellar.
Scene Seven—The Hall of Candles.
Scene Eight—The Chapel.

ACT II

Scene One—The Vault.
Scene Two—The Royal Barge.
Scene Three—Count Matteo's Study.
Scene Four—The Road to Orvieto.
Scene Five—The Villa.
Scene Six—The Ducal Palace.
Place: Venice. Time: Eighteenth Century.

Score

"Blade of Mine" (George Bagby–Grace Henry)
*"Wicked Old Willage of Wenice"
"Fioretta" (G. Romilli)
"Dream Boat" (Bagby–Henry–Jo Trent)
*"Doing a Dance"
"Carissima" (Romilli–Henry)
"Roses of Red" (Romilli)
"Alone with You" (Romilli–Henry–Trent)

Dec. 31, 1928–Jan. 5, 1929	Ford's Opera House	Baltimore, Md.
1929 Jan. 6–12	National	Washington, D.C.
Jan. 14–Feb. 2	Erlanger	Philadelphia, Pa.
Feb. 5–May 11	Earl Carroll	New York, N.Y.

FANNY BRICE
Orpheum Vaudeville

1929 Nov. 16–29	Orpheum	Los Angeles, Calif.

RKO Vaudeville

1930 Feb. 8–14	Palace	New York, N.Y.
Feb. 15–28	———	
March 1–7	Albee	Brooklyn, N.Y.
8–11	Madison	Brooklyn, N.Y.
12–14	Keith's	Flushing, N.Y.
15–21	Palace	New York, N.Y.
22–25	Coliseum	New York, N.Y.
26–28	58th Street	New York, N.Y.
March 29–April 1	Fordham	New York, N.Y.
April 2–4	86th Street	New York, N.Y.
5–11	———	
12–15	Kenmore	Brooklyn, N.Y.
16–18	81st Street	New York, N.Y.

19–25	——	
26–29	Franklin	New York, N.Y.
April 30–May 2	Jefferson	New York, N.Y.

SWEET AND LOW

An Intimate Musical Revue in Two Acts and Twenty-Five Scenes. Sketches by David Freedman. Dances by Danny Dare. Additional Dances by Busby Berkeley. Settings by Jo Mielziner. Costumes by James Reynolds. Produced by Billy Rose.

ACT I

Scene One—Song—"Outside Looking In" (The Ladies)
Scene Two—"Poor Mr. Jessel"
Scene Three—Song—"Dancing with Tears in Their Eyes" (James Barton, Fanny Brice, and George Jessel)
Scene Four—Song—"Cheerful Little Earful" (Hannah Williams and Jerry Norris)
Scene Five—"Babykins"

Baby	FANNY BRICE
Doctor	ARTHUR TREACHER
Father	ROGER DAVIS·
Mother	PEGGY ANDRE
Nurse	LUCILLE OSBORNE

Scene Six—Song—"When a Pansy Was a Flower" (George Jessel)
Scene Seven—Song—"Ten Minutes in Bed" (Paula Trueman)
Seven Eight—"The Mad Dog" (James Barton)
Scene Nine—"Venetian Reprise" (Moss and Fontana)
Scene Ten—"In a Venetian Box" (The Ladies)
Scene Eleven—Stereopticon Slides (George Jessel)
Scene Twelve—Song—"Would You Like to Take a Walk?" (Hannah Williams, Hal Thompson, and Ladies)
Scene Thirteen—Shirley Richards and Sam Krevoff
Scene Fourteen—"Stocks and Blondes" (Hannah Williams)
Scene Fifteen—"Mr. Barton Still Alone"
Scene Sixteen—"Strictly Unbearable"

Isabel Paisley, a Southern girl	FANNY BRICE
Count Gus de Raviola, of Italy	GEORGE JESSEL

ACT II

Scene One—"Customary Spanish Number"
   (a) Song—"For I'm in Love Again" (Jerry Norris and Ladies)
   (b) Dance (Moss and Fontana)
   (c) "I Knew Him Before He Was Spanish" (Fanny Brice)
Scene Two—"East St. Louis Toodle-O"
Scene Three—Song—"Overnight" (Fanny Brice)
Scene Four—Sketch—"Overnight"

Lady   FANNY BRICE
Gentleman   GEORGE JESSEL

Scene Five—"Song in a Solarium" (Hannah Williams, Jerry Norris and Ladies)
Scene Six—Mr. Jessel
Scene Seven—"Chinese White"

Lize   FANNY BRICE
Chang JAMES BARTON

Scene Eight—Borrah Minevitch and His Musical Rascals
Scene Nine—Finale—"Rose's Rendezvous" (James Barton, Fanny Brice, George Jessel and Company)

Score

"Outside Looking In" (Harry Archer–Edward Eliscu)
"Mr. Jessel" (Charlotte Kent)
*"Dancing With Tears In Their Eyes" (Wm. Irwin–Rose–Mort Dixon)
"Cheerful Little Earful" (Harry Warren–Ira Gershwin–Billy Rose)
"When A Pansy Was a Flower" (Irwin–Rose–Malcolm McComb)
"Ten Minutes In Bed" (Ned Lehak–Allen Boretz)
"Would You Like To Take a Walk?" (Warren–Dixon–Rose)
"Reival Day" (Irwin–McComb)
"For I'm In Love Again" (Mischa Spoliansky–Dixon–Rose)
*"I Knew Him Before He Was Spanish" (Dana Suesse–Rose–MacDonald)
*"Overnight" (Louis Alter–Rose–Charlotte Kent)
"You Sweet So and So" (Philip Charig–Joseph Meyer–Ira Gershwin)

1930	Oct. 14–25	Sam S. Schubert	Philadelphia, Pa.
	Oct. 27–Nov. 1	Sam S. Shubert	Newark, N.J.
	Nov. 10–15	Majestic	Brooklyn, N.Y.
Nov. 17, 1930–Jan. 17, 1931		Chanin's 46th Street	New York, N.Y.
1931	Jan. 19–April 25	44th Street	New York, N.Y.

CRAZY QUILT

An Intimate Musical Revue in Two Acts and Twenty-Seven Scenes. Sketches by David Freedman. Additional Dialogue by Herman Timberg. Staged by Billy Rose. Musical Numbers Staged by Sammy Lee. Technical Direction by Ira Ashley. Lighting by Clark Robinson. Costumes Designed by Fanny Brice.

ACT I

Scene One—"Mr. Healy Produces"
Scene Two—Song—"Sing a Little Jingle"
Scene Three—"Rest Room Rose" (Fanny Brice)
Scene Four—Phil Baker and his men; Ted Healy without his men
Scene Five—Song—"I Found a Million Dollar Baby in a Five-and-Ten Cent Store" (Ted Healy, Phil Baker, Fanny Brice, Lew Brice, and Ensemble)
Scene Six—"Customary Waltz" (Gomez and Winona)

Scene Seven—"The 'Crazy Quilt' Sextette"
Scene Eight—Sketch—"Mill's Grand Hotel" (Fanny Brice, Phil Baker, Ted Healy, Lew Brice, Marion Bonnell)
Scene Nine—Song—"I Want to Do a Number with the Boys" (Fanny Brice, Ted Healy, Roger Davis, Lew Brice, and Mr. Healy's Men)
Scene Ten—Song—"Under the Clock at the Astor" (Phil Baker)
Scene Eleven—"In a Museum with Mr. Healy" by Herman Timberg
Scene Twelve—"Mr. Healy Explains"
Scene Thirteen—Song—"Peter Pan" (Fanny Brice)
Scene Fourteen—Song—"In the Merry Month of Maybe"
Scene Fifteen—Song—"Kept in Suspense" (Phil Baker and Four Little Ladies)
Scene Sixteen—Song—"Crazy Quilt" (Marion Bonnell, Lew Brice, Vale & Stewart, and Ensemble)

ACT II

Scene One—Song—"Would You Like to Take a Walk?"
Scene Two—"The 'Crazy Quilt' Sextette Again"
Scene Three—"Professor Heinidine" (Ted Healy, Lew Brice, Roger Davis, and Mr. Healy's Men) by Clark and McCullough
Scene Four—Miss Brice and Mr. Baker
Scene Five—"Mr. Healy's Dressing Room" (Ted Healy, Phil Baker, and Roger Davis) by James Dyrenforth and Herman Timberg
Scene Six—"Million Dollar Baby" (Mr. Healy's Men)
Scene Seven—"Strictly Unbearable"

Isabel Paisley, a Southern Girl   FANNY BRICE
Count Gus de Raviola, of Italy   TED HEALY

Scene Eight—"And Again"
Scene Nine—Gomez & Winona (Mr. Baker at the Accordion)
Scene Ten—Mr. Healy (Assisted)
Scene Eleven—Finale

Score

"Sing a Little Jingle" (Harry Warren–Mort Dixon)
*"Rest Room Rose" (Richard Rodgers–Lorenz Hart)
*"I Found a Million Dollar Baby in a Five-and-Ten Cent Store" (Warren–Billy Rose–Dixon)
*"I Want to do a Number with the Boys" (Rowland Wilson–Ned Wever)
"Under The Clock At The Astor" (Manning Sherwin–Wever)
"Peter Pan" (Carroll Gibbons–Rose–James Dyrenforth)
"In the Merry Month of Maybe" (Warren–Ira Gershwin–Rose)
"Kept in Suspense" (Gibbons–Rose–Dyrenforth)
"Crazy Quilt" (Warren–Bud Green)
"Would You Like to Take a Walk?" (Warren–Rose–Dixon)

*Barred from Minneapolis as "indecent and obscene"

1931	May 19–July 25	44th Street	New York, N.Y.
	Sept. 28–Oct. 3	Alvin	Pittsburgh, Pa.
	Oct. 4–Dec. 19	Apollo	Chicago, Ill.
Dec. 25, 1931–Jan. 2, 1932		Cass	Detroit, Mich.
1932	Jan. 3	———	Fort Wayne, Ind.
	4–5	English's Opera House	Indianapolis, Ind.
	6–7	National	Louisville, Ky.
	8	———	Nashville, Tenn.
	9	———	Memphis, Tenn.
	10	———	Peoria, Ill.
	11	Shrine Temple	Cedar Rapids, Iowa
	12	Shrine Auditorium	Des Moines, Iowa
	13	Coliseum	Sioux Falls, S.D.
	14	Auditorium	Sioux City, Iowa
	15–16	Brandeis	Omaha, Nebr.
	17–23	Sam S. Shubert	Kansas City, Mo.
	24	Memorial Hall	Joplin, Mo.
	25	Convention Hall	Tulsa, Okla.
	26	Forum	Wichita, Kan.
	27	Shrine Auditorium	Oklahoma City, Okla.
	28	Municipal Auditorium	Amarillo, Tex.
	29	Memorial Auditorium	Wichita Falls, Tex.
	30	State Fair Auditorium	Dallas, Tex.
	31	Municipal Auditorium	Shreveport, La.
	Feb. 1	City Auditorium	Houston, Tex.
	2	Auditorium	San Antonio, Tex.
	3	Liberty Hall	El Paso, Tex.
	4	Fox	Phoenix, Ariz.
	5–6	Fox California	San Diego, Calif.
	7–20	Biltmore	Los Angeles, Calif.
	Feb. 21–March 5	Curran	San Francisco, Calif.
	March 6–12	———	
	13–16	Fox	Seattle, Wash.
	17	Fox	Spokane, Wash.
	18	———	
	19	Broadway	Butte, Mont.
	20–26	(Holy Week lay-off)	
	27	———	
	*28–30	Metropolitan Opera House	Minneapolis, Minn.
	March 31–April 2	Metropolitan Opera House	St. Paul, Minn.
	April 3–9	Davidson	Milwaukee, Wisc.
	10–16	Shubert-Rialto	St. Louis, Mo.
	17–19	———	Evansville, Ind.
	20	Shrine Auditorium	Mansfield, Ohio
	21	———	Canton, Ohio
	22	Auditorium	Columbus, Ohio
	23	Goodyear	Akron, Ohio
	24–30	Hanna	Cleveland, Ohio

FANNY BRICE

Presentation House Vaudeville

1932	Sept. 16–22	Paramount	New York, N.Y.
	23–29	———	
	Sept. 30–Oct. 6	Paramount	Brooklyn, N.Y.
	Oct. 7–Nov. 10	———	
	Nov. 11–17	Oriental	Chicago, Ill.
	Nov. 18–Dec. 1	———	
	Dec. 2–8	Paramount	New York, N.Y.
	9–15	Paramount	Brooklyn, N.Y.

ZIEGFELD FOLLIES OF 1934

A Musical Revue in Two Acts and Twenty-Six Scenes. Lyrics by E. Y. Harburg. Music by Vernon Duke and Samuel Pokrass. Staged by Bobby Connolly. Production Lighted and Additional Numbers Stged by John Murray Anderson. Dialogue Staged by Edward C. Lilley. Additional Dances Staged by Robert Alton. Costumes Designed by Russell Patterson, Raoul DuBois, Charles LeMaire, Kiviette. Settings by Watson Barratt and Albert R. Johnson. Presented by Mrs. Florenz Ziegfeld (Billie Burke).

ACT I

Scene One—Opening
Scene Two—"All Quiet in Havana" by H. I. Phillips
Scene Three—Song—"Soul Saving Sadie" (Fanny Brice)
Scene Four—Song—"Water Under the Bridge"
Scene Five—"Barnyard Theatre, Inc." by Fred Allen and Harry Tugend

Manager	WILLIE HOWARD
Constable	BUDDY EBSEN
Phoebe Colt	EVE ARDEN
A Gentleman	JOHN ADAIR
A Lady	LORETTA DENNISON
Meyer Lonsdale	VICTOR MORLEY
Rennie	OLIVER WAKEFIELD
Julia	FANNY BRICE
Ladies and Gentlemen	
of the Audience	

Scene Six—Dance (Cherry & June Preisser)
Scene Seven—"Ivory and Old Gold"
Scene Eight—Mr. Oliver Wakefield
Scene Nine—"The Follies Choral Ensemble" by Harburg and Pokrass
Scene Ten—"Fifth Avenue"
Scene Eleven—"Before the Black Fire Curtain"
Scene Twelve—"Baby Snooks" by David Freedman

Father	VICTOR MORLEY

Mother   EVE ARDEN
Baby Snooks   FANNY BRICE

Scene Thirteen—Song—"Man About Town" (Jane Froman)
Scene Fourteen—"Reviewing Stand" by H. I. Phillips
Scene Fifteen—Song—"Countess Dubinsky" (Fanny Brice)
Scene Sixteen—Song—"To the Beat of My Heart"

ACT II

Scene One—"Street Scene"
Scene Two—"The Last Round-Up" by Billy Hill
Scene Three—"Careful with My Heart" by Harburg and Pokrass
Scene Four—Betzi Beaton and the Follies Girls
Scene Five—"Sailor, Behave!" by David Freedman

Rosie   VIVIAN JANIS
Annie   FANNY BRICE
Moe   WILLIE HOWARD

Scene Six—Song—"Green Eyes" (Jane Froman)
Scene Seven—Dance—"The Maxixe" (Vilma and Buddy Ebsen)
Scene Eight—Song—"Wagon Wheels" (Everett Marshall)
Scene Nine—"The Man Who Came Back" by David Freedman
Scene Ten—Song—"This Is Not a Song"

Score

"That's Where We Come In" (Samuel Pokrass–E. Y. Harburg)
* "Soul Saving Sadie" (Joseph Meyer–Ballard MacDonald–Billy Rose)
"Water Under the Bridge" (Duke–Harburg)
"I Like the Likes of You" (Harburg)
"Suddenly" (Duke–Harburg–Rose)
"Moon About Town" (Dana Suesse–Harburg)
* "Countess Dubinsky" (Meyer–McDonald–Rose)
"To the Beat of My Heart" (Pokrass–Harburg)
"What Is There to Say?" (Duke–Harburg)
"Careful with My Heart" (Pokrass–Harburg)
"This Is Not a Song" (Duke–E. Hartman–Harburg)

1933	Nov. 2–18	Sam S. Shubert	Boston, Mass.
	Nov. 20–Dec. 2	Forrest	Philadelphia, Pa.
	Dec. 4–9	National	Washington, D.C.
	11–16	Nixon	Pittsburgh, Pa.
	18–23	———	
	25–30	Sam S. Shubert	Newark, N.J.
1934	Jan. 4–June 9	Winter Garden	New York, N.Y.
	Sept. 4–Nov. 3	Grand Opera House	Chicago, Ill.
	Nov. 5–10	Municipal Auditorium	St. Louis, Mo.
	12–17	Sam S. Shubert	Cincinnati, Ohio
	19–24	Hanna	Cleveland, Ohio

Nov. 25–Dec. 1	Cass	Detroit, Mich.
Dec. 3–5	Hartman	Columbus, Ohio
6–8	English's Opera House	Indianapolis, Ind.
10–15	Davidson	Milwaukee, Wisc.
17–22	Metropolitan	Minneapolis, Minn.
Dec. 25, 1934–Jan. 1, 1935	Sam S. Shubert	Kansas City, Mo.
1935 Jan. 3–5	Broadway	Denver, Colo.
7–8	Paramount	Salt Lake City, Utah
10–26	Curran	San Francisco, Calif.
Jan. 28–Feb. 3	Biltmore	Los Angeles, Calif.
Feb. 4	Orpheum	Phoenix, Ariz.
5	Rialto	Tucson, Ariz.
6	Plaza	El Paso, Tex.
8	Paramount	Austin, Tex.
9	Texas	San Antonio, Tex.
10–11	Majestic	Houston, Tex.
12	Texas	San Angelo, Tex.
13	Paramount	Amarillo, Tex.
14	Majestic	Wichita Falls, Tex.
15	Texas	Fort Worth, Tex.
16–17	Melba	Dallas, Tex.
18	Convention Hall	Tulsa, Okla.
19	Technical High School	Little Rock, Ark.
20	Ryman Auditorium	Nashville, Tenn.
21	Tivoli	Chattanooga, Tenn.
22	Tennessee	Knoxville, Tenn.
23–24	Memorial Auditorium	Louisville, Ky.
25	Victory	Dayton, Ohio
26	Colonial	Akron, Ohio
27	Park	Youngstown, Ohio
Feb. 28–March 2	His Majesty's	Toronto, Ont.
March 4–9	His Majesty's	Montreal, Que.
11–12	———	
13	Court Square	Springfield, Mass.
14	Parsons'	Hartford, Conn.
15–16	Sam S. Shubert	New Haven, Conn.

ZIEGFELD FOLLIES OF 1936

A Musical Revue in Two Acts and Twenty-Four Scenes. Sketches by David Freedman. Lyrics by Ira Gershwin. Music by Vernon Duke. Scenery and Costumes Designed by Vincente Minnelli. Modern Dances by Robert Alton. Ballets by George Balanchine. Sketches Directed by Edward Clarke Lilley. Entire Production Staged by John Murray Anderson.

ACT I

Scene One—Song—"Time Marches On"
Scene Two—Song—"He Hasn't a Thing Except Me" (Fanny Brice)
Scene Three—Song—"Red Letter Day"

Scene Four—Sketch—"Of Thee I Spend"
Scene Five—Song—"West Indies"
Scene Six—Sketch—"The Sweepstakes Ticket"

Norma Shaffer	FANNY BRICE
Messenger Boy	DUKE MCHALE
Monty Shaffer	HUGH O'CONNELL
Mr. Martin	JOHN HOYSRADT

Scene Seven—"Words Without Music" (A Surrealist Ballet)
Scene Eight—Song—"The Economic Situation" (Eve Arden)
Scene Nine—Song—"Fancy, Fancy"

Zuleika	FANNY BRICE
Sir Robert	BOB HOPE
Sir Henry	JOHN HOYSRADT

Scene Ten—"Night Flight" (Harriet Hoctor)
Scene Eleven—"Baby Snooks Goes Hollywood"

Mrs. Higgins	EVE ARDEN
Director	BOB HOPE
Baby Snooks	FANNY BRICE
Cameraman	GEORGE CHURCH
Clark Gable	RODNEY MCLENNAN
Joan Crawford	JANE MOXON
Photographer	ROGER DAVIS
Official	JOHN HOYSRADT

Scene: A Stage in a Hollywood Studio
Scene Twelve—"Maharanee" (Josephine Baker)
Scene Thirteen—The Nicholas Brothers
Scene Fourteen—"The Gazooka" by David Freedman and Ira Gershwin

Conductor	ROGER DAVIS
Father	JOHN HOYSRADT
Mother	JUDY CANOVA
Bing Powell	BOB HOPE
Aviator	DUKE MCHALE
Ruby Blondell	FANNY BRICE
Casting Agent	GEORGE CHURCH
Dolores Del Morgan	GERTRUDE NIESEN
Producer	HUGH O'CONNELL

Scene 1—A Railway Station.
Scene 2—A Casting Office.
Scene 3—Backstage.
Scene 4—"The Gazooka" in Techniquecolor on the Widescope Screen.

ACT II

Scene One—"Moment of Moments" (Gertrude Niesen)
Scene Two—"Sentimental Weather"
Scene Three—"Amateur Night"

Major Bones	HUGH O'CONNELL
Attendant	ROGER DAVIS
Juggler	STAN KAVANAGH
Elvira Mackintosh	JUDY CANOVA
Lady DeVere	EVE ARDEN
Myrtle Oppenshaw	FANNY BRICE

Scene: A Broadcasting Studio

Scene Four—Stan Kavanagh
Scene Five—"The Voice of Friendship" by Ogden Nash (Bob Hope)
Scene Six—"Five A.M." (Josephine Baker)
Scene Seven—"I Can't Get Started with You" (Bob Hope and Eve Arden)
Scene Eight—"Modernistic Moe" (Fanny Brice)
Scene Nine—"The Petrified Elevator"
Scene Ten—"Dancing to Our Score"

Score

"Time Marches On!"
"He Hasn't a Thing Except Me"
"My Red-Letter Day"
"Island in the West Indies"
"Words Without Music"
"The Economic Situation"
"Fancy, Fancy"
"Maharanee"
"The Gazooka"
"That Moment of Moments"
"Sentimental Weather"
"Five A.M."
"I Can't Get Started"
"Modernistic Moe"
"Dancing to Our Score" (Lyrics by Ira Gershwin and Billy Rose)

1936 Jan. 13–25	Boston Opera House	Boston, Mass.
Jan. 30–May 9	Winter Garden	New York, N.Y.

THE NEW ZIEGFELD FOLLIES OF 1936–1937

A Musical Revue in Two Acts and Twenty-Five Scenes. Sketches by David Freedman. Lyrics by Ira Gershwin. Music by Vernon Duke. Scenery and Costumes Designed by Vincente Minnelli. Modern Dances by Robert Alton. Sketches Directed by Edward Clarke Lilley and Edward D. Dowling. Entire Production Staged by John Murray Anderson.

ACT I

Scene One—"Time Marches On"
Scene Two—"He Hasn't a Thing Except Me" (Fanny Brice)
Scene Three—Song—"Nice Goin' " by Bob Rothberg and Joseph Meyer (Cass Daley)
Scene Four—"Of Thee I Spend" (Bobby Clark and Gypsy Rose Lee)
Scene Five—"Isle in the West Indies" (Jane Pickens)
Scene Six—"The Sweepstakes Ticket"

Norma Shaffer	FANNY BRICE
Messenger Boy	MARVIN LAWLER
Monty Shaffer	BOBBY CLARK
Mr. Martin	HUGH CAMERON

Scene: A Small Apartment Uptown

Scene Seven—"Words Without Music" (Jane Pickens)
Scene Eight—"The Economic Situation" (Gypsy Rose Lee)
Scene Nine—"Fancy, Fancy" by Ira Gershwin

Zuleika	FANNY BRICE
Sir Robert	BOBBY CLARK
Sir Henry	HUGH CAMERON

Scene Ten—Song—"You Don't Love Right" by Tot Seymour and Vee Lawnhurst (Cass Daley)
Scene Eleven—"Baby Snooks Goes Hollywood"

Mrs. Higgins	GYPSY ROSE LEE
Director	BOBBY CLARK
Baby Snooks	FANNY BRICE
Cameraman	BEN YOST
Clark Gable	JAMES FARRELL
Joan Crawford	VIRGINIA LANGDON
Photographer	BERNARD PEARCE
Official	HUGH CAMERON

Scene: A Stage in a Hollywood Studio

Scene Twelve—Song—"Ridin' the Rails" by Edward Hayman and Harold Spina (Ben Yost's Varsity Eight)
Scene Thirteen—Gypsy Rose Lee
Scene Fourteen—"The Gazooka"

Pilot	MARVIN LAWLER
Father	JAMES FARRELL
Mother	CASS DALEY
Bing Powell	BOBBY CLARK
Ruby Blondell	FANNY BRICE
Casting Agent	WM. QUENTMEYER
Dolores Del Morgan	GYPSY ROSE LEE

Producer   HUGH CAMERON
Dance Director   GEORGE SPELVIN
Minister   STAN KAVANAGH

CHERRY and JUNE PREISSER
BEN YOST'S VARSITY EIGHT
Ziegfeld Follies Show Girls
Ziegfeld Follies Dancing Girls
Male Dancers

Scene 1—A Railway Station.
Scene 2—A Casting Office.
Scene 3—Backstage.
Scene 4—"The Gazooka" in Techniquecolor on the Wide-
    scope Screen.

ACT II

Scene One—"Moment of Moments"
Scene Two—"Sentimental Weather"
Scene Three—"Amateur Night"

Major Bones   BOBBY CLARK
Attendant   BEN YOST
Juggler   STAN KAVANAGH
Elvira Mackintosh   CASS DALEY
Lady De Vere   GYPSY ROSE LEE
Myrtle Oppenshaw   FANNY BRICE

Scene: A Broadcasting Studio
Scene Four—Stan Kavanagh
Scene Five—Song—"Harlem Waltz" by Richard Jerome and Walter Kent (Sung
    by Cass Daley. Danced by Cherry & June Preisser.)
Scene Six—"Dr. Fradler's Dilemma"

Mrs. Bigley   MARJORY LEACH
Nurse   GYPSY ROSE LEE
Dr. Fradler   BOBBY CLARK
Mrs. Phoebe Schwartz   FANNY BRICE

Scene Seven—Song—"Midnight Blue" by Edgar Leslie and Joe Burke (Jane Pickens
    and James Farrell)
Scene Eight—"I Can't Get Started with You" (Bobby Clark and Gypsy Rose
    Lee)
Scene Nine—"Modernistic Moe" (Fanny Brice)
Scene Ten—"The Petrified Elevator"
Scene Eleven—Finale (Fanny Brice, Bobby Clark and the Entire Company)

1936   Sept. 14–Dec. 19   Winter Garden   New York, N.Y.
Dec. 25, 1936–Jan. 2, 1937   Nixon   Pittsburgh, Pa.

1937	Jan. 4–March 13	Grand Opera House	Chicago, Ill.
	March 14–17	Davidson	Milwaukee, Wisc.
	18–20	———	
	22–27	Music Hall	Kansas City, Mo.
	March 29–April 3	American	St. Louis, Mo.
	April 5–8	English's Opera House	Indianapolis, Ind.
	9–10	Hartman	Columbus, Ohio
	11–24	Cass	Detroit, Mich.
	April 26–May 1	Hanna	Cleveland, Ohio
	May 3–5	Royal Alexandra	Toronto, Ont.
	6	Masonic Auditorium	Rochester, N.Y.
	7–8	Erlanger	Buffalo, N.Y.
	10–15	National	Washington, D.C.
	17–22	Ford's Opera House	Baltimore, Md.
	24–25	Mosque	Richmond, Va.
	26	Community	Hershey, Pa.

CHARLOT'S REVUE

A Musical Revue Devised and Staged by Andre Charlot.

Cast

Reginald Gardiner, Freddie Bartholomew, June Lockhart, Mary Brian, Richard Haydn, Mary Parker, Billy Daniels, John Garrick, Rita Hayworth, June Clyde, Mischa Auer, Leni Lord, C. Aubrey Smith, Fred Leslie, Jackie Cooper, Bonita Granville, Anna Neagle, Fanny Brice, Hanley Stafford, Vyola Vonn, Frank Nelson, Buster Keaton, Carol Adams, The King's Men, Billy Burt, Heather Thatcher, Eric Blore, J. Carroll Nash, Simone Simon, Henry Fonda, Rod LaRocque, Chester Morris, Alan Mowbray, Ronald Colman, George Sanders, Mitchell Leisen, Elsa Maxwell, Shirley Chambers, Lorraine Bridges.

Note: The Players' Theatre presented this All-Star Revue at the El Capitan Theatre in Los Angeles from September 20 to October 19, 1940. Proceeds went to the British War Relief Association.

Fanny Brice was in one scene, as follows:

Scene Twelve—"Baby Snooks' First Flight" by Phil Rapp

Baby Snooks	FANNY BRICE
Daddy	HANLEY STAFFORD
Stewardess	VYOLA VONN
Passenger	FRANK NELSON

Filmography

MY MAN
(Warner Bros., 1928)

Production:	July–September, 1928
Premiere:	December 21, 1928, Warner Theatre, New York
Length:	99 minutes

Director:	Archie Mayo
Scenario:	Joe Jackson, James Storr, Robert Lord
Source:	A story by Mark Canfield (Darryl F. Zanuck)
Photography:	Frank Kesson
Film Editor:	Owen Marks

Cast

Fannie Brand	FANNY BRICE
Joe Halsey	GUINN "BIG BOY" WILLIAMS
Edna Brand	EDNA MURPHY
Landau, the producer	ANDRE DE SEGUROLA
Waldo	RICHARD TUCKER
Sammy	BILLY SEAY
Thome	ARTHUR HOYT
Mrs. Schultz	ANN BRODY
Forelady	CLARISSA SELWYNNE

Songs

*"I'd Rather Be Blue" (Fred Fisher–Billy Rose)
*"I Was a Floradora Baby" (Henry Carroll–Ballard MacDonald)
*"Second Hand Rose" (James F. Hanley–Grant Clarke)
*"I'm an Indian" (Leo Edwards–Blanche Merrill)
*"If You Want the Rainbow" (Fred Fisher–Rose)
*"My Man" (Maurice Yvain–Channing Pollock)

NIGHT CLUB
(Paramount, 1929)

Production: March, 1929, Astoria, Queens, N.Y.
Premiere: August 11, 1929, Little Carnegie, New York, N.Y.
Length: 28 minutes (in addition to 12-minute prologue talk by Donald Ogden Stewart)

Director: Robert Florey
Source: Inspired by the novel by Katherine Brush

Cast

Master of Ceremonies	JIMMY CARR
Performers	FANNY BRICE
	ANN PENNINGTON
	TAMARA GEVA
	BOBBE ARNST
	MINNIE DUPREE
	PAT ROONEY II
	PAT ROONEY III

BE YOURSELF!
(United Artists, 1930)

Production: August–September, 1929
Premiere: March 6, 1930, Rialto Theatre, New York, N.Y.
Length: 65 minutes

Director: Thornton Freeland
Scenario: Thornton Freeland, Max Marcin
Source: Based on a story by Joseph Jackson
Photography: Karl Struss, Robert H. Planck
Film Editor: Robert J. Kern
Sets: William Cameron Menzies, Park French
Costumes: Alice O'Neill
Production Numbers Maurice L. Kusell

Cast

Fannie Field	FANNY BRICE
Jerry Moore	ROBERT ARMSTRONG
Harry Field	HARRY GREEN
Lillian	GERTRUDE ASTOR
McCloskey	G. PAT COLLINS
Step	BUDD FINE
Lola	MARJORIE (BABE) KANE
Jessica	RITA FLYNN
Jimmy Tolson	JIMMY TOLSON

Songs

*"Sascha, The Passion of the Pascha" (Greer–Rose–McDonald)
*"When a Woman Loves a Man" (Ralph Rainger–Rose)

*"Kicking a Hole in the Sky" (Greer–Rose–McDonald)
*"Cooking Breakfast for the One I Love" (Tobias–Rose)

CRIME WITHOUT PASSION
(Paramount, 1934)

Fanny Brice and Helen Hayes appeared as extras in this Ben Hecht–Charles MacArthur crime drama starring Claude Rains as "Lee Gentry," a thinly veiled portrayal of New York criminal lawyer William J. Fallon.

THE GREAT ZIEGFELD
(M-G-M, 1936)

Production:	Brice sequence filmed in October, 1935
Premiere:	March 23, 1936, Astor Theatre, New York, N.Y.
Length:	170 minutes

Director:	Robert Z. Leonard
Screenplay:	William Anthony McGuire
Source:	Life of Florenz Ziegfeld, Jr.
Photography:	George Folsey, Karl Freund, Merritt B. Gerstad, Ray June, Oliver T. Marsh
Film Editor:	William S. Gray
Conductor:	Arthur Lange
Choreographer:	Seymour Felix
Art Director:	Cedric Gibbons
Costumes	Adrian

Cast

Florenz Ziegfeld, Jr.	WILLIAM POWELL
Anna Held	LUISE RAINER
Billie Burke	MYRNA LOY
Billings	FRANK MORGAN
Sampston	REGINALD OWEN
Sandow	NAT PENDLETON
Audrey Lane	VIRGINIA BRUCE
Sidney	ERNEST COSSART
Joe	ROBERT GREIG
Sage	RAYMOND WALBURN
Fanny Brice	FANNY BRICE
Mary Lou	JEAN CHATBURN
Ann Pennington	ANN PENNINGTON
Ray Bolger	RAY BOLGER
Harriet Hoctor	HARRIET HOCTOR
Julian Mitchell	CHARLES TROWBRIDGE
Gilda Gray	GILDA GRAY
Will Rogers	A. A. TRIMBLE
Patricia Ziegfeld	JOAN HOLLAND
Buddy Doyle	EDDIE CANTOR
Pierre	CHARLES JUDELS

Leon Errol	LEON ERROL
Marie	MARCELLE CORDAY
Prima Donna	ESTHER MUIR
Customer	HERMAN BING
A. L. Erlanger	PAUL IRVING
Gene Buck	WILLIAM DEMAREST
Stage Door Man	ALFRED P. JAMES
Little Egypt	MISS MOROCCO
Miss Blair	SUZANNE KAAREN
Wardrobe Woman	SARAH EDWARDS
Bill	JAMES P. BURTIS
Telegraph Boy	MICKEY DANIEL
Husband	WILLIAM GRIFFITH
Wife	GRACE HAYLE
Alice	ALICE KEATING
Marilyn Miller	ROSINA LAWRENCE
Detective	JACK BAXLEY
Carriage Starter	CHARLES COLEMAN
Desk Clerk	ERIC WILTON
Miss Carlisle	MARY HOWARD
Jim	BERT HANLON
Fat Woman	EVELYN DOCKSON
Allen	FRANKLYN ARDELL
Sam	JOHN LARKIN
Clarence	DAVID BURNS
Press Agent	PHIL TEAD
Girl with Sage	SUSAN FLEMING
Wife of French Ambassador	ADRIENNE D'AMBRICOURT
French Ambassador	CHARLES FALLON
Willie Zimmerman	BOOTHE HOWARD
Charles Froman	EDWIN MAXWELL
Lillian Russell	RUTH GILLETTE
Dave Stamper	JOHN HYAMS
Broker	WALLIS CLARK
Inspector Doyle	RAY BROWN

Songs

"A Pretty Girl Is Like a Melody" (Irving Berlin)
"You Gotta Pull Strings"
"You" (Walter Donaldson–Harold Adamson)
"She's a Ziegfeld Follies Girl"
"You Never Looked So Beautiful"
"A Circus Must Be Different in a Ziegfeld Show"
"Rhapsody in Blue" (George Gershwin)
"On with the Motley"
"One Fine Day"
"Humoresque Number 7 in G Flat"
"If You Knew Susie" (Joseph Meyer–B. G. DeSylva)
*"Yiddle on Your Fiddle"

*"My Man" (Maurice Yvain–Channing Pollock)
"Won't You Come and Play with Me?"
"Parade of the Glorified Girls"
"Queen of the Jungle"
"Look for the Silver Lining" (Jerome Kern–DeSylva)
"March of the Musketeers"
"Ol' Man River" (Kern–Oscar Hammerstein II)
"Makin' Whoopee" (Walter Donaldson–Gus Kahn)
"Rio Rita" (Harry Tierney–Joe McCarthy)
"Tulip Time" (Dave Stamper–Gene Buck)
"Someone Loves You After All"
"It's Delightful to Be Married" (Vincent Scotto–Anna Held)

EVERYBODY SING
(M-G-M, 1938)

Production: July–November, 1937
Premiere: March 10, 1938, Capitol Theatre, New York
Length: 80 minutes

Producer: Harry Rapf
Director: Edwin L. Marin
Screenplay: Florence Ryerson, Edgar Allen Woolf
Additional Dialogue: James Gruen
Photography: Joseph Ruttenberg
Film Editor: William S. Gray
Conductor: Dr. William Axt

Cast

Ricky Saboni	ALLAN JONES
Olga Chekaloff	FANNY BRICE
Judy Bellaire	JUDY GARLAND
Hillary Bellaire	REGINALD OWEN
Diana Bellaire	BILLIE BURKE
Jerrold Hope	REGINALD GARDINER
Sylvia Bellaire	LYNNE CARVER
John Fleming	MONTY WOOLLEY
Boris	ADIA KUZNETZOFF
Signor Vittorino	HENRY ARMETTA
Madame Le Brouchette	MICHELETTA BURANI
Miss Colvin	MARY FORBES

Songs

"Swing, Mr. Mendelssohn, Swing"
"The One I Love"
"Down on Melody Farm"
"The Show Must Go On"
"I Wanna Swing"
"Never Was There Such a Perfect Day"
*"Quainty Dainty Me"

* "Why? Because"
"Snooks"
"Cosi Cosa"
"Swing Low, Sweet Chariot" (traditional)

ZIEGFELD FOLLIES
(M-G-M, 1946)

Production: August 1944–June 1945
Premiere: March 22, 1946, Capitol Theatre, New York
Length: 110 minutes

Producer: Arthur Freed
Director: Vincente Minnelli
Photography: George Folsey, Charles Rosbher
Technicolor: William Ferrari
Film Editor: Albert Akst
Conductor: Lenny Hayton

Art Directors: CEDRIC GIBBONS
JACK MARTIN SMITH
MERRILL PYE
LEMUEL AYERS
Set Directors: EDWIN B. WILLIS
MAC ALPER
Costumes: FLORENCE BUNIN, IRENE
Choreographer: ROBERT ALTON
Make-Up: JACK DAWN

Scenes

1. Ziegfeld Days
    a. William Powell as "The Great Ziegfeld"
    b. Bunin's Puppets as Old-Time Ziegfeld Stars
    c. Fred Astaire sings "Here's to the Beautiful Girls"
    d. Lucille Ball and the Ziegfeld Girls in "Merry-Go-Round"
    e. Virginia O'Brien sings "Here's to the Wonderful Men"
2. A Water Ballet featuring Esther Williams
3. "Number, Please" with Keenan Wynn
4. "Traviata" sung by James Melton and Marian Bell
5. "Pay the Two Dollars" with Victor Moore and Edward Arnold
6. "This Heart of Mine" with Fred Astaire and Lucille Bremer
7. "A Sweepstakes Ticket" with Fanny Brice, Hume Cronyn, and William Frawley
8. "Love" sung by Lena Horne
9. "When Television Comes" with Red Skelton
10. "Limehouse Blues" with Fred Astaire and Lucille Bremer
11. "An Interview" with Judy Garland
12. "The Babbit and the Bromide" with Fred Astaire and Gene Kelly
13. "Beauty" sung by Kathryn Grayson

Radiography

Compiled by Peter Tatchell with Larry F. Kiner and Herbert G. Goldman

STARRING RADIO SERIES
Royal Vagabonds (NBC Red)

Time slot: Wednesdays, 8:00–8:30 P.M.
Sponsor: Standard Brands
Conductor: George Olsen

Broadcast from New York: March 15–October 4, 1933

Total broadcasts: 30

Ziegfeld Follies of the Air (CBS)

Time slot: Saturdays, 8:00–9:00 P.M.
Sponsor: Colgate-Palmolive
Conductor: Al Goodman

Supporting talent: James Melton (February 22–March 21, 1936)
Benny Fields (March 28–June 6, 1936)
Patti Chapin

Broadcast from New York: February 22–June 6, 1936

Total broadcasts: 16

NOTE: Fanny Brice missed the first broadcast due to illness. Minerva Pious appeared in her place.

Miss Brice left the show after the broadcast of May 2, having appeared on only ten shows in the series.

Revue de Paree (NBC Blue)

Time slot: Wednesdays, 8:00–8:30 P.M.
Sponsor: R. L. Watkins Co.

Announcer: Ford Bond
Conductor: Victor Arden

Broadcast from New York: September 30–December 23, 1936

Total broadcasts: 13

Good News of 1938 (NBC Red)

Time slot: Thursdays, 9:00–10:00 P.M.
Sponsor: General Foods
Conductor: Meredith Wilson

With: Robert Taylor (host, January 6–April 21)
Robert Young (host, April 28–June 9)
Frank Morgan (December 2–June 30)
Hanley Staffo5rd

Broadcast from Los Angeles: November 4, 1937–June 30, 1938

Total broadcasts: 35

M-G-M weekly guest stars:

1937	Nov. 4	Jeanette MacDonald, Allan Jones, Sophie Tucker
	11	Joan Crawford, Spencer Tracy, Robert Young
	18	Allan Jones, James Stewart, Judy Garland
	25	Allan Jones, Sophie Tucker, Judy Garland
	Dec. 2	Allan Jones, Wallace Beery, Freddie Bartholomew
	9	Allan Jones, Clark Gable, Freddie Bartholomew
	16	James Stewart, Spencer Tracy, Freddie Bartholomew
	23	James Stewart, Nelson Eddy, Eleanor Powell
	30	James Stewart, Wallace Beery, Myrna Loy
1938	Jan. 6	Judy Garland, Gilbert Russell
	13	Sophie Tucker, Gilbert Russell
	20	Judy Garland, Virginia Grey, Allan Jones
	27	Allan Jones, Edna May Oliver, Robert Young
	Feb. 3	Judy Garland, Allan Jones, Billie Burke
	10	Allan Jones, Betty Jaynes, Virginia Bruce
	17	Jack Benny, Judy Garland, Allan Jones
	24	Luise Rainer, Melvyn Douglas, Warren William
	March 3	Connie Boswell, Mickey Rooney, Billie Burke
	10	Connie Boswell, Robert Montgomery
	17	Connie Boswell, Rita Johnson
	24	Connie Boswell, Mickey Rooney, Lewis Stone
	31	Connie Boswell, Maureen O'Sullivan
	April 7	Judy Garland, Sam Levene
	14	Judy Garland, Freddie Bartholomew
	21	Judy Garland, Clark Gable, Myrna Loy
	28	Judy Garland, Maureen O'Sullivan, Una Merkel
	May 5	Judy Garland, Clark Cable, Una Merkel
	12	Robert Montgomery, Rita Johnson
	19	Joan Crawford, Douglas McPhail, Zarova
	26	Robert Montgomery, Virginia Bruce, Gus Kahn

June 2 Robert Taylor, Margaret Sullavan, Mary Martin
    9 Robert Taylor, Mary Martin, Douglas McPhail
  16 Robert Taylor, Mary Martin, Freddie Bartholomew
  23 James Stewart, Mary Martin, Una Merkel
  30 Robert Taylor, James Stewart, Mary Martin

NOTE: Fanny Brice did not appear on the first four broadcasts.

Good News of 1939 (NBC Red)

Time slot: Thursdays, 9:00–10:00 P.M.
Sponsor: General Foods
Conductor: Meredith Wilson

With: Robert Young
       Frank Morgan
       Hanley Stafford

Broadcast from Los Angeles: September 1, 1938–June 29, 1939

Total broadcasts: 44

M-G-M weekly guest stars:

1938 Sept. 1 Spencer Tracy, Mickey Rooney, Alice Faye
        8 Judy Garland, Norma Shearer
  15, 22, 29 ———
    Oct. 6 Wallace Beery, Mickey Rooney, Joe E. Brown
      13 Allan Jones, Eleanor Powell, Lew Ayres
      20 Judy Garland, Billie Burke, Joan Crawford
      27 Clark Gable, Lionel Barrymore, Rita Johnson
   Nov. 3 Ralph Morgan, Ruth Hussey, Betty Jaynes
      10 Lionel Barrymore, Maureen O'Sullivan
      17 Margaret Sullavan, Joan Crawford
      24 Mickey Rooney, Lewis Stone, Fay Holden
   Dec. 1 Tony Martin, Clarence Muse
      8 Tony Martin, Rosalind Russell
     15 Tony Martin, Lionel Barrymore
     22 Tony Martin, Robert Taylor
     29 Lionel Barrymore, Douglas McPhail
1939 Jan. 5 Melvyn Douglas, Virginia Bruce
     12 Meliza Korjus, Dennis O'Keefe, Tony Martin
     19 Lionel Barrymore, Melvyn Douglas
     26 Lionel Barrymore, Mickey Rooney, Zarova
   Feb. 2 Mickey Rooney, Rex Ingram, Tony Martin
      9 Eleanor Powell, Tony Martin, Harry Warren
     16 Rosalind Russell, Robert Montgomery
     23 Gertrude Niessen, Meliza Korjus
 March 2 Joan Crawford, Gertrude Niessen, Lew Ayres
      9 Robert Taylor, Lionel Barrymore
     16 Robert Montgomery, Gertrude Niesen
     23 Wallace Beery, Gilbert Russell
     30 Walter Pidgeon, Virginia Bruce

April 6 Lionel Barrymore, Kitty Carlisle
    13 Melvyn Douglas, Virginia Bruce
    20 Mickey Rooney, Lewis Stone, Cecilia Parker
    27 Clark Gable, Eddie Cantor, Robert Taylor
May 4 Robert Taylor, Myrna Loy, Connie Boswell
    11 Ed Sullivan, Rita Johnson, Connie Boswell
    18 Wallace Beery, Connie Boswell
    25 Melvyn Douglas, Virginia Bruce
June 1 Connie Boswell, Frances Arms, Carey Wilson
     8 Connie Boswell, Lionel Barrymore
    15 Connie Boswell, Carey Wilson, John S. Young
    22 Connie Boswell, Frances Arms, Tony Martin
    29 Judy Garland, Ray Bolger, Bert Lahr

Good News of 1940 (NBC Red)

Time slot: Thursdays, 9:00–10:00 P.M.
Sponsor: General Foods
Announcer: Warren Hull
Conductor: Meredith Wilson

With: Walter Huston (September 7–October 26)
       Edward Arnold (November 2–February 22)
       Dick Powell (February 29)
       Frank Morgan
       Connie Boswell
       Roland Young
       Hanley Stafford

Broadcast from Los Angeles: September 7, 1939–February 29, 1940

Total broadcasts: 26

M-G-M weekly guest stars:

1939 Sept. 7 Gladys George
        14 John Huston
        21 Ann Shirley, Zarova
        28 Lucille Ball
    Oct. 5 Isabelle Jewell
        12 Edith Fellows
        19 Minna Gombel, Maxie Rosenbloom
        26 Paulette Goddard
    Nov. 2 Maxie Rosenbloom, Billy Hallop
         9 Nan Sunderland
        16 Marlene Dietrich, Maxie Rosenbloom
        23 Raymond Walburn
        30 Fay Wray, Lou Holtz
    Dec. 7 Frank Travis
        14 Mary Martin, Allan Jones, Walter Connolly
        21 Lanny Ross, Jessica Dragonette
        28 John Boles, Lucille Ball

1940 Jan. 4   Raymond Walburn, Ann Sothern
      11   Hattie McDaniel, Raymond Walburn
      18   Lola Lane, William Gargan
      25   Alice Faye, Brenda Joyce, Richard Greene
  Feb. 1   Claudette Colbert, Alan Marshall
      8   Ida Lupino, Ronald Colman, Frank Parker
      15   Virginia Bruce, Benny Rubin, William Gargan
      22   Warren William, Eric Blore, Benny Rubin
      29   Gracie Allen, Una Merkel, William Gargan

Good News (NBC Red)

Time slot:	Thursdays, 9:00–9:30 P.M.
Sponsor:	General Foods
Announcer:	Warren Hull
Conductor:	Meredith Wilson
With:	Dick Powell (March 7–July 25)
	Connie Boswell
	Roland Young
	Hanley Stafford

Broadcast from Los Angeles: March 7–July 25, 1940

Total broadcasts: 21

Maxwell House Coffee Time (NBC Red) FIRST SEASON

Time slot:	Thursdays, 8:00–8:30 P.M.
Sponsor:	General Foods
Announcer:	Don Wilson (September 5–December 26)
	John Conte (January 2–July 10)
Conductor:	Meredith Wilson
With:	Mary Martin (September 5–December 5)
	Frank Morgan (January 2–July 10)
	Hanley Stafford

Broadcast from Los Angeles: September 5, 1940–July 10, 1941

Total broadcasts: 45

NOTE: The show was titled *Good News* for the first six broadcasts. Remaining 39 broadcasts under title *Maxwell House Coffee Time,* beginning October 17.

Maxwell House Coffee Time (NBC Red) SECOND SEASON

Time slot:	Thursdays, 8:00–8:30 P.M.
Sponsor:	General Foods
Announcer:	John Conte
Conductor:	Meredith Wilson
With:	Frank Morgan (September 4–June 4)
	Hanley Stafford
Guests:	1940 Nov. 20 Jack Benny
	1942 June 11 Groucho Marx

	18	Groucho Marx
	25	Pat O'Malley
July	2	Ralph Morgan
	9	Jimmy Durante
	16	Frank Fay
	23	Mark Hellinger

Broadcast from Los Angeles: September 4, 1941–July 23, 1942

Total broadcasts: 47

NOTE: Fanny Brice did not appear on the first four broadcasts; October 2 marked her first appearance of the season.

The show was titled *Post Toasties Time* for the last eight broadcasts of the season, beginning on June 4.

Maxwell House Coffee Time (NBC Red) THIRD SEASON

Time slot: Thursdays, 8:00–8:30 P.M.
Sponsor: General Foods
Announcer: John Conte
Conductor: Meredith Wilson (September 3–December 10)
Frank Tours (December 17–June 17)

With: Frank Morgan
Hanley Stafford

Broadcast from Los Angeles: September 3, 1942–June 17, 1943

Total broadcasts: 42

Maxwell House Coffee Time (NBC Red) FOURTH SEASON

Time slot: Thursdays, 8:00–8:30 P.M.
Sponsor: General Foods
Announcer: John Conte
Conductor: Frank Tours

With: Frank Morgan (September 2–March 16)
Hanley Stafford

Guests: Dec. 30, 1943 Marilyn Maxwell
April 6, 1944 George Burns & Gracie Allen
June 15, 1944 Charles Ruggles, Cass Daley

Broadcast from Los Angeles: September 2, 1943–June 15, 1944

Total broadcasts: 42

NOTE: Fanny Brice did not appear on the broadcasts of March 30 and April 6.

Toasties Time (CBS)

Time slot: Sundays, 6:30–7:00 P.M.
Sponsor: General Foods
Conductor: Carmen Dragon

With: Hanley Stafford
Danny Thomas

Producer: Al Kaye
Script: Everett Freeman

Broadcast from Los Angeles: September 17 1944–June 10, 1945

Total broadcasts: 39

The Baby Snooks Show (CBS) FIRST SEASON
Time slot: Sundays, 6:30–7:00 P.M.
Sponsor: Sanka Coffee

Announcer: Harlow Wilcox
Conductor: Carmen Dragon

With: Hanley Stafford
Bob Graham
Lois Corbett

Broadcast from Los Angeles: September 16, 1945–June 9, 1946

Total broadcasts: 39

NOTE: Miss Brice missed first three broadcasts due to illness. Eddie Cantor, Robert Benchley, and Kay Kyser were on the respective shows.

The Baby Snooks Show (CBS) SECOND SEASON
Time slot: Fridays, 8:00–8:30 P.M.
Sponsor: Sanka Coffee

Announcer: Harlow Wilcox
Conductor: Carmen Dragon

With: Hanley Stafford
Arlene Harris
Ben Alexander

Broadcast from Los Angeles: September 6, 1946–May 30, 1947

Total broadcasts: 39

The Baby Snooks Show (CBS) THIRD SEASON
Time slot: Fridays, 8:00–8:30 P.M.
Sponsor: General Foods (Jell-O)

Announcer: Harlow Wilcox
Conductor: Carmen Dragon

With: Hanley Stafford
Arlene Harris
Ben Alexander

Broadcast from Los Angeles: September 5, 1947–May 28, 1948

Total broadcasts: 39

The Baby Snooks Show (NBC) FIRST SEASON
Time slot: Tuesdays, 8:30–9:00 P.M.
Sponsor: Lewis-Howe (Tums)

Announcer: Don Wilson
Conductor: Carmen Dragon
Producer: Al Kabaker
Director: Artie Stander
Script: Artie Stander, Robert Fisher

Cast: Fanny Brice
Hanley Stafford
Arlene Harris
Leone Ledoux
Ken Christy
Hans Conried
Doris Singleton

Broadcast from Los Angeles: November 8, 1949–May 2, 1950

Total broadcasts: 26

The Baby Snooks Show (NBC) SECOND SEASON
Time slot: Tuesdays, 8:30–9:00 P.M.
Sponsor: Lewis-Howe (Tums)

Announcer: Don Wilson
Conductor: Carmen Dragon
Producer: Al Kabaker
Directors: Artie Stander, William Karn
Script: Artie Stander, Robert Fisher

Cast: Fanny Brice
Hanley Stafford
Arlene Harris
Leone Ledoux
Frank Harris

Broadcast from Los Angeles: October 10, 1950–May 22, 1951

Total broadcasts: 33

PRINCIPAL GUEST RADIO APPEARANCES

Colgate-Palmolive Hour (NBC) Dec. 9, 1927, New York
Philco Show (CBS) Feb. 5, 1930, New York
Philco Show (CBS) March 19, 1930, New York
RKO Hour (NBC) April 1, 1930, New York
Wise Shoes Program (CBS) Nov. 24, 1930, New York
International Shoe Company Program (CBS) Aug. 12, 1931, New York
Ziegfeld Follies of The Air (CBS) May 22, 1932, New York
Fleischmann Hour (NBC) Jan. 12, 1933, New York
Fleischmann Hour (NBC) June 28, 1934, New York
Fleischmann Hour (NBC) Oct. 4, 1934, New York
Palmolive Beauty Box (CBS) Feb. 22, 1935, New York
Borden Sales Program (NBC) June 14, 1935, New York
Shell Chateau (NBC) Sept. 14, 1935, New York

Shell Chateau (NBC) Oct. 26, 1935, New York
American Can Co. Program (NBC) Nov. 15, 1935, New York
Fleischmann Hour (NBC) Aug. 20, 1936, New York
Fleischmann Hour (NBC) June 17, 1937, New York
Camel Caravan (CBS) Oct. 3, 1938, Los Angeles
March of Dimes (CBS) Jan. 22, 1939, Los Angeles
March of Dimes (CBS) Jan. 20, 1940, Los Angeles
Philco Radio Hall of Fame (NBC) Jan. 9, 1944, Los Angeles
Screen Guild Theatre (NBC) Dec. 30, 1948, Hollywood
Operation Tandem: The Big Show (NBC) Nov. 12, 1950, Los Angeles

Discography

February 18, 1916. New York, N.Y.
With Columbia Orchestra under direction of Charles A. Prince.

46427   "I Don't Know Whether to Do It or   Columbia A-1973 (1)
       Not"
       (Leo Edwards–Blanche Merrill)

46428   "If We Could Only Take Their Word"   Columbia A-2122 (1)
       (Part One)
       (Leo Edwards–Blanche Merrill)

46429   "If We Could Only Take Their Word   Columbia A-2122 (1)
       (Part Two)
       (Leo Edwards–Blanche Merrill)

46430   "Becky Is Back in the Ballet"   UNISSUED
       (Leo Edwards–Blanche Merrill)

September 7, 1916. New York, N.Y.
With Columbia Orchestra under direction of Charles A. Prince.

46428   "If We Could Only Take Their Word"   Columbia A-2122 (3)
       (Part One)
       (Leo Edwards–Blanche Merrill)

46429   "If We Could Only Take Their Word"   Columbia A-2122 (3)
       (Part Two)
       (Leo Edwards–Blanche Merrill)

46430   "Becky Is Back in the Ballet"   UNISSUED
       (Leo Edwards–Blanche Merrill)

November 8, 1921. Camden, N.J.
With Victor Orchestra under direction of Rosario Bourdon.

B-25751   "Second Hand Rose"   Victor 45263 (3)
       (James F. Hanley–Grant Clarke)

B-25752   "My Man"   Victor 45263 (6)
       (Maurice Yvain–Channing Pollock)

November 15, 1921. Camden, N.J.
With Victor Orchestra under direction of Rosario Bourdon.

B-25762 "Oh! How I Hate That Fellow, Na-   Victor 45303 (3)
          than"
          (Albert von Tilzer–Lew Brown)
B-25763 "Irish-Jewish Jubilee"   UNISSUED
          (Harry Ruby–Bert Kalmar)

November 18, 1921. Camden, N.J.
With Victor Orchestra under direction of Rosario Bourdon.

B-25769 "I'm an Indian"   Victor 45303 (3)
          (Leo Edwards–Blanche Merrill)

July 13, 1922. Camden, N.J.
With Victor Orchestra under direction of Rosario Bourdon.

B-26588 "On the Shores of Rockaway"   UNISSUED
          (Tony Martin–Bert Hanlon–Howard
          Johnson)
B-26599 "Becky Is Back in the Ballet"   Victor 45323 (3)
          (Leo Edwards–Blanche Merrill)

July 14, 1922. Camden, N.J.
With Victor Orchestra under direction of Rosario Bourdon.

B-25763 "Irish-Jewish Jubilee"   UNISSUED
          (Harry Ruby–Bert Kalmar)
B-26588 "On the Shores of Rockaway"   UNISSUED
          (Tony Martin–Bert Hanlon–Howard
          Johnson)
B-26800 "The Sheik of Avenue B"   Victor 45323 (3)
          (Harry Ruby–Cliff Friend–H. Down-
          ing–Bert Kalmar)

December 20, 1927. New York, N.Y.
With Victor Orchestra under direction of Nat Shilkret.

BVE-25752 "My Man"   Victor 21168 (7)
          (Maurice Yvain–Channing Pollock)
BVE-41187 "Mrs. Cohen at the Beach" (Part One)   Victor 21211 (3)
          (Billy Rose)
BVE-41190 "The Song of the Sewing Machine"   Victor 21168 (2)
          (Jesse Greer–Ballard MacDonald–
          Billy Rose)

Note: Matrix BVE-41187 is a humorous monologue with piano introduction by Nat Shilkret.

December 21, 1927. New York, N.Y.
With Unidentified Actor.

BVE-41194 "Mrs. Cohen at the Beach" (Part Two)   Victor 21211 (1)
          (Billy Rose)

December 22, 1927. New York, N.Y.
With Victor Orchestra under direction of Nat Shilkret.

BVE-25752	"My Man"	Victor 21168 (11)
	(Maurice Yvain–Channing Pollock)	
BVE-41199	"Is Something the Matter with Otto Kahn?"	UNISSUED
	(Jesse Greer–Ballard MacDonald–Billy Rose)	
BVE-41500	"Sascha (The Passion of the Pascha)"	UNISSUED
	(Jesse Greer-Ballard MacDonald–Billy Rose)	

December 14, 1928. New York, N.Y.
With Victor Orchestra under direction of Leonard Joy.

BVE-49260	"If You Want the Rainbow"	Victor 21815 (2)
	(Fred Fisher–Billy Rose)	
BVE-49261	"I'd Rather Be Blue Over You"	Victor 21815 (3)
	(Fred Fisher–Billy Rose)	RCA Victor LPV-561 (2)

December 17, 1928. New York, N.Y.
With Victor Orchestra under direction of Leonard Joy.

BVE-25752	"My Man"	Victor 21168 (12)
	(Maurice Yvain–Channing Pollock)	
BVE-49261	"I'd Rather Be Blue Over You"	UNISSUED
	(Fred Fisher–Billy Rose)	

January 15, 1930. New York, N.Y.
With Victor Orchestra under direction of Leonard Joy.

BVE-57995	"When a Woman Loves a Man"	Victor 22310 (3)
	(Ralph Rainger–Billy Rose)	X LVA-1006 (1)
BVE-57996	"Cooking Breakfast for the One I Love"	Victor 22310 (3)
		X LVA-1006 (1)
	(Henry Tobias–Billy Rose)	

June 21, 1950. Los Angeles Calif.
With Hanley Stafford.

| 6154 | "Baby Snooks—Crossing Streets" | Capitol CAS-3117 |

July 7, 1950. Los Angeles, Calif.
With Hanley Stafford.

| 6155 | "Baby Snooks—Truthfulness" | Capitol CAS-3115 |

July 12, 1950. Los Angeles, Calif.
With Hanley Stafford.

6156	"Baby Snooks—Cleanliness"	Capitol CAS-3116
6157	"Baby Snooks—Kindness to Animals"	Capitol CAS-3117
6158	"Baby Snooks—Table Manners"	Capitol CAS-3115
6159	"Baby Snooks—Good and Bad"	Capitol CAS-3116

Index